PSYCHOTHERAPY OF PREOEDIPAL CONDITIONS:

Schizophrenia and Severe Character Disorders

PSYCHOTHERAPY OF PREOEDIPAL CONDITIONS:

Schizophrenia and Severe Character Disorders

by Hyman Spotnitz, M.D., Med. Sc.D.

JASON ARONSON, INC.
NEW YORK

Copyright © 1976 by Jason Aronson, Inc.

ISBN: 0-87668-242-5

Library of Congress Catalog Number: 75-37489

typeset by Jeanne Lombardi
      New York, N.Y.

Manufactured in the United States of America

Preface

This book spans more than a quarter of a century. Its contents blend papers that are now out of print and currently in demand with previously unpublished lectures or other oral presentations and some of my most recent contributions to multi-authored books on issues in contemporary practice. All of the material has been reedited, some of the early reports have been extensively revised, and the book has been organized to reflect the evolution of contemporary individual and group approaches to patients with severe but psychologically reversible problems originating in the preoedipal phase of development. These include psychosomatic conditions, psychotic states, and character and behavior disorders that can be traced back to psychological disturbances during the first two years of life.

The book focuses on two subjects with which I have been preoccupied since I began the private practice of psychoanalytic therapy in 1939. One is the treatment of schizophrenia and other preoedipal disorders; the other, analytic group psychotherapy, as applied for the same purpose. I was drawn into the latter area during the 1940s as consulting psychiatrist to the treatment agency where S. R. Slavson and his associates were intent on the systematic development of group procedures.

The book is intended for psychiatrists, psychologists, psychiatric social workers, and members of the other behavioral sciences, or those preparing to enter these fields, who are interested in achieving significant results in the treatment of severe forms of emotional illness. Understanding of the many forces that serve to create the mature personality is essential in this difficult work; but this needs to be combined with knowledge of therapeutics if one wants to help individuals with crippling preoedipal problems achieve their potential in life.

When students enter supervision, their main interest is usually in filling the requirements for carrying on the practice of psychoanalytic therapy. Operating under the pressure for accreditation, they tend to forget what they learn. If they return to supervision later, they generally demonstrate more serious concern about treating patients more effectively.

It has been my privilege to carry on a second round of supervision for students and colleagues already trained in classical psychoanalysis who solicit further guidance in their work with schizophrenic and other preoedipal patients. These supervisees, like practitioners who consult me when problems arise in their management of such patients, have shown much interest in tracing the evolution of the modern methods of treating them. Knowledge of the various stages in the development of the approaches I recommend has not only increased their security and comfort in working with these patients; it has also stimulated new and original contributions in the spirit of these approaches.

In making the same knowledge available through this book, I hope to open up new perspectives in the treatment of the preoedipal disorders and to facilitate more consistently effective results in these cases.

Six of the papers in this book were collaborative works, as indicated in the text. They are reprinted here with the permission of Mrs. Yonata Feldman, M. S. W., Mrs. Betty Gabriel, Philip Resnikoff, and the estate of Leo Nagelberg, Ph.D.

I am pleased to acknowledge the cooperation of Julia Older Bazer in the presentation of the book. Her assistance encompassed the organization and editing of its contents and the revision of some of the chapters.

HYMAN SPOTNITZ

Acknowledgments

For permission to reprint material to which they hold copyright, grateful acknowledgment is made to the following sources:

Introduction: "My Philosophy of Psychotherapy." JOURNAL OF CONTEMPORARY PSYCHOTHERAPY, 1973 (6:43-48). Copyright, the Long Island Consultation Center, Forest Hills, N.Y.

Chapter 2: Discussion of "Irrational Trends in Contemporary Psychotherapy" (E. K. Schwartz and A. Wolf). PSYCHOANALYSIS AND THE PSYCHOANALYTIC REVIEW, 1958 (45 [1-2]:74-78). Chapters 2, 4, and 9 reproduced by courtesy of the Editors and the Publisher, National Psychological Association for Psychoanalysis, New York, N.Y.

Chapter 3: "Strengthening the Ego through the Release of Frustration-Aggression." AMERICAN JOURNAL OF ORTHOPSYCHIATRY, 1958 (28:794-801). Chapters 3, 15, and 16; Copyright, the American Orthopsychiatric Association. Reproduced by permission.

Chapter 4: "The Maturational Interpretation." THE PSYCHOANALYTIC REVIEW, 1966 (53:490-495).

Chapter 5: "The Toxoid Response." REPORTS IN MEDICAL AND CLINICAL PSYCHOLOGY, Monograph No. 3, 1963. Chapters 5, 10, and 11: Copyright, Psychology Department, Stuyvesant Polyclinic, New York, N.Y.

Chapter 6: "A Psychoanalytic View of Resistance in Groups." THE INTERNATIONAL JOURNAL OF GROUP PSYCHOTHERAPY, 1952 (2:3-9). Chapters 6, 21, 22, 23, 27, 28, 29, and 30: Copyright, American Group Psychotherapy Association, Inc.

8   ACKNOWLEDGMENTS

Chapter 7: "Psychoanalytic Therapy of Aggression in Groups." CURRENT PSYCHIATRIC THERAPIES, 1968, Volume 8, edited by J. Masserman. Copyright, Grune & Stratton, Publishers, New York, N.Y.

Chapter 8: "The Management and Mastery of Resistance in Group Psychotherapy". THE JOURNAL OF GROUP PSYCHOANALYSIS AND GROUP PROCESS (now GROUP PROCESS), 1968 (1[2]:5-23).

Chapter 9: "The Myths of Narcissus." THE PSYCHOANALYTIC REVIEW, 1954 (41:173-181).

Chapter 10: "The Narcissistic Defense in Schizophrenia." REPORTS IN MEDICAL AND CLINICAL PSYCHOLOGY, Monograph No. 1, 1961.

Chapter 11: "The Need for Insulation in the Schizophrenic Personality." REPORTS IN MEDICAL AND CLINICAL PSYCHOLOGY, Monograph No. 3, 1963.

Chapter 12: "Techniques for the Resolution of the Narcissistic Defense." PSYCHOANALYTIC TECHNIQUES: A Handbook for the Practicing Psychoanalyst, edited by B. B. Wolman. (C) 1967 by Basic Books, Inc. Publishers, New York.

Chapter 13: "Group Psychotherapy with Schizophrenics." GROUP PROCESS TODAY: Evaluation and Perspective, edited by D. S. Milman and G. D. Goldman, 1974. Charles C Thomas, Publisher, Springfield, Ill.

Chapter 14: "Initial Steps in the Analytic Therapy of Schizophrenia in Children." THE QUARTERLY JOURNAL OF CHILD BEHAVIOR, 1952 (4:57-65). Chapters 14 and 20, Copyright, Jelliffe Trust.

Chapter 15: "The Attempt at Healthy Insulation in the Withdrawn Child." AMERICAN JOURNAL OF ORTHOPSYCHIATRY, 1953 (23:238-251).

Chapter 16: "Ego Reinforcement in the Schizophrenic Child." AMERICAN JOURNAL OF ORTHOPSYCHIATRY, 1956 (26:146-162).

Chapter 17: "Adolescence and Schizophrenia: Problems in Differentiation." ADOLESCENTS; Psychoanalytic Approach to Problems and Therapy, edited by S. Lorand and H. I. Schneer, 1961. Copyright, Medical Department, Harper & Row, Publishers, Inc., Hagerstown, Maryland.

Chapter 18: "Object-Oriented Approaches to Severely Disturbed Adolescents." THE ADOLESCENT IN GROUP AND FAMILY THERAPY, edited by M. Sugar, 1975. Brunner/Mazel, Publishers, New York, N.Y.

Chapter 19: "Observations on Emotional Currents in Interview Group Therapy with Adolescent Girls." JOURNAL OF NERVOUS AND MENTAL DISEASE, 1947 (105:565-577). Copyright, Jelliffe Trust.

Chapter 20. "Resistance in Analytic Group Therapy: A Study of the Group Therapeutic Process in Children and Mothers." THE QUARTERLY JOURNAL OF CHILD BEHAVIOR, 1950 (2:71-85).

Chapter 21: "The Borderline Schizophrenic in Group Psychotherapy." THE INTERNATIONAL JOURNAL OF GROUP PSYCHOTHERAPY, 1957 (7:155-174).

Chapter 22: "The Concept of Goals in Group Psychotherapy." THE INTERNATIONAL JOURNAL OF GROUP PSYCHOTHERAPY, 1960 (10:383-393).

Chapter 23: "Touch Countertransference in Group Psychotherapy." THE INTERNATIONAL JOURNAL OF GROUP PSYCHOTHERAPY, 1972 (22:455-463).

Chapter 24: "Acting Out in Group Psychotherapy." GROUP THERAPY 1973: An Overview, edited by L. R. Wolberg and E. K. Schwartz, 1973. Copyright, Intercontinental Medical Book Corporation, New York, N.Y.

Chapter 25. "Group Therapy in Perspective." THE AMERICAN JOURNAL OF PSYCHIATRY, 1972 (129:606-607). Copyright 1972, the American Psychiatric Association.

Chapter 27: Book Review, *A Psychotherapy of Schizophrenia: Direct Analysis* (A. E. Scheflen). THE INTERNATIONAL JOURNAL OF GROUP PSYCHOTHERAPY, 1962 (12:267-269).

Chapter 28: Discussion of "Accelerated Interaction: A Time-Limited Approach" (F. H. Stoller). THE INTERNATIONAL JOURNAL OF GROUP PSYCHOTHERAPY, 1968 (18:236-239).

Chapter 29: "Resistance Reinforcement in Affect Training of Analytic Group Psychotherapists." THE INTERNATIONAL JOURNAL OF GROUP PSYCHOTHERAPY, 1958 (8:395-402).

Chapter 30: Discussion of "Harassed! A Dialogue" (L. S. Brody). THE INTERNATIONAL JOURNAL OF GROUP PSYCHOTHERAPY, 1966 (16:491-494).

Contents

PSYCHOTHERAPY OF PREOEDIPAL CONDITIONS:

Schizophrenia and Severe Character Disorders

Introduction

When I entered medical school some forty years ago, I did not contemplate a conventional practice in any field of physical or psychological medicine. I turned to neurology and psychiatry because the investigation of severe mental illness was opening up as a major research area at that time. While a student at the University of Berlin, I enrolled as a voluntary research assistant at the Kaiser Wilhelm Institute for Brain Research, in order to study the microscopic structure of the brain. My investigations of nervous and mental functions were continued later at the New York Neurological and Psychiatric Institutes. What I learned in the course of these studies—especially through investigation of the rationale of the "talking cure" and experimentation with pharmacologic treatment—gradually drew me into the practice of psychotherapy.

As a medical student, I had checked some of the assumptions on which Freud based his working hypotheses and also obtained some unexpected dividends from amateurish ventures in self-analysis. But I have always been more impressed with the value of psychoanalysis as a method of investigating human functioning than as a self-contained technique of therapy. I underwent formal training in psychoanalysis primarily to learn and test out the classical procedures; this was necessary to determine the extent to which these procedures would have to be modified in the formulation of a scientifically well-grounded approach to the treatment of schizophrenic patients and others suffering from severe emotional disorders. I had a strong desire to contribute to the development of an operational theory, flowing out of the basic working concepts of resistance and transference, that would facilitate the systematic treatment of the preoedipal conditions and attain results as predictable as those secured in the mild oedipal conditions.

As a research psychiatrist specializing in psychoanalytic therapy, I combine the study and treatment of the preoedipal disorders in my practice. And strive through words and attitudes to advance the science and art of helping each person produce in his own physico-chemical organization—the body's own chemical laboratory—whatever rearrangement of his physiological and psychological functioning would permit him to feel, think, an and accomplish what he wants to in life. My own interventions are designed to stimulate this laboratory to produce the physico-chemical and psychological changes the patient needs to become well, stay well, and determine his own destiny.

ROLE OF MATURATIONAL AGENT

In recent years, I have conceptualized my clinical role as that of a maturational agent helping people with psychologically reversible disorders resolve whatever obstacles to personality maturation they have experienced. In these terms, the goal of the case is to bring the patient's personality to full term—emotional maturity. The goal may be spelled out in different ways; in the course of a favorably developing treatment relationship, it usually subsumes a succession of intermediate goals, which both parties agree to pursue. Accurate diagnosis of the factors impending personality maturation, and interventions focused on the immediate growth needs of the personality, are essential for achieving the ultimate goal of the case.

I operate indirectly as a maturational agent unless I discover that this goal can be achieved more readily and easily through a direct approach. In other words, I address myself to the obstacles to personality maturation, working to resolve them when they operate as resistances to communication. And in working with patients with the most incapacitating blockages, those rooted in the preoedipal stage of development, I usually accept full responsibility at the beginning of treatment for resolving these obstacles, provided that the patient agrees to adhere to the treatment schedule, lie on the couch, talk, and pay for the treatment. I have been increasingly impressed with the fact that it is the psychotherapist who has the primary task of making change possible.

EXPANSION OF INTERVENTIONS

At the beginning of my practice, I tried to adhere to the basic model technique of psychoanalysis; that is, I endeavored to resolve the patient's resistance patterns exclusively through the use of interpretation. I still regard interpretation as the primary intervention, but the extent to which I use it in each case depends on its effectiveness in resolving the immediate obstacle to personality maturation. Experience has substantially expanded the range of interventions I regard as permissible in analytic psychotherapy. In addition to various types of verbal communications, I now utilize nonverbal and emotional communications. I refer to this approach as modern psychoanalysis (1969a).

In my early years of practice, I conducted treatment exclusively in the one-to-one relationship. I now use the group therapeutic setting as well, treating both groups of strangers and the family group. I have found the dyad to be the preferred setting for patients with the preoedipal disorders. But the results achieved to date in exposing some of these patients to both settings, concurrently or in sequence, suggest that a highly specific combination of individual and group therapy will eventually emerge as the treatment of choice for the most severe disorders.

The rapid expansion of the field of psychotherapy that began in the 1960s stimulated a great deal of experimentation with therapeutic methods. Widespread dissatisfaction with the time-consuming nature of the traditional methods and increasing recognition of the need to help a greater number of people motivated this experimentation, by and large. Some of it has been ingenious, even creative, but because of the trial-and-error nature of experimentation in psychotherapy, it has led to the use of ineffectual as well as effectual treatment procedures.

Experimentation played a vital role in the development of psychotherapy and is the key to its further advancement; but the lack of adequate criteria for the critical evaluation of results has always plagued the experimenter in our field. It is often difficult to determine whether one is engaging in responsible psychotherapy or in irresponsible experimentation. The misleading impression that treatment that affords gratification is also therapeutically effective creates other problems. Some disarray and corruption is therefore inevitable, but I believe that the vast majority of psychotherapists who are testing out new methods dedicate themselves to the development of approaches that will significantly benefit patients.

Under strong pressure to meet the community's need for expanded psychotherapeutic service, however, some investigators have focused on demonstrating how much can be accomplished at minimal cost. This puts the cart before the horse. Figuring out the best method of treating particular categories of patients *regardless of expense* merits top priority. After this has been determined, the next step is to find out how to apply that method in the least costly way.

IMPROVING MENTAL HEALTH PRACTICES

The role of psychotherapy transcends the commitment of its practitioners to the relatively few persons each of them works with in his own professional quarters. Knowledge thus acquired of the complexities of human behavior and of the relation between individual and social psychopathology needs to be disseminated to improve the emotional well being of society as a whole. As a profession, we have an obligation to teach the principles of mental health to the community at large, to exert our influence to improve their application, and to constructively direct the attention of other disciplines and educational institutions to specific practices that violate these principles. All of this entails cooperation with the other behavioral sciences, educators, and various social agencies.

First and foremost, in the interests of prophylaxis, there is a great need to expand the school curriculum to include courses in emotional education. The present high incidence of mental illness suggests that such training is too difficult to be entrusted almost exclusively to parents. If society were to accept this responsibility, just as it accepted responsibility for intellectual training when it became too onerous for parents, far fewer children would suffer emotional damage. Some school systems now provide group psychotherapy for those already damaged, but this does not attack the broader problem. Courses conducted to teach children how to handle their feelings and to help them understand the distinction between the "sayable" and the "doable" are no less important than training them to work with figures, letters, and other intellectual tools.

The emotional realities of growing up in an era of quickening social and technological change, and of marriage and parenthood would also be included in a broadly based program of emotional education in the schools. Parents may train their offspring to behave well *as children;* but the high divorce rate attests to general neglect in the training of children to become good husbands or wives. This is fully as important, if not more so, than courses in sex education.

Our influence might contribute, too, to the outmoding of potentially harmful techniques to which young people are often exposed. For example, in a college physiology class attended by one of my patients, the instructor suddenly chopped off the head of a guinea pig. Observing the general state of shock precipitated by this "experiment," and responding to members of the class who voiced objections to being forced to witness it without any forewarning, the instructor explained that he had sacrificed the animal to demonstrate human reactions to sudden and violent death. Exposing students to such an ordeal without preparing them for it and securing their consent to undergo it can be a severely damaging experience.

Psychotherapeutic knowledge ought also to be applied to the task of providing optimal working conditions for those who staff the medical institutions of this country. Resident physicians, nurses, and orderlies cannot perform well when they are not given enough time to eat, sleep, relax and function as social beings. That is one reason why acutely ill patients in general hospitals are often deprived of the type of service they need. The remuneration of hospital employees is now astronomically higher than when I was an intern; the hospital could not afford to pay me more than fifteen dollars a month. But earnings are only one aspect of the problem. When there's a will, ways of improving working conditions can also be found, and perhaps more expeditiously through our cooperation with hospital administrations.

Probably we would be more successful in helping other disciplines remedy damaging practices in their respective provinces if we were able to exert the influence of a united profession. Psychotherapy today is a fragmented domain. The various schools of psychotherapy go their own ways. The knitting of psychotherapy into a discrete profession has also been retarded by the diverse educational backgrounds of those who work in the field and their primary allegiance to other disciplines—medicine, psychology, psychiatry, social work, education, and so forth. Under these circumstances, I anticipate that psychotherapy will ultimately become a major field of application in an integrated science of human behavior.

TREND TOWARD SPECIFICITY

The many blinders that are worn in the field of psychotherapy today hamper its scientific progress. The fact that a practitioner's ministrations lead to improvement in a patient is no indication that the patient is being exposed to the treatment method that will solve his emotional problem. The placebo effect is a pervasive element in psychological treatment. Nonspecific approaches to this problem, even the fact that one is interested in the patient and agrees to treat him, have positive effects. Moreover, there is no justification for the claim that any one method is superior to others *for all patients*. Rigidity in theoretical allegiance, personal predilections, training, and expertise on the part of the practitioner the patient happens to consult may deprive the patient of the precise type of treatment experience he needs.

Although I dislike the analogy, the human psyche does in some ways resemble the automobile motor. Both are composed of many different assemblies, and both are subject to defects that cannot be corrected by a single technique. When we are confronted with symptoms of psychic malfunctioning, we need to know what assembly is implicated and what technique to apply to correct the defective functioning in that assembly. For a person with excessively disturbing feelings of emptiness and unreality, for example, the choice of interventions indicated depends on the impulses that are producing the feelings. We need to know what types of communications and attitudes would modify these feelings. But today the correction of the problem entails more tinkering than really circumspect interventions.

When psychotherapy is more uniformly based on accurate diagnosis, and when we know how to correct defects in each psychic system most expeditiously, and with minimal disruption, specificity in psychological treatment will become the rule rather than the exception.

The field of psychotherapy will probably continue to expand, and the trend toward specificity will foster the emergence of subspecialties. As in medicine, general practitioners will treat patients presenting a variety of readily reversible conditions; specialists in the field will probably devote themselves exclusively to one or another category of more intractable patients.

We know now much more about the constructive application of psychotherapeutic procedures than about their destructive potentialities. Detailed descriptions of the types of errors that are made are needed. All of us make errors, and this is not wholly undesirable; to err is human, and no patient wants to be with a therapist who functions perfectly at all times. But to condone all errors is as objectionable as to refuse to tolerate any.

Consistently constructive emotional interchange with our patients and the elimination of errors that are grossly contraindicated would be facilitated by the development of a science of *toxipsychology*, which would perform a service similar to that of toxicology in clinical medicine. I anticipate that toxipsychology will eventually come into being and provide vital information about the toxic effects of certain psychological communications and attitudes, in contradistinction to therapeutic psychology and psychotherapy. As this knowledge of therapeutic versus toxic psychology and psychotherapy accumulates, it is reasonable to assume that psychotherapy in the many areas of psychological and psychosomatic illness will become more efficient.

OCCUPATIONAL HAZARDS AND REWARDS

There are occupational hazards in the practice of psychotherapy. The most serious for me are confinement to my office for many hours of the day and the limitations imposed on my physical activity. Another hazard is associated with the somatization of repressed emotions, which exposes one to the development of organic illness. We have begun to recognize feelings as a source of needed therapeutic leverage in the treatment of many patients;

but it is as important for the preservation of our own health as for the recovery of our patients that we be able to feel our own feelings and the feelings induced in us by those we treat.

No other profession provides a better opportunity to experience the full spectrum of human emotions. From the bewildering variety of feelings communicated by patient after patient in diverse sequences and tempos, and at different levels of intensity, one distills from this unfolding panorama of psychic change the essence and the flux of human existence. To really succeed in helping people achieve their emotional potential is always a rewarding experience. And helping them invest this potential in zestful and creative achievement makes all of the psychotherapist's efforts—and torture—worthwhile. It gives him a sense of complete personal and professional accomplishment.

PART ONE:

Latent Emotional Processes

Human beings influence one another through actions, impulses, and emotions. Less widely recognized than the reciprocal effects of the impulses and feelings that are communicated deliberately through language or behavior is the impact of their unexpressed attitudes. The chapters in this section are concerned with the import of some of these unconscious emotional processes for psychotherapy.

Early observations on certain sources and operations of such emotional influence between patient and psychotherapist are reported in Chapter 1.

Chapter 2 concerns the varying effectiveness of the consciously or unconsciously communicated attitudes of the psychotherapist. Their immediate impact, it is suggested, depends on the emotional state of the patient exposed to them, and the timing of the exposure.

Chapter 3, particularizing this idea, introduces a theme that is reiterated frequently in subsequent chapters; that is, the crucial role of aggressive impulses in personality formation and functioning. Since destructive manifestations of aggressive impulses dominate the treatment of the severe emotional disturbances, various techniques for dealing with them are described and illustrated.

Chapters 4 and 5 are also concerned with the potentially damaging forces that are aroused in the psychotherapeutic relationship. Processes of diminishing the patient's vulnerability to these forces, and then of immunizing him against them are suggested.

Chapters 6 constitutes a general guide to the recognition and application of the psychoanalytic concept of resistance in the therapeutic group setting. The general theory and value of dealing with all obstacles to progress in terms of resistance are outlined in this early study.

Chapter 7 focuses on the specific problem of handling manifestations of destructive aggression in the course of group treatment.

Chapter 8 presents specific guidelines for the systematic application of the concept of resistance in conducting group therapy.

Emotional Induction

It is well known that the presence of emotions in one individual may significantly influence the emotional state of another. This phenomenon is most dramatically illustrated by social psychologists (for example, McDougall, 1924) whose studies of the effect of the spread of similar emotions upon the actions and thoughts of large multitudes have facilitated the understanding of social and mass behavior. The significance of the phenomenon for psychotherapy has received little attention. Freud wrote about thought transference—mental telepathy—but did not report on the interpersonal transference of emotions. Brill (1949) explicitly referred to the latter process in stating, "Of course, emotions beget emotions" (p. 224); he also observed that any marked emotional affect tends to arouse some patients from a "congealed state" (p. 219). He did not, however, pursue the import of emotional induction for ego formation. Its therapeutic implications for people with emotional problems are focused on here.

VALUE OF EMOTIONS

What is the value of emotions per se? What role do they play in our functioning? All of us are aware that it is much easier to do something when we feel like doing it than when we do not. Behavior is facilitated by compatible emotions. The possession of a rich supply of compatible emotions eases our adjustment to immediate realities; the constant availability of such emotions enables us to function well spontaneously.

Based on a paper presented at the annual meeting of the American Psychiatric Association in 1949.

How does emotional induction occur? Observations suggest that it is an unconscious process that operates constantly among human beings. However, the conditions under which they are most likely to react to this unconscious emotional influence are not known. Studies suggest that the greatest sensitivity to such influence obtains in the child-mother relationship, particularly in the infant, who seems to sense the parent's emotional state. Support for these observations has emerged from the psychoanalytic study of children and also of adults, such as the physically handicapped, for whom sensitivity to the emotions of others serves a self-protective purpose.

ORGANIZATION OF EMOTIONS

It is important to distinguish between impulses toward emotional discharge and actual emotional discharge. The experiencing of an emotion appears to coincide with the acceptance of an impulse toward emotional discharge. When two individuals have the same impulse and the same attitudes about discharging it, both experience the same emotion. They will not do so, however, if these attitudes differ. In other words, similar impulses that are unconsciously held in check by different defense processes lead to the experiencing of dissimilar emotions, or the absence of emotions in the second individual. Impulses that are inhibited become intensified.

The fact that emotions can be induced therefore suggests that the induction in a patient of a specific emotion or emotions whose relative absence has interfered with his achieving his potential in life might well be accepted as an essential aspect of the psychotherapeutic endeavor. The application of this principle, however, would not be easy. Considerations of timing and the appropriateness of one or another mode of functioning would be involved in the exploitation of the emotional induction factor for therapeutic purposes. Moreover, the possibility of inducing unhealthy emotions needs to be recognized and controlled. Hence, careful and prolonged therapeutic work may be entailed in the effective use of emotional induction.

CLINICAL ILLUSTRATIONS

When one individual induces emotions in another, the latter may be aware of the source of these emotions. For instance, a psychiatric social worker reporting on the case of a 12-year-old girl with a tendency toward anxiety and depression, reported that her young client naively remarked, "I caught my fear of mice from my sister." In thus describing one factor in the development of this fear, she seemed to take it for granted that emotions could be "caught" in the same way as a contagious disease.

Frequently, however, the individual in whom an emotion is induced is unable to account for it. A young man who was describing his introduction to a young woman at a party a few nights earlier, said, "She was a beauty, but I muffed it. I just felt too disagreeable to be nice to her. I haven't the slightest idea why." Eventually, they met again and the young woman told him that he had aroused disagreeable feelings in her at first sight; he reminded her, she said, of someone who had always rubbed her the wrong way. This patient had known he was sensitive to his own feelings, but it came as a great surprise to him that he was also sensitive to the feelings of others.

It has been repeatedly noted that members of therapy groups react to one another's emotions. Often they appear to be governed by the emotional attitude of the preceding speaker.

At times they act in harmony with the induced feelings. This is illustrated by the successive reactions of adolescent girls to the suggestion of the group therapist that, instead of having refreshments at the social agency where the group held its sessions, they have it elsewhere when they finished their work. The therapist recorded the following material:

Fay said that if she were to stop and eat before coming here, it would be too late, and she doesn't have enough money to eat out. Ethel works in a factory, where she polishes diamonds. She carries her lunch, and feels it would be too difficult to carry food for both meals. Belle, too, would find it difficult, because she rushes to her job as soon as she leaves school, and she does not know how she could manage. And so it went down the line.

Material from the same group session illustrates how differently individuals may react to the same emotional influence. At a time when their communications were unconsciously dominated by reproductive urges, one girl described a dream about having a baby, other verbalized sexual fantasies or recalled their childhood interest in dolls. At that point, another girl responded more maturely:

Hilda expressed surprise as she heard these girls talking because it seemed to her that they all liked to indulge in impersonal things. They seemed to have imagination; they daydreamed. She and her sister, particularly her sister, never had any imagination. Her sister was just a "regular down-to-earth person." As for Hilda herself, she never played with dolls; what she wanted was a real baby. Actually, she began early to take care of babies.

VARIED EFFECTS

Induced emotions may significantly influence the emotional attitude of the analysand toward the analyst. For instance, at a time when I was trying to find out how some of my analysands would respond to a feeling of self-restraint, I conveyed that feeling by remaining silent for a prolonged period. Six different reactions were noted.

One woman was delighted. She remained quiet for 45 minutes. At the next session, she said that she could not recall a situation in which she had felt "more free to do nothing and really enjoy it."

To another woman, my attitude of self-restraint signified anger. She said she could not bear feeling that she had made me angry.

A young man did not object to my self-restraint. In the next session, he said that he had felt free to talk about whatever he pleased.

Another man experienced my attitude as lack of interest. He felt that he was talking to himself during the session.

A tense verbal outburst of hostility was the response of the fifth patient. Even though, the night before, she had enjoyed an orgasm during intercourse with her husband for the first time in several years, she felt that she was not benefiting in any way from the analysis.

The sixth patient felt that the same attitude communicated criticism.

An investigation of these reactions suggests that they were similar to those induced in the child-parent relationship when one or the other felt restrained. For example, the woman who experienced the self-restraint as criticism said, "Mother was dissatisfied with me from the day I was born. She would restrain herself for a long time and then explode, so I got to expect that her silences would end with some expression of disapproval."

Emotional induction is an important factor to bear in mind when one is treating schizoid or schizophrenic patients. They sense the therapist's emotional attitude and may react to it with compliance or defiance.

A schizoid man in his early twenties entered treatment because of psychosomatic symptoms, general malaise, and bizarre behavior. In the initial interview, after the preliminary arrangements had been made, he was directed to lie on the couch but not told what he was to do there. The analyst was aware that he hoped the patient would spontaneously begin to talk. To his surprise and amazement, however, the young man spent the rest of the period relaxing on the couch, smoking cigarettes, crossing and recrossing his legs, stretching, and generally luxuriating in his newfound freedom—without uttering a word. He appeared to be extremely comfortable.

That impression was verified more than a year later, when he told the analyst that the first session was the most pleasant of his analysis. Accustomed as he was to being driven by his parents, he experienced the absence of pressure as permission to do as he pleased.

It was subsequently confirmed that his silence had been based on a distinct emotional perception that the analyst wanted him to talk. Reacting to this desire, he had indulged his unconscious attitude of defiance because he had not been specifically instructed to talk.

RECIPROCAL INDUCTION

In analytic therapy, emotional induction is a reciprocal process. As the patient develops a transference, the therapist usually develops a counter-transference, which is based on unconscious reactions to the patient's transference attitudes and behavior. The effectiveness of the therapy depends in large measure on the therapist's ability to "feel" the patient's tendencies toward instinctual discharge. The capacity to sense his latent emotions and help him feel them determines whether their relationship is grounded in genuine emotional understanding or is primarily an intellectual exercise. In working with a severely disturbed patient, it is extremely important that one have the capacity to experience the emotions he induces and to help him verbalize them in the process of dealing with his resistances.

Influencing the patient to feel his latent emotions is often difficult, because he usually has no intimation of their existence. When exposed to them, his ego cannot function, and his symptoms are defenses against such feelings. The therapist comes to feel them gradually, and guides their discharge in language by working on the defenses. In the course of this work, the discharge patterns become more and more spontaneous and ego-syntonic. The pressure to behave rigidly diminishes, and the patient becomes a more flexible and adaptable human being.

Studies of patients undergoing psychoanalytic therapy lead to the recognition that integrated functioning of the ego requires that impulses be only partially gratified. The patient needs to become aware of his impulses *gradually*, and also to restrain them sufficiently so that they become emotions—the driving fuel of the ego. An evolving ego is one that continually utilizes primitive impulses for emotions with which to perceive and react to external situations.

Such studies have also consistently revealed that the damming up of aggressive impulses causes the most dangerous disruptions of personality functioning. If the patient feels these impulses in their full intensity, he tends to inhibit their release. They are therefore held in check by various devices. Thus inhibited they give rise to destructive emotions in the patient, and also tend to stimulate aggressive impulses in others. With the reciprocal induction of such impulses, an eruption of destructive behavior in the therapeutic situation becomes possible. Damaging changes in the patient and therapist or damaging action by either one or both parties are prevented by facilitating the rapid verbal discharge of the negative feelings aroused.

On the other hand, if the patient has positive impulses toward the therapist and these induce similar impulses in the therapist, they will experience these impulses as mutual affection. This leads to the formation of a cooperative relationship, in which they can help each other achieve the goals of the treatment. Furthermore, their joint analytic activity will tend to be more productive if they limit themselves to discharging their positive emotions in language. Such restraint will intensify these emotions, and the stronger the emotions the more energy they will command for pursuing their common purpose.

Cognizance of the emotional induction factor appears to facilitate the maturation of the preoedipal personality. Negative impulses can be neutralized by helping the patient discharge them in language, and healthful feelings can be induced by positive impulses in the therapist.

CHANNELIZATION AND ACTION

Impulses to action in one individual may arouse similar impulses in another. When their patterns for discharging an impulse are similarly organized, they experience the same type of emotions—characterized as induced emotions. Discharge processes stimulated in an individual whose discharge patterns are dissimilar to those of the inducing individual may lead to different emotions or to the absence of emotions.

Inability to channelize primitive impulses in socially desirable ways may account for various psychological disturbances.

A psychotherapist who has the capacity to sense the patient's impulses to action, and also to recognize impulses and emotions they induce in himself, can utilize these emotions to help the patient resolve his resistances. The induced emotions provide an additional source of therapeutic leverage in the treatment of the severely disturbed patient.

Induced emotions are of particular importance in the treatment of patients with preverbal problems. The aggressive impulses of such patients require primary attention because they may develop into physically destructive patterns. These impulses can be neutralized by helping the patient discharge them in language.

The presence of positive impulses in the therapist can induce healthful feelings in the patient, and helps him channelize his destructive impulses into emotions which can be regulated.

Unconscious Attitudes of the Therapist

It has long been my impression that the psychotherapist whose primary interest is to provide patients with the benefits of his own wisdom and solutions for the problems of life risks the danger of violating the scientific integrity of his role. Almost inevitably, his concern with being a therapeutic force in the lives of the fellow beings he deals with in his treatment relationships leads him into the untenable position of volunteering his personal judgments on moral and ethical issues and of deciding what is rational or irrational, desirable or undesirable for his patients.

The temptation to exceed the limits of his professional role is not one to which the "pure" scientist is exposed. His task is to describe an existing situation as accurately as he can and to develop the particular hypotheses which make it possible to foretell the subsequent course of events. Since he can measure his predictions against the events which actually do flow out of the situation, he can determine for himself the correctness of his position.

One cannot operate so fortuitously in an applied science. In this area it is more difficult to decide which hypothesis or approach is best, which will stand the test of time. Additional considerations, such as practicality and the immediacy of benefits, figure in the decisions. Frequently what is best in theory has to be discarded for utilitarian motives, or for the rapid amelioration of a situation.

These are factors which often confront the psychotherapist. If he is more interested in being as therapeutic as possible than in functioning with scientific objectivity, he tends to set up a system of values whereby he decides what is good and what bad for his patients, what is to be encouraged and what discouraged. Personal wishes—what pleases the therapist himself—influence his judgment; the wishes of society—social approval—also enter into this system of values.

INTRUSION OF VALUE JUDGMENTS

With these to draw upon, he can do more than provide a patient with an objective description of events, their correct analysis and the prediction of their consequences—the province of psychoanalytic psychotherapy. Why limit himself to pointing out various courses in life when it is within his power to select the course and pattern of behavior which would be best for a patient, thus saving him the trouble of making his own selection? Hence, the goal of healing the mind and making it capable of operating healthfully in its own interests tends to be lost sight of as value judgments adulterate the analytic process.

Another impression I have gained from the paper by Drs. Schwartz and Wolf (1958) is that they feel that they have discovered a way to do psychotherapy that is universally good or right, in contradistinction to a bad or wrong way to do it. Sharing the fruits of their discovery with us, they argue eloquently in support of the first, and warn against the second or unapproved way. I would be the last to quarrel with them on this score. They are rather to be congratulated if they really have found one right way to do psychotherapy and if it works for them.

If I understand correctly, this "right way" encompasses such attitudes, beliefs, and procedures as the following: Reinforcing the positive, constructive aspects of a patient's personality and exploiting to the utmost his healthy resources; balancing psychotherapy with psychosanity and taking care not to become submerged in the pathological and irrational; distinguishing between seed and weed by making reasonable demands and imposing limits; upholding reason, judgment, intelligence, learning, science, and the objective point of view; a multidimensional approach to human behavior; consistent, persistent vigilance; determining the outcome through the application of therapeutic ingenuity.

Is there one among us who would disagree with any of these ideas? All that the authors recommend figures in good analytic psychotherapy and also, one might add, in good human relationships. It must be pointed out, though, that all of these values can be distorted or injected inappropriately into some treatment situations and that they may prove useless in others. An objective point of view, reason, and esteem of learning, to give a few examples, have their own time and place.

But that is also true of attitudes and practices that they vigorously denounce. Among these are preoccupation with the negative or pathologic aspects of the personality; exclusive concern with feelings; being personal; being interested in the dead; ideology which is non-rational, alogical and spiritualistic; viewing the analyst as peculiar and bizarre; destroying pathology with stronger pathology; telepathy; induced psychosis; going into depth; mistaken permissiveness and numerous other things.

NEED FOR PRAGMATISM

I do not agree that such attitudes and practices are invariably bad. These too can have their time and place. Indeed, after reviewing what the authors implicitly categorize as virtues or vices in psychotherapy, I must admit that almost every item in the approved list I have found to be an ineffective procedure, while those they decry have proved on occasion to be most helpful in moving a patient forward on the road to health. The truth of the matter is that there are no absolutes in this area. What is very effective in one situation can be relatively less effective in another, and of no therapeutic value whatsoever in still other situations.

The same principle operates in the fields of clinical medicine and pharmacology, where almost every kind of medication or procedure has its indications and contraindications. The drug that is therapeutic in one dosage can be toxic for the same person in a larger dosage, or for someone else in the original dosage. A surgical procedure that is curative in one case can be fatal in another. To enable a bone to heal properly, it may be necessary to fracture it.

What all of us want is effective psychotherapy—the method that will lead to the best results with the least expenditure of time and energy. It is not brought any closer by the advocacy of "good" psychotherapy, by invective, or by the blanket condemnation of procedures which we do not personally approve. What we need to know are the *organization, application, and sequence of psychotherapeutic principles and attitudes that are essential to achieve the best results*. In other words: What is effective and what is ineffective in each psychopathological condition, and what psychological instruments are the most efficacious for dealing with various kinds of psychological situations and problems?

LEARNING FROM ERRORS

Had the authors made the point that many psychotherapists use methods that are unproductive because of improper timing or inappropriateness to specific situations, I would have agreed with them. All of us make errors time and again.

Instead of advocating the good and condemning the bad in general terms, it seems to me that, at the present time, the task confronting us is to report on the effectiveness of psychotherapeutic measures in specific situations and about the timing or sequence in which particular measures have produced the best results. Patients and society as a whole are making demands on us for the more precise application of specific procedures. These demands can be met by illuminating the still dark areas of psychotherapy with fresh knowledge.

Dealing with Aggressive Impulses

Coauthor: Leo Nagelberg, Ph.D.

In the life equation of every human being, the aggressive drive is an x force whose value is determined by what he does with it. Constructively released toward the outside world by a mature ego, the drive serves as a precious raw material for productive living; but if it is suppressed and repressed, the finished products are likely to be social maladjustment and emotional illness. What an individual does with the drive depends, in turn, on how his primary needs were met by his mother or other significant objects in his childhood experience. As Glover points out, aggressive impulses radically influence the mind from the very beginning of life and, besides contributing to normal development, "can be responsible for the most severe forms of mental breakdown" (1949, p. 40).

For example, the individual who was exposed early in life to extreme frustration of his basic needs habitually responds to frustration by mobilizing excessive aggressive impulses. Our present concern is with the patient who responds in this manner and, especially, with the development of healthy patterns for the release of his frustration-aggression.

A prodigious amount of psychotherapeutic effort is expended in undoing the evil consequences of suppression and repression. One of the reasons why play therapy and activity group therapy (Slavson, 1943) are commonly employed with children, and various educational, inspirational and counseling procedures with adults, is to secure the release of suppressed energy. These are among the generally recommended methods of stimulating emotional discharge and facilitating the formation of new release patterns.

But the patient who has developed stubborn infantile defenses against the release of aggressive impulses may require something more fundamentally reconstructive than new opportunities and outlets for emotional release. Unless the actual *patterns* of his pathological behavior are resolved—that is, mastered and outgrown—the pressure to revert to them may prove irresistible. To be of permanent value, his treatment must be oriented to the resolution of these patterns. The psychic energy which has been so unprofitably invested in maintaining them can then be put at the ego's service for its own maturation and other desirable purposes.

That is why the preferred form of treatment for such a patient is intensive analytic psychotherapy, with consistent interpretation and working through of the infantile defenses. As a rule, this process serves to reawaken images and memories of the relationship and situations—usually preverbal ones—in which these patterns of response to frustration were originally formed and experienced. If catharsis takes place the resolution of the patterns becomes possible.

THERAPEUTIC IMPASSE

In a problem case or particular stage of treatment, however, a patient may fail to experience catharsis despite the accurate and well-timed interpretation and working through of his infantile defenses. The failure may be associated with too strong an attachment to the original object, which often militates against the development of a full negative transference toward the therapist.

Such a patient may remark, for example, that he is utterly worthless and that is why his therapist won't talk to him. Time and again it may be explained that he feels that way because he is attacking himself, and intellectually the patient may be able to grasp the validity of that interpretation. He does not feel any the better for it, though, unless the defense pattern it reactivates leads to a kindling of images and memories of the early experiences in which the defense was patterned. That, we repeat, is the *sine qua non* for resolving the pattern: the bringing to consciousness of the original experience and the discharge of aggressive impulses in new feelings, thoughts and language.

How is one to proceed when the ego attitudes of a patient who has been consistently receiving judicious interpretation block catharsis? Can the release of his hate tensions be instigated in some other way, or must treatment grind to a standstill?

We have found that such an impasse can generally be averted if the therapist psychologically reflects the infantile defense patterns as one aspect of treatment. We shall suggest certain theoretical concepts underlying this ego-strengthening approach,* and indicate how it has been employed by the

---

*For a fuller account of the therapeutic process, see Spotnitz and Nagelberg (1960).

authors and their colleagues for more than a decade in administering intensive analytic psychotherapy to several hundred patients who had proved refractory to consistent objective interpretation.

JOINING AND REFLECTING RESISTANCE

The long-range treatment goal, one to which the therapist needs to be constantly oriented, is the resolution of the patient's various resistances to telling the story of his life in a spontaneous and meaningful manner. As long as he has a strong need to maintain these resistances, no pressure is exerted on him to overcome them. Quite the reverse. The therapist supports and reinforces the resistance patterns—*joins* them. In a well-structured and favorably developing relationship, the psychological needs which gave rise to them gradually diminish. As the patient becomes more and more capable of functioning without these resistances, he tends to give them up voluntarily. Eventually they are mastered and outgrown—fully resolved.

How do the infantile defenses fit into this general plan? They are reactivated in frustrating treatment situations, and help the patient resist talking significantly about his life. They therefore fall into rank among the resistances which the therapist joins. One of the ways he does this is by psychologically reflecting their patterns.

Psychological reflection is a therapeutic approach which is not used exclusively to deal with the problem we are discussing. We shall not attempt to examine this approach, however, except as a specific means of facilitating the refractory patient's pathological response to frustration.

For this purpose, two forms of psychological reflection are often employed. We shall refer to one as an echoing procedure and the other as a devaluating procedure. Each is designed to resolve a different aspect of a defense pattern which is probably not too unfamiliar: the pattern of the worthless ego attacking its "low-down" self or worshiping a wonderful and distant object.

Echoing the Ego

The ego's pattern of self-attack is highlighted through the echoing procedure. The therapist uses it to repeat—at times with dramatic emphasis—the patient's expressions of low regard for himself. The unequivocal echoing of his ego in the process of "low rating" itself strengthens his attitude that he is not fit company for a wonderful object. And yet, however black the ego, the object never moves away. It dedicates itself to meeting the ego's constant need for psychological closeness to an object, the kind of object that will stick with the ego through thick and thin. That is the crucial factor.

Hypothetically, this procedure may be said to reverse the original process of ego formation, when the infantile mental apparatus failed to release hostile feelings toward its earliest object since the latter was experienced as being too distant. Feelings of being neglected, and of being deprived of an object that could be depended on to receive the aggressive impulses which were mobilized, contributed to the formation of a pattern of directing these impulses back upon the mental apparatus. A similarly frustrating situation is created in treatment when the object echoes the ego's attacks upon itself, but with this vital difference: The once distant object has been replaced by one constantly within reach, one always close enough to serve as a target for the ego's aggressive impulses. Sooner or later the psychological twin image which faithfully stands by and joins in the ego's attack upon itself arouses sufficient resentment to reverse the flow of mobilized aggression from the ego to the object.

As it is repeatedly demonstrated that expressions of hostility do not drive the object away, the patient tends to discharge his aggression more and more freely in feelings and language. The feelings of hate and aggressive fantasies with which he characteristically responds to the echoing procedure often lead to the hoped-for recall and release. That is, the hateful situations in which the infantile defenses were structured and activated are recalled, and aggressive impulses are released in the form of emotionally crystallized and verbally discharged energy.

The Case of Mr. A.

To demonstrate how the echoing procedure may be used and what may result from it, we shall report some interaction which took place in the treatment of Mr. A. This prosperous and respected businessman regarded himself as a faker and could see little satisfaction in his life—past, present, or future. His attacks upon his own ego were psychologically reflected to help him resolve this pathological response pattern and develop a healthier pattern of attacking the object without fear of losing it. The four successive interviews drawn upon took place within a two-week period during the third year of treatment.

First interview. Dispiritedly, Mr. A complained that he was a rank failure. The therapist paraphrased the complaint and agreed that Mr. A could be regarded as a rank failure. Almost at once, the patient became more animated. He accused the therapist of looking for an excuse to drop the case. Then he added, "I resent your looking upon me as an inferior person. If I really was one, how could I solve my problems? But I have to admit that I really don't believe you when you say nice things about me. Words of approval don't give me the strength to fight. The first time something stirred inside me was when you criticized me."

Second interview. The patient began speaking about himself in very discouraging terms and the therapist echoed his remarks. This irritated Mr. A, and he declared, "My situation really is hopeless, but I don't want *you* to say so. Do you think I want to feel this way?" Battling against his feelings of hopelessness, the patient went on to say, "Instead of always attacking me, why can't you be helpful?" The therapist asked, "Why must I always be helpful? Why can't I attack you too?" After some consideration, the patient replied, "When you give me the idea you might not want to be helpful, you do seem more alive to me. That makes me feel more alive too; and I want to fight back. The trouble is I still feel I shouldn't attack you."

Third interview. Mr. A declared that no one loved him; probably this was so because he wasn't worth loving. He was asked, "Is there anything about you that makes you worth loving?" The patient quickly answered, "That's just your way of saying you have no love for me. I ought to quarrel with you for saying such things, but I know there are many things about me which people hate." He proceeded to recall occasions when he had felt resentful toward his associates.

Fourth interview. He hated most of the people he knew, Mr. A said, and he distrusted all of them, even the therapist. The latter asked, "Do you think that you yourself can be trusted?" The patient exclaimed, "Well, you really rang the bell that time. You should have asked me that a long time ago. I complain that people put pressure on me, and they really do; but I certainly put pressure on them. I don't give them any reason to trust me." As the session went on, the patient became more and more emotionally involved. He said to the therapist, "I'm beginning to get somewhere now, but you're no longer an easy mark for me. You make me feel like a baby beginning to walk." This led to the statement that the therapist was beginning to make Mr. A feel as he had once felt with his father. Early childhood experiences which had made the patient feel tense and numb were then recalled. He said that he had always bottled up his true feelings because he did not dare to give his father any reason to disapprove of him.

Devaluating the Object

There is more than one way of psychologically reflecting an ego in the process of "low rating" itself. Instead of echoing the ego's complaint about itself, the object may respond: I'm just as bad. In effect, that is what happens when the therapist employs the so-called devaluating procedure. He picks up the same cue as for the echoing process to resolve another aspect of the infantile defense pattern: the tendency toward object-worship. The lowly ego makes deep bows before the wonderful object perched way above it; such a superior object cannot be treated with hostility without risking the loss of its valuable services. Hence, the therapist acts upon an appropriate cue from time to time to make the object less wonderful, to move it down to the ego's level. He suggests that instead of being an omnipotent therapist, he is just like the patient—equally inadequate or equally in need of help. Since they are really brothers under the skin, he deserves to be attacked and will welcome it.

The specific element in the process of ego formation which is being reversed through this maneuver, it is hypothesized, is closely related to that on which the echoing procedure is based. The greatly needed original object which was experienced as too rarely available also came to be regarded as too valuable to attack. Rather than risk damaging such a wonderful object or driving it even farther away, the infantile mental apparatus began to bottle up its aggressive impulses. The therapist's disillusioning attacks expose the ego to the frustrating experience of looking on while its cherished object is painfully devaluated. But it is transformed into an object that can be attacked with relief and with impunity, so that it eventually receives the verbal attack it has been inviting.

The two procedures described may be used singly or in combination at any phase of therapy. The one that we have generally employed first is the echoing procedure, with its focus on the patient. The process of object devaluation is usually set in train after the patient has acquired some feeling for the therapist as an external object. Interpretation, by the way, becomes an increasingly important aspect of the treatment process as the infantile defense patterns are gradually resolved. After the patient has become fully capable of expressing in the treatment relationship the aggression that objective interpretation may mobilize, the therapist shifts from psychological reflection to interpretation as his judgment dictates.

The Case of Betty

We shall now demonstrate the devaluating procedure—its use and characteristic effect. Betty, the patient, was an attractive single woman in her late twenties. Though advancing in her profession, she habitually complained that outside her office she felt like a robot or "lifeless shadow" who had to conform totally in order to survive. The therapist's interpretations of her behavior would help her for a while to assert herself more freely in her social relationships; but she could not be budged from the attitude that she herself was defective, and too dependent on the godlike creature who was deigning to treat her to express any hostility. Material is presented from a therapy session during which the devaluating procedure was employed to facilitate the resolution of this stubborn defense. The session took place after she had been in treatment for several years, with different therapists.

Betty complained that she didn't trust herself to go out socially; besides, no one ever asked her for a date. The therapist told her it was obvious that he hadn't helped her; had he done a better job, many men would have been taking her out. Betty responded that he couldn't be serious, and she apologized for painting such a gloomy picture. At any rate, if anyone had failed, it was herself, not the therapist. When he repeated that he had failed her and was responsible for her lonely evenings, Betty said that he was making her feel uncomfortable. She preferred to think that *she* was at fault. She added, "I tell you I'm a failure to annoy you, but I'm really not because I don't do or feel a thing."

Again the therapist shouldered the blame, and again she disagreed. He could show her how to walk, she said, but he couldn't do her walking for her. Betty went on, "What's the use of blaming you if I don't want to move? In a way, though, you are right, I ought to be wanting a husband instead of always sitting alone and doing nothing. Now you're making me feel terrible. Why must you get me so worked up about things? I hate to say it, but you really should have helped more than you have. No, that isn't true. I haven't cooperated. I should have talked more freely."

She *had* talked freely, she was told. Bewildered, Betty asked the therapist if he was certain of that. Then, after pausing briefly, she exclaimed, "You're right! I told you everything but it hasn't helped. What about all the time and money I've put into this treatment? If you get me to believe you, I'll be too mad to ever come again."

The therapist asked, "Why can't you be mad and still come? Even if I have failed, all this can change. I can begin to understand you if you'll help me."

"That would be a cheap way out for you," Betty shouted, "But if you haven't helped me by now you never will. Besides, since when is it *my* job to help *you*? If you need help, go and see an analyst yourself."

The therapist's next statement was that, although Betty had spoken freely, she had made no attempt to help him make her as popular as she wanted to be. They could work together to accomplish this if she would display more initiative about it.

Betty made no effort to conceal her anger as she shot back, "I could help you, and I'm smart enough to point out all the mistakes you've made, but I hate you too much to help you. My foot! I'll help you into the grave. If I let it sink in that you've botched up my treatment, I'd go crazy, scream and cut my throat. No. It's you who ought to go to prison for getting me in such a state. I was too nice to tell you what I thought of you before, but now I'm so mad I don't care. I ought to report you and sue you for my money. If I tore you to pieces I could plead insanity and get off scot-free."

After Betty's rage had somewhat subsided, she calmly—almost apologetically—told the therapist that he had gotten her into a mess, and would have to get her out of it.

"Why don't you get *me* out of it?" he asked her.

"I wouldn't lift my little finger to help you," Betty replied. Then she laughed. "You see how I hate you when you don't let me have my way. If you won't let me win, I won't let you either, even if my whole treatment goes up in smoke. Now you've seen how furious I can get when I let myself go. And there's still plenty of anger inside me."

Later in the session Betty remarked that she had never felt free to vent her anger until the therapist had told her he had failed her. The patient continued, "That made me want to fight because you wouldn't let me take the blame. Then I was able to feel my real feelings. I know that I can succeed: I really don't have to be so meek and apologetic. . . . But I still feel that you're on the defensive. I know it's absurd, but I also feel that you're still afraid of me and jealous, like the enemy I used to feel my mother was. I would try to convince her that I was good, so she wouldn't keep on being my enemy and attack me. But I was never as innocent as I tried to appear. I'd fight Mother tooth and nail, and I wanted her to die. All the time I was afraid she wouldn't go on taking what I was dishing out. I felt she was scared but would pay me back some day. I expected that would happen today when I hit at your feelings of importance. I was afraid you couldn't take it and would turn against me."

Betty stopped suddenly and appeared to be thinking over what she had just said. Then she told the therapist that she now realized she was taking the same attitude toward him that she had once had toward her mother. "I've been living all these years with my mother's image inside me," Betty declared. "I never dared to disobey her and show her my true colors. I was always against her but never felt it before. Now I'm going to begin thinking for myself."

In conclusion, brief presentations focusing on clinical practices often create a misleading impression. Inadvertently, we may have conveyed the notion that psychological reflection is a sort of gimmick, or a device that can be flicked on mechanically at any time in any treatment relationship. We therefore wish to make it clear that what we have been discussing is *not* an artificial technique. It is, rather, a general approach which the therapist has to develop in his own way and assimilate comfortably to his own personality. To be spontaneous and therapeutic, his responses must be motivated by genuine feeling for, and a sincere desire to help the patient. That is the key to the effective use of psychological reflection.

4

The Maturational Interpretation

Significant stages in the growth of understanding about the curative factors in analytic psychotherapy are reflected in changing emphases in interpretation. Half a century ago it was thought that what healed a patient was the recall of memories. Treatment was then regarded as incomplete unless "all the obscurities of the case are cleared up, the gaps in the patient's memory filled in, the precipitating causes of the repressions discovered" (Freud, 1917, pp. 452-453). When it became evident that the memories were less important than what prevented their recall, interpretations were made to overcome the repressive forces in the guise of resistance. Later resistance was recognized as an essential source of interpretive data because it told the story of the ego's development. The focus shifted to the constrictive influence that resistance, in order to create more favorable psychological conditions for ego functioning. Explanations were oriented toward the integration of the ego and the acquisition of insight.

More recently, widening appreciation of the communication function of resistance has stimulated other approaches to interpretation. As yet, these have not dispelled the misleading notion that therapeutic change issues primarily from objective understanding of one's behavior. In the professional literature, "interpretation" is still commonly laced together with such verbs as "convince," "point out," "demonstrate," "prove," "confront," and "unmask." But the use of interpretation primarily for veil-lifting purposes is waning, with the recognition that other aspects of the treatment relationship are often more significant than the development of self-understanding. The patient usually acquires this, but it is rarely the decisive factor in the case.

INADEQUACY OF OBJECTIVE UNDERSTANDING

Objective understanding of his behavior does not invariably make it easier for him to change it. Of course, the therapist has to understand what motivates this behavior, but he does not intervene just to transmit insight. Scientific understanding is the raw data for therapeutic understanding, that is, some knowledge of what goes on in the patient which is given to him if and when it will unlock the door to personality change. Instead of trying to overcome resistance by explaining problems, the analyst uses interpretation to create the precise emotional experience that will resolve the problems.

In many cases I find it helpful to operate on the hypothesis that interpretation is consistently employed for maturation purposes. The treatment itself is conceptualized as a growth experience. In this context, the problems which motivate a person to undergo treatment are attributed, to some extent, to inadequacies in his interchanges with the environment from conception onward. These interchanges—physiochemical and biological as well as psychological—are with different configurations of environmental forces which, in a sense, constitute maturational teams. During infancy, mother and child form the team. When the oedipal level is reached, the child's maturational interchanges are more specifically with his family. Then the social team takes over and the reciprocal processes encompass an expanding circle of peers and adults.

The candidate for psychotherapy is viewed as a person who is unable to deal comfortably with the exigencies of his life because he sustained some damage in these early maturational interchanges. He commits himself to a supplementary series of interchanges with a therapeutic object because he suffers from the effects of failures, or memories of failures. Deleterious experiences with his natural objects caused fixations or arrests in growth. In attempting to cope with them, he developed maladaptations: certain repetitive patterns that drained off energy needed for maturation into circuitous processes. Consequently, he presents two distinctly different problems. One is that his maturational needs were not met. The other is that his maladaptations prevent him from effectively assimilating the experiences that would reduce these needs. The operation of these patterns block maturation.

REVERSAL OF MALADAPTATIONS

Maladaptations are not totally reversible, but it is sufficient for the analyst to intervene to loosen their compulsive grip and to nullify the effects of the original blockages. If he does so, the patient usually requires little help in obtaining and assimilating experiences that will reduce his maturational needs.

In theory, therefore, the therapist does not intervene to reduce maturational needs directly; nor does he address himself to maladaptations (defenses) that do not interfere with maturation. Rather, he intervenes to lay the foundation for new growth by freeing the patient from the stranglehold of pathological maladaptations. As these patterns are reactivated in the relationship (transference) they are studied until the analyst understands how they were set up and why they come into play in a given situation. He relates to the patient in terms of this understanding but does not share it unless the patient desires an explanation that would facilitate his talking and cooperative functioning. In that case, an interpretation is indicated. By and large, maladaptation patterns are dealt with when they have been reactivated with sufficient intensity to be reducible.

Although patients enter treatment in different degrees of immaturity, there are few who do not require some period of preparation before they reach the stage in which interpretation alone will resolve maturational blockages. Preverbal patterns are responsive only to symbolic, emotional, and reflective interventions. Affective nonverbal communications, even the analyst's state of being, give the preoedipal personality freedom to grow. During this preparatory period, the emotional logic of the patient's behavior on the couch is not explained to him. The therapist listens to him, silently analyzes, and generally maintains the attitude of the thoughtful parent with a young child. Intimacy may flow out of this attitude, but it is not fostered deliberately.

After the preoedipal maladaptations are more or less resolved, the patient becomes accessible to verbal interpretation. Thereafter the analyst gives the response which, in his opinion, will resolve whatever maturational blockages are hampering the patient at that moment.

MOTIVATION AND TIMING

In my experience, interpretation is ineffective unless it is motivated by a specific therapeutic intent. The response of the patient is a more important consideration than the accuracy of the explanation. The analyst should be able to anticipate the patient's reaction to an interpretation, and then voice it only if the anticipated reaction would be desirable at that time.

The hit-or-miss effect of interpretation given to convey the general understanding of a problem is illustrated by a report which recently came to my attention. The patient was a young man who had been brought out of the depths of a severe depression. While the more serious factors in this case were dealt with, the analyst had withheld comment on the patient's disclosures regarding his perverse tendencies. Then one day the analyst decided that he ought to call attention to their implications. In an absolutely correct, even brilliant interpretation, he pointed out the harmful consequences of the perverse behavior. The patient agreed that it was interfering with his recovery. He went on to say that the perverse activity gave him little gratification, and that the time had come for him to give it up.

In recalling what happened, the therapist said, "He knew exactly what I meant, and thanked me for opening his eyes, but I never saw him again."

The interpretation, which would probably have been helpful at another time, apparently stimulated an unconscious battle to defeat the therapist, whatever the cost. The patient was in such an intense state of negative suggestibility that, had he been told that giving up the perverse activity forthwith would make him miserable and mobilize his old suicidal urges, he might still be in treatment. That, at any rate, would have been the maturational interpretation at that time.

I have focused in this discussion on the science of interpretation. Its skillful use takes us into another realm. Intuition, inspiration, and empathy are among the personal qualities which are entailed in the sensing of the exact constellation in which an interpretation will be dynamically effective, and in expressing it in words that will ring bells at the patient's own level of communication. The art of interpretation cannot be taught. It can, however, be nurtured by mastery of the scientific principles.

5

The Toxoid Response

A certain defensive preoccupation with the unrecognized and inappropriate reactions of the analyst to his patient has characterized the literature on countertransference since Freud introduced the term to encompass "what arises in the physician" as a result of the patient's influence on his [the physician's] unconscious feelings" (1910, p. 144). The "perfectly analyzed" practitioner having been conceded as nonexistent—a derivative of the Myth of the Hero (Glover, 1955, p. 4)—deliverance of the human instrument from the insidious clutches of the "patient's influence" has been the major concern. In striking contrast to the reliance on transference as a conceptual tool, the "counter" phenomenon has been viewed, by and large, as a wholly unwelcome intruder bent on disrupting the analytic process. Vigilant attention to the analyst's subjective and unconscious reactions as a contribution to therapeutic failure has tended to obscure, or at least to retard the recognition of those reactions that are realistically induced in him by the patient as a valuable component of psychoanalytic therapy.

These objective derivatives of the therapeutic encounter are destined to gain increasing acceptance in the future. Their potential value is now being explored as an aspect of various developments in the field. For example, the application of psychoanalytic therapy to a broadening spectrum of psychiatric conditions entails the investigation of new modes of functioning to meet the special requirements of those who are severely disturbed. Continuing efforts to expedite the therapeutic process and enhance its effectiveness for patients in all categories also expose the traditional attitudes and practices to searching inquiry. Some modifications are suggested by our growing understanding of the ingredients of a corrective emotional experience, and by the related new concept of facilitating the meeting of maturational needs. These considerations presage a more discriminating approach to countertransference.

The attitude most prevalent today, however, is that the development and expression of feelings for the patient are out of order. In most respects this attitude is unassailable, for reasons too familiar to detail here. It is in the interest of patients that the analyst remain free from emotional involvement with them. Such freedom also facilitates his professional functioning. Moreover, there can be no quarrel with the strictures against his exploiting the treatment relationship as an outlet for his own emotional gratification. But what if the patient has a maturational need to experience feelings from his partner in the relationship? His need challenges the attitude of emotional detachment. And observations of the therapeutic effectiveness of certain types of countertransference reactions strengthen the challenge.

A more flexible approach is encouraged, for example, by reports of cases being expedited by the direct communication of the analyst's negative feelings about a patient's resistant behavior. In the light of Breuer's abrupt termination of the case of Anna O. when he became aware of the strong reaction she was provoking in him (Jones, 1953; Karpe, 1961), and of the still respectable policy of referring patients to other practitioners as a solution to countertransference problems, it is novel to read of treatment relationships that were preserved and even moved forward dramatically *after* the analyst had communicated his feelings.

Such an incident is disclosed by Alexander (1956, pp. 90-92); he reports having ended an apparent stalemate by venting his impatience, explaining the transference situation, and admitting his dislike of the patient. Stekel (1950, p. 180) and others have also reported cases that took a good turn after the analyst had expressed his anger to the persons concerned. Tower (1956) acted out extreme irritation with an abusive woman by "unconsciously and purposely" forgetting their appointment one day. After the incident, the analysis proceeded more productively.

ACCEPTANCE OF OBJECTIVE COUNTERTRANSFERENCE

In these cases the therapeutic effectiveness of the analyst's emotional confrontations was inadvertent. In each instance the analyst had reached the limits of his tolerance, but the frank admission of that fact had by no means been calculated to further the progress of the provocative patient. Another breach in the recommended attitude of emotional detachment is more fundamental. It involves the acceptance of countertransference as a dynamic tool in the therapeutic armamentarium.

Excluded from this formulation are subjective reactions based on the practitioner's unanalyzed or insufficiently analyzed adjustment patterns. Feelings developed for significant figures in his personal history and transferred to the patient are differentiated from those that are justified by objective observation of the latter. The influence and communication of such transferred feelings may continue to be regarded as highly undesirable, whereas feelings that are empathically induced in the analyst by the patient may be utilized in various way to meet the patient's treatment needs.

Induced feelings may be employed solely as an aid in the fact-finding process—that is, to facilitate the understanding of the patient or an issue in the case. Saul points out that these feelings are a "sensitive indicator of what is going on in the patient" (1958, p. 140). But more active use may also be made of induced emotions. Rado utilizes them to "provoke a relieving outburst" (1951, p. 240) in a depressed patient whose retroflexed rage reaches an alarming degree. Winnicott reports that his feelings are at times the "important things in the analysis of psychotic and antisocial patients." Carefully sorted out from subjective reactions, he reserves the "truly objective countertransference," especially hatred, until it can be used interpretively.

PLANNED COMMUNICATION OF INDUCED FEELINGS

My own experience and findings with respect to induced feelings agree with the observations just outlined. Emotional states created in me by objective study of a patient's personality and behavior serve as a direct tap on his unconscious; these states also influence and eventually enter into my interpretations. However, my communications to the patient based upon induced feelings are as a rule planned, rather than adventitious, and are not limited to interpretation. I also communicate these feelings as an additional method of dealing with the resistances of the highly narcissistic patient.

In cases of schizophrenia, psychotic depression and other severe disturbances, one encounters resistances, chiefly preverbal, that do not respond to objective interpretation. Their resolution is thwarted by toxic affects that have interfered with the patient's maturation and functioning. In my experience, these resistances yield to an emotional working-through process, in contradistinction to the customary working-through on an intellectual basis.

The troublesome affects are of two kinds. They are either those of the patient himself or the negative affects of the original object to which the patient's infantile ego was unduly sensitive. Exposure to these emotions creates either similar or antithetical states—induced neurosis or psychosis—in the analyst. If he is able to recognize and tolerate these emotional states indefinitely without acting on them, they can be utilized to neutralize the pathological effects of the patient's past experiences and immunize him against sensitivity to similar emotions stimulated by other people in the future.

Emotional Immunization

It might be pointed out that successful analysis and interpretation of the defensive and repressive forces that hold toxic emotions in check may secure their discharge in language. Nevertheless, the kind of patient we are considering is highly vulnerable to recurrences of the pathological affects. The precise nature of the emotional upheavals to which he is inordinately sensitive depends on the pattern of his life experience; whatever that has been, the affects are approached as foreign bodies that have impeded maturational processes. To reduce his disposition to these upheavals in the future, he is given verbal injections of the emotions he has induced in the analyst, carefully "treated" to destroy their toxicity and to stimulate the formation of antibodies. In brief, *the induced emotions are employed as a toxoid.*

The science of immunology contributed to the elaboration of this concept, but it is compatible with the spirit and principles of resistance analysis and has been suggested in the literature. Ackerman, for one, writes about the need for injecting the "right emotions to neutralize the patient's wrong ones" (1959). Rado refers to "emotional neutralization" as the therapeutic task and the "contagiousness of emotions" (1953, pp. 265, 266) as a significant mechanism in the interaction of patient and therapist. Coleman and Nelson write about the "gradual dosing" of patients with specific responses to immunize them against pathological reactions (1957, p. 39). Freud himself, in describing the permanent change wrought in the mental life through the successful handling of resistances, stated that the patient is "raised to a high level of development and remains protected against fresh possibilities of falling ill" (1917, p. 451).

Communication of Negative Feelings

The assumption prevails that Freud was fundamentally opposed to the exertion of emotional influence by the psychoanalyst. Indeed, references to it are absent from his statements on technique, and he developed a system of analyzing all of the induced feelings and of interpreting them in an unemotional manner. But one of his most illuminating statements on countertransference contradicts this belief. In a letter written to Binswanger in 1913 (but not published until some forty years later), Freud refers to countertransference as one of the most difficult problems in psychoanalysis, one more easy to solve in theory than technically. The letter continues:

> What is given to the patient should indeed never be a spontaneous affect, but always consciously allotted, and then more or less of it as the need may arise. Occasionally a great deal, but never from one's own unconscious. This I should regard as the formula. In other words, one must always recognize one's countertransference and rise above it, only then is one free oneself. To give someone too little because one loves him too much is being unjust to the patient and a technical error (Binswanger, 1957, p. 50).

The exclusion of any reference to the negative feelings induced by the analysand is characteristic of Freud. A letter he wrote in 1915 refers to a patient who "actually has been running away from me, since I was able to tell her the real secret of her illness (revengeful and murderous impulses against her husband)." He then dismisses the woman in these words: "analytically unfit for anyone" (Binswanger, 1957, p. 62). If Freud ever confronted this patient or any others with feelings of hatred, he appears not to have done so through the "consciously allotted" affects that he had already advocated for conveying feelings of love. This may help to explain his pessimistic views about the treatment of the narcissistic disorders.

Subsequent experience has borne out Freud's conviction that the resistances of narcissistic patients cannot be safely overcome by the customary analytic method; but we have also learned that they respond to other methods (Spotnitz and Nagelberg, 1960). Like Hill (1955), Winnicott (1949), and others who have focused on the destructive impulses as the most troublesome in such cases, I have found that the narcissistic defense can be resolved when it is dealt with as a defense against feelings of hatred and self-hatred, and joined and reinforced until it is outgrown (Chapter 10).

Apart from Freud's failure to address himself to the induced feelings of hatred, his 1913 statement on countertransference is entirely compatible with the modern psychoanalytic approach to the deeply narcissistic person.

The utilization of the induced neurosis or psychosis as an ally in treatment represents a preliminary foray into the psychodynamics of the psychoanalyst, an area that requires more thorough exploration in the future. Nevertheless, it is my impression that many analysts, who do not accept the giving of feelings as an essential part of the therapeutic process, do expose their patients to feelings that facilitate appropriate behavior and thus ease their adjustment to reality. Their need to experience feelings consonant with their maturational needs probably accounts in some measure for the time-consuming nature of the working-through process, even in cases of neurosis. Some patients manage to pick up toxoid emotions from other people at the same time as their progress in the analytic situation is slowed up by the intellectual nature of the established working-through process.

This process will be expedited, I believe, when both the phenomenon of emotional induction and psychological needs at each level of maturation are better understood. Effective utilization of the objective countertransference to meet these needs would then become an important aspect of all forms of analytic psychotherapy.

USE OF OBJECTIVE COUNTERTRANSFERENCE

Early in my psychiatric practice I treated a young woman, suffering from paranoid psychosis and epilepsy, who was regarded as unsuitable for classical psychoanalysis. The case was handled on a research basis during the period when I was undergoing my personal analysis. In investigating her responsiveness to various techniques, I operated mainly on the assumption that, since I was intensely interested in curing her, verbalizations of the feelings induced in me by her personality and behavior would benefit her.

My unconscious could not have carried the burden that this approach entailed had I not been working on the subjective countertransference problems, one by one as I became aware of them, with my own training analyst. The identification and understanding of reactions associated with my own adjustment patterns helped me to recognize and work for the verbal discharge of the patient's latent emotions. These created reactions which I felt free to voice. The induced feelings also prompted me to make occasional comments on her functioning and appearance. I knew when she aroused anger in me and, in due time, let her know it.

An interpretation of her paranoid attitude was responded to as if it were a signal to dominate the treatment situation. Calm explanations of her problems branded me in her mind as a weakling bent on forestalling another outburst of rage. On the other hand, when I confronted her with the emotions induced by her psychotic tendencies, my interventions had a tremendous impact. She developed some respect for me and became amenable to therapeutic influence.

That was the first case in which I operated on the basis of the induced feelings. In verbalizing my reactions, I attempted to be sufficiently stimulating to produce movement in the case and yet not so stimulating as to force the patient off the couch. How to achieve the first and avoid the second effect I learned chiefly by trial and error.

Tempering Of Communications

It soon became clear that to act immediately on an impulse to respond to an unconscious resistance with an emotional communication was not consistently therapeutic. Spontaneous verbal expressions of my reactions rarely met with indifference, but they were harmful at times rather than helpful. A communication that stimulated an outpouring of anger in one situation could crush the patient into silence in another. But when my interventions were predicated on a study of what was going on between us—the emotional dynamics of the session and her discharge tendencies from moment to moment—she behaved in a more controlled way. The withholding and tempering of my communications until they became acceptable and meaningful to her ego permitted a therapeutic process to develop.

This process was conceptualized as one of immunizing a patient against toxic affects long before the pivotal role played by emotional induction in our relationship was recognized. Mutual contagion emerged as a basic factor: The analyst has to experience the patient's feelings in order to "return" them to him; the patient, through experiencing them from the analyst, is helped to discharge the feelings in language. The significance of this discharge became clearer after I had accumulated considerable evidence that nonverbal resistance patterns could be effectively dealt with when they were approached as primitive forms of communication rather than as manifestations of outright defiance of the rule of free association. When the patient is helped to maintain these resistance patterns, they are eventually outgrown. These three formulations—emotional induction, immunization, and resistance reinforcement—are integrated in my clinical approach.

Resistance Reinforcement

The more ill the patient, the less capable he is of talking about himself in an emotionally significant way. Presumably, he is forced to use infantile modes of communication because of his previously unmet maturational needs; their nature is reflected in the type of resistance patterns to which they give rise and which the patient stubbornly maintains. But feelings that were intolerable to his infantile ego come into awareness when the analyst expresses the similar or complementary feelings induced in him by the patient. By "matching" the feelings in this way, the analyst apparently helps the patient to meet his maturational needs because he becomes capable of discharging the warded-off feelings in language. As he feels and verbalizes these toxic affects through his identification with the emotionally responsive analyst, the resistance pattern is outgrown and the patient commits himself more easily to spontaneous self-revelation through language.

Departures from a passive attitude are not indicated while a resistance pattern is being investigated early in treatment. The standard approach is maintained as long as the patient functions cooperatively or remains self-absorbed. The timing of the emotional response is regulated by the patient's contact functioning; that is, his direct attempts to elicit some personal information about the analyst or to involve the analyst in some emotional problem he (the patient) is unable to express in words. The induced feelings, tempered with understanding of their origin, may then be "returned" to the patient by the analyst through a response that reflects the pattern of the patient's resistance.

Timed and Graduated Confrontations

The confrontations are carefully timed and graduated to prevent uncontrollable reactions. The duration of the exposure and strength of the dosage are regulated by the intensity of the emotions generated. If the patient proves indifferent or is overstimulated, the emotional confrontation is discontinued. Otherwise, it goes on as long as it produces new understanding or ideas the patient was unable to deal with previously.

CLINICAL APPLICATIONS

Emotional responses figured prominently in the resolution of the resistances of the highly narcissistic young man I call Fred (Chapters 10, 11).

Early Stage of Treatment

Directly or indirectly, during the early stage of his treatment, he would start to verbalize thoughts of getting off the couch to attack me and then quickly lapse into silence. My interventions at the time were designed to help him talk about his destructive impulses and to tame them somewhat through such release. Feelings of guilt about what he might say clammed him up. He also had strong fears that talking about his impulses would force him to act on them. He was convinced that his destructive urges proved that he was incurable.

I noticed that the repetitive quality of his threats aroused a great deal of resentment in me; even more, I was aroused by his insistence that his troublesome feelings and fantasied acts of primitive violence made him unique. He fought strenuously against accepting the notion that such impulses were natural and that an important aspect of one's rearing was to learn to control them.

It occurred to me that the way to solve this problem was to demonstrate to Fred that I had similar thoughts and feelings about him. My first attempts to convey this idea were ineffectual. "Don't try that stuff," he said when one of his threats was turned back at him. "You're repeating what I say but you don't really feel it." But I had the impression that he was unconsciously egging me on. I bided my time until the feelings induced by his outbursts of rage permitted me to respond with equal vehemence.

Fred appeared to be ready for such a response when he shouted in a moment of fury: "I'll bash your head in." "No you won't," I exploded back at him, "because I'll bash yours in before you can get off the couch." Though he felt no need to defend himself against attack, he responded to this expression of genuine feelings by exclaiming: "You really do hate me as much as I hate you, and you can be even more vicious!"

He garnered relief and security from my emotional responses. As his terror of speaking about his destructive urges gradually diminished, they lost their toxic quality. If someone he respected and relied on could accept and verbalize such urges, so could he. When he permitted himself to dwell voluntarily on long outlawed feelings and thoughts of violence and found that he could do so without acting impulsively, the toxoid responses were discontinued.

As positive feelings for his own ego mounted, Fred matured sufficiently to accept, either spontaneously or with the aid of interpretation, many libidinal as well as aggressive impulses that had been ego-alien. By that time, the induced feelings I had stored up for long periods during the first two years of the case were rarely employed as a therapeutic instrument. Interpretations tend to dissipate these feelings; but I made no effort to sustain them when the interpretations were acceptable to his ego.

Late Stage of Treatment

Toxoid responses are often employed late in the treatment process to immunize a patient against the return of resistant attitudes. Daniel, a businessman in his forties, demonstrated the need for a "booster" during the last few months before I discharged him (1961, pp. 145-147). He had pulled out of a severe depression and resumed his normal activities, but from time to time he slipped back into despondency. In one such interlude he complained of bungling the impromptu talk he had given earlier in the day before a trade convention. After castigating himself for half an hour he paused, obviously appealing to me to lift his spirits.

Instead, I vigorously reproached him, expressing surprise that a man of his experience had not prepared some remarks for the occasion. The feelings of irritation and annoyance that he induced were mobilized for the response; the expression of these feelings had been withheld during the many months when he was too sick to defend himself. At that point, however, my reflection of his self-attacking attitude stimulated a lively counter-attack. This was a signal to proceed and step up the dosage.

To my criticism that he had muffed his opportunity and had been a rank failure, Daniel retaliated easily. He insisted that he had not acquitted himself so badly; it would have been in poor taste for him to "hog the occasion." Eventually his gloom vanished. With dramatic self-esteem, he ended the heated exchange with these words: "Enough, enough. What have I done to get your bowels in such an uproar? Why did you get involved in my business anyway? You're just my analyst."

After he had won the argument on rational grounds, he was rewarded with an interpretation. "All you ever want is to be attacked; you just beg for it. I gave it to you and now you feel better."

Daniel readily accepted the interpretation. In fact, all he needed at that time were a few more reminders of the connection between his once unconscious need to secure love by making "mother" sorry for him and the self-attacking tendency that had reasserted itself once again in that session. The final toxoid responses were administered in the case to invigorate him with sufficient understanding to recognize and protect himself in the future under circumstances that might encourage a revival of this tendency. A few more confrontations of this sort were helpful in dissolving the resistance.

RESOLUTION OF THERAPIST'S RESISTANCE

To provide a gravely narcissistic person with "treated" doses of the toxic emotions he experienced in childhood and re-experiences in the transference facilitates the therapeutic task of releasing the intense emotions he has held in check. However, the very fact that the emotional quality of the transference reactions is thereby intensified introduces the possibility of a new source of error: contamination of the analytic situation by an incorrect confrontation.

An incorrect confrontation can be more damaging than an incorrect interpretation. Transference reactions are damped by the neutral attitude of the analyst who limits himself to the classical approach. The treatment edition of the patient's nuclear conflict is weaker, so that wrong interpretations are of relatively little significance. They do not create reactions in the patient that are likely to distort or change the toxic emotions of the transference neurosis.

Such distortion is a greater danger if the patient is exposed to feelings developed by the analyst in relation to other people. Hence, countertransference cannot be utilized with complete confidence unless it has been purged of its subjective elements. These "foreign" influences have to be "analyzed out" of the objective countertransference before they contaminate the transference reaction. The toxoid response is compounded in the pure culture of the feelings induced in the analyst by the patient.

The time may come when we will discover that certain types of contaminated responses are also helpful. However, my own experience leads me to believe that the only emotional confrontations that are consistently therapeutic for the deeply narcissistic patient are those based exclusively on the feelings he induces. Certainly, the induced feelings promote a transference climate; in a sense, they add an important new dimension to transference.

Clinical Illustration

A situation about which a student analyst recently consulted me illustrates how the presence of subjective elements of countertransference can take one off on a tangent. The case she brought up for discussion was that of a young male schizophrenic who had been in treatment with her for about two years. In the negative transference he had already resolved his fears of becoming violent if he verbalized his destructive urges, but he was still in a state of conflict about remaining infantile or growing up. He repeatedly complained that his year-old marriage was going on the rocks because his wife was prodding him to get a better job.

During one session that his analyst discussed with me, the man said that when his wife brought up the subject, he would become aware of pains in his head. He felt like "sticking a knife through it."

"At that point," the analyst continued, "I wanted to say something that would make him feel that I was as hostile as his mother had been. I asked him: 'Why don't you go ahead and do it?' He replied: 'I think you are trying to destroy me.' If I had followed up by asking what difference that could make when he was set on destroying himself anyhow, he would have in all probability vigorously denied the self-destructive impulse and verbalized the feeling. But somehow I just couldn't give him that response. I said instead that I was just trying to get him to say whatever occurred to him. A little later he said that he was getting to feel hopeless about his treatment. I seem to have developed a resistance to responding as I should, and this is what is holding up the case. Since that session I've had a couple of dreams about it."

In the first dream, her patient repeated his statement: "I think you are trying to destroy me." Then he got off the couch and stood before her. "I was terrified that he would kill me," she went on. "That ended the dream, but the next night I had another one about him. In the midst of a session, a stranger walked in and my patient left the office with him. The stranger returned alone and tried to rape me. I cried for help but no one heard me. I woke up in a state of terror."

Associating to the first dream, the analyst connected it with a fear that the patient really believed that she wanted to harm him. His standing up in the dream probably signified that he intended to attack her sexually. The second dream indicated to her that she actually wanted to be raped, but by someone other than the patient. The stranger in the second dream represented the supervising analyst.

Eventually she recognized that her difficulty in responding to her patient in harmony with the induced feelings of anger was linked with her own sexual needs. Because of her husband's extended absence abroad, she labored under an unconscious wish to have someone "stand up" for her. This wish had checked her readiness to verbalize hostility. The analysis of her own sexual feelings and their influence on the case was necessary to resolve her counterresistance.

Dealing with Countertransference Problems

The ideal way to deal with countertransference problems that tend to develop when one works with profoundly narcissistic patients is to be in analysis oneself when one begins to treat them. As I have already indicated, this helped me to understand my resistances to treating narcissistic patients and also increased my tolerance for the feelings they induced. Even experienced practitioners who have no difficulty in treating neurotics may find it necessary to return to their training analyst or secure other aid in resolving personal problems they become aware of when they start to work with more intractable patients. The therapist who is unable to analyze the severe neurosis or psychosis they induce courts the actual development of psychotic or psychosomatic reactions unless he secures immediate help.

For the well-trained analyst who approaches treatment as an intellectual undertaking and has inhibitions about expressing his emotional reactions, the approach I have described above will be repugnant. On the other hand, the practitioner who can permit himself to experience the induced feelings, convert them into toxoid responses, and communicate these as necessary in the course of resistance analysis, works comfortably with narcissistic patients. As a matter of fact, such an analyst is more comfortable when he works in harmony with the induced emotions than when he tries to suppress them; to keep them out of his interventions entails the expenditure of considerable energy.

If the practitioner's personality is adapted to this approach, emotional induction operates in his interest as well as in the interest of his patients. A therapy based on the empathic understanding that develops in the analytic situation is beneficial for patient and therapist alike. For the recovery of the severely narcissistic person, this type of treatment experience is essential. Ultimately, we shall learn how best to create it.

6

Resistance in Groups

Freud called attention to the concept of resistance in analytic psychotherapy and emphasized its great importance in the following statement:

> An analytic treatment demands from both doctor and patient the accomplishment of serious work, which is employed in lifting internal resistances. Through the overcoming of these resistances the patient's mental life is permanently changed, is raised to a high level of development and remains protected against fresh possibilities of falling ill. This work of overcoming resistances is the essential function of analytic treatment; the patient has to accomplish it and the doctor makes this possible for him with the help of suggestion operating in an *educative* sense. For this reason psychoanalytic treatment has justly been described as a kind of *aftereducation* (1917, p. 451).

It is noteworthy that Freud regarded the labor of overcoming resistances as the essential achievement of analytic treatment. Experience indicates that this is as true of analytic group psychotherapy as it is of individual analytic psychotherapy. To the extent to which the group psychotherapist is successful in helping patients to deal with their individual resistances as they appear in treatment, their mental life is permanently changed, lifted to higher levels of development, and subsequently remains proof against fresh possibility of illness. Therefore, application of the concept of resistance is basic for analytic group psychotherapy as a scientific form of therapy.

The question then arises as to what are resistances in analytic therapy groups. The hypothesis was advanced (as reported in Chapter 20) that if a group of patients in analytic group therapy were directed to give emotionally significant accounts of their life experiences, they would respond to this direction with powerful forces opposing these revelations. These opposing forces or contrary tendencies were found to be analogous to the resistances to free association that develop in the course of individual analytic therapy. The success or failure of analytic group therapy thus depends on how these resistances are dealt with.

One might think that group therapy is easy: All one has to do is overcome resistances, get the patients to tell their life stories, and they will be "cured." Unfortunately, the process is not so simple. The modesty and reluctance of patients, the resistance of the individual members and that of the group as a whole have a social and personal value.

TYPES OF RESISTANCE

Individual resistances during psychoanalytic therapy are of five types: (1) ego resistance, (2) superego resistance, (3) id resistance, (4) secondary gain resistance, and (5) transference resistance (Freud, 1926). Ten or more defense mechanisms are involved in their utilization. The same resistances appear in the course of analytic group psychotherapy. However, a special complication is the fact that each type operates not only against the therapist in his efforts with each group member but also against the group members in relation to each other; and finally these individual resistances of the group members may unite to become a group resistance, of which there are also five types—(1) group ego resistance, (2) group superego resistance, (3) group id resistance, (4) group secondary gain resistance, and (5) group transference resistance.

A "group resistance" is understood to be the same form of resistance used by all or the majority of the members of the group at the same time.

Thus analytic group psychotherapy is a complicated process; administering it effectively requires skill and experience in individual psychotherapy as well as in group psychotherapy. It would be much more difficult to deal with resistances in the group setting than in individual treatment were it not for the fact that, in the initial stages of treatment in the group, the therapist can enlist the assistance of the members in dealing with each other's resistances. Frequently the success or failure of a group will depend upon the therapist's skill in enlisting their cooperation. The more planfully he does so, the greater will be the group's success in dealing with the members' resistances.

THERAPEUTIC VALUE

It is certainly not desirable to destroy resistances when they are of therapeutic value, nor is it desirable to remove them until their nature is fully understood: what form they take, what useful function they perform, and what would be the consequences of their removal. An obvious illustration of the therapeutic value of resistance may be drawn from a situation referred to by Freud (1921), in "Group Psychology and the Analysis of the Ego"—that is, a group may be dominated unconsciously by impulses toward parricide.

Let us suppose that the individuals in a therapeutic group are defending themselves against such impulses by ignoring the "leader" and acting as if he were not present. It is as though they were saying: "There is no need to destroy the group therapist; the group therapist does not exist." Someone who is not present cannot be destroyed. This transference resistance serves a useful purpose: The group members can tolerate their impulse to destroy the "leader" because, as far as they are concerned, there is no "leader"; at least, they feel, think, and may even act as if he were not there. They behave as though the dangerous act of destroying the therapist, having already been carried out, cannot be performed again. This resistance is of value for the psychotherapist too. He would not want the group to become enraged and attack him physically in a real attempt to destroy him, and the patients in the group do not wish actually to destroy the group "leader."

How then does the group therapist go about dealing with this resistance pattern of ignoring his existence as an unconscious means of defense against acting out or verbalizing their parricidal impulses? Of course, the general principles for dealing with resistance are well known; but in the group setting, where the therapist is dealing with continually changing and intense emotional processes, both in his patients and in himself, it is amazing how the simple and obvious principles involved in human relationships can be forgotten again and again when a different set of emotions appears.*

PRINCIPLES APPLIED

It is impossible to cope with a resistance successfully if one cannot see and feel it. The first task of the therapist, then, is to study the group over several sessions (the number varying with the experience of the therapist and the character of the group) in an attempt to recognize the main resistances the group is using. Secondly, the therapist must attempt to understand the

---

*For a detailed description of technical methods to be used with resistances in individual analytic therapy, the reader is referred to Glover (1927-1928).

significance of the resistance. What useful function does it serve? What is its possible origin, history, and meaning? Into what classification does the resistance fall? Is it one of the ego, superego, id, transference, or secondary-gain type?

Once the therapist has had sufficient time to study the various forms of resistance being presented by the group, he needs to decide which resistance is to be dealt with first. On this highly important decision may depend the success or failure of a therapy group. For example, if the therapist deals first with a resistance that helps the individuals to cooperate, its removal would inevitably result in a less cooperative group. If the balance of forces becomes such that the group becomes less rather than more cooperative, it may be temporarily or permanently disrupted. Should a permanent disruption occur, needless to say, the therapist can no longer help its members toward emotional health.

After selecting the resistance to be worked on first, the therapist is confronted with the task of dealing with it in the group setting. While dealing with resistance is to a certain extent a science, it is also an art. Application of the scientific principles does not depend on the therapist's personality and talent, but dealing with a resistance artistically can be a thrilling experience, for both the therapist and the group, rather than a dull or painful operation. It is desirable that the therapist foresee the consequences of dealing with the resistances and approach them so as to help each patient gain control over his own resistances as painlessly as possible.

The first of several steps involved is to call attention to the resistance. It may be necessary to help the individuals in the group recognize the pattern that is being focused on at the moment. For example, during a period when the group is ignoring the therapist, it may be necessary for him to call attention to this fact repeatedly before the patients recognize it. Then the therapist may enlist sufficient interest in the group so that the members will attempt to understand the significance of their resistance, what caused it, how it developed, and why it is operative at that time. This should be a slow process, so that there is little, if any, chance for impulses held in check by the resistance to be freed into action.

Verbal Discharge of Hostile Impulses

To return to the situation in which a group is defending itself against acting on parricidal impulses: The therapist needs to overcome this resistance very slowly so that there be no danger of his being physically attacked. It may first be necessary to "educate" the group to the fact that the acting out of hostile impulses is not acceptable. The therapist might convey the idea that everyone feels hostile impulses, but these are appropriately discharged in a controlled, measured manner—through language, if necessary, but not in aggressive action.

It is amazing how many people in ordinary life situations cannot allow themselves to feel angry when they wish to, and cannot discharge hostile impulses in an organized manner, through language. They do not seem to have control over their temper, do not permit themselves to generate anger when anger is appropriate, and cannot control it when it is necessary. Many a person even finds it difficult to raise his voice to express anger or to lower and change the tone of his voice to hold the expression of anger in check. It may turn out that only after the members of the therapy group have been "educated" to speak up in hostile tones and have become aggressive verbally rather than in action, will they be able to recognize the fact that they have collectively ignored the group therapist as an expression of hostility.

When, after months of treatment, the patients have developed a sense of security in the group setting, have experienced aggressive and even murderous impulses, and come to feel that they can control overt discharge of feelings through language, they also discover that no harm resulted to themselves or to the group therapist from doing so. It is this security and emotional flexibility that makes it possible for them to understand the origin, history, and meaning of their hostility toward the therapist and the resulting resistance. When this point of self-acceptance and dissolution of guilt and fear is reached, one patient will recall ignoring his father as a defense when the latter became angry at him; a second will recall that once, as a child, when he felt like killing his brother, he ignored him for several days, but found that he could tolerate his brother after winning the approval of his parents.

RATIONALE OF THIS APPROACH

The significance of such a method of dealing with resistance is twofold. (1) The group members are helped to recognize that they are resistive. (2) The circumspect therapist, understanding the emotional tension held in check, does not expect that the patients give up the resistance until (*a*) the emotional forces held in check are sufficiently discharged or converted so that they no longer threaten the safety of the therapist or the group, and (*b*) each member has come to understand the meaning of the resistance in terms of his life history and experience.

Thus, once the emotional energy has been drained off through therapy, and the individual comes to understand the meaning and the cause of his behavior in the group, one can then expect that this form of resistance will no longer appear as a compulsory, unconscious defense. When and if it is used in the future, it will be employed individually and collectively in a conscious, purposeful, and controlled way.

Differences from Individual Therapy

How does the method of dealing with resistance presented here differ from that used in individual analytic therapy? There are two fundamental differences. (1) In the group, when the resistances of the various members are different, there is a natural tendency for each to deal with resistances of the other patients. They may do so in a constructive or a destructive manner. One of the tasks of the therapist is to enlist their cooperation in dealing constructively with each other's resistances. If this process is successful, there is an increasing tendency for the individuals in the group to develop a *common* or *group* resistance; that is, all of the group members tend to use the same resistance simultaneously. One may say that, in a sense, there develops out of their individual neuroses a *common neurosis*, which is reinforced by the group situation. (2) The basic task of the therapist then is to deal with the "common neurosis." This does not mean that a new type of neurosis has developed. It means rather that the neurotic patterns that all or the majority of the patients have in common come into play. Each member is emotionally reinforced by the other members and the instinctual energy held in check by the neurosis fortifies the common resistance.

RESISTANCE IN THE GROUP THERAPIST

The common resistances of the group tend to stimulate counterresistances, and the common neurosis tends to incite an *induced neurosis* in the group therapist. Self-analysis and self-control are therefore much more difficult problems for the therapsit who treats groups than for the analyst treating individual patients. In order to help the group members deal with their group resistances, the therapist must become aware of much more powerful resistances within himself as they are generated by the group, and he must be able to understand them.

In the literature on individual analytic psychotherapy, the counterresistances of the analyst are discussed in connection with countertransference problems. His identification with the analysand is recognized as the source of problems related to the induced neurosis. This is present in the analyst during the course of individual analysis and it is more or less easily recognized, analyzed, and controlled by him. The instinctual forces brought into play are, after all, only those stimulated by one individual (the analysand).

In group therapy, on the other hand, the therapist is exposed to instinctual forces operating collectively and simultaneously in several individuals. While it is true that the group psychotherapist tends to identify with the group members, there are in addition especially strong reaction-formations against conscious and unconscious identifications. Under these conditions, the group therapist finds that his induced neurosis is much more intense and requires more thorough and more prolonged self-analysis.

Application of the principles presented here involves the use of mature judgment, a sense of timing, a sensitivity to the state of excitation of the group, and a regard and respect for human beings. This culminates in a group experience that is not only therapeutic but also has the inspirational characteristics we have come to associate with a work of art.

7

Dealing with Aggression in Groups

The adults treated in our group setting usually have undergone individual treatment for narcissistic or character disorders or severe psychoneurotic conditions. They have demonstrated gross inability to invest aggressive impulses in personally and socially desirable activity. Some of them too are, by force of circumstances or the restricting influence of their illness, cut off from opportunities to learn to function without anxiety in multipersonal encounters. They are assembled in mixed groups, composed to balance divergence in personality structures with reasonable compatibility in educational and social backgrounds. A blending of phlegmatic and volatile individuals with good instigators and regulators of emotional release facilitates the analytic group process (Chapter 21).

INDIRECT METHOD

The therapy of aggression is indirect. Regardless of the etiology of the individual problems of the patients, their symptomatic patterns of dealing with aggressive impulses are activated by frustration in the treatment situation. To schematize the psychodynamic events to be influenced: frustration $\rightarrow$ aggressive impulses $\rightarrow$ defensive operations stifling the release of energy $\rightarrow$ inability to assimilate or provide narcissistic supplies $\rightarrow$ frustration of the personality growth. The therapist applies himself to interrupt this vicious cycle and establish the following progressive sequence of events: frustration $\rightarrow$ aggressive impulses $\rightarrow$ verbal discharge $\rightarrow$ intake of narcissistic supplies $\rightarrow$ personality maturation. The point of intervention is the defensive maneuvers. When these interfere with cooperative functioning in the group, they are dealt with as resistance.

Resistance in the shared treatment experience encompasses the various methods, voluntary or involuntary, by which a group member avoids giving—or helping the other members to give—a spontaneous and emotionally significant account of past psychic realities in his life and his feelings and thoughts in the treatment session. Urgent attention is given to resistance patterns that obstruct the verbalization of frustration-aggression. No attempt is made to demolish such patterns; they are respected as "holding" operations that help the patients preserve their equilibrium in the group.

Negative transference is fostered in a way that makes it possible to deal therapeutically with the problem of aggression, that is, by giving minimal directions and explanations and generally maintaining a reserved attitude. In the initial phase of treatment, the therapist intervenes only when some communication from him is solicited verbally; as an important exception to that principle, he deals urgently with behavior that threatens the integrity of the group or the elimination of one of its members. The relative sparsity of the therapist's communications discourages the development of a positive-transference climate, in which patients tend to bottle up anger. Descriptions of the dynamics of present impulse states are rarely made at this stage because they provoke narcissistic mortification, which it is undesirable to inflict on individuals who have difficulty venting negative feelings. Injuries to self-esteem and the intensification of self-preoccupations are avoided by communicating understanding when the patients really desire and request it, and in the form and tempo at which explanations of defective functioning can be healthfully assimilated.

From the beginning of treatment, the patients are educated (as implicitly as possible) to the idea that they are to do nothing but talk together, that they compose a *nonactivity* group. Behavior that is obstructive is not foreclosed, but the members themselves are able to identify it and help one another distinguish between the appropriateness of saying what one feels like doing and actually doing it. In the sharing of time as well as in the identification of resistance, a basis for democratic functioning is established because they recognize that they may talk or not talk, as they prefer. Versatility in talking, not time-sharing on a mathematical basis session after session, is the objective.

In working on the obstacles to the discharge of hostile aggression, it is borne in mind that, if it can not be freely verbalized, it may erupt into impulsive behavior, whereas *too* freely expressed, it may become a source of sadistic gratification. The therapist does not respond with retaliatory hostility to provocative remarks, but vilification that does not serve the purpose of therapy is interpreted as a perverse form of pleasure and thus discouraged. The objective is to mobilize just enough frustration to permit the group members to go on talking, hour after hour, about their true feelings, neither withdrawing nor coming to blows over the most hateful things they say to each other. This process is facilitated by providing enough gratifying experience to preserve the group until its members, having learned appropriate ways of getting hatred out of their systems, have developed new patterns of relatedness.

MOBILIZATION OF AGGRESSIVE IMPULSES

Group treatment per se is a good instrument for mobilizing aggressive impulses and investigating how patients deal with them. It is inherently more frustrating than the one-to-one relationship owing to the necessity of sharing time and attention, as well as the stress of divulging intimate and painful experiences to strangers. The more or less noncommunicative attitude of the therapist applying the method just outlined arouses resentment. The lack of directions about how to proceed creates some anxiety. The patients enter the group with cravings for attention, appreciation, admiration, and affection, and are confronted with pressures that lower their spirits.

In the substance of their verbal interchanges, too, there are potent mobilizers of negative feelings. These are aroused in a group member when he is ignored, neglected, or isolated. Neglect provokes despair and anger. Verbal attacks that are regarded as merited reinforce self-attacking attitudes or motivate retaliation, depending on the group member's immediate state. False accusations, undeserved censure, and much ado about trivial lapses, such as arriving 30 seconds late for a session, stir up anger or rage. Outpourings of anger lift a patient dramatically out of a state of depression. Expressions of sympathy, on the other hand, fixate the depressed individual in his despair. Injury and violence are common themes of the communications and also tend to dominate the dreams reported.

Primitive patterns of ego and id resistance are observed as the group members try to conceal, disguise, or bury their anger and resentment. Instead of expressing dissatisfaction, they may maintain embarrassed or stony silences or deliberately withhold information. Caustic remarks are made about the therapist, and veiled insults are traded with other members. Sadistic jokes and flippant comments cover up anger and hatred; references to perverse sexual activities may serve the same purpose. One member may monopolize attention with an irrelevant soliloquy while the others ignore him or refrain from comment.

Some ganging up on a silent group member may occur—frequently displacing a desire to attack the therapist. If the scapegoat refuses to accept the attack and runs out of the room, this behavior may be repeated if it is not immediately challenged by reminders of the distinction between talking about what one feels like doing and actually doing it. Similar reminders discourage tendencies to physical contact, such as the touching or striking of another member. But destructive behavior rarely occurs when there is common agreement on what constitutes cooperative functioning in the sessions.

TYPES OF INTERVENTIONS

The therapist intervenes in various ways to deal with patterns that operate to check the release of hostile aggression. He describes the resistant behavior; he also asks questions about it. The questions are object-oriented, and formulated to help the patients talk out their immediate reactions. Other techniques include the psychological reflection (with or without feelings) of resistance patterns and emotional communications. The standard interpretive procedures are employed with increasing frequency after the group members have developed the ability to verbalize their frustration-tensions spontaneously and comfortably. The resistant behavior is conceptualized as consistently as possible as an element of the total constellation of behavior—that is, as an interference with the functioning of the group as a unit.

Responding to this approach, the group members tend to work as a team in recognizing the individual problems that interfere with progressive communication. An interesting phenomenon is observed: Each patient tends to call attention to the uncooperative attitudes and behavior that differ from his own. Consequently, in addition to monologue and dialogue, the therapist is equipped with a third resistance solvent—"groupalogue." It provides opportunities to experience simultaneously different reactions to one's own behavior and thus to scrutinize it more objectively.

Clinical Illustration

Overwhelmingly negative—or positive—feelings are often tempered through groupalogue. But it makes an impressive contribution to emotional involvement in the treatment experience. Its influence in dissolving intellectualization as a defense against feeling and expressing objectionable emotions is illustrated below.

The patient, an unmarried actor in his early thirties, had been functioning in an amazingly detached way in individual treatment. It was hard for him to respond feelingly in the more intimate relationship.

During his first few group sessions, he fenced himself off just as rigidly from painful feelings. He expressed contempt for the more emotionally involved patients. He was "too sane to be happy" and they were too childish to be entrusted with his "head" problems. He did not talk about himself, and chided those who did with an air of superiority. Two of the three women members took strong exception to the brutal objectivity of his criticism. Their angry reactions soon crept under his skin. "Just listening to you here makes me feel naked," he said. Although he remained aloof from the group give-and-take, it began to animate and agitate him. He became angry with himself when he realized that he was experiencing rage. However, pressure to discharge it steadily mounted.

A month later he made his first disclosure of intense emotions to the group. He began, "I'm boiling mad"; and he looked it. He also revealed that he was experiencing more feeling outside the group situation. He was "finally" falling in love with a young woman of his acquaintance. However, like the women in the group, she was driving him out of his mind. "I'm not mean or malicious," he continued. "I just try to show her how she really is." She was not accepting his constructive criticism and that was "rubbing him the wrong way, just as you women do here. . . . No woman is lovable once you get to know her." He was afraid that his affection would drown in her anger.

The group experience, after mobilizing feelings that he had not been aware of, helped him to modify his inconsiderate manner of expressing them. (1961).

FOCUS ON GROUP AS A UNIT

In supplementing the influence of groupalogue, the therapist focuses on the group picture, particularly the increasing tendency of the patients to present a solid phalanx of resistant behavior as the idiosyncratic patterns are mastered. However, he may have to intervene to deal with individual resistances that continue to operate because they mesh in with the communicative activity of the group as a unit. When resistance is approached in this broader context, the uncooperative member is not exposed to undue pressure to participate; moreover, no one is neglected in the exploratory process.

Before calling attention to the protracted silence of one member, for instance, the therapist first tries to determine whether he wants to talk and whether the others want him to talk, and formulates his interventions accordingly. This approach enables the other members to mobilize and express feelings that were latent in the situation and thus help the resistant patient to talk.

Clinical Illustration

How the resolution of a depressive pattern was initiated is illustrated below.

May, a middle-aged woman, had become more and more isolated in the group sessions. Her gloomy attitude and occasional tearfulness had elicited no comment; but she appeared no less willing to be ignored than the others were to ignore her.

The therapist asked whether a plan was afoot to help May escape attention. Various explanations were advanced: One patient said she had noticed May's tears but had been respecting her silence. Another said, "She'll talk when she feels like it." A third reported the impression that the therapist preferred that no comment be made on May's unhappiness for the time being.

May challenged these explanations. She was sure they had been neglecting her because they disliked her, she said. If they had noticed the paralyzing effect of her despair, why hadn't they talked to her? Why hadn't she experienced any consideration from them? She was not a person who isolated herself by choice.

"How was I to know this?" one man asked. "I'm not a mind reader." Others spoke up to the same effect: Why blame us? Why didn't you let us know you felt like talking?

May reacted strongly. Did they have to attack her for misinterpreting their neglect? The battle, thus joined, was followed by animated discussions, in which she expressed anger with increasing ease, and learned to tolerate it from others. Defenses that had been patterned in a severely traumatic childhood were given up. Eventually, she developed and experienced genuine attachments to other members of the group.

When the frustration-gratification situation is managed to deal first with the problem of aggression, the group serves as a forensic training ground. In the process of countering verbal thrusts and parries, a person who has never enjoyed a real argument in life gradually relinquishes his pathological defenses. To explode verbally in anger at someone else when he feels like it, or to endure being the butt of anger, gives him a much-needed sense of power. The overtalkative patient also benefits from these interchanges. The inhibiting presence of less garrulous members helps him control his impulses and behave in a more disciplined manner.

COUNTERTRANSFERENCE RESISTANCE

Constant exposure to the instinctual forces operating simultaneously in the group members generates strong feelings in the therapist. If these are conceptualized as countertransference, they should be differentiated from feeling responses related to his own adjustment patterns. The feelings that are induced by the members' transference emotions are realistic reactions to what is going on in the group.

The therapist will tend to identify with its members; he will also develop powerful reaction-formations against these conscious or unconscious identifications. When, for instance, he is exposed to a great deal of latent aggression, he may want to talk a great deal to steer the patients away from subjects that might stimulate hostile reactions. He may become aware of impulses to cancel sessions, start them late, or even to disband the group when the behavior of its members is difficult to control. He may find himself pacifying or consoling or advising when he meant to be silent and focus on understanding a problem. He may prefer to allay anger when he meant to bring it into the open. Because of the intensity of the group-induced neurosis, self-understanding and self-control are stringent necessities in carrying out one's planned interventions. Too much suppression of personal feelings one can not cope with may lead to psychosomatic reactions. The task is not without its hazards!

Although it is undesirable to respond purely on the basis of the induced feelings, if the therapist understands them and can sustain them, they are not only a perceptual aid but a source of therapeutic leverage as well. Communicated in a goal-oriented way—to resolve a resistance that is being dealt with—the induced feelings contribute to the resolution of preverbal defenses against the release of frustration-aggression.

CHANGES IN FUNCTIONING

Marked improvements in functioning are observed in the treatment sessions and the patients report that these benefits carry over into their lives. The most important change is that they experience less tension and find themselves operating more easily and consistently in their own best interests. Pressures to behave in self-destructive ways are reduced. Some patients find it easier not to operate on impulse. Self-punitive behavior, whether manifested in somatically damaging habits, accident proneness, and the like or in emotional withdrawal and states of depression, is significantly alleviated.

The patients become less egocentric, more comfortable in social situations, and more considerate of others. New feelings of health and maturity help them develop personally and socially wholesome patterns of relatedness. Once they are in control of their aggressive drives, they experience a sense of security and power with which to carry out their immediate and long-range goals.

8

Resistance Management in Groups

The body of knowledge on group psychotherapy and group process offers much more evidence on the emotional impact of the shared treatment experience than on its theoretic rationale. Some contributors to the literature, perhaps the majority, provide a wealth of impressions of behavioral changes in patients but account for it vaguely if at all. Reports on phenomenology rarely indicate how the therapist harnesses the group properties and forces at his disposal, thus suggesting that he is beholden to them when progress is made and at their mercy when stalemate occurs. To the uninitiated reader, the therapist's task may seem to be one of giving interpretations whenever the spirit moves him, in the hope that the group members will be sufficiently mated to his aims and efforts to respond accordingly. In my experience, this laissez faire approach often leads to disappointing results; at best it wastes rich and unique potentials of the group setting. I shall therefore spell out in this article an objective answer to the question: How does the analytic group therapist work systematically to produce the sought-for changes in patients?

Analytic group process is an indirect form of psychotherapy. As in other methods based on psychoanalytic principles, the practitioner works to facilitate change by addressing himself to the obstacles to change. These interfering factors are numerous and highly diverse. Besides the intrapsychic forces, there are external obstacles to therapeutic progress—socioeconomic and family problems, environmental emergencies and so on. When these forces interfere with therapeutic progress, they are designated as *resistance*; in Freud's words, "whatever interrupts the progress of analytic work is a resistance" (1900, p. 517). Since we now possess a substantial amount of information on resistance in the group setting and a variety of techniques for investigating and influencing it therapeutically, the broad application of this working concept affords a basis for schematizing analytic group process.

ELABORATION OF WORKING CONCEPT

When Freud reported his discovery of resistance as a clinical phenomenon (Breuer and Freud, 1893-1895), his method of dealing with it was consonant with his belief at that time that the recovery of pathogenic ideas that had been repelled by the ego was the curative mechanism. He was interested in resistance only as the force that opposed these ideas "*becoming conscious (being remembered)*" (p. 268). Concentrating on getting the ideas verbalized, he tried to overcome the resistance to free association by "making use of psychical compulsion to direct the patient's attention to the ideational traces of which he is in search," (p. 270). But working to elicit them directly by circumventing the opposing forces got Freud into various difficulties. Although time-saving, this approach proved traumatizing to the patient, giving rise to feelings of disturbance, strangeness, withdrawal and the like which inhibited or even blocked communication.

Freud found later that, when he addressed himself instead to the interfering factor, the force of the pathogenic idea came into awareness, eventually freeing the patient to recall and verbalize it. This finding is crystallized in his statement that the "work of overcoming resistances is the essential function of analytic treatment" (Freud, 1917, p. 451).

Since the spadework era of theory building, interest has shifted from resistance as an artefact of the analytic situation to resistance as an expression of the living personality—the patient's characteristic modes of functioning. Any impulse or type of behavior may produce resistance, but it is prominently identified with the early defenses patterned by the ego in the interests of environmental mastery and psychological survival. These protective devices are activated in the treatment situation by transference, and when their mobilization interferes with communication, they are identified as resistance. In short, defenses activated by the charge of transference become resistance.

Equally significant has been the recognition that resistance, originally equated with the blocking of communication, actually performs a communication function—provided that someone is present to decipher its meaning. To the analytically trained observer, it frequently conveys, in a disguised or primitive way, otherwise unobtainable information about the patient's psychic history. Some forms that commonly operate in the group setting, for example, point back to patterns of adjustment to family life. Moreover, by giving clues to the developmental stage in which a maladaptation was formed, the pattern of the resistance suggests the type of therapeutic intervention needed to influence it.

Resistance operates on different levels in the course of therapy, and the lower the level the more difficult it is to deal with it through the medium of communication. Patterns associated with preoedipal development are rarely responsive to interpretations; symbolic, reflective, and emotional interventions are needed to resolve them. But by committing himself first to these more demanding and time-consuming procedures to master the deepest resistances, the therapist helps the patient move up into those levels of functioning where the impact of "adult" interpretation is more consistently impressive and can facilitate the emergence of the mature personality.

Recognition of the survival and communication functions of resistance has engendered a more tolerant attitude to it. It is generally present to some degree, and an important aspect of the science and art of analytic therapy resides in learning from resistance, and influencing it through techniques that help the patient become capable of giving it up easily and voluntarily. The forcible approach—efforts to abolish or cut through resistance—falls by the wayside when one applies oneself to facilitate personality maturation in the patient. Viewed in that context, a pattern of resistance is gradually diminished in force and eventually, as a byproduct of emotional growth, loses its compulsive grip on the personality.

Consonant with that approach, I do not couple resistance with a value-judgment. It is not good, but neither is it bad. As the best adjustment the patient was able to make at the trauma level, resistance is simply a force that needs to be recognized and dealt with throughout the treatment.

REVIEW OF THE LITERATURE

The validity of the working concept for treatment in the group setting was more or less taken for granted by the pioneers in the field. Trigant Burrow reported (1927) that the group method "offers its most distinctive advantage" in the dissolving of resistances; passing references to the reduction of resistance in groups were made by Paul Schilder (1936) and Louis Wender (1936). To mention other relevant views: Nathan Ackerman (1949) observed differences between resistance patterns in group and individual analytic therapy; James Shea (1954) discussed these differentials and provided clinical illustrations. Alexander Wolf (1949-1950) detailed his methods of dealing with resistance and described a variety of patterns. Leslie Rosenthal (1963) reported on a longitudinal study of resistances observed in one member of a group.

Group Resistance

Fritz Redl, in an important contribution, stressed the existence and signif-icance of "group psychological expressions of resistance" and suggested that these be called *group resistance* (1948, p. 308); he pointed out that these group-wide phenomena serve as a cover-up for individual resistance. Group resistance has been defined as the "same form of resistance used by all or the majority of the members of the group at the same time" (Chapter 6). The same report called attention to the counterresistances originating in the feelings induced in the therapist by the "instinctual forces operating collec-tively and simultaneously in several individuals."* Voicing the growing concern about the intensification of negative feelings toward the therapist, Henrietta Glatzer (1953) commented: "Unless individual resistance is pene-trated, there is danger it may spill over and turn the whole group against the therapist even to the point of departure." F. Powdermaker and J. Frank (1953) viewed group resistance as "one of the greatest challenges to the ther-apist's skill" (p. 384), accepted the idea of dealing with it, and suggested some techniques for that purpose. S. H. Foulkes and E. J. Anthony (1957) referred to "*something in the total situation*, some difficulty, some barrier, which the group has in common" (p. 149) and recommended that the pa-tients be made aware of the resistances of the "group as a group." Benjamin Kotkov (1957) reported that the resistances of individual members "become mobilized as resistances of the group."

More recently, objections to dealing with group resistance phenomena, and even to the use of the term (Schwartz and Wolf, 1960) have figured in the controversy over the significance of group dynamics for psychotherapy (Durkin, 1964). Slavson (1964) described patterns of group-induced resis-tance and mentioned specific situations when it should be analyzed. Re-flecting the sharp divergences in the field on group resistance, Marvin Aron-son (1967) attributed its presence to therapeutic error and Louis Ormont (1968) suggested that the ability to recognize and resolve it enhances the therapist's effectiveness. Ormont also discussed the "ever-present problem of drop-outs" (p. 147) in relation to group resistance.

Sources of Resistance

Freud's postulates on a libidinal drive and an aggressive drive fail to en-compass completely the multiplicity of internal and external forces that operate in the scheme of human experience. I referred to "constellations of forces" in reporting on emotional currents in the group setting (Chapter

---

*Space limitations preclude the discussion of countertransference resistance in this report.

19). In that contribution and a later one (1952), three such constellations were distinguished: (1) a reproduction constellation—forces that make themselves felt in desires for sexual congress, and to conceive and rear a healthy, happy child superior in all respects to oneself; (2) a negative reproduction constellation of forces, which operates to prevent the fulfilment of those desires; and (3) an inadequacy constellation encompassing the physical, emotional, and integrational deficiencies that prevent individuals from realizing the ultimate aims of the reproduction constellation. To an extent depending on the organizational level of the ego, each member of the group of adolescent girls reported on was found to be aware of those forces, which expressed themselves through her impulses, feelings, thoughts, and behavior in the sessions.

Group process was found to be constructive when it permitted some partial and immediate gratification of the instinctual energies of the reproduction and inadequacy constellations, and destructive when it severely blocked or delayed their gratification. The forces of the negative reproduction constellation operated in a non-therapeutic way *unless* they were released in language with feeling—anger, resentment, and the like.

When the emotions generated by these three constellations press for discharge and are verbalized, group process serves as a therapeutic agent. Feelings give rise to resistances *only* when they are denied such release; this point is stressed because resistance is sometimes equated with the expression of hostility. The presence of resistance may indicate that patients are inhibiting the verbalization of feelings aroused by the currents and cross-currents that operate in the group setting.

Understanding of these emotional constellations is important to the clinician because they supply the energy for the various forms of resistance he has to deal with. Moreover, he can help to maintain these forces in a state of healthy equilibrium when he comprehends their nature and senses their presence. In other words, these states of excitation are not only sources of resistance; they also provide therapeutic leverage.

Research in the field of group dynamics has facilitated understanding of the shifting emotional currents observed in the therapeutic group setting. Readers who are familiar with W. R. Bion's studies of group phenomena may have noted that the emotional constellations discussed above and his so-called basic assumptions are conceptualizations of the same forces; inadequacy constellation and basic assumption of dependency; reproduction constellation and basic assumption of pairing; negative reproduction constellation and basic assumption of fight-flight (Bion, 1961). For the clinician, Bion's basic assumptions are of value primarily as a classification of the major sources of resistance in the group setting.

GENERAL STRATEGY

The plan of treatment, in essence, is to deal with the group as a unit as much as possible, the individual member either when he demonstrates a problem that requires special attention or as a representative of the group. Formulating this strategy in terms of dealing with resistance, the therapist applies himself to facilitating personality maturation through the analysis and resolution of group resistance (Spotnitz, 1961). In addition to the same patterns concurrently manifested by all or most of the members, their dissimilar but interlocking patterns are conceptualized as group resistance. After the total configuration is resolved, its individual components are worked through when the group is in a cooperative state.

Operating on the assumption that attempts to forcibly overcome or eliminate resistance are rarely successful and usually anti-therapeutic, the therapist is prepared to *work with* resistance. He accepts responsibility for keeping it within manageable proportions (controlling its intensity) and nullifying its destructive potential. An important dimension of management is dealing with some forms of resistance more urgently than others.

When one or more members engage in behavior that threatens the continuance of the treatment or suggests that severely regressive tendencies are operating in a member, the therapist addresses himself to the forces that interfere with the verbalization of pent-up feelings. (No attempt is made to influence the feelings.) Whereas these so-called treatment-destructive patterns are dealt with promptly, to neutralize their immediate impact, other patterns are not "touched" until they have developed into full-blown transference resistances. The strategy is to focus first on the negative-transference resistances (Mann, 1955). After the tendencies to retain aggressive impulses (aggression-constipation) have been resolved, the forces that interfere with the verbalization of positive-transference reactions are dealt with.

By concentrating on group resistance, the therapist takes full advantage of the patients' natural tendencies (conscious and unconscious) to reduce the individual resistances. When they do so destructively, however, such as ganging up on a silent member to force him to talk, the therapist intervenes to discourage defense-attacking maneuvers and to support or reinforce the resistance until the patient is able to give it up without detriment to his psychic economy.

The therapist intervenes consistently in terms of dealing with resistance, but that does not mean that he intrudes into the group interchanges whenever he detects its presence. In theory he intervenes only in response to the following cues: the presence of treatment-destructive forms of resistance; when the group members are dealing with an individual resistance in damaging ways; when he is confronted with a fully developed group transference resistance; and when a communication from him is specifically requested (contact functioning).

When the treatment begins, patients who ask what they are expected to do in the sessions are told only that they are supposed to do nothing but talk together. They are slowly educated to the distinction between verbalizing feelings and thoughts and acting on them during the sessions. In calling attention to modes of behavior that interfere with progressive verbal communication, the therapist characterizes them as improper or uncooperative; he does not say that they are not allowed. Thus liberated from undue pressure to give up their resistant behavior, the group members get to understand that they have the *right to resist*.

The group is conducted on democratic principles, a policy that applies to the process of securing recognition of the presence of resistance. In other words, resistance is not what the therapist arbitrarily decides that it is. After he has called attention to a mode of behavior that he regards as resistant, its pros and cons may be explored repeatedly before the patients consciously accept it as an obstacle to therapeutic process. Until they do, the behavior is not dealt with as resistance but as a pattern for further study.

Unanimity of opinion on the presence of resistance is worked for because it creates the best conditions for the group members to participate in the detection and resolution of resistance. Situations may develop, however, when the individual or group resistances are not unanimously recognized as such. Special techniques for handling these gray situations (necessarily omitted from this general discussion) often resolve the issue. Otherwise, the therapist may have to settle it through majority decision or dictate when he is certain that the behavior interferes with the group's functioning as a unit or with that of an individual member.

STAGES IN MASTERING RESISTANCE

Arousal

Individuals beginning group treatment are immature in at least one aspect of their personality. Their emotional problems cannot be influenced in absentia; the therapeutic experience has to be structured to bring them to the fore. In brief, the creation and maintenance of a transference climate is necessary to activate the problems with sufficient intensity to resolve them in the group situation.

The patients are instructed to talk and the therapist remains relatively silent. Frustrated by his apparent failure to help them or join them in self-exposure, they develop states of tension and irritation in which they demonstrate their pathological modes of relatedness. Each member who freely verbalizes his own feelings and thoughts, however hostile and disagreeable, and permits and helps his co-members to do the same, is regarded as functioning cooperatively. But when progressive verbal communication is hampered by his emotional immaturities, these are identified as resistance.

The therapist works for the maximal arousal of therapeutically manageable patterns of resistance. This is achieved when the forces that interfere with verbal communication are strong enough to be recognizable but not so strong as to give rise to destructive behavior or a severe deterioration in mental functioning.

Arousal, though basically a function of the intensity of transference, is to some extent a matter of technique. The therapist can increase resistance by silence or by lengthy and authoritative communications; manifestations of resistance are vivified in either way. He can mitigate it, on the other hand, by brief interventions at well-spaced intervals.

Recognition

As the therapist studies the group, session after session, he identifies the resistances that come into play, and silently analyzes them. Each type is labeled in terms of its intrapsychic origin—ego, superego, or id—and the scope of its operation—individual, subgroup, group (Spotnitz, 1969b). He is then in a position to evaluate the effect of the behavior on the group's functioning at that time and also to decide, when more than one form of resistance operates, their respective claims for attention. On the basis of these determinations, he decides whether the pattern should be tolerated because its influence is relatively inconsequential; encouraged because it serves a useful purpose at that time; or discouraged because it is seriously disruptive.

Most particularly, the therapist keeps his weather eye open for any type of behavior which, if permitted to continue, would imperil the group's existence or be seriously damaging to any of its members. If, for example, all of the members sprawl on the floor and refuse to talk—an extreme example but six teen-agers actually did so when assembled for treatment in a community clinic—the group's future is obviously very dim.

The ordinary functional resistances are simply studied during the early months of treatment. As already mentioned, no attempt is made to influence them until they become fully developed transference resistances. For the therapist himself to try to resolve them before then would be a waste of time because, even when he succeeds, they return at the height of the transference. However, early study of the group members' characteristic hedging maneuvers prepares him for the crucial task of dealing with them later.

When all or most of the group members are bogged down in saying the same thing over and over again, talking chit-chat, or "fooling around," it is easy to conceptualize the behavior as a group resistance. More difficult to recognize are the overt and covert patterns that mesh together to block communication. One member, for example, may be looking out of the window, while another daydreams, two others talk idly about a current event, and so forth. But in this situation too, the group as a whole is killing time, refusing to go on with the work it is supposed to do, or ignoring the therapist as the cause of their frustration instead of enlisting his cooperation.

Investigation

The therapist calls attention to the resistance he has decided to deal with and initiates the investigation of its origin and history and the reason for the activation of the behavior in the immediate situation. Other than pointing out the behavior, he limits his interventions, by and large, to verbal descriptions when the pattern is clear enough to be demonstrable. Questions are asked to stimulate the group members to talk out the thoughts and feelings bound up in the pattern. When, for instance, they are bogged down in voicing the same idea ad infinitum, a brief comment to that effect often helps them resume progressive communication. The therapist does not explain why he is calling attention to the behavior when those engaging in it have difficulty in verbalizing hostility.

Although the therapist may barge into the group interchanges without "invitation" to neutralize a treatment-destructive resistance, interventions to deal with the lower categories of resistance are cued to what I have referred to as contact functioning—questions and comments that the members address to him to elicit some words from him. Although this maneuver is usually a manifestation of resistance, it may give notice that the group is really interested in hearing from the therapist and is probably receptive to his influence. Interventions at the point of contact are, in effect, verbal feedings on a self-demand basis, the effectiveness of which is more predictable than that of an intervention made simply because the therapist feels like talking.

Resolution and Working Through

The process of resolving a transference resistance gets under way when the therapist has some understanding of its historical antecedents and the forces that brought it into play at that time.

When addressing himself to a group resistance, he contends first with the united opposition of the group by clarifying the psychodynamics of the grand design; the specific role played by each member is then explained. After the total configuration has been loosened up, the components that were insufficiently influenced by the group interpretation are worked through individually.

Repeated interpretations usually resolve the relatively mild oedipal-type resistances. Depressive reactions, withdrawn behavior, threats, and other preoedipal patterns rarely respond to interpretation; the patient may experience it as an attack, or it may expose him to undesirable pressure to relinquish a mode of behavior that helps him maintain his equilibrium in the group. When such resistances are effectively joined, he usually gives them up voluntarily when the need for them has been outgrown. Until then, questions and brief comments reflecting the patient's attempts at contact functioning, and emotional communications are given.

When he is able to utilize insight in the interests of personality development, the early resistance patterns are often interpreted retrospectively. However, interpretations by the other group members or, preferably, by the patient himself are encouraged. The therapist, if requested to comment, may limit himself to expressing agreement with those that accord with his own understanding.

Resolving resistance means more than analyzing it. The therapist accepts the idea of helping the patient meet the maturational need upholding the pattern. The presence of other patients, responding in divergent ways with genuine feelings, tends to create the precise experiences needed to reduce maturational needs; hence, the therapist himself does not need to do more than enlist participation. When the old symptomatic patterns are given up, new modes of relatedness are "rehearsed." Collective feedback plays a more important role in this emotional working-through process than the therapist's explanations.

SYSTEM OF PRIORITIES

The sequence in which resistance patterns are presented below reflects the relative urgency of recognizing and influencing characteristic modes of uncooperative behavior that patients indulge in during the course of the treatment. As I have already mentioned, approaches to the first category, treatment-destructive resistance, are regarded as emergency measures to preserve the group or protect a member from a potentially damaging contact. The reason for dealing with the other four categories in the order indicated is to facilitate forward movement in the group.

Treatment-destructive resistance: Among the patterns so identified are absences without prior notice, chronic tardiness, destructive forms of acting-in such as striking another member, running out of the room rather than accepting a verbal attack, refusing to talk or to permit others to talk; protracted and unexplained delays in the payment of fees. Since the treatment contract, whether implicitly or explicitly established, is to attend regularly and promptly, to talk together to facilitate understanding, and to pay for the treatment on schedule, such behavior constitutes serious violations of the contract.

Repetitious indulgence in conduct of this nature is called to the group's attention, and its implications for treatment are pointed out, but the behavior is not interpreted.

Prolonged states of narcissistic preoccupation, protracted and stressful silence, sudden exacerbations of symptoms, and silent crying are indications for prompt attention to a patient with a serious emotional disturbance. The therapist intervenes primarily to help the patient talk. Verbal feeding to lower the frustration level for that member is helpful in managing such resistance.

When communication and attention are needed to check defensive regression at a time when the patient is being totally ignored by his co-patients, their attention is called to the problem. This may temporarily deactivate it as a group resistance; they become interested in his difficulties and try to draw him into the interchanges. Later, if the individual resistance is not eased, the therapist himself focuses on the problem. A series of object-oriented questions usually eliminates the danger of a patient leaving the session in a state of psychotic regression.

A member who withholds information from the group may be attacked in a damaging way. In that situation, the therapist would join his resistance, pointing out that any patient has the right to conceal sensitive information until he wants to disclose it, but that it is appropriate to explain why it is being withheld. No invasion of privacy is entailed in the statement that talking about a particular subject at that time would be too painful or might be disadvantageous, and the non-defensive approach rarely provokes potentially harmful forms of retaliation.

Status quo (inertia) resistance usually puts in an appearance after the first six months, as the group members become acclimated to the treatment situation and their presenting problems have been somewhat alleviated. At times they will conceal their "bad" feelings and thoughts, building up the idea that maintaining their present state is all that can be asked of them. When desires to drift along aimlessly and have a good time together become strong transference resistances, the members may, for example, communicate the attitude that they are stalling because the therapist would welcome stalemate. He may then respond with a series of questions inviting them to account for his alleged interest in standing still. Their attitudes may be reflected without approval (Stay where you are but don't expect any worthwhile results), or they may be interpreted. The immediate functioning of the group determines the choice of procedure.

Resistance to analytic progress is associated with more anxiety than the status quo patterns, fear of change, and apprehension about moving ahead into unknown areas of experience. Manifestations of such reluctance to move forward, to verbalize what they really think and feel without regard for the consequences are the patterns that some beginning therapists like to deal with in the opening stage of treatment. To do so makes it possible to achieve manifest improvements quickly and to impress patients with the benefits of the group experience. The more impressed they are, however, the greater their reluctance to verbalize their negative feelings in the sessions. Moreover, treatment-destructive resistance is activated in patients who tend to bottle up aggressive impulses when they feel that they are being "pushed" ahead. This category of resistance is therefore accorded third priority.

Resistance to teamwork: Exclusive concentration on oneself, cravings for undivided attention, unwillingness to listen to others and learn from them; tendencies to ignore some co-members and indulge in tete-a-tetes with others or with the therapist are prominent among these patterns. A similar obstacle, referred to above, entails a member's refusal to give the group specific information about himself or to state why he is withholding it. In joining this resistance, the therapist conveys the message that it may be necessary to withhold the information and helps the patient delay the disclosure until he wishes to share it with the group (Spotnitz, 1969b).

Resistance to termination: A backsliding into patterns of uncooperative behavior that seemingly had been outgrown is observed during the final months of treatment (and also during preceding stages before the vacation break). Well in advance of the projected closing of a case (or scheduled vacation), the group is given due notification because the systematic working through of this resistance, particularly in patients with serious disturbances, is a time-consuming process. In addition to interpretive procedures, the therapist employs the joining approaches and emotional communications that resolved the patterns when they were first activated in the group sessions. The permanence of behavioral change is tested out through interventions charged with the feelings that the group members' collective functioning has induced in the therapist. These toxoid responses are repeated until the patients demonstrate that they have been well immunized against a return to their old resistant attitudes (Chapter 5; 1969b).

RECIPROCAL EFFECTS

When either the group or the one-to-one relationship is used as an accessory procedure to work on specific resistances that were difficult to resolve in the other setting, reciprocal influences are observed. These patterns are often easier to resolve in individual treatment after they have been dealt with in the shared treatment experience. For example, initial difficulties in talking on the couch usually diminish appreciably after a patient has learned to talk in the group. Similarly, the clearing up of a problem dealt with as a component of a group resistance eases the resolution of that problem in the individual relationship. On the other hand, as a consequence of dealing effectively with a resistance in the one-to-one relationship, the pattern is easier to resolve in the group. In short, each setting serves as a resistance solvent for the other.

The permanent resolution of a resistance in individual therapy does not mean that it will not reappear under the greater impact of the shared experience. For instance, a patient who outgrows a tendency to run out of the room during individual sessions may revert to the same behavior later in the group. The resolution of a resistance pattern in both settings seems definitely to enhance the capacity to cope appropriately with environmental stress.

It is my impression that the analysis and resolution of group resistance is a more powerful therapeutic mechanism than the analysis and resolution of individual resistance in either setting. But it does not necessarily follow that a person who finds a new solution to an interpersonal problem through the resolution of a group resistance will adhere to it after completing treatment. Changes in behavior to please the group — perhaps a variant of transference cure — are not unknown. The permanence of the resolution of group resistance and its long-range effects are both unanswered questions.

Another unknown is how much working through in individual treatment may be rendered superfluous by the resolution of group transference resistance, and the working through of its individual components in the group. The latter approach consumes less time than the resolution and working through of the same pattern in the one-to-one relationship, and also impresses me as making a deeper impact. But both issues merit further investigation.

DEALING WITH GROUP RESISTANCE

From what other therapists report on their modus operandi, it appears that the majority focus on the patients as individuals, showing little regard for their collective behavior or interest in facilitating their simultaneous emotional evolution in the group setting. In principle, I see no objection to this approach; it produces good results and eliminates the appreciably greater stress entailed in dealing with group resistance.

Reluctance to deal with it is understandable. To permit and study in a goal-oriented way the unfolding of a situation in which patients band together and attempt to unseat the unhelpful group therapist is inevitably a threatening experience. There is good reason for trying to forestall their united opposition — to "buy it off" by helping each of them resolve his own resistances as quickly as possible. Individual feedback is easier to tolerate than the collective feedback when the group as a unit is in a strong state of resistance. Counterresistance originating in the induced feelings can even blind one to the presence of group resistance — self-protection for the therapist who prefers to deal with individual resistance. The countertransference situation is basically similar to that in the individual treatment of severely disturbed patients (Spotnitz, 1969a).

But to work for therapeutic change in one person at a time with a treatment tool powerful enough to produce it concurrently in six or eight persons is, in a sense, like shooing away an insect with an instrument designed to subdue a lion. Moreover, I prefer not to weaken the group feeling. When its members are permitted to be themselves and to experience their full power and strength vis-á-vis the therapist, they discover what they can do and become together. They get to appreciate the value of belonging to a group, and this is reflected in their improved social functioning. Utilized in this manner, analytic group process represents a transition to rewarding social experience.

PART TWO:

The Schizophrenic Patient

The section opens with a symbolic presentation of schizophrenia, based on an investigation of several ancient versions of the myth of Narcissus and the properties of the narcissus plant. I engaged in this study because my early experience with schizophrenic patients suggested that Freud overlooked the role of internalized aggression in the illness; in formulating his views on narcissism, it seemed to me that he placed undue emphasis on the aspect of self-love. Freud's formulations coincide with the well-known version of the myth by Ovid, in which the presence of aggressive impulses in Narcissus are as effectively concealed by the youth's attractive appearance as is the presence of poisonous substances in the beauty of the narcissus flower. By comparing this popular version with less complex versions of the myth, by writers with different attitudes toward love and hate, and studying the scientific findings on the plant, I learned that many of its properties are embodied in these myths.

The other papers in this section (Chapters 10 through 13) were written after I had assembled the clinical evidence to confirm the impression that internalized aggression is the primary problem to work on in the treatment of schizophrenic patients. Experience with many such patients crystallized this general approach and enabled me eventually to develop the working hypothesis I now employ in the treatment of these patients. This hypothesis is presented in Chapter 13.

9

The Myths of Narcissus

Coauthor: Philip Resnikoff

It is noteworthy, in view of the fundamental role assigned to narcissism by Freud (1914b), that there exists no detailed analysis of the myth that immortalized the handsome youth Narcissus and provided psychoanalysis with so felicitous a term. Certain essential features of the myth are well known, and these may conveniently serve as initial material for analysis, the more so as they raise problems of considerable importance for investigation.

Narcissus, as will be recalled from the most frequently cited version of the myth, preserved in Ovid's *Metamorphoses* (1951), was a youth of extraordinary beauty who fell in love with his image as he leaned over a pool of water. Fascinated by his own reflection, he pined away and died. There appeared in his stead the flower that bears his name.

What is usually emphasized in this touching story is the extreme self-love that Narcissus manifests, the very quality designated by the term *narcissism*. But is self-love the only essential aspect of the myth? Apparently what has been less emphasized is the fact that the death of Narcissus is by self-neglect and that the myth, therefore, is as much concerned with the fate of destructive impulses as with libidinal impulses. Moreover, is the relationship between the youth and the narcissus plant as superficial as the myth would seem to indicate, or is there a more significant tie between the two?

THE YOUTH

The peculiar manner in which Narcissus met his death lends itself more easily to analysis than do other, more obscure features of the myth. Analysis must explain not only the nature and object of Narcissus' infatuation, but also the circumstances surrounding the manifestations of this infatuation, namely, his gazing into a pool of water and the manner of his death, self-neglect.

Parentage

Concerning his gazing into the pool, there are indications of the solution to the problem in the events that led to the conception of Narcissus. According to Ovid, "the river-god, Cephisus, embraced [Liriope] in his winding stream and ravished [her] while imprisoned in his waters. When her time came the beauteous nymph brought forth a child, whom a nymph might love even as a child, and named him Narcissus (p. 149)."

Evidently the tendency that overcame Narcissus as he looked into the water was determined by the fact that his father had found a desired love object there. Narcissus by identification with Cephisus was predestined to seek the love object in water. Hence, part of the fascination exerted on Narcissus by the image he saw reflected in the pool stemmed from his incestuous strivings, i.e., his yearning for his mother.

Identity of the Loved Object

As to the nature of the image seen by Narcissus, the matter is not as simple as this popular version of the myth would suggest. In other versions, there is no unanimity of opinion on the identity of the figure that so absorbed Narcissus. Whereas Ovid is positive that Narcissus saw his own reflection in the pool, Pausanias (1935) states that

it is utter stupidity to imagine that a man old enough to fall in love was incapable of distinguishing a man from his own reflection. There is another story about Narcissus, less popular indeed than the other, but not without some support. It is said that Narcissus had a twin sister; they were exactly alike in appearance, their hair was the same, they wore similar clothes, and went hunting together. The story goes on that Narcissus fell in love with his sister, and when the girl died, he would go to the spring, knowing that it was his reflection he saw, but in spite of this knowledge, finding some relief for his love imagining that he saw, not his own reflection, but the likeness of his sister (p. 31).

Cause of Death

In the Ovid version, the death of Narcissus is attributed to his unrequited love for his own image. The Pausanias version emphasizes the aspect of mourning. In his grief over the death of his twin sister, Narcissus gazes at his own image in order to find relief from the intense suffering occasioned by the loss of an essential love object.

According to Ovid, then, the loved object is the self. Even in his version, the most highly organized, there is some question whether Narcissus immediately recognized the reflected image as his own. In the other versions, it is stated that he loved someone other than himself. Evidently, the loved object was not completely introjected. Narcissus was mourning the death of an external object with whom he was not completely identified, namely, his twin sister. But it is agreed that his death occurred because of his inability to withdraw his libidinal cathexis from the beloved image sufficiently to seek new object relationships and survive.

Referring to an explanation that he challenges, Pausanias states, "They say that Narcissus looked into the water, and not understanding that he saw his own reflection, unconsciously fell in love with himself . . . " This suggests that the loved object was a male, and that Narcissus was dominated by homosexual impulses that developed during the period when the distinction between self and not-self was relatively absent. If Narcissus actually recognized his own image, he was dominated by primarily narcissistic impulses. If the image represented his twin sister, the attachment to a heterosexual, incestuous object was causing the disturbance. If all three possibilities are accepted, Narcissus unbeknown to himself was driven by impulses for the fusion of both sexes into scopophilic union (primal scene fantasies).

Role of Aggression

The aggression that led to the death of Narcissus was not directed only toward his own ego. Narcissus was universally known to have attracted many suitors, both male and female. He rejected all of them. According to Ovid, "At last one of these scorned youths, lifting up his hands to heaven, prayed: 'So may he himself love, and not gain the thing he loves.' The goddess, Nemesis, heard his righteous prayer" (p. 153), "righteous" emphasizing the aggressive way that Narcissus rebuffed his suitors after exciting them.

In the Conon version of the myth (Smith, 1904), Narcissus was more than just rejecting; he even invited a suitor he despised to commit suicide! Narcissus sent a sword to this rejected suitor, Amenias. After calling on the gods to avenge him, Amenias slew himself at the doorstep of Narcissus. Later Narcissus, after being tormented "by love of himself and by repentance," killed himself.

In the Probos version (Smith, 1904), which is probably the earliest, the death of Narcissus is not related to his ego attitude toward himself. The youth was killed by a suitor he had rejected.

It is thus possible to arrange the different versions of the myth in a series dealing with the role of aggression in relation to objects. In the simplest version, by Probos, Narcissus is killed by a rejected suitor—a completely external object. As narrated by Conon, Pausanias, and Ovid, the myth becomes more complicated and more highly organized. Paralleling that organization is the fact that the death of Narcissus involved a relationship with an object that was more and more like himself and, finally, was actually his own image.

Ego Structure

In the Conon version, Narcissus destroyed himself because he repented of what he had done to Amenias. In the Pausanias version, Narcissus died because he longed for a sister who was like himself. In the Ovid version, Narcissus died because he could not receive enough self-love from his own image. These versions appear to progressively describe an increasing internalization and assimilation of an external object that passed the judgment of death on Narcissus because of his sexually exciting and yet frustrating and unsympathetically rejecting attitude. What these versions seem to describe is an ego formation produced by a fusion of the images of a sexually excited object (father) and a sexually exciting yet frustrating object (mother) who had a deadly hatred for her ravisher.

That a child from a union of two such persons would be in danger of an early death was suspected by the mother, Liriope. In the Ovid version, after giving birth to Narcissus, she approached Tiresias (the seer who foretold the doom of Oedipus) and asked him whether her child would live to a "well-ripened age." The seer replied, "If he ne'er know himself" (p. 149).

Summarizing what seems obvious thus far, it is notable that Narcissus, a handsome youth of marked scopophilic appeal, tended to provoke aggressive impulses in those who sought to have sexual relations with him. The mounting tension released aggression that led eventually to the death of Narcissus. In one version of the myth, his death was caused by an unrelated external object. In others, it was related to his twin sister and, finally, to his preoccupation with his own image. The most popular version was that Narcissus, when he became both the subject and object of his own love, also became the subject and object of his own aggression and died.

IDENTITY OF PERCEPTION

It is well known that there is a tendency in human beings to establish an identity of perceptions between old and new experiences (Freud, 1900, VII). Did the narcissus plant provide an opportunity for establishing an identity of that nature? Were there any biological properties of the plant that aroused scopophilic impulses and also served to provoke and release libidinal and destructive impulses?

Wieseler (1856) to whom we owe the classic study of the Narcissus myth, believed that it was created in order to explain the origin of the plant. He pointed out, however, that some doubt existed about the flower the ancients had in mind when they referred to the narcissus. (Similarly, the myths reflect some doubt about the identity of the person who provoked the death of Narcissus.) Various plants were mistakenly referred to as narcissuses, the niceties of plant taxonomy being unknown to the Greeks at the time the myths were elaborated.

But it is most probable that the flower designated as narcissus was the Narcissus tazetta. At that time, the Madonna lily (*Lilium candidum*) and the poet's narcissus (*Narcissus poeticus*) may have been roughly classified as narcissuses. This is not at all surprising since both the lilies and narcissuses belong to the same botanical order, the *Liliales*. *Narcissus* is the name of a species to which daffodils and jonquils also belong; *Lilium* is the corresponding name of the species to which the lilies belong. *Lilium*, incidentally, is the Latin term, the Greek name for the same species being *Lirion*. Hence, Liriope, the name of Narcissus' mother.

Duplicated Properties

To what extent are the botanical features of the plant represented in the myth? Wiesler mentioned some such properties but omitted others that appear to be more important. Four features of the plant that are duplicated in the myth are the following:

1. The plant has an affinity for water; it grows along the banks of pools and springs. In the myth, Liriope was raped in a stream; Cephisus, father of Narcissus, was a river god, and Narcissus leaned over a pool when he was overcome with passion. Incidentally, the flowers of *Narcissus tazetta*, characteristically bend over (*decline* is the botanical term) as they grow from their slender stalks, thus suggesting the youth inclining over the water.

2. While the narcissus plant is capable of both sexual and asexual reproduction, the asexual mode is the more obvious, the bulbs simply reproducing other bulbs. The sexual mode of reproduction by pollination is not so self-evident and was unknown to the Greeks. In the myth, Narcissus eschews all attempts at sexual intimacy. It may be said that Narcissus, in dying, reproduced in an asexual fashion the plant that bears his name.

3. The plant is poisonous. Numerous authorities have attested to its toxicity. According to Burbridge and Baker (1875), for example, "the odour of *Tazetta* and *N. poeticus* in close rooms has proved extremely disagreeable, if not actually injurious to delicate persons, many of whom are extremely sensitive to the effects of perfumes. All parts of the plant are narcotic and highly poisonous." Bowles (1934) states that the crystals found in the sap of narcissus bulb scales "are responsible for the irritation of the skin known as Lily rash among those who pick the flowers for market. Some people are more liable to be affected by it than others, but it is always dangerous to allow the juice to get into a cut or abrasion of the skin." Pliny mentioned that *Narcissus jonquilis*, or at least what moderns have identified as this plant, is an emetic. Current scientific literature is replete with evidence of the toxic effects of an ingestion of narcissus bulbs. Macht (1933) reported cases of poisoning that resulted from eating Narcissus tazetta bulbs, which were mistaken for onions. According to Kobert (1906), cows, pigs, and dogs have died after eating the plant. Ably summing up the literature on the subject, Cook and Loudon (1952) discuss the chemistry of the bulbs and trace the relevant scientific research.

The various versions of the myth leave no doubt that Narcissus was dangerous to those who tried to become intimate with him. Tiresias made this amply clear in predicting that the youth would even endanger himself if he got to know himself. His very name connotes danger, being derived from the Greek root *Narke* (stupor, lethargy), which is also found in English words conveying toxicity, such as *narcotic* and *narcolepsy*. Indeed Pliny, who denied that the narcissus received its name from the youth, thought that it was derived directly from *Narke* because of the plant's toxic effects.

4. The beauty of the plant is duplicated in the myth. Even today the narcissus flower with its pure white petals fascinates many who see it, so it is not surprising that the youth whose name is associated with the flower is depicted as unusually beautiful. Moreover, it is not implausible to link the emphasis on scopophilia in the myth with the visual attraction of the narcissus plant. The fact that both plant and myth utilize the same sensory sphere as a medium of pleasure is a significant duplication.

The myth ends with the search for the remains of Narcissus and the discovery of the flower on the spot where he pined away. In conveying the idea that the flower preserves the memory of the youth, mythographers apparently reversed the actual sequence of events. The duplication of the significant characteristics of the flower in the personality of Narcissus leads to the conclusion that the flower preceded, and is personified in the youth. The myth actually anthropomorphizes the flower.

DIVERGENT PERSONALITIES OF THE NARRATORS

Psychological needs are characterized by specific structures in each individual, with some impulses playing a more central role than others. From time to time there may be changes in these structures; but certain patterns persist, and these define the personality. Each of the four recorded versions of the myth investigated bears the imprint of the patterns of the narrator's psychological needs interacting with the properties of the narcissus plant. In other words, the different versions reflect the variable influence of these properties on divergent personality structures.

All of the versions are, in our view, the product of fantasies about the flower. The particular fantasies that each narrator wove about it, like those stimulated by the ambiguous structure of the Rorschach ink blot, give some indication of his psychological makeup.

For example, the fact that self-love and self-absorption were obviously understandable to Ovid, whereas they were so inconceivable to Pausanias that he replaced self-love with the love for a twin sister, suggests that Ovid was the more introverted and complex personality. Again, whether Narcissus was murdered, took his own life, or just pined away (making the involvement of destructive impulses invisible to an observer) suggests that the authors differed in the degree of freedom they could comfortably permit for the expression of aggression toward objects.

SURVIVAL OF OVID'S VERSION

Beauty arouses pleasurable emotions in people and the idea of self-love has a great appeal. In all versions of the myth, Narcissus is presented as a paradigm of male beauty and as a youth who loved himself (or someone he identified with his own image). The pervasiveness of these themes, coupled with the ethical and psychological issues to which they give rise, would explain the survival of the myth. But how does one account for the fact that Ovid's version steadily gained in popularity through time and the other versions became relatively unknown and are rarely referred to today?

Increasing Internalization of Aggression

The ascendancy of the Ovid version seems to parallel the psychological evolution of human beings. Mastery, even adjustment to a life environment that has become more and more complex, has led to the emergence of the more complex personality of the present era. As we have evolved, for example, social restraint has forced us to become more restrained in discharging our aggression. In the Ovid version of the myth, aggressive impulses are internalized so effectively that their presence is virtually concealed—a psychic phenomenon that is comprehensible and relevant to contemporary life experience.

Infantile Aggression

Children are born without the ability to be directly damaging to others. An infant who is neglected during the early weeks of life can be destructive only to himself. And the most primitive manner of self-destruction, the only one within the grasp of the helpless infant, is self-neglect. That was the suicidal method pursued by Narcissus. Although this self-destructiveness was effectively covered by manifestations of self-love and self-admiration, he actually behaved in a way that could only end in death.

In the personality and fate of the handsome youth whose primitive, helpless self-destructiveness prompted him to stand, motionless, gazing at his own reflection in a pool of water, it is easy to recognize the life cycle of the beautiful, immobile, defenseless, and orally destructive narcissus plant.*

The survival of the version of the myth that deals with the complete intrapsychic internalization of libido and aggression for an object suggests that the internalization of aggression provoked by the beauty of frustrating personalities like Narcissus and his mother has become an increasingly popular pattern of response in human beings.

Implications for Treatment

The psychotherapeutic problem inherent in the myth encompasses more than the presence of excessive self-love—the factor that has been emphasized. Analysis of the myth suggests that it is important to deal with the tendency to idealize beautiful but excessively frustrating objects and to wrap up in a cloak of self-love the destructive impulses provoked by such objects.

---

*Some elements in the myth invite more speculative interpretations. For example, the death of Narcissus beside a pool of water, his gazing at his own image, and the flower that replaces him suggest that the myth might deal with problems of birth, the attitude a newborn child might have toward his mother's breast and her attitude toward the child. The flower might symbolize the breast whose beauty serves to conceal the poisonous nature of the milk it supplies. However, we have refrained from pursuing the more speculative interpretations and have limited ourselves to ideas that follow directly from the material available.

The Narcissistic Defense

My experience over the past thirty years has implanted the impression that each person has a highly specific threshold for the development of schizophrenia. The height of the threshold seems to be overdetermined. In each case, three mutually interacting factors appear to operate; these are heredity, constitution, and life experience. Understandably, the psychotherapist focuses on the factor which is readily accessible to psychological influence—the effects of life experience.

Most investigators seem to agree that the relationship with the mothering figure during the first few years of life plays a major role in schizophrenia, and that it signifies developmental arrest on—or regression to—the oral level. Studies of the relevant events have, by and large, stressed the traumatizing effects of an inadequate diet of emotional nourishment. Much less recognition has been given to that aspect of the young child's upbringing which seems to me to be even more crucial: namely, what he learns to do with aggressive impulses mobilized in his mental apparatus through exposure to excessive frustration, excessive gratification, or both.

The child who tends to discharge frustration-aggression into his body, for example, is a likely candidate for psychosomatic illness later in life. The highway to depression is paved with frustration-aggression poured characteristically into the superego, which then attacks the ego. If the child does not discharge this impulsivity at all, but lets it accumulate in an emotionally impoverished ego, the corrosive effects of the mobilized frustration-aggression may fragment his ego and push him over the threshold into schizophrenia. This particular pattern of response to unfavorable environmental pressures is what I mean by the narcissistic defense.

Though Freud did not use this term, to the best of my knowledge, he alluded to what I conceive to be the narcissistic defense as the "narcissistic wall" and the "wall which brings us to a stop." The narcissistic neuroses are inaccessible to cure by psychoanalytic therapy, the resistance being "unconquerable." Freud went on to say: "Our technical methods must accordingly be replaced by others; and we do not know yet whether we shall succeed in finding a substitute" (1917, p. 423).

It is still pretty generally agreed that the wall of narcissism cannot be successfully scaled by the customary psychoanalytic approach. The search for other methods has, however, led to the recognition that the wall is not as impenetrable as Freud considered it to be. The concept of the narcissistic defense developed out of many attempts to outflank the wall, so that the schizophrenic patient could enjoy its protection while being prepared to undergo the more conventional analytic procedures. The clinical value of the concept is that it provides a key for the resolution of his early resistances.

HISTORY OF THE CONCEPT

Though *narcissistic* and *defense* are very familiar words, both separately and linked together they are susceptible to widely divergent meanings. Marked changes have taken place in our understanding and use of the terms. To establish precisely what is implied by "narcissistic defense" within the context of schizophrenia, I shall therefore outline briefly the historical development of the concept.

Defense

Freud began to formulate his concept of defense (*Abwehr*) in two early papers on the defense neuropsychoses. In the first, he states that patients are able to "recollect as precisely as could be desired their efforts at defence, their intention of pushing the thing away, of not thinking of it, of suppressing it" (1894, p. 47). The ego treats the unbearable idea as *non-arrivé*, something that has never existed. This undertaking is bound to fail, he points out, because the memory-trace and affect attached to the idea cannot be extirpated from the mental apparatus.

In the second paper (1896), Freud differentiates primary from secondary defenses and describes compromise formations. Though inadequate in terms of our present understanding, this paper suggests the highly complex and overlapping sequences and mechanisms which are aroused by the desire to reject some painful reality.

At that time Freud evidently regarded defense as a conscious process, a means of forgetting painful realities. Indeed, he referred subsequently to a process of rejection "called 'defence' and later, 'repression' " (1914a, p. 11).

What purpose does a defense serve? It prevents the occurrence of some undesirable action by the self, by someone else, or through natural process. That is my understanding of its primary purpose. Defense is also defined in the literature as a protection against anxiety (Gero, 1952). Of course, the anticipation of action which is felt to be undesirable does give rise to anxiety and result in tensions, but the defense comes into operation basically to prevent the action from taking place. For example, the person who engages in masochistic acts to combat his sadistic strivings is counteracting and curbing such impulses not only because of the anxiety they cause but also to prevent himself from engaging in sadistic acts.

Narcissism

The word *narcissistic*, derived from the ancient Greek myth of Narcissus, suggests a more picturesque and controversial concept. Countless generations of school-children have mused sadly over the handsome youth who pined away while gazing at his own reflection in a pool of water, until only a flower could be found there to remind us of his fate. The best-known version of the myth, by Ovid, provides a striking personification of self-love and self-absorption in their most extreme form.

The love motif is responsible for the introduction of Narcissus into modern psychological literature. Havelock Ellis was the first to hark back to it. In a study of auto-eroticism published in 1898, Ellis calls attention to the "Narcissus-like tendency . . . for the sexual emotions to be absorbed, and often entirely lost, in self-admiration" (1955, p. 103). In a German abstract of this paper, Dr. P. Nacke translated "Narcissus-like tendency" into *narcismus*, calling it the "most classical form" of auto-eroticism. Freud adopted the term in 1910, and modified and extended the concept four years later in his well-known paper on the subject (1914b). Here, in agreement with Otto Rank's views that narcissism represented an ordinary stage of sexual development, Freud refers to primary narcissism as "the libidinal complement to the egoism of the instinct of self-preservation" (pp. 73-74). Since that time these ideas have been further modified and elaborated on, by Freud and his colleagues, and also by later generations of psychoanalysts.

Narcissism is now commonly associated with the erotic feelings aroused in a person by his own body and personality. The term is also applied to that early stage of normal development when the infant who has felt himself to be wholly one with his mother becomes aware of himself as a separate and unique personality and directs practically all of his emotional interest toward himself, becoming both the self-loving ego and its beloved object.

Mythology has been called the "dust of former beliefs" (Scott, 1898, p. ix). Whether we like it or not, this dust appears to have settled permanently on the pages of psychoanalytic literature. To the extent to which words derived from this source succinctly and unmistakably summon to mind the character formations and emotional states encountered in psychotherapeutic activity, these grafts from mythology enrich our understanding. They create difficulties if they give rise to conflicting usages and interpretations, as is the case with "narcissism" and its derivatives.

The person whose development is favorable behaves only briefly like someone in love with himself. But even after he has formed good object-relations, he persists in narcissistic activity to some extent and generally increases it late in life. We commonly recognize the value of narcissism, as well as the vital role it plays in creative activity. If we regard sleep as the quintessence of absorption in the self, we agree that narcissism is essential for self-preservation.

Need I point out that "narcissistic defense" does not involve these kinds of normal activity? What we are concerned with is narcissism in a pathological sense, with self-love that serves as a cloak for self-hatred. The polarities of self-hatred and self-love are linked together in the defensive system, but the nuclear problem is the self-hatred. *

ORIGIN OF THE DEFENSE

What is the foundation of the narcissistic defense? It is not total emotional deprivation. This leads to marasmus and death, not schizophrenia. The defense seems to originate in a relationship which was gratifying to the infant in some respects, especially in meeting his biological needs for the intake of stimuli, but failed to meet the need of his mental apparatus for cooperation in discharging destructive energy. Nevertheless, he was not totally abandoned; he was sufficiently gratified to develop a strong craving for more gratification and, consequently, to place an unduly high value on the source of this bounty. The infant got to understand that his mother might be damaged by his rage; perhaps she discouraged such reactions by withholding her favors.

---

*For other expressions of this point of view, see Hill (1955) and Stuart (1955).

At any rate, the infantile ego which was not trained to release mobilized aggressive energy toward its object in feelings and language responded to prolonged periods of frustration by internalizing its destructive impulses. Much of the energy that would otherwise have been available for maturational processes was expended to bottle up this impulsivity.

As one explores the dynamic processes underlying the narcissistic defense, it should be borne in mind that very young children engage in narcissistic behavior in a random and voluntary way. Characteristically, they become self-absorbed when they are undergoing an inordinate amount of frustration. They console themselves through some type of activity directed toward their own bodies. One infant sucks at his thumb or a pacifier, for example, while another may scratch his face or bang his head against the crib.

These and various other self-preoccupations assume a defensive character only if the infant resorts to them whenever he feels threatened by mobilized frustration-aggression which he cannot cope with in any other manner. Under those circumstances, the narcissistic behavior gradually becomes patterned into a defense against undesirable action—that is, action that would injure the object. The child who started out to console himself with self-love thus compensates for a specific type of damage incurred in the course of maturation by becoming the object of his own hatred. Sacrificially, he attacks his ego to preserve his external object.

The attitude conveyed by the narcissistic defense is like that of the baby who feels that there must be something wrong with his own body when it is pricked by an unfastened pin in his diaper. The immediate reaction of anyone mature enough to recognize and cope with the source of the pain would be to eliminate it by removing the pin. The schizophrenic doesn't want to feel the pain either, but his immediate reaction is anger at the part of his body which feels it. If an expression of hostility to some person responsible for his pain is in order, the schizophrenic will typically try to curb any destructive impulses by blotting the offender—and the pain—out of his awareness. Excessive preoccupation with himself protects him against acting on impulses which he has disowned and outlawed.

CLINICAL OBSERVATIONS

Self-Hatred

The hypothesis that self-hatred is the paramount factor to be worked on in treating a schizophrenic patient is not one that was advanced in medical schools during the thirties. Indeed, very little was heard at that time about the possibility of treating him. Academic psychiatry then placed its emphasis almost exclusively on diagnosis—classification of the various forms of the disease. However, I became interested in understanding and helping the human being behind the diagnostic facade because schizophrenia then offered the greatest challenge to the research-minded student of psychiatry.

Everything these people thought or felt was of enormous interest to me while I was learning the nature of this baffling illness. Since it was easy to discern that they had suffered much emotional deprivation, it seemed important to give them sympathy, support, and reassurance while I went on studying their psychotic states as thoroughly as possible. I tried to track down the visions and sensations they reported. I listened interminably to descriptions of their weird feelings and the mysterious voices that sounded in their heads.

The first schizophrenic patient I treated was a beautiful young woman, not long married, who had been institutionalized following an acute schizophrenic episode. In her acute catatonic state she blotted out her feelings completely. Cigarette stubs that were burning her finger had to be taken from her; she did not respond to the pain. Several hours a day, five to seven days a week, I listened to her sympathetically, drawing her out on her symptoms, laughing with her when she laughed at her own wisecracks, and making numerous other efforts to get her to make some emotionally significant communication. This made her no better.

Then, during a session when I said some harsh words to her, she immediately came out of her stupor and hurled a glass ashtray that missed my head by an inch. The miss was intentional, she later told me, but she had felt like killing me. When I stopped being supportive and just maintained sincere interest in trying to understand her, standing my ground before her frequent outbursts of rage, the case began to move. The precipitation factor, brought to light during the analysis, was an abortion she had undergone about a month before the psychotic episode leading to her hospitalization. She had been overwhelmed with rage against her husband, whom she believed had tricked her into an unwanted pregnancy.

Extensive treatment in her childhood and adolescence, as well as the fact that her illness was recent and acute rather than chronic, made her readily accessible to psychotherapy. She talked out her hostility in six months and was then discharged from the hospital as a cured case.*

Fate of Aggressive Impulses

Looking back at the case, it clearly pointed to the problem of mobilized frustration-aggression, but at the time this clue went unnoticed. The connection between the illness and the fate of aggressive impulses eluded me

*This case is reported in greater detail elsewhere (Spotnitz, 1961).

until, years later, I reviewed evidence accumulated from a number of schizophrenic patients. The clinical approach to their narcissistic defense as a protection against the wish to destroy slowly emerged from this series of observations.

An early link in this chain was forged by a schizophrenic woman who was preoccupied with death; in her sessions, she consistently communicated the feeling that she was dead herself. I asked her if she had experienced any interruption in these feelings. During the past several years, she said that she could remember only one incident which had made her feel alive. When she finally resolved her resistance to talking about it, she recalled sitting at her window one day and hearing a sudden thump from the adjoining yard. She looked out and saw blood trickling from the mouth of a man who had jumped to his death from the roof of the building. The sight electrified her. She told me: "The moment I saw death in front of me, I came to life."

Eventually, it became clear that this woman labored under a strong urge to kill which had been satisfied, momentarily, by the sight of the corpse. The feelings that she was dead herself was her defense against this urge.

A schizophrenic woman in her forties was very withdrawn until the session when I made some reference to her being middle-aged. She became livid with rage on hearing this, and, after a brief silence, said to me, "If I hadn't blotted you out just now, I would have gotten off this couch and killed you." In outbursts of rage as a child, she had blotted out her mother in the same way.

"When I feel like killing you, I kill my feelings instead." This is a statement I have frequently heard from schizophrenic patients. Some of them say they don't feel that I am in the room with them. Feelings of emptiness are another characteristic complaint.

Patient's initial attitude: At the start of treatment, I expect patients to make few demands on me, and I am rarely mistaken in this assumption. Even though I apply myself in as non-stimulating a manner as possible to the initial task of fact finding—studying them and uncovering the kind of problems their parents had in raising them—they manifest extreme sensitivity to specific types of stimuli. But while the defense is operating, they tend to attribute their misery to what one man frequently referred to as "my own rotten self" rather than to my lack of communication and other frustrations of the treatment situation.

At a time when another patient was experiencing a great deal of discomfort, I inquired whether he wanted me to do anything to relieve him. *"Can you?"* he asked. The idea that someone else could relieve his distress startled him. He expected no more than he had received from his mother, who had trained him to "stew in his own juice."

Recently a schizophrenic youth entering psychotherapy informed me that he knew what it would entail for him. Besides doing all the talking in the sessions, he would have to figure out everything for himself. When I asked what I was supposed to do, he replied: "Sit quietly in your chair, listen to me, and collect your fee." To one who felt so "utterly nothing," the use of my couch and a lien on my attention at the appointed hour seemed like a bonanza.

Therapist's initial attitude: Though the therapeutic impulse is to respond to such suffering with kindness, this would not really be kindness to the schizophrenic patient. It would block the release of the poison that sickened him and may lead toward permanent deteriorated schizophrenia. The self-hatred that has choked up his ego has to be unmasked, transformed into object-hatred, and steadily tapped off without endangering his ego or his object.

The hate tensions which accumulate can take only one direction. The patient must release them in his sessions toward his treatment partner. These impulses must be "tamed" and worked through in feelings and language without improper action. Needless to say, a schizophrenic being treated in one's office requires protection against going too far in the working-through process. The release of his hostility has to be facilitated without exposing him to those dangerous pressures from high accumulations of destructive energy which might lead to further ego fragmentation and psychotic attacks.

Destructive action is blocked by helping the patient maintain his narcissistic defense, and by strengthening it when necessary until it can be relaxed with safety. He is permitted to outgrow the need for it, at his own pace.

Initial interchanges: After instructing him to tell the story of his life in any way he wishes, I study the various ways he resists doing so. What has been conceptualized as the narcissistic defense patterns many of his resistances. Trying to overcome resistances puts too much strain on a schizophrenic. His resistances are analyzed; but objective interpretation, which exposes him to narcissistic injury and tends to inhibit him from talking, is avoided. In fact, the classical psychoanalytic approach is rarely employed until the narcissistic defense has been resolved. Instead, the resistances are joined to the extent that they do not damage the patient, the analyst or the treatment situation. By releasing the patient from any pressure to talk, this method of dealing with his resistances actually facilitates verbal communication.

There are numerous ways to get a schizophrenic patient to begin to talk about himself; this is a matter of technique which I shall not discuss at length here. Sooner or later, he will make some effort to get in contact with his therapist, usually by asking a casual question or by soliciting some personal information from him. This form of resistance, which I call "contact functioning", often suggests what technique would be effective in the situation.

By reflecting the attempts at contact, the therapist provides the precise kind of verbal gratification his patient needs, when he needs it. The attempts can also be utilized to investigate why he doesn't feel or express his hostility—exactly how he defends himself against it.

When the therapist limits his own communications to responding to the patient's direct attempts at contact, and responding in kind, the narcissistic defense is reactivated rather quickly and promotes the development of the transference on a narcissistic basis. In other words, the patient is permitted to mold the transference object in his own image. He builds up a picture of his therapist as someone like himself—the kind of person whom he will eventually feel free to love and hate.*

My immediate objective at the start of treatment is to help the patient develop a narcissistic transference. On the surface it looks positive. He builds up this attitude: "You are like me so I like you. You spend time with me and try to understand me, and I love you for it." Underneath the sweet crust, however, one gets transient glimpses of the opposite attitude: "I hate you as I hate myself. But when I feel like hating you, I try to hate myself instead."

I operate as a gratifying object to the extent necessary to prevent aggressive impulses pressing for discharge from shattering the narcissistic defense. However, my primary concern is the negative transference. I investigate how it is utilized to prevent the release of hostility and work to drain it off in verbal discharge as quickly as possible.

CLINICAL ILLUSTRATION

To illustrate how a schizophrenic patient with a narcissistic transference oscillates between self-love and self-hatred, on the one hand, and object-love and object-hatred, on the other hand, I shall present some clinical material. The case which I now draw upon is that of the patient I have referred to elsewhere as Fred. The early phase of his treatment has been described in another paper (Spotnitz and Nagelberg, 1960). Fred is now a comparatively well-adjusted human being, married, and earning a good salary. He is regarded by himself, his family, and others who know him as a healthy and happy person.

*The use of psychological reflection in the treatment of children is illustrated in Chapter 16.

This highly intelligent young man was on the verge of a full-blown psychosis when he entered treatment at the age of twenty, shortly after various suicidal attempts, sexual escapades, arrests for reckless driving, and feuds with teachers and classmates had abruptly terminated his college career. The episodes that follow illustrate how he tended to defend himself while his negative transference was slowly being resolved.

Material From One Session

One day, near the end of his first year in intensive analytic psychotherapy, Fred called my attention to his new suit as soon as he entered my office. He said it was the first he had picked out for himself, and asked me to feel the material. I did not touch it, but I praised him for making such a good purchase. By the way, the session ended on the same note. Before leaving, he invited me to admire his new tie, and thanked me profusely when I did.

On the couch Fred's first statement was that his face was rather ugly. (Actually, it was not unattractive. He was responding to my praise, really telling me: Though I want to be admired, I don't deserve to be.) In the spirit of his attempt to contact me, I told Fred that he did look "somewhat beast-like." He laughed, and said he knew that I was exaggerating. But he liked to hear me agree with him, he went on, because his parents used to contradict him when he said that he was ugly. This had always disturbed him. (Being regarded as an ugly beast gave him some feeling of protection in the presence of a frustrating object, who would be warned by Fred's appearance that he was a dangerous person.)

Fred then recalled that, during the last session, when he had asked me if I didn't think he was very stupid, I had answered: "Why not be stupid?" He had been very relieved to hear this. It meant that he did not have to drive himself to be intelligent, to reassure himself that he wasn't a moron. Being told to be stupid gave him permission to be a happy infant. (In other words, to attain an early love object.) "I feel like a nude baby looking himself over," Fred remarked. "I feel just like wiggling my ears and hands and saying wiggle-woggle."

When he got up in the morning, Fred said that he had to rush to get rid of his troublesome thoughts. Could he hear some words at the end of every session to prevent him from torturing himself? Asked what kind of words he would like to hear, Fred replied: "Words of praise would do it." (Praise and admiration, which discouraged him from attacking his ego, figured prominently in his defense.)

Fred was soon immersed in thoughts of violence and self-torture. He said he had a choice between killing two co-workers in the office where he had a part-time clerical job, but he wouldn't harm Robert because Robert had a family. Jack was a single man. Though personally clean, Jack's desk always looked like a pig-sty. "My lips are chapped all the time," Fred immediately went on. "I feel it like a pain. When I think of someone else, I think I don't have any right to like him. I'm afraid the self-torture is coming back. It's plaguing me again, like an octopus." (Once again, Fred was demonstrating his fear of getting too close to people; if he came to like them, he might also come to hate them. And then he might want to injure them.)

"If I am getting to enjoy something," Fred continued, "I say to myself that I can't enjoy it because I have to torture myself. . . . I was just thinking of torturing myself. I try to think of something disturbing. That's my old balancing way. I will lie here and *not* think of torturing myself. I'll think of people pulling away from me. . . . Give me some magic words. Help me make up my mind that what I do is torture myself."

(Fred frequently suspected that he might actually be enjoying himself. He was disturbed about this because he wanted to feel that he was really punishing himself, to expiate the suffering he had brought to his mother. He wanted to feel that his self-torture equalled her pain on giving birth to him, when she had been near death, as well as her disappointment—frequently sensed by him in early childhood—that he was not a girl.)

Shortly before the end of the session, Fred said he was thinking of being a male with a vagina. He asked me: "Aren't you supposed to cut off my penis?" I asked him how that would give him a vagina. Fred answered: "I am trying to figure that out. . . . When I am afraid of castrating myself, I think of the most horrible tortures. Maybe I'll die. That would make things all right with mother. I'd walk down the stairs, throw my balls on the table and say to everybody, 'There—that is reality.' I like historical novels because they deal with basic things—castration and sex. No dinner without castration. Who the hell knows what I'm talking about? I ought to show you the wonderful pictures I have of sharks and snakes."

Later Sessions

Fred's communications during the sessions that followed continued to reflect divergent associations and considerable fragmentation. The case record also indicates that puffs of anger came with increasing frequency. He talked repetitiously about what he called "the excruciating torture of torturing myself about torturing myself," and he was also preoccupied with his fantasies of cutting off his testicles and dramatically presenting them to his mother.

When he asked me if he should do this, I asked Fred if he would cut off his testicles for me. The question made him speechless with terror. Why, I went on, didn't he ge furious with me for asking him such a question? I suggested that if his mother or anyone else ever made such a demand on him, he should tell whoever it was to "go to hell."* On hearing that, Fred roared with laughter for five minutes. After that, the thought of castration ceased to terrify him

A few sessions later, there was evidence that the pressure for discharge was building up. The long-smouldering volcano tried hard for several minutes not to erupt, but finally, with a bang, the torrent of abuse came out. Fred shrieked that I hadn't done a thing for him except give him horrible feelings he'd never had before. I'd made him hate me so I could enjoy his misery. I was a faker and a thief; he'd report me to the AMA and the Academy of Medicine for taking his money. Then he ran out of the office.

After this outburst, Fred clammed up for several sessions. To relieve him of his shame and guilt, I employed a technique for reflecting his abuse and turning it back on him, when this could be done within the context of the treatment situation. He heard me out without saying a word. Then Fred got off the couch and solemnly shook my hand. "If you can take what I've dished out here and give it back to me," he said, "you're my friend for life."

RAGE REACTIONS

When primitive hatred, the kind which has been walled up for years behind the narcissistic defense, finally explodes into language, considerable fortitude and a strong desire to cure the patient may be needed to tolerate the insults and threats that spill forth. The boiling fury and onrushing flow of larval venom are hard to describe. Fred's threats were relatively mild. For sheer passionate hatred, the productions of some schizophrenic patients I have worked with can be compared only with the performance of Judith Anderson as Medea. I am inclined to believe the report that playing the role of Medea made her anemic. Some patients have been just as emotionally exhausting—and they were not play-acting.

In one session a man who had been blocked from emotional communication for more than a year began cursing and making the worst threats he could think of. He would start off by tearing my office to shreds. Then he would kill my wife and children. When my turn came, quick death would be too good for me, but he'd figure out something bad enough. I would die through some form of torture. He would stretch it out "inch by inch" and enjoy my anguish as long as possible. Then he dashed out of the office.

He expected to be thrown out the next day, rejected as his mother had rejected him when he lost control. But a few weeks later, he had trouble re-

---

*To demonstrate to Fred how he should behave were he exposed to similar demands in the future, I mobilized the appropriate feelings in making this communication. This is an example of paradigmatic strategy (Coleman and Nelson, 1957).

calling exactly what he had said. A sort of amnesia settles over such episodes.

A woman complained that I made her feel and say things she had been fighting all her life not to say to another human being. Only a monster would want people to become aware of the kind of feelings she experienced. She said: "If Freud really suggested this form of treatment, he belongs where he is. And you should join him."

Changing from the rage-withdrawal to the rage-combat reaction has a terrific impact on schizophrenic patients. One of them asserted: "It's like being dissected while you're still alive."

Some have stated that they would never have entered treatment had they known what they would feel and say. After the defense has relaxed, they usually change their minds. They begin to recognize that exercises in "verbal combatability" are an essential aspect of their emotional reeducation.

TRANSFORMATION OF TRANSFERENCE

Eventually, the general character of the relationship changes. When the positive and especially the negative aspects of the narcissistic transference have been verbalized—the energy discharged in feelings and words towards an object *like* the self—the patient becomes concerned with the therapist as someone *different* from the self. (This is an emotional concern, generally, not to be mistaken for the intellectual interest in the therapist which develops earlier in treatment.) The patient wonders: Is this person toward whom I have come out with all my hatred really different from me and, if so, how different?

With the exploration of these questions, new feelings toward the therapist come into awareness and an object transference gets under way. As it develops, the patient becomes amenable to objective interpretation of his resistances.

RAGE REACTION IN PSYCHOSIS

When I am called on today to bring a patient out of an acute psychotic episode, I employ the same approach. In my experience, too much attention to his symptoms tends to perpetuate the illness. Delusions, hallucinations and the like can take one on an interminable detour. A brief history of their onset and development is sufficient. Once I have this history, the symptoms are explored to the extent necessary to get to the roots of the narcissistic defense. In the process the patient's contact functioning is utilized to resolve his resistance to the verbal release of hostility as quickly as possible.

A few months ago I treated a woman who had entered a mental hospital in an acute schizophrenic condition. It was her delusion that her husband wanted to kill her, and that the entire staff of the hospital was in on the plot. She wanted to beat everyone to the punch by killing herself. I spent an hour a day resolving her negative narcissistic transference. Her "voices" warned her that it was my intention to poison her and cut up her body. Such questions as *"Why* do I want to kill you?" helped her to verbalize hostility to me. In return for the admission that she felt like tearing me up, she found out that I liked her. At that point she showed remarkable improvement. Psychotherapy and thorazine brought this woman out of a full-blown psychosis in two weeks' time. She was then discharged from the hospital and is now being treated privately by a psychotherapist in the city where she lives.

With the therapeutic discharge of the destructive hostility, I have found that the psychosis is regularly resolved. However, this approach to the narcissistic defense does not invariably produce cure. External realities may require the perpetuation of the illness. One schizophrenic woman came out with all of her aggression while in treatment with me and grew to recognize the key contribution it made to her illness. Then, she discontinued psychotherapy in the conviction that her own mental health was less important to her than the concealment of her hatred from her husband. Acting in terms of her feelings would have compelled her to leave him, a step that she refused to take because he was a sick man and needed her. After he died of cancer, she resumed treatment with another analyst and obtained successful results.

RAGE REACTION AND DEPRESSION

In some severe cases of schizophrenia, as in the case of Fred discussed above, one has to contend with a depressive component in the narcissistic defense—that is, strong feelings of negativism and hopelessness. The patient releases his frustration-aggression but doesn't feel loved. The tendencies toward emotional withdrawal are corrected, but basic feelings of being worthless and incurable remain. They do not dominate the situation as they do in a case of severe depression, where the chief danger is that the patient will run off into death. In schizophrenia, rage and fright make homicide a greater danger than suicide; still, there may be a strong enough depressive component in the personality to make the differential diagnosis exceedingly difficult.

One may hypothesize that feelings of being worthless, hopelessly "bad", were introjected very early in life, and that the patient has been fighting against them ever since. To put the dynamic process as simply as possible: The mother acted out feelings of hatred to the child while telling him to love her. Then the child patterned feelings of love into a defense against the stronger feelings of hatred induced in him. To reverse these induced feelings, the therapist conveys feelings of love while telling the patient, in effect: Hate me because I'm not curing you. Hate yourself because you're hopeless.

In this way, the original situation is reversed. The negativistic patient defends himself against loving and feeling loved with feelings of hatred. When this defense is eventually resolved, he works hard to demonstrate that he and the object are both worthy and lovable human beings. The discharge of his hatred enables him to accept his early love objects. Such acceptance is essential for the healing of the fragmented ego as well as for counteracting any depressive component.

THE THERAPIST'S PREDICAMENT

Some may not agree with the hypothesis that self-hatred is the nuclear problem to be worked on in treating a schizophrenic patient. Some may suspect that I just prefer to work with the negative transference; in fact, I have been accused of enjoying it much more than the positive transference. That would take care of me, but it would not account for the fact that the number of psychotherapists who share this clinical approach is growing. It is becoming increasingly difficult to attribute the formulation I have offered to personal idiosyncrasy.

However, the view that the schizophrenic's problem is one of libidinal withdrawal is still the more prevalent. The schizophrenic is more commonly approached as a person who took himself off to a fantasy world because he was inadequately loved in this one. The difficulties of persuading him to abandon self-love for object-love and to accept the harsher realities of life are most likely to be attributed to the fact that he is having too wonderful a time as king of his fantasy world to leave it.

It may be that the schizophrenic was not adequately loved, and that he pursues a way of life which helps him compensate for his emotional deficiencies. I am nevertheless convinced that the *primary* reason why he withdraws from society is to prevent himself from acting as his impulses tell him to act.

When I have analyzed, hour after hour, the megalomania, the non-feeling states and the various other manifestations of the narcissistic defense, what emerges from behind these posturings of self-love is the bitter kernel of self-hatred. The grandeur of the fantasies is a measure of how potentially destructive the patient feels himself to be. Once his aggressive energy is drained off in verbal discharge, he admits to feeling less and less wonderful. Then it becomes amazingly clear that his self-preoccupations have served the purpose of defending his object and his ego against his own hostility. The schizophrenic patient may be anti-social in his behavior, but actually he is a very social-minded human being. Too social-minded, in fact, for his own good. He unconsciously sacrifices his ego to preserve his object. What he has to learn is that both can survive.

To employ the concept of the narcissistic defense in teaching this lesson, the therapist must, so to speak, throw himself in the direct line of fire. He may expose himself to injurious action even as his self-preservative instincts are warning him that he would be better off if his treatment partner were shut up or locked up. The therapist may unconsciously tend to identify with his patient's anxiety about acting destructively if he permits himself to "blow his top." That is probably why we hear so much about the necessity of serving as a reassuring presence to reduce the patient's anxiety, or about helping him carry his hostility.

That is much safer for the therapist. But if carrying buried hostility is what made the patient ill, helping him to go on carrying it won't make him well. That is the predicament of the therapist who chooses to work as I do on the problem of frustration-aggression (Spotnitz, 1969a).

The Way Out

Reinforcement of the narcissistic defense as long as the patient needs its protection is the way out of this predicament. He has to be educated to feel the urge to destroy you—slowly educated, so that he will feel that urge comfortably enough to control his behavior. As he oscillates between positive and negative transference, his ability to control his actions is repeatedly put to the rest. The therapist does not work for the resolution of the narcissistic transference until he is certain that his patient can talk out his destructive impulses, not act on them. Teach him to *feel* like killing you, to *tell* you about it, and *not* to do it, I advise my students.

Meanwhile, he has to be provided with enough gratifying experiences over an extended period of time to change the feeling-tone of his communications. Ideas of disintegration and alienation usually dominate him when he enters treatment. An understanding relationship with a therapist who has a genuine interest in treating him, and feels comfortable in his presence, enables the schizophrenic patient to acquire a more positive orientation to his family and his society. But this kind of re-education is a time-consuming process. A minimum of five years is usually required to predispose him to accept the pain and suffering which the realities of his life may entail.

Major factors in the resolution of the narcissistic defense are the strengthening of the protective barrier against stimuli and the development of new action patterns for the healthful and productive discharge of impulsivity.

11

The Need for Insulation

The clinical approach to be explored and the concept of narcissistic defense (Chapter 10) are related aspects of a general theoretical framework for understanding the dynamic processes which operate in schizophrenia. This understanding, derived from experience with schizophrenic patients, appears to be of vital significance for their treatment.

In my discussion of the narcissistic defense, it was hypothesized that the excessive self-love and self-preoccupations of these patients serve as a cloak for self-hatred. Their pathologically narcissistic behavior is patterned very early in life into a primitive defense system against the discharge of high accumulations of mobilized frustration-aggression. The ego is sacrificed to prevent the release of destructive impulsivity in action that would injure the object.

The tendency of the schizophrenic patient to accumulate destructive impulsivity in his ego appears to be connected with two pathogenic situations: the historic failure of his infantile mental apparatus to acquire a good protective coating, and the under-development, or strangulation, of its discharge patterns. Abnormally weak barriers against the encroachment of external and internal stimuli force the schizophrenic ego to resort to unhealthful forms of protection against overstimulation; the insufficiency of self-protective action patterns, including verbal patterns, expose it to overwhelming types of discharge characteristic of the most sever psychotic states. Schizophrenia itself appears to be a pathological process of compensatory insulation that is set in train by these developmental circumstances.

CONCEPT OF PROTECTION

In a picturesque passage in "Beyond the Pleasure Principle," Freud (1920) calls attention to the need of the personality to be shielded against environmental forces that serve to interfere with its natural growth processes. He compares the living organism to a tiny vesicle "suspended in the middle of an external world" whose energies would overpower the vesicle if it did not possess a protective shield against this continuous bombardment. Freud writes: "*Protection against* stimuli is an almost more important function for the living organism than *reception* of stimuli. The protective shield is supplied with its own store of energy and must above all endeavor to preserve the special modes of transformation of energy operating in it against the effects threatened by the enormous energies at work in the external world— effects which tend towards a levelling out of them and hence towards destruction" (p. 27).

The notion of a protective coating against the dangerous impact of the environment may be rendered more clear through a brief incursion into the principles of electrodynamics. The term *insulation,* applied in its technical sense to the personality, suggests the dynamic processes by which the mind copes with pressures to prevent its energy systems from being overloaded.

The efficient operation of an electrical system testifies to the presence of so-called non-conducting materials between the energized elements of its circuit. These materials confine the current to the wires or other components of the circuit where it is designed to flow. The non-conductors would be more aptly referred to as poor conductors or as materials that are highly resistant to the flow of electric current, because they cannot prevent the current from flowing through other regions if the voltage gradient exceeds a certain point. If it does, what ensues is called a breakdown or puncture.

Justification for applying this concept to mental functioning comes from the science of electroencephalography. It has taught us that the brain operates like an electrical apparatus, generating those rhythmic electrical currents that we call brain waves. Alternating currents of variable frequency are produced by the billions of nerve cells in the brain, and these currents can be measured when a large enough number of the cells repeatedly fire together. Although we are still far from understanding the basic mechanics of this very intricate human apparatus, it has become clear that the nervous system receives, correlates, stores, and generates countless signals which apparently determine our behavior.

It is reasonable to assume that the brain, too, requires insulation for healthful functioning—that is, that there be present certain substances which are poor conductors or are highly resistant to electrical or emotional currents. In a sense, emotional currents are also electrical currents. The neurophysiological investigations of Wilder Penfield (1959) and his associates at the Montreal Neurological Institute have demonstrated that electrical stimulation of certain areas of the brain mobilizes the recall of long forgotten experiences. Events stored beyond the voluntary reaches of memory were awakened in patients undergoing brain surgery when an electrode was applied to the temporal lobe. Instead of requesting a patient to recall past experiences, the neurosurgeon applies an electrical current. Obviously, he does not have any time to spend in overcoming psychological resistance. I doubt that this method will ever be introduced into psychotherapy.

Presumably, the more insulation the brain possesses, the greater its capacity to store energy, the waves of electricity in the brain. When its insulation is weak and the pressure for discharge of the energy—the voltage, so to speak—is very high, it may be incapable of confining the flow of the current to the regular pathways. Instead, a breakdown or puncture may occur, as in an epileptic seizure or the explosive outbursts of the schizophrenic with a full-blown psychosis. The same thing appears to take place in a diffuse way in schizophrenia generally. In other words, abnormally high voltage in the brain—that is, a great deal of emotional tension—can lead to a failure in insulation.

Of interest in this connection is the report of an intensive study of epileptics. The authors, a group of French investigators, present an electronic theory of the cause of epilepsy. They develop the hypothesis that the brain is a condenser which requires insulation, and that excessive discharges of electric current in the brain produce epilepsy. The seizures stopped when the abnormal electric currents were drained off (*World-Wide Abstracts of General Medicine, 1961*).

INADEQUACY OF PROTECTION

The transference relationship provides ample evidence of the schizophrenic's lack of insulation. His general oversensitivity to the impact of the environment, or to a specific aspect of it, is frequently observed. Testimony on this point, which I have drawn from my own cases and supervisory work, can doubtless be duplicated by others who work with schizophrenic patients.

Their extreme sensitivity to the unverbalized and even the unconscious pre-feelings of others is consistently noted. They may be so swept up in these "borrowed" feelings that they feel impelled to act on them. "I was so dominated by my mother's feelings that I never stopped to think about my own," a schizophrenic woman told me. "I ate or did not eat depending on how my mother felt about it. My own needs were of no interest to me."

Another woman complained of being lacerated by her husband's feelings of mild disapproval, even when he did not voice them. "I can sense when he feels like scolding me," she said early in her treatment, "and I get panicky about it. I get to feel that I am falling apart."

Even the movements of others may be overstimulating to these people. It was amazing to observe how one man used to move his arm or change his position on the couch the moment I moved my arm or shifted my position in the chair behind him. It was impossible for him to see me doing it and, as far as I could tell, there was no way of his hearing or sensing that I was moving. Somehow, though, he seemed to become aware of my discomfort and invariably responded to it himself, and exactly as I did.

Another patient would say, "Don't talk. I can't stand the sound of your voice." Later he came to recognize that he had tried to numb himself as a child in order not to feel his parents' anger, which had the effect of persuading him that he was absolutely no good. He, too, had operated consistently in response to his parents' feelings. In the course of his treatment, he had to learn to distinguish the feelings of others from his own.

Some of these patients are unduly stimulated by their own feelings. A youth who had been in treatment a year ran out of the office in the middle of a session. A few minutes later, he rang the bell and returned. My silence had aroused feelings that he could not tolerate. To feel like committing some act they disapprove of implants fears in many schizophrenic patients that they will actually commit it. Mildly positive feelings for attractive women were a source of terror to one young man; it was his fear that such feelings would force him to "cheat" his steady girl friend. He said that he felt like an alley cat when he merely experienced a wish to date anyone else. This man had fought for years against becoming aware of his feelings. The only one he did not object to was elation, the feeling associated with his pleasurable contact with his mother.

Bodily sensations may also be fought, especially those that awaken memories connected with impulses to engage in destructive activity. To a man who had been sensitive to his mother's rough physical handling of him as a young child, sexual excitement was a source of torment. It evoked the recall of her painful punitive measures, thus giving rise to disagreeable fantasies. These fantasies, in turn, aroused strong impulses to obliterate the sensations by cutting off his genitals.

Some patients are hypersensitive to their own thoughts One of them referred to the prolonged silences he had required during the early phase of his treatment as periods of escape from ideas which occurred to him. The thought that business associates might watch him while he worked was very disturbing.

I treated a schizophrenic woman who lived in perpetual fear of killing her husband and young child. To read a news report of a murder or just to think about one put her under so much pressure to act out her urge to kill that her control was threatened. Temporarily she eased this pressure by running off into fantasies of being judged insane and committed to a mental institution for life. So much panic was created by these fantasies that they became more threatening to her than the danger of killing someone. Repeatedly she implored me to tell her why she worried so much about being locked up, but she had little to say about her real problem.

Another woman made this statement: "When my mother asked me whether she might commit suicide, I gave her permission because at that moment I felt only her feelings. I was completely identified with her. My own feelings and wishes were unimportant." The thought of being touched by someone overstimulated this patient, who dreaded any kind of physical contact.

Attempts at Compensation

Harry, a teen-ager whose treatment I supervised, gave abundant evidence of his lack of insulation. His case history (Chapters 15, 16) illustrates how the schizophrenic personality attempts to compensate for this weakness. When he entered psychotherapy, Harry communicated many feelings of being overstimulated by his mother's closeness and seductive behavior. He frequently spent the whole day in bed, rolled up in blankets like a mummy and with his head practically glued to his radio. When he did go outside, he kept close to buildings and avoided speaking to acquaintances.

When asked why he clung obsessively to the same topic session after session, he said that he always hammered away at one subject at a time. "It's like shutting myself up in a back room and shutting out everything else," Harry explained. "I hammer away and it is like grabbing for some security and also justifying myself that I am right." In this situation, the youth employed simultaneously five characteristic patterns of insulation: self-isolation, shutting out stimuli, forceful repetition as a protective pattern against new stimulation, clinging to one idea, and self-justification.

A person entering treatment for some condition other than schizophrenia may also be inadequately insulated, but whereas he generally appears to have some confidence in his eventual ability to control his own behavior, the schizophrenic betrays a complete lack of confidence in this respect. His attempts to deal with the pressure of his needs are, in consequence, much more primitive, and they engross his whole personality. The ego, which remains relatively free in other conditions, becomes involved to an all-encompassing degree in schizophrenia. All of its energy is invested in compensating for the inadequate insulation. To remove himself from the danger of being overstimulated, the schizophrenic resorts to pathological narcissism and emotional seclusion. He sacrifices his ego to insulate himself against the danger of destroying his object (Chapter 10).

THE NORMAL PROTECTIVE COATING

It is important to understand why the schizophrenic's life experiences tend to overexcite him and prepare the ground for impulsive behavior. A review of the processes by which the mind normally acquires its protective coating may help to clarify the precise type of emotional training that the schizophrenic patient needs to experience.

Insulation of the human organism begins before birth. The mother's body, prototype of the protective barrier, provides a shock-free atmosphere where the insulative process begins as an aspect of the physiological growth of the embryo. It is protected in various ways from the excessive impact of the surrounding organs—the impinging environment. For example, shortly after conception, the organism is securely implanted in the uterine cavity and encircled by protective membranes. The placenta mediates its needs with the maternal economy. The amniotic fluid cushions the soft tissues, maintains a comfortably warm temperature for the embryo and, in due time, eases its birth. Need I say more about the insulating properties of intrauterine life? The analyst is familiar with this lost paradise and the traumatic experience of being expelled from it.

With the birth of her infant, the mother continues to perform her insulative role; but she shifts from the involuntary biological operations of the gestation period to voluntary activity that will facilitate his adjustment and growth in a more rigorous environment. To take over voluntarily and consciously the role that she performed involuntarily and unconsciously for nine months is a task that she generally finds very difficult. She must now minister to the baby's physical needs and their psychological concomitants. Chief among these needs are nourishment, sleep, bodily contact, mild tactile stimulation, protection from noise, glare, and other intense sensory influxes that would give rise to instinctual tensions. By meeting the infant's maturational needs through the proper balance of gratification and frustration, she helps to prepare his body and mind to take over the task of insulating himself.

The growth process itself also lays down protective coatings. Nervous tissue is sheathed in myelin, its insulating substance, during the first few years of life. Motor coordination is very important; when the child is able to walk, he can remove himself physically from dangerous situations. Talking is another skill that can be employed to reduce tension. The child who can tell his mother explicitly that he is cold or wet or has a bellyache is spared the distress of the woman I treated who recalled having a bottle stuffed into her mouth every time she cried. About the age of four, the youngster begins to acquire the outer layer of its protective coating—powers of comparatively rational thought and actions. At that point the mother's role becomes less significant.

An important aspect of this cooperative enterprise is the exchange of positive feelings. In the infant who experiences love from his mother, feelings of love toward her and toward himself are stimulated. Eventual awareness of these shared feelings is a great new source of gratification for him. The capacity to love the self and the object develops through the introceptive feelings that a loving mother generates in her infant by sensing his needs and responding to them with intuitive understanding. Her reinforcement of his love responses has an insulative value. On the other hand, strongly negative feelings stimulated in him tend to reduce the strengthening effect of positive feelings and lead to distorted perceptions of the parent. It is my impression that schizophrenic patients, as infants, were oversensitive to negative introceptive feelings—their own and those of the mother and other adults.

FAILURE TO ACHIEVE PROTECTIVE COATING

External Stimuli

If the maturational team does not succeed in building up a good protective barrier in the child, who is to be held accountable? I do not subscribe to the tendency to attribute this failure to either the "schizophrenogenicity" of the mother or some irreversible genetic or constitutional deviance in the child. Let us just say that they did not click as a team. For one reason or another, equilibrium between the mother's handling and the child's impulsivity was impossible to achieve. There may have been tension in the relationship from the beginning. The mother may have found the child exceedingly difficult to bring up, hypersensitive and hard to understand or please even if his needs were within normal limits. If she did not sanction overt expressions of hostility, she may have responded to the child perfunctorily when he provoked murderous impulses in her, and trained him to regard the discharge of hate tensions, either in rage or action, as highly undesirable.

Patients often report that they were not allowed to hate their parents. Not only were they not supposed to say that they did; even to think or feel it was prohibited. Some patients, terrified that the presence of their negative thoughts and feelings would be recognized by their parents, did everything possible to prevent themselves from becoming aware of them.

To a certain extent these are speculations, but the behavior of the schizophrenic patient points back to early bouts with overstimulation and prolonged frustration during which he developed a pattern of going out of contact to buttress himself against the mobilization and discharge of his destructive impulsivity. To stifle impulses to attack his object physically, he ran away from it psychologically into non-feeling states and self-preoccupation—an involuntary and impulsive narcissistic defense. The pressure of this impulsivity fragmented his ego and disrupted its insulation function. Hence, the regulatory mechanisms that normally maintain the reservoir of psychological energy at a pleasurably low level either failed to develop or became inoperative.

Internal Stimuli

It is important to keep in mind the two aspects of the schizophrenic problem: too much stimulation and too little discharge. The absence of adequate discharge patterns has been obscured to a considerable extent by the tendency to focus on the inadequacy of the mind's protective barrier against external and internal stimuli. But the building up of intermediate barriers between stimuli and discharge that serve to delay or store up the response to stimuli is at least as important as the initial screening out of stimuli. It is my impression that the early failure to develop adequate discharge patterns plays a larger role in producing the illness than the weakness of the barrier against stimulation.

This impression may not be supported by the clinical picture, but neither does the clinical picture of the person suffering from autointoxication indicate that the key to his recovery is the elimination of the poisonous substances that have accumulated in his body. The would appear to be a fair analogy. The resemblance between the manifest symptoms in the two conditions has often been noted; indeed, the theory that schizophrenia is a psychological form of autointoxication was frequently discussed several decades ago.

The somnolence, nausea, cramps and other symptoms of the victim of autointoxication may create acute tension, but the direct alleviation of these symptoms does not cure the condition. The physician focuses his attention on draining the toxic substances from the body and, if the condition is chronic, on setting up a regimen for the patient that will prevent the toxins from being produced in the future. Similarly, in schizophrenia, the alleviation of the anxiety caused by the pressure of high accumulations of destructive impulsivity dammed up in the mental apparatus will not resolve the illness. The patient's fundamental need is to develop the ability to engage in the verbal release of feelings, especially aggressive feelings. It goes without saying that this encompasses a great deal more than simple cathartic release, which gives only temporary relief. Treatment has to be structured to provide the patient with the situations required for the creation of action patterns that will facilitate the discharge of aggressive energy in socially desirable ways whenever it builds up in the future (Chapter 3).

FREUD'S EARLY FORMULATION

In the emotional training of a child, the building up of the protective barrier against stimulation is probably more important than the organization of action patterns. Under normally favorable conditions, the mind acquires sufficient patterns as an aspect of maturational processes. This may help to explain why Freud tended to focus on the problem of oversensitivity, as in the passage quoted above.

However, exactly twenty-five years before this work was published, he addressed himself to the problem of discharge and, in a sense, actually suggested the rationale of the clinical approach we are exploring. In an unfinished manuscript written and sent to Wilhelm Fliess in 1895, Freud identified discharge as the mind's primary function. This manuscript, though a product of that early period when his collaboration with Breuer had scarcely ended, did not come to public attention until 1950, when it was published in the original German with the letters to Fliess.

The editors of the English version, issued a few years later, entitled the document, "Project for a Scientific Psychology" (1950). Freud himself refers to it, in the text, as a study on the "structure of quantitative psychology" (p. 311). The study was undertaken, he writes, with the intention of furnishing "a psychology that shall be a natural science" (p. 295). In other words, he was attempting to integrate the findings and terminology of other sciences into psychology, and to discuss the mind without resorting to the aura of mysticism that usually surrounds such a discussion. Some of the formulations in this paper were further developed and appear piecemeal in Freud's later works, but he abandoned the general scheme, apparently in the belief that it was taking him up a blind alley. Nevertheless, the 1895 draft is well worth reviewing now, in view of its amazing relevance to some of the most recent findings in neurophysiology.

Freud's project in quantitative psychology was based on clinical observations, especially those concerned with "excessively intense ideas" (p. 295). Approaching such excitation as "quantities," he suggests that the nerve cells or neurons operate in accordance with "the principle of *inertia*" (p. 296); that is, they tend to divest themselves of these quantities, discharging the excitement into various connecting paths in order to get rid of it. Freud continues: "This discharge represents the primary function of the nervous systems" (p. 296).

Clearly, Freud in 1895 regarded discharge as more important than stimulation. The correctness of this view becomes pretty obvious when one stops to think about it. The reception of stimuli is not crucial for the survival of the organism, but action is crucial. Birth is contingent on both mother and infant engaging in activity. To survive, the neonate must breathe. From the point of view of the nervous system, breathing is a discharge process. Although different sets of muscles are involved in inhaling and exhaling, activity of these muscles always initiates discharge by the nervous system. The discharge of nervous energy is the first requirement of human life.

What Freud calls "contact-barriers" (p. 298) hold up the discharge of nervous excitement between the cells. He theorizes that there are at least three groups of these cells, one group governing the intake of stimuli, another governing memory, and the third consciousness. The stimulus system tries to keep the energy received down to zero. The endings of the nerve cells in this peripheral system perform the function of screening or damping down the amount of energy flowing through the system, thus holding back the energy or discharging it. The reservoir of psychological energy is usually maintained at a low level through these screening and discharge processes, which figure in the concept of insulation.

The group of cells dealing with memory has the additional insulative effect of being out of direct contact with the external world. However, overexcitation and eruptions of large quantities of external stimuli indirectly reactivating the memory system cause pain, according to Freud. Pain signifies a failure or breach of continuity in the contrivances he describes.

The thesis that the schizophrenic's pathological defensive maneuvers represent an unconscious attempt to flee from painful stimulation would appear to coincide with this early formulation by Freud. He makes other points relevant to our discussion; unfortunately, we cannot linger any further on this interesting study in quantitative psychology. However, I want to make brief mention of another idea that he stated in 1895 because it is so reminiscent of the latest findings on the physiology of the brain. Stimuli are registered in the nervous system in what are called "periods" in this study. It suggests that the sense organs operate not only as screens against quantity of stimuli but also as sieves, which admit stimuli from "only certain processes with a particular period" (p. 310). This comes remarkably close to current notions of energy waves and "scanning" in the brain.

PENFIELD'S STUDIES

Further support for Freud's theories detailed above has come from published reports of neurophysiologists, especially Wilder Penfield and his associates who have continued his investigations at the Montreal Neurological Institute. I have already referred to their findings derived from electrical stimulation of the temporal lobe of epileptic patients undergoing brain surgery. In 1936 Penfield initiated a study of the so-called stream of consciousness that the brain seems to preserve; he likens it to a continuous film strip with a sound track. He summarizes his findings in *Speech and Brain Mechanisms*.

As I cite a few passages from the book (Penfield and Roberts, 1959), it would be helpful to bear in mind that the processes he describes are similar to those observed in patients in the course of analytic psychotherapy. Especially pertinent is the following passage:

> The business of the brain is carried out by the passage of nervous impulses from ganglion cell to ganglion cell in an orderly and controlled manner. The impulses pass quickly along the *insulated nerve fibers* like an electrical current. . . . If some area is injured by disease or pressure or lack of oxygen, the gray matter, although it may continue to function, may do so with abnormal additions of its own. There seems to be a *defect in the regulating mechanisms which normally limit excessive discharge* (p. 6). [italics added]

As this statement suggests, healthful activity of the brain requires moderate discharge. Maximum discharge is dangerous; this is what produces the epileptic fit and leads to psychosis, homicide, and suicide. When the integration of brain functions does not insulate the mind adequately, it resorts to regulatory inhibitory mechanisms to provide more insulation. Indeed, the defenses which operate in patients during psychotherapy, notably the narcissistic defense in schizophrenia, might be regarded as sluice gates that limit discharge, to prevent it from reaching the danger point.

A central integrating system within the higher brain stem appears to coordinate the numerous forms of activity that go on in the nervous system. Its psychical responses to stimulation are of two kinds, designated as *experiential* and *interpretive*. Electrical stimulation of certain portions of the temporal lobe cortex produces these responses, according to Penfield.

The stimulation of one area produces a flashback to some past experience of emotional significance. As the patient lives over some previous period in his life, he becomes aware of something more than his memory of that time. "He has a double consciousness. He enters the stream of the past and it is the same as it was in the past, but when he looks at the banks of the stream he is aware of the present as well" (p. 45). This should sound familiar. One of the goals of analytic treatment is the verbal discharge of the stream of the past.

Application of the electrode to another area of the temporal lobe produces the interpretive responses, those concerned with the process of comparing past and present that figures in the making of useful judgments. In some cases, however, electrical stimulation of the area led to false interpretations of the present—*deja vu* phenomena and other perceptual illusions. Emotions not justified by the relation between the new stimuli and past events were produced. For instance, fear was aroused by the anticipation of some threatening perception even though there was no realistic basis for the fear. In brief, neurophysiologists confirm the findings of psychoanalysts that people may suffer from memories and that overcharged memories can lead to inappropriate emotions and improper actions.

In the most primitive type of functioning, stimuli are received and discharged immediately into action. Discharge into feelings and language has been demonstrated to be a much more complex operation, involving many more brain cells, brain systems and integrating mechanisms. It has been estimated that more than two hundred muscles and their controlling brain centers engage in coordinated activity when a person speaks.

IMPLICATIONS FOR PSYCHOTHERAPY

The findings just reviewed shed some light on what transpires in a patient's nervous system during the psychotherapeutic process. They also suggest that, when we ask him to cooperate in the two-fold task of developing healthful forms of insulation and the appropriate verbal discharge patterns he needs, we are actually making enormous demands on the patient. These demands involve the reorganization and reintegration of his nervous system.

Any kind of talking won't do this job. The exceedingly intricate neurophysiological mechanisms involved in talking are utilized to secure the release into language of certain feelings that were associated with highly charged emotional experiences. The patient must verbalize the destructive impulses that he has been holding in check through pathological forms of insulation. If he does not possess sufficient patterns for verbal discharge, he has to be assisted in developing additional patterns. Meanwhile, healthful forms of insulation must be built up to enable him, eventually, to give up his narcissistic defense. But until these more desirable methods of inhibiting destructive action are fully established, the narcissistic defense has to be maintained (Chapter 10; Spotnitz and Nagelberg, 1960).

With this understanding, I conduct the treatment of a schizophrenic patient entering analytic psychotherapy in accordance with three general principles: (1) to provide him with a non-stimulating treatment climate; (2) to train him not to discharge his feelings into action in my presence; and (3) to work from the beginning of treatment to build up the insulative capacity of his ego, reinforcing it as necessary in the process.

Initial Climate

The problem of oversensitivity is focused on from the opening session. External and internal stimuli expose the schizophrenic ego to undue pressure. The reservoir of psychological energy has to be maintained at a low level while the insulative capacity of the ego is being built up. Hence, the need for a non-stimulating climate is obvious.

It might appear that such a climate would be created if the analyst kept quiet. However, silence may at times be more stimulating than words. A great deal of anxiety can be produced by too much silence as well as by too many words. The anxiety level of the patient has to be studied, to determine whether silence or a communication would be more therapeutic in a particular situation.

Although generally a good clue, the anxiety level does not invariably indicate how to protect the patient from overstimulation; anything one does raises the anxiety level in some people. In these cases it may be helpful to space communications instead of operating in relation to the anxiety level. For example, one woman I am treating became extremely anxious when I was quiet. On the other hand, communications to reduce her anxiety had the opposite effect; her recognition that anxiety was rewarded with communication served to increase her anxiety. The best way out of this dilemma, I found, was to alternate brief periods of communication with brief periods of silence. Thus far, this schedule has proved therapeutic for this woman; but if she becomes aware of what I am doing it may be necessary to change the schedule or devise some other means of protecting her from overstimulation.

Discouraging Destructive Action

The process of educating a patient to the idea that his feelings should just be articulated, not acted on, gets under way with the start of treatment. In accordance with the general principle of keeping my own interventions at a minimum, if a patient appears able to proceed and behave appropriately without explicit instructions, I prefer that he continue that way. Otherwise, he is instructed to tell the story of his life in any way he wishes. He is also permitted to remain silent when he prefers that to talking. But it is important to inculcate the idea that talking and keeping quiet are the only activities encompassed in the treatment relationship.

I formalized this principle after several narrow escapes from murder convinced me that I did not want patients to engage in motor activity when in the room with me. I decided that, if I wanted to live and continue to function in the field, I had better lose no time in conveying, preferably by implication, the message: Just talk; don't act. Of course, this serves to heighten the transference because, as I pointed out earlier, survival depends upon discharge—action. When a patient with a terrific drive to act is told, "Don't act," aggressive forces are mobilized in his personality. He feels that you are trying to destroy him. However strongly he feels this, the freedom granted him to verbalize the feeling signifies that you will permit him to live.

Increasing Insulative Capacity

Once the hostility has been drained off, communications that are specifically designed to stimulate are involved in the process of increasing the insulative capacity of the patient's ego. Other communications are planned to provide substitute forms of insulation; these are required to reinforce the healthful non-conducting materials the ego possesses, and to help it outgrow the need for pathological forms of insulation. In a sense, the therapist serves as the protective barrier as long as may be necessary to tame the patient's impulses to act, to block up destructive action patterns which short-circuit emotionally significant verbal communications, and to prevent the puncturing of weakly insulated areas of the ego.

The degree to which an individual will be stimulated by the presence and behavior of another is difficult to control, let alone anticipate. My most reliable guide is the patient's contact functioning: his conscious or unconscious attempts to elicit some response from me as he resists talking about himself in a mature way. I study these attempts and psychologically reflect them in my own communications.

Contact functioning generally operates as a resistance in the analytic situation, but its investigation and reinforcement have two special values in working with a schizophrenic patient. His attempts to make contact clarify the nature of his relationship with his original objects, thus providing clues to his precise needs for insulation. In other words, his contact functioning tells one how to go about insulating his ego. Moreover, the reflection of the attempts at contact—that is, acting as a twin image—gives the patient the feeling that he is doubly protected against improper behavior.

Reinforced in this way, the ego feels more secure. Feelings of security have a high insulation value. So do healthy identifications. Positive introceptive feelings are strengthened; negative ones are detoxified through this psychological method of child rearing. This approach is designed to create the special kind of object relationship that a severely regressed patient needs to work effectively on his preoedipal problems and put his ego in good control of his energy systems.

By responding in the manner indicated by the patient's contact functioning, the therapist presents stimuli that are carefully controlled by the patient and will thus tend to reduce his narcissistic activity.

Frustration Dosage

Resistances are handled in an entirely different way than that dictated by the standard procedure (Spotnitz and Nagelberg, 1960). The patient is not put under any pressure to overcome them; as a matter of fact, he is helped to preserve his resistances and even to strengthen them at times because of their insulative value. The aim is to prevent him from accumulating more destructive impulsivity than he is able to release verbally. Hence, the frustration dosage to which he is exposed is mild. He is not overindulged with gratification either. He is given just enough to make him want to struggle for more, and to convince him that the struggle is worthwhile.

Some analysts concentrate first on the positive transference. The negative aggressive patterns receive relatively little attention. But I have not found this approach effective with a patient who has stored up intense rage reactions, at great cost to his ego (Chapter 10). His primary need is to discharge his hate tensions in socially acceptable ways. Libidinal impulses may also be troublesome for a schizophrenic but, in my experience, his hostile ones are far more dangerous to himself and others.

Some schizophrenic patients talk hour after hour about their incestuous feelings for a parent without getting any better; but they clam up at the thought of damaging the object. Had Oedipus been a well-defended schizophrenic instead of the prototype of a psychoneurotic, he might still have committed incest with his mother, but he would have run away from his father. The schizophrenic does not kill his object unless his ego is completely overwhelmed by psychosis and compelled to engage in destructive behavior.

The first lesson the schizophrenic patient has to learn—and the hardest to teach him—is that frustration-aggression *can* be discharged appropriately in words, that language *is* powerful enough to liberate him from the most hateful situations.

Goal-Oriented Interventions

When to talk and when not to talk is an elementary concern to the analytic psychotherapist. "Talk when you have something to say," though a good rule of thumb for the treatment of neurotic patients, does not meet the special needs of one who is schizophrenic. I may talk to such a patient when I have the impression that a particular communication will facilitate his development of additional discharge patterns. I have already referred to the use of communication to reduce the anxiety level of the patient. Other types of communications may be helpful in producing verbal discharge or in keeping his hostility from reaching unbearable heights. The important consideration is that all of the therapist's communications be goal-oriented.

Goading, reassurance, or emotional support are inadvisable. Early in treatment, I give interpretations only when they will help the patient improve his immediate functioning. Interpretations are contraindicated when they tend to make him more absorbed in himself or are felt as narcissistic injury. Experience has demonstrated that exposure of a schizophrenic patient to objective evaluations of himself before his protective barrier has been built up may easily compound his difficulty because, right or wrong, they tend to puncture his ego.

The theoretical formulations presented here are addressed to the twin problems of overstimulation and inadequate verbal discharge patterns, primary concerns in the early stages of the psychotherapeutic process. In order to resolve these problems, the therapist operates in such a way that the patient feels that he and the therapist are one. This facilitates the development of a strong transference on a narcissistic basis. The security derived from this relationship eventually makes it "safe" for the patient to become aware of the therapist as a different object. At that point, the narcissistic transference is superseded by an object transference. After this develops, the treatment of the schizophrenic is not basically different from that of a neurotic undergoing psychoanalytic psychotherapy, and presents no special problems to the goal-oriented therapist.

CLINICAL ILLUSTRATION

To illustrate how the concept of insulation is implemented in treatment, I shall return to the case of the schizophrenic youth I refer to as Fred.*

During his first two sessions, Fred talked freely about childhood events and his quarrels with his parents following the breakdown which had cut short his college career. He complained that he felt dead; agitated and restless, he asked if he was talking the way he was supposed to talk. Repeatedly he called my attention to his distress. Frightened by it, he made several rather feeble attempts to solicit some response. For example: What was I interested in? Did I have any hobbies? Questions such as these were followed by provocative remarks, such as, "This couch must be older than I am."

I psychologically reflected these communications; that is, I directed a similar question or remark to Fred but gave no factual information. His resentment mounted with each response. A therapist who objects to working with an angry patient will undoubtedly regard this strategy as improper,

*Material from the same case was presented in earlier papers to illustrate other aspects of treatment (Spotnitz and Nagelberg, 1960; Chapters 5, 10).

because my reflection of Fred's contact functioning made him very angry with me. However, the more I talked as he did, the more secure he felt, and his mounting feelings of security enabled him to verbalize a great deal of anger. Toward the end of the second session, he threatened to tear the office apart. Asked what damage he would do, he replied that he would break the windows and smash the desk lamp. But that would just be the beginning. He was reminded that he was supposed to verbalize his feelings, not act on them.

This instruction was repeated during the third session. Fred answered that he had no intention of cooperating. He hadn't wanted to come in the first place. What right did his father have to force him into treatment?

"Then why don't you stop?" I asked him. "If you don't want to be treated, you don't have to be."

"You're only saying this because you know my father won't let me stop," he replied. "You know I can't buck him."

"No, I'm serious about this," I told Fred. "If I tell your father that you should stop, he will believe me."

I meant what I said, but Fred did not believe it until we had talked and talked about his leaving treatment for the next two sessions. By that time, he was convinced of my sincerity. Needless to say, had I not meant what I said, this strategy would have led to failure. He shook my hand for the first time, and thanked me profusely. As he was about to close the office door, I called out after him, "Remember now. Don't come back unless you yourself really want to be treated."

The series of interventions just reported represented a therapeutic maneuver to increase the insulative capacity of Fred's ego so that he could defy his father and refuse to be forced into treatment. The maneuver also made it possible for him to express his objections to having anything to do with me at that time.

Fred's father telephoned two days later, and was informed that the young man had not misrepresented the situation. He himself was not heard from for ten days. Then he telephoned and pleaded for an appointment "right away." He added, "I really want to come no." His return to treatment was arranged for the same day.

Fred's ego was now able to accept the idea of treatment. Successful defiance of his father made it possible for him to commit himself to it voluntarily.

When he came to the office later in the day, Fred explained that he had come to the previous sessions just to "see how things would go." He had felt too cracked up to talk. But he had been so miserable at home during the last few days that treatment couldn't possibly make him feel worse. Although he experienced great difficulty in involving himself in the therapeutic process, only one more break in treatment occurred.*

Fred's resistance patterns were psychologically reflected at times to communicate my awareness of his misery. To cite one example: He talked about wanting to take a trip to California, proceeding from there to Alaska. "That sounds like a wonderful idea," I told him, "but why limit yourself to this continent? There's so much more to see in the rest of the world. Why not make the trip really worthwhile by taking a boat to Australia, especially New Zealand?" I joined Fred in his wanderlust to insulate him more adequately against his strong impulses to throw up the sponge and spend the rest of his life as a footloose hobo. At that time, he really relished the idea of becoming a hobo.

He made many attempts to control his anger by asking me to relieve him of his emptiness and misery. I did not offer reassurance, but asked why I should relieve him. This insulative maneuver produced an outburst of rage. He thundered, "I hate you for permitting me to go on tormenting myself."

Fred tended to attribute his continuing improvement wholly to my communications, ignoring the importance of his own verbalizations. Hence, he sought to control situations to obtain whatever emotional nourishment he craved. When this verbal feeding was not forthcoming on demand, he was apt to explode again. In one moment of fury, he reached for a bronze ashtray and shouted, "Stop this stalling and talk to me." Of course, the immediate response was a reminder that all force was to be turned into language. "No action, just talking, please."

When he threatened bodily assault during another outburst of rage, it was pointed out that he did not hold the whiphand. Plenty of damage could be done to him before he had time to get off the couch. Reflection of Fred's own threats helped to insulate him against carrying them out. My repetition of the threats served to assuage his guilt about them. He felt no need to defend himself since he was convinced that I would not harm him; but the fact that I could comfortably say I would made him feel more secure about verbalizing his own destructive impulses.

In other situations questions were put to Fred to help him talk about any subject that came to his mind. His attention was directed away from himself toward the consideration of objects.† He was educated to the idea that it is

---

*This took place about four years later, when Fred missed a session because he suddenly felt a "call" to visit a childhood sweetheart he hadn't seen for ten years. His irresistible urge to find out whether their love had survived the long separation led Fred into a disappointing experience. His trip of several hundred miles ended, surprisingly, in a maternity hospital, where he was greeted by a young woman holding a newborn baby in her arms. Obviously, she was very much in love with her husband.

†This maneuver, which has an insulative effect, is sometimes employed in the initial interview with a person who becomes very disturbed in talking about himself, especially when he focuses on his functional difficulties. Steered into an object-oriented discussion, he usually becomes more relaxed.

normal to express feelings of hostility when one's emotional needs are being frustrated. Other interventions helped him discharge instinctual tensions while he was being insulated against action. The verbal release of the tensions also tamed his impulses to behave inappropriately.

Fred was conditioned to the verbal discharge of his object interests. Such conditioning figures significantly in the insulating process. When he felt secure enough to attach himself to new objects, Fred found that he could satisfy his emotional hunger without being overstimulated. He developed a terrific drive for work, went to night school, and made friends with several of his fellow students. He also started to date girls.

His narcissistic preoccupations waned as he discovered that his work, studies, and social activities brought him much more satisfaction. He began to operate like a confident human being with a well-insulated ego.

FUNCTIONING WITH ADEQUATE INSULATION

The clinical material presented above supports the hypothesis that schizophrenia represents a pathological mode of insulation against the destructive effects of undischarged aggressive energy. When the goal-directed therapist operates in terms of this understanding to build up the insulative capacity of the ego, and help it develop appropriate patterns for the discharge of this energy,* the patient is able to function without recourse to ego-sacrificing forms of insulation.

The scarring of the ego caused by the schizophrenic process cannot be completely obliterated, but evidence of past pathological tendencies will only be found through careful diagnostic testing or interviewing in later life. The acquisition of a mature ego—that is, a well-insulated ego commanding an abundance of patterns for verbalizing emotions—tends to immunize a person against the return of the illness.

Experience with schizophrenic patients convinces me that one cannot help them meet their maturational needs solely, or even to a major extent, through the use of words alone. It should be emphasized that the use of special techniques is subordinate to the genuine desire of the therapist to understand such a patient and help him preserve his ego. The therapist with the right feelings can develop maneuvers which, properly timed and applied, will build up the insulative capacity of the patient's ego and enrich its patterns of self-expression.

---

*Perhaps this is analogous to setting an example for the patient, an illustration of paradigmatic strategy (Coleman and Nelson, 1957).

Resolving obstacles to the meeting of the patient's maturational needs is the objective of those therapists who, though guided by psychoanalytic understanding, use whatever ingenuity is required to develop the appropriate emotional and thought responses, rather than limiting themselves to any single procedure. Ultimately, I believe that the special approaches being developed for the treatment of the preverbal personality will facilitate the emergence of a more efficient form of psychotherapy for both verbal and preverbal personalities—a modern form of psychoanalysis.

12

Techniques for Resolving
the Narcissistic Defense

The clinical phenomena analyzed in the present chapter inspired Freud's reference to the "wall which brings ut to a stop. . . . In the narcissistic neuroses the resistance is unconquerable; at the most, we are able to cast an inquisitive glance over the top of the wall and spy out what is going on on the other side of it" (1917, p. 423). Subsequent explorations substantially modified the bleakness of Freud's impression and emphasized the conclusion he drew from it: His own therapeutic method would have to be replaced to deal effectively with the narcissistic defense. Such a method can, nevertheless, be formulated and conducted within the basic framework of Freudian psychoanalysis.

The method described here has been employed for many years by analytically trained psychotherapists in the treatment of adults, adolescents, and children, with appropriate modifications, in private practice and psychiatric clinics. An application of the method in a short-term therapy program for six hospitalized patients is reported by Davis (1965-1966). Although the majority of patients have been schizophrenic or borderline cases, this approach has been applied also in other conditions marked by regression to preverbal levels of functioning, notably severe depression, hypochondriasis, and psychosomatic disorders. A gross inability of the patient to manage the release of aggressive impulses in healthful and socially appropriate ways has been viewed as an indication for the use of the method.

Effective application of the method is contingent on recognition of hostile impulses in the patient and the effects they induce in the practitioner (Win-

nicott, 1949), and the ability of the patient to control the release of potentially explosive forces without damage to himself, the analyst, and the treatment situation. Goal-oriented functioning, emotional resiliency, and self-
command are required. Characteristic countertransference problems and
the use of the realistically induced emotions as a source of therapeutic leverage are discussed in earlier publications (Chapters 5, 10).

RATIONALE OF THE METHOD

The candidate for psychoanalytic therapy is an individual who has used
faulty patterns of self-expression in adjusting to his environment and the
exigencies of life. The treatment is designed to reactivate these pathological
patterns of adjustment, to help the patient outgrow any need to use them
compulsively or involuntarily, and to provide the highly specific defense-
freeing and psychological-growth experiences that will facilitate his emotional evolution.

The pathological narcissistic defense is attributed to the disorganizing influence of unconscious aggressive impulses. The defense is understood to be
a primitive mental structure, set up in the undifferentiated stage of emotional development, that interfered with the completion of maturational sequences. The structure appears to be in part innate, in part environmentally
conditioned. A high potential for aggressive impulsivity may be a genetic or
constitutional predisposition. There may have been disequilibrium between
the mother's early emotional training and the child's impulsivity.

It is reasonable to assume that the aggressive impulsivity was mobilized
by frustration. Even in those cases where the frustration experience appears
to have been relatively inconsequential, frustration-aggression presents itself as the central problem because of the pattern that was set up early in life
to deal with the impulsivity.

Many failures reported in the early psychoanalytic treatment of extremely narcissistic people may be attributed, to some extent, to the fact that the
narcissistic defense conveys the impression that its nuclear force is self-love.
Clinical experience does not support this notion. The patient appears to be
wholly wrapped up in himself, but self-love cloaks self-hatred, which is the
core problem. Hatred was turned back upon the ego, and the object field of
the mind was obliterated to protect the external object against the discharge
of destructive impulsivity (Bloch, 1965; Clevans, 1957). Running away psychologically from hostile impulses into nonfeeling states and self-preoccupations eventually becomes a compulsive operation. The polarity that
figures significantly in the narcissistic defense is self-hatred and object love.
The treatment is based on this working hypothesis, which has been formulated more extensively in other publications (Spotnitz and Nagelberg, 1960;
Chapter 10; Spotnitz, 1969a).

In the sense that the bottling up of destructive impulsivity drains off energy from vital mental processes, the narcissistic defense is dealt with as a specific maladaptation that interfered with maturation of the personality and blocked its further growth. The patient is approached as an individual whose spontaneous emotional evolution was impeded in his earliest interchanges with natural objects and who requires a corrective series of interchanges with a therapeutic object.

In that role, the analyst helps the patient to maintain the narcissistic defense and gradually develop more healthy defenses. To enable him to reach as quickly as possible the goal of the treatment—personality maturation—the analyst addresses himself to the resolution of the forces that block maturation.

The analyst operates indirectly as a maturational agent. His communications are *not* designed to appease the patient's maturational needs. Nor are they designed to transform unconscious into conscious material, to help him experience catharsis, to gain an understanding of himself, or to acquire new insights. Catharsis per se is not regarded as significant, but it is experienced by the patient as he is trained to articulate whatever he feels, thinks, and remembers without engaging in the analytic sessions in any other motor activity. Insight and the other just-mentioned phenomena may emerge as by-products of the relationship, but they are of secondary value. The crucial task is to nullify the effects of the forces that interfered with the patient's growth and to catalyze maturation.

INVESTIGATION OF TRANSFERENCE RESISTANCE

All personality deviations are dealt with under the operational formula of investigating transference-resistance phenomena and intervening only for the sake of their resolution. Symptoms are not analyzed per se and are dealt with only to the extent to which they interfere with analytic progress. The analyst's reaction to symptoms must not either encourage or discourage the patient from revealing psychotic material.

The treatment is conceptualized as a therapeutic process of resistance analysis. All obstacles to meaningful verbal communication fall under the heading of resistance; thus they must be resolved and not overcome. Resistance to the verbalization of negative feelings requires attention from the beginning of the treatment. Resistance is dealt with on a priority basis throughout each case, the five classic types of resistance (Freud, 1926) being observed in each category.

Transference is evoked in a nonstimulating way, and the patient's need to experience it in a state of mild tension is respected. Negative-transference manifestations are dealt with first. Transference, which develops first on a narcissistic basis and is superseded by object transference, is dealt with as resistance when it interferes with progress, and fully resolved.

The treatment is structured to prevent regression too severe to be dealt with in the course of the session. To avoid the danger of precipitating an acute psychotic episode, a distinction is made between a purposeful engaging in a retrograde process and running away involuntarily from the treatment situation into the past to prevent the release of frustration-aggression. Regressive tendencies are dealt with as resistance until the patient is capable of appropriately expressing his reactions to the frustrations experienced in the relationship. He is trained to stay in the present and simply remember the past.

INITIAL INTERVENTIONS

The opening of a case may be preceded by a series of maneuvers reflecting the need of a highly narcissistic individual to defend himself against the stresses of the analytic situation. Letters or telephone calls are often received from relatives or friends inquiring about the availability of the practitioner's services, or these may be repeatedly solicited by the prospective patient himself before he mobilizes himself to make a definite appointment and come to the office. The patient is motivated to do so primarily by a strong desire to be relieved of his misery, and his arrival may signify no more than that he has decided to investigate the possibility of finding such relief.

The initial interview is devoted to formulating a tentative diagnosis and establishing the treatment contract. A brief family history is also taken. Names of parents, siblings, and grandparents, occupations, divorces, and causes of death, for example, often contain clues to family patterns of emotional illness as well as the nature of the candidate's own childhood experience. The identity of the person referring him may also be of some significance, and this information or the reason for the referral is also discussed if he wishes to do so.

A brief history of the onset of the illness and development of symptoms is desirable but not indispensable. The candidate is placed under no pressure to give information that he has withheld; the diagnostic impression is based on his voluntary disclosures. One of the few questions I usually ask a prospective patient is why he wants treatment. Whatever answer he gives clears the way for an exploration of his attitude about it, and for an evaluation of his willingness and ability to cooperate under mutually agreeable arrangements.

The patient's questions are usually countered with the analyst's questions. A full and straightforward explanation of pathology is undesirable because it may be experienced as a narcissistic injury, an attack on his ego by someone who does not like him, understand him, or speak his language.

It is equally undesirable for the practitioner to reveal information about himself. Even if solicited, such disclosures may be interpreted as a sign of weakness, lack of self-confidence, or professional insecurity.

It is preferable not to volunteer information on the treatment under consideration, especially with respect to its length, difficulties, and the results anticipated. Promises, explicit or implicit, of a successful outcome are out of order. Such assurances are rarely helpful. In a negatively suggestible person, for example, they may unconsciously stimulate a strong resolve to defeat the analyst. When a question regarding outcome is raised by a person who indicates a specific need for an answer, it is advisable to investigate the unconscious meaning of the question before formulating a response.

In my experience, uncertainty and ignorance "anesthetize" the preoedipal patient against the discomforts and stresses of the therapeutic undertaking that lies ahead. The less he knows about either its tribulations or potential benefits and the less aware he is of what is actually going on in the relationship prior to its final stage, the more capable he will be of concentrating his energy on the crucial task of verbal communication. Moreover, if the emotional tone of the practitioner's statements throughout the interview is one of genuine interest without warmth or urgency, the counterforce operating in a person who is apprehensive about committing himself to the undertaking is minimized. A trial period of about six weeks is usually suggested. The analyst attributes the discontinuance to his own incapacity if the relationship is terminated at that time.

Practical Arrangements

The establishment of a relationship in which analytic work can go on systematically is one of the early goals of treatment, but the ability to function accordingly is not a prerequisite for it. The practitioner shoulders virtually all responsibility for developing an effectual alliance when the case opens. As it proceeds, the patient becomes more and more cooperative; as termination approaches, he usually is fully cooperative.

The minimum demands consistent with the treatment of his condition on an ambulatory basis are that the patient lie on the couch and talk. He is not instructed to free-associate. As the opening move in educating him to do so, he may be asked to tell his "life story" or simply to talk of his experiences; a severely disturbed individual may begin by recounting how he traveled to the office, what he ate for breakfast, and the like.

Time and fee are fixed during the first interview, but no formal declaration is volunteered on other contractual matters. Arrangements and rules are flexibly formulated as dynamic tools of therapy. The patient is told that talking is the only activity that is "cooperative" during his sessions and is gradually educated to the idea that he is expected to verbalize his impulses, thoughts, feelings, and memories. It is also impressed on him, in due time, that regularity and promptness in attendance and payment of fees are expected of him. Early in treatment, resistance tends to cluster around these areas and, in some cases, the couch position.

I prefer to start a patient on one session a week and investigate the maximum intensity of treatment desirable for the case during its first stage. He may be seen more often if he is capable of digesting psychological nourishment at a faster tempo. Under exceptional circumstances he may respond to five or even six weekly sessions; however, from one to three sessions usually provide as much emotional feeding as can be healthfully assimilated.

The patient is assisted to continue for two years, the minimum period necessary for significant change to occur. At the end of that period, he is usually given the option to discontinue and return later if he wishes to make further progress. A minimum of five years is required for personality maturation for an individual who enters treatment to resolve the narcissistic defense. The case may go on much longer, its ultimate duration depending on the willingness of both parties to work together and the mutual recognition that worth-while progress is being made and is likely to continue. Otherwise, termination is recommended.

ROLE OF ANALYST

By functioning as an ego-syntonic object, the analyst facilitates the development of transference on a narcissistic basis as well as its eventual transformation into object transference.

As the patient re-experiences the emotional charge of his early object relations, the pathological patterns he set up for blocking the release of negative feelings come into play. These blockages are systematically studied from the beginning of the treatment, but the analyst reveals no interest in them until his present and more powerful influence makes them reducible.

To permit the narcissistic transference to develop fully, interventions are cued to the patient's *verbal* attempts to solicit some information about his characteristic preoccupations, to satisfy his personal interest in the practitioner, or to convert silence or monologue into dialogue through a casual question. In previous reports, such behavior has been referred to as "contact functioning," and its use as a timer and operational guide to goal-oriented communication has been discussed (Chapters 10, 16). Study of the patient's immediate contact functioning helps the analyst to provide frustration and gratification in the precise balance needed to prevent aggressive impulses from shattering the narcissistic defense.

To facilitate the release of such impulsivity on what is, in effect, a self-demand basis, the analyst reflects the verbal attempts to establish contact without giving the information requested. Instead, he investigates why the patient wants it. At times, contact functioning helps him engage in meaningful communication, but generally it operates as resistance. In joining or psychologically reflecting the pattern, the analyst is usually oriented toward the following objectives:

The attitude expressed by the patient is met with unspoken acceptance. He is not contradicted; no attempt is made to modify his thoughts and feelings. The analyst refrains from asserting himself as a personality. He does not explain, for instance, why the patient relates to him as an extension of himself rather than as a separate and different person. The possibility of serving as a narcissistic-transference object is foreclosed if the analyst corrects the misperceptions and distortions of reality. The "feeding back" of his own attitudes gives the patient feelings of being understood; more than that, he tends to move away from the original position.

When the occasion presents itself, the patient's attention is directed to external objects. What motivated him to set up the narcissistic defense has to be determined. Usually the attitudes he experienced from his earliest objects had something to do with its establishment.

As much as possible, pressure is taken off the ego and shifted to the object. When, for example, the patient is bogged down with worry over his deviant tendencies, it may be indicated to him there is nothing seriously amiss aside from the fact that he was not trained properly. Undoubtedly, he can be retrained; the only question is whether the analyst is capable of doing it.

TRANSFERENCE RELATIONSHIP

When the transference is established, the patient may talk about what he imagines is going on in the analyst's mind. The patient may feel that the analyst does not want him to relax his defenses, especially in expressing hostility. Instead of attributing it to the frustration inherent in the treatment situation, he says, in effect, "I am making myself miserable." The "I" may be the object rather than the ego. On the other hand, the "you" he talks about may actually be the ego. In other words, some of the feelings transferred reflect attitudes of significant objects that were incorporated in the infantile ego. Unless such feelings are sorted out from those which the patient originally experienced himself, it is impossible to reconstruct his earliest object relations.

It has been pointed out that the analyst begins to deal with this melange of ego-object attitudes when he has become more emotionally significant to the patient than his original objects. Narcissistic-transference manifestations that interfere with communication are then joined or psychologically reflected.

Negative transference is dealt with first. To facilitate the discharge of frustration-aggression, the analyst presents himself as a willing target for verbal abuse. As an essential safeguard against explosive behavior, the patient's own resistance to *acting* on his destructive impulses is consistently joined and even reinforced if necessary. Moreover, another line is drawn between therapeutically desirable utterances and those that yield sadistic gratification.

By identifying with the patient in feelings and thoughts, the analyst helps the patient to identify with him in behavior. The patient also becomes more and more aware of positive feelings for his transference object. As he oscillates between states of negative and positive transference, what was at first little more than an ego percept becomes a real object.

After the compulsive grip of the narcissistic defense has been relaxed and new modes of behavior have been established with the aid of the ego-syntonic object, the patient feels secure enough to relate to a different object. He becomes aware of strong cravings for a livelier one. The development of object transference is facilitated by demonstrations of how the patient should handle himself, especially in those interpersonal situations in which he tends to resort to the narcissistic defense (Chapter 10; Nelson, 1962a). In a state of object transference, he explores the differences between himself and his object. Having acquired the ability to experience and give expression to his feelings, he is in a position to defy, comply, or cooperate, depending on his own preference. By that time he has passed the emotional age of two and is much less narcissistic.

RESISTANCE MANAGEMENT

A counterforce is mobilized when the patient is directed to talk at the beginning of the treatment. As this counterforce waxes and wanes in the case, it gives rise to countless manifestations, which the analyst recognizes and deals with as resistance. Attempts to overcome the resistance of an extremely narcissistic patient serve to intensify the counterforce. In order to diminish it, the pressure for progress is carefully controlled.

Although the counterforce must be weakened, it must also be preserved because it represents the totality of the patient's experience in the perceptual field. He is therefore permitted to maintain the old field until he can function with integrity in the new perceptual field that is created in the analytic relationship. Until he feels secure about his behavior, can release his psychological energy healthfully and constructively, and relates appropriately to an object that is regarded as cooperative and reliable, the patient needs the freedom to return to the old experiences. Some failures in treatment occur because the old perceptual field is not re-created with sufficient intensity or preserved long enough for the patient to make an unequivocal choice between the two fields.

To help him make this choice, his undifferentiated ego-object percepts are permitted to become highly charged with emotion before they are dealt with in the context of resistance. Coincidentally, freedom from undue pressure to commit himself to the new perceptual field diminishes the counterforce. What motivates him ultimately to give up the narcissistic defense is difficult to determine. However, when the counterforce to progress is approached in the manner just suggested, one observes that the patient outgrows his immature attitudes. He begins to feel that anything is preferable to the old mode of functioning.

The analyst also operates on the premise that resistance performs a communication function. Inadequate, incomplete, and indirect forms of communication are characteristic of a person at the preoedipal level and are accepted as such rather than being regarded as the absence of communication. His nonverbal messages and primitive modes of behavior as he resists the instruction to talk out his feelings, thoughts, and memories usually provide some information about him that is grist for analysis. He is educated, not forced, to communicate consistently in adult language.

It is also recognized that many resistance patterns of a severely regressed patient are the "holding" operations he unconsciously resorts to in other interpersonal situations, in the interests of self-preservation and object protection. Their survival function is respected. The analyst does not attempt to resolve them until they can be given up without detriment to the patient's psychic economy.

Special Problems

The analyst intervenes promptly to nullify the influence of any pattern of behavior that, if permitted to continue, would break off the treatment (Brody, 1964). Whereas the chronic and stable defenses are preserved, new symptoms, sudden exacerbations of old ones, and mounting evidence of the stiffening of the narcissistic defense are focused on, if only to deactivate those forms of resistance that could destroy the therapeutic relationship. At any time when the corrosive effects of destructive impulsivity become manifest and the patient's characteristic defense against explosive behavior is strongly activated, it is a matter of extreme urgency to provide some communication that will help him verbalize his hostility as forcefully as possible.

First priority. Also included in the category of treatment-destructive resistance—patterns connected with accumulated frustration-aggression blocked from verbal discharge or being discharged indirectly through aberrant behavior—is extreme tardiness or absence without notice of a person who has previously been punctual and faithful in attendance. These and similar problems—unwillingness to leave promptly at the end of the session or impulsive behavior such as jumping off the couch—are repeatedly discussed. The analyst does not wait for the patient to bring them up.

The storing up of frustration-aggression in a pattern that is conducive to personality fragmentation is one of the two special forms of resistance to which the narcissistic defense gives rise. The other form is directly connected with the tendency of a severely disturbed patient to communicate primarily through nonverbal behavior. If these resistances to appropriate verbal communications are beyond the comprehension of the practitioner, they may put a great strain on the relationship. Neither of these special forms of resistance responds to interpretation until the patient is capable of communicating consistently in adult language.

Whether or not a resistance to talking will disrupt the treatment depends on the meaning of the silence. An important clue is the anxiety level in the immediate situation. As long as the patient remains comfortable and relaxed, he is permitted to maintain silence, especially in the early stage of treatment, but if he is suffering or in a state of conflict, it is desirable to find out why he cannot talk and remove the obstacles to verbal communication. What he says is of no immediate consequence; any utterance is preferable to prolonged silence in those circumstances. If it cannot be interrupted by asking questions, the analyst may have to talk for a while, preferably about impersonal matters, which often stimulates the patient to follow suit. Recognition that the analyst is not particularly eager for him to talk about himself temporarily diminishes the resistance. In other words, the counterforce is worked on by controlling the display of eagerness.

Second priority. The analyst is in a position to deal with other resistances when the treatment-destructive patterns do not operate. Accorded second priority are the patterns that communicate inertia and disinterest in change —status quo resistance. These attempts to "stay put" in treatment are usually observed after the patient begins to feel relatively comfortable in his sessions, and they may continue for protracted periods. The resistant attitudes convey the impression that the need for ameliorative change is minimal. Problems are concealed, and the general picture presented is that of the "good" patient.

Third priority. The third category of resistance shifts from the clinging to the current situation toward apprehension concerning the effects of new experiences. The patient resists learning how to make progress; he may ask for rules and directions and resist meaningful communication. He may demonstrate unwillingness to move ahead into a new territory or to say what he really thinks and feels, with or without regard for the consequences.

Fourth priority is given to the resistance to cooperating with the analyst. The patient may prefer to remain self-preoccupied rather than to discuss or share the responsibility for problems that develop in the relationship. He tends to follow instructions literally and to react negatively to the idea that he has reached the point where it is incumbent on him to contribute more broadly to the solution of his emotional problems. The patient has reached an important milestone when these resistances are resolved. In a cooperative frame of mind he can voluntarily check the expression of his feelings of hostility in nondamaging ways. Analytic progress along the standard lines then becomes possible.

The treatment-destructive resistances disappear when the forces preventing the release of frustration-aggression in feelings and language are permanently resolved. To the extent to which the other categories of resistance mentioned above also operate to check such release, their resolution is secured in the same way. However, these three forms of resistance are maintained in part by the paucity or defective nature of the patient's identification patterns. The use of paradigmatic techniques (Nelson, 1962b) and analytic group psychotherapy (Chapter 21; Ormont, 1964; Spotnitz, 1961) are recommended procedures for dealing with that aspect of the problem, especially for a person whose life provides few opportunities to form wholesome identifications.

READYING PATIENT FOR INTERPRETATIONS

The excessively narcissistic patient tends to react negatively to explanations of what is going on in his mind. Information may traumatize the relationship by provoking resentment and mortification, which he is unable to verbalize at the time; thus his withdrawal tendencies may become even stronger. Until he is able to communicate in adult language, interpretations are withheld unless they would improve his immediate functioning.

The analyst needs to keep in mind the unconscious significance of the patient's feelings, thoughts, memories, and nonverbal activity in the session. Emotional communications are provided to help the patient verbalize his own insights. When his questions are psychologically reflected and repeatedly countered with questions, he usually answers them himself. The analyst limits himself to placing the stamp of approval on correct self-interpretations when the opportunity presents itself. He does not reveal interest in investigating disturbing feelings or thoughts, especially in psychotic material, nor does he give any information about them

Attention to Dreams

Dreams are responded to in the same manner. The patient's tendencies to flood the analyst with dreams when the patient is eager to please and to withhold such disclosures when he is inclined to displease are thus discouraged. Dreams are studied as part of the total production of the session rather than as a special form of communication, and the analyst does not work actively to secure associations to them. Whatever is reported is usually included in the summary of unconscious problems. Occasionally a few questions are asked about a dream, primarily to clarify it. The danger that the patient will be influenced by the analyst's attitude to provide one or another kind of material is thus minimized, as Freud pointed out (1925).

As the case proceeds, understanding is communicated at the rate at which it can be healthfully assimilated. Interpretation of unconscious mechanisms usually beging during the second year of treatment.

When the patient is permitted to emerge from his misconceptions and distortions of reality while being weaned away from his defective identifications, he gradually sharpens the distinctions between himself and others. When his new perceptual field is established with the aid of appropriate e-motional communications, cravings for self-understanding and contact with reality begin to develop. After manifesting interest in finding out what the analyst thinks and feels, the patient becomes aware of similar strivings in relation to people on his own horizon and, eventually, genuine concern with the world-at-large, or with a specific activity or area of knowledge.

In the final stage of treatment, oedipal problems are dealt with, and object-transference resistance is resolved. Interpretations may be provided, but as much as possible the explanations of unconscious mechanisms are permitted to emerge through what occurs in the relationship. Insight into the pathological tendencies mastered earlier in the case often develops in the course of discussions of resistance patterns. Explanations of how they were permanently resolved may also be given to a patient who is keenly interested in understanding the therapeutic maneuvers. Interpretations and self-interpretations of the narcissistic defense on a retrospective basis often dominate the last months of treatment.

MANEUVERS IN WORKING THROUGH

Working through of the narcissistic defense is a process of repeating the same emotional communication over and over again until the patient is sufficiently impressed to give up resistant behavior. Instead of working through an interpretation, the analyst, in essence, works through *to* the interpretation.

When he recognizes a resistance pattern that commands his attention on the basis of the priority system already mentioned, he analyzes it and devises some strategy for dealing with it. In one session he may use one joining procedure consistently or two or more alternatively. Observing the patient's response to the emotional communication, the analyst may develop various hypotheses about the resistant behavior, which he is joining in one way or another through these procedures. The theory that leads to the permanent resolution of the resistance pattern is assumed to be the correct interpretation.

It is also assumed that repeated explanations of a preverbal pattern will be ineffectual, other than to resolve it temporarily, as long as it yields some needed gratification. The psychological need that is being appeased is called to the patient's attention when the pattern operates, and the analyst applies himself to drain it of gratification—provided that he can respond with genuine feeling at the moment (Chapter 5).

To secure the release of the emotional charge motivating a preverbal pattern, the analyst often reflects its configuration in his own communication. When the patient's pathological pattern of bottling up frustration-aggression comes into operation, he resists talking in a meaningful way about himself; his expressions of low regard for himself are then echoed by the analyst to reverse the flow of mobilized aggression from ego to object. After the patient has acquired some feeling for the therapist as an external object, the procedure of "low rating" the object is employed to help the patient discharge the hostility with which he is attacking his own ego (Chapter 3). The procedure of "outcrazying the patient," (Spotnitz, 1969a) that is, exaggerating to the point of absurdity an imaginary exploit or invention the patient talks about, is also effective in securing the release of aggressive impulses in the form of emotionally crystallized and verbally discharged energy.

As the narcissistic defense is gradually mastered and outgrown, interpretation becomes an increasingly important aspect of the working-through process. The task of resolving resistance permanently approaches a successful conclusion when the patient is capable of cooperating actively without developing undesirable states of tension. Thereafter, the analyst shifts from emotional communication to interpretation as his judgment dictates.

In the course of the case, resistance is dealt with at all levels, and each component of a pattern is examined. Working through is not compartmentalized or approached as a discrete operation. It is conceptualized as an aspect of the progress of understanding the origin and history of each resistance pattern and of recognizing why it operates in the current situation.

APPROACHING TERMINATION

There is relatively little evidence of the narcissistic defense in the final stage. The patient demonstrates the ability to verbalize spontaneously both negative and positive feelings. But the progress made earlier in the case has to be stabilized. The patient needs to be educated to use voluntarily and intentionally the normal defense mechanisms, in contradistinction to the old involuntary and compulsive defenses he has outgrown. Exercises in "defense maneuverability" are provided. Otherwise, treatment at this stage is not basically different from that of the oedipal patient.

The analyst broaches the subject of termination as soon as it appears feasible because it meets with prolonged opposition. The patient tends to revert to the old narcissistic behavior and complains of new problems cropping up. Resistance to termination includes both patterns.

Although the old ones have been drained of their compulsive force, they are still at his disposal. Tendencies to reactivate them are especially difficult to deal with if his current life experience is not conducive to emotional reactiveness. In the process of learning how to behave appropriately without shutting out feelings, the patient may communicate that he feels like an actor trying out several roles in succession in order to determine which is most appealing, or he may equate undisciplined behavior with being "genuine." However, the old resistance patterns can be resolved with relative ease by applying the procedures that were effective early in the treatment.

It is desirable to test out the patient's inclination to return to the old modes of functioning. The feelings he has induced in the analyst are therefore "fed back" to him in graduated doses until any tendencies to "clam up" or react explosively are resolved. The use of this procedure, which I refer to as the toxoid response (Chapter 5), has served its purpose when he verbalizes his insights and indicates that he has had enough of the "old stuff."

The patient displays intense interest in understanding his personal history and in exploring every aspect of his current behavior. Formal interpretations are provided when he demonstrates the ability to talk of himself with some detachment. However, the artful use of "why," which gives him the opportunity to formulate his own explanations, is often preferable.

The patient talks spontaneously, in an animated voice, and appears thoroughly at ease during the last six months of treatment. He lies on his back, arms and legs uncrossed; on occasion he may sit up on the couch by prearrangement, but he feels no need to behave impulsively during the session. He reports his current activities and tries to relate them to his memories of events in the remote past. Dreams are also reported regularly, and he participates actively in their analysis. The free associations of each session include references to his sex life, and he talks freely of his thoughts and feelings about the analyst. He remains within the normal range of variability in attendance and payment of fees.

THE RECOVERED PATIENT

The communications of a highly narcissistic individual in the early months of treatment often remind me of an old-fashioned music box playing the same thin tune over and over again. The narcissistic patient appears to be bogged down in the basic and essentially gross feelings of childhood. Effective treatment slowly enriches his personality with more feeling tones, and eventually the communications become fully "orchestrated." The hierarchy of feelings that characterize emotional evolution appear to develop in the patient. This is one aspect of the emergence of the mature personality, which is equated with successful outcome of the case.

Effective treatment also equips the patient with an abundance of action patterns that facilitate the discharge of feelings, so that he no longer has to go out of contact with reality to prevent himself from behaving destructively. He is able to feel and express appropriately, and also to accept, both love and hate and the derivatives of both emotions. The give-and-take is important and often changes his whole orientation to life. The patient can relate comfortably to people even while experiencing rage and faces up to painful realities without the support of the old narcissistic defense. It is virtually impossible to secure any evidence of the resolved pathological patterns except through careful diagnostic testing or skillful interviewing.

But their resolution does not mean that he has solved all of his emotional problems, nor is it a guarantee that he won't encounter new ones in the future. Cure is not cure-all, but it encompasses a notable increase in the patient's capacity for self-fulfillment and happiness, the ability to behave appropriately in all normal situations, and to meet the impact of abnormally traumatic ones with considerable resiliency. He has sufficient understanding of himself to deal independently with conflicts of ordinary magnitude.

The recovered patient is a much more sociocentric human being than when he entered treatment. His family and associates are impressed with the improvements of his functioning at home, at work, and in social situations. He is more understanding of other people and finds it easier to get along with them regardless of differences in perspectives and attitudes. He discovers that it is possible to live among them with a sense of emotional integrity and self-respect instead of living alone behind the stone wall of narcissism.

The Modern Group Approach

A series of lectures conducted by Edward Lazell for World War I veterans confined to the schizophrenic wards of St. Elizabeth's Hospital in Washington, D.C. initiated the literature on the group treatment of schizophrenic patients in 1921. This venture, which served to attenuate feelings of isolation among the young psychiatrist's audience, was later characterized by him as "mental re-education." In the half-century that has elapsed since then, the literature has focused primarily on improving the lot of hospitalized schizophrenics, alleviating their psychotic symptoms, and restoring them to community life at their premorbid level of functioning.

Notably absent from a review of 404 reports published from 1956 to 1966 (Schneiwind, Day, and Semrad, 1969) are claims of curing the condition or suggestions that anyone works, let alone knows how, to produce such an outcome. When Stotsky and Zolik scanned the literature from 1921 through 1963, they found no "clear endorsement for the use of group psychotherapy as an independent modality" for psychotic patients (1965, p. 339). The common theme running through the reports was that a group therapeutic experience can help these patients achieve a "more successful treatment outcome" when combined with other therapies and an "aggressive interest" in helping them.

The copious literature on inpatient group treatment highlights the paucity of reports on group psychotherapy with ambulatory schizophrenics. A large majority of practitioners are reluctant to accept patients with a firm diagnosis of schizophrenia for groups conducted in private practice; others place one or two such individuals in a heterogeneous group and do not report the specific results achieved in these cases.

Most therapists conducting such treatment adhere to the basically supportive goals that are typically pursued in the inpatient group treatment of psychotic patients. Hence, descriptions of group psychotherapy with schizophrenics that is addressed to more ambitious goals, usually as one aspect of a total treatment program, sound an exceptional note in the literature. The authors of these reports, rejecting the notion of helping the patient "learn to live with" his illness because "once a schizophrenic, always a schizophrenic," strive to provide a group experience that will "transform schizophrenics into nonschizophrenics" (Berne, 1961, p. 290).

Against the backdrop of many years of psychotherapeutic activity oriented to socialization, the emergence of this more optimistic treatment philosophy parallels two other historical developments: (1) a change in views about the nature of the core problem in schizophrenia that significantly influences the clinician's approach to the patient; (2) the ongoing transformation of group procedures from a miscellany of relatively crude and more or less similar instruments for "doing psychotherapy in a general sense into an armamentarium of different instruments fashioned to achieve highly specific objectives" (Spotnitz, 1971, p. 81).

Consonant with these broader developments in the field, new ideas about how schizophrenic patients should be treated, and a definitive technique that exploits the potentials of group process more fully for that purpose, have been evolving.

EVOLUTIONARY TRENDS

Some of these changes can be retrospectively traced in two books on group psychotherapy published a decade apart—one by Powdermaker and Frank (1953) and the other by Johnson (1963).

From Anxiety to Aggression

The observations and clinical experiences reported in the books just mentioned reflect a gradual shift in interest from anxiety to aggression as the fundamental factor to be dealt with in the group treatment of schizophrenic patients. The psychotherapists who conducted groups of chronic schizophrenics under the Veterans Administration research project reviewed by Powdermaker and Frank addressed themselves primarily to allaying anxiety and its manifestations. Hostility was viewed at that time as one of the prominent defenses against anxiety. Nevertheless, the material reported suggests that progress in the group was a function of securing the appropriate discharge of aggressive energy in language. Much evidence is advanced that the patients did well in the group when the therapist could accept their hostility. When, for some reason, they had to inhibit its expression, they manifested catatonic or withdrawal reactions. The counter-hostility of unconsciously antagonistic therapists was repeatedly observed to make these patients more upset and eventually unmanageable.

Three of the first four groups had to be reshuffled at the end of the first year. The group that remained intact was the one that had "reached the stage of expressing intense hostility to a hostility-inviting" therapist (Powdermaker and Frank, p. 363). What was therapeutic was not the expression of the hostility but the therapist's ability to accept it undefensively and help the members of the group verbalize and eventually understand it.

Ten years later, Johnson too stressed the focal role of anxiety. However, his approach reflects definite movement toward dealing with the defenses against massive rage, awareness of guilt over the rage, fears of retaliation from others, and fears of close relationships. He recognized that such feelings were the source of much of the anxiety demonstrated by schizophrenic patients in group relationships.

It is evident that Johnson worked on the problem of hostility. He viewed the symbolic and metaphorical communications of the schizophrenic as a "necessary and safe means of expressing hostility to the group therapist" (p. 396). Early in treatment, displacements of hostility from the therapist protect the patient from examining feelings that might evoke fantasies of rejection, retaliatory hostility, or loss of dependency. Indefinite delay in confronting the patient with these feelings was recommended because of his acute need for love, dependency, security, and help from the group.

Foreshadowing another element of the modern theoretical approach—the need to inhibit action—, Johnson commented on the tendency of schizophrenics to control homosexual impulses triggered in group relationships. He also called attention to their "highly developed radar" (p. 395) for detecting the unconscious feelings of others. He recognized the importance of the therapist having the proper feelings for them.

The initial concentration on anxiety as the crux of the illness has been abandoned because it proved to be therapeutically unrewarding. The unconscious ego-sacrificing attitudes that bind aggression—the primitively patterned defenses of the schizophrenic against the acting out of destructive impulses—are now regarded as primary and his anxiety as a sign that the defenses are threatened. In the contemporary literature, one finds far fewer references to the patient's anxiety than to that he arouses in the therapist. Projection of the therapist's anxiety onto the patient apparently helped to confuse the issue. Countertransference reactions that make it difficult to provide the type of emotional experiences that facilitate the reversal of the schizophrenic reaction are now viewed as the main obstacle to effective treatment.*

Specific goals were not formulated for the groups of hospitalized schizophrenics treated under the Veterans Administration project. Each therapist was permitted to set his own. The leaders of these groups tended to err "in the direction of overambitiousness" (Powdermaker and Frank, p. 5) because of their research orientation. Johnson, pointing out that group therapy does not produce a high percentage of recoveries, advocated limited goals in the treatment of schizophrenic patients, as follows: increasing repression, bringing about new, positive identifications, sociability, expiation of guilt, strengthening of old defenses and establishment of new defenses, and the lessening of inner tensions.

The current tendency, as already mentioned, is not only to resolve the fundamental problem but also to help the patient continue on the road to personality maturation. Outpatient treatment is recommended to a post-psychotic patient leaving the hospital. The prognosis has brightened over the years. The specific nature and severity of the condition become less significant when the patient is helped to manage his aggression. Techniques are available to help him achieve a mature personality and his potential for creative accomplishment and happiness in life.

Composition of Groups

Retrospective study of the Powdermaker-Frank and Johnson books elucidates other revolutionary trends that are of interest in the present context.

The first inpatient groups in the V.A. research project were formed on the basis of diagnosis, each group being composed of patients with the same subtype of the illness. Inter-member relationships developed in these groups but they remained at a primitive level. One patient tended to monopolize the sessions of the group of paranoids; silences that could not be broken developed in the catatonic group; the hebephrenic group, after barraging the therapist with intense hostility, subsided into hostile silence. None of the so-called pure or homogeneous groups fared as well as those subsequently formed on the basis of blending patients with different diagnoses and behavior patterns, and giving consideration to the personal characteristics, tolerance of aggressive reactions, and techniques of the therapists. One of them said, for example, that he felt more comfortable when the members of his group were openly hostile in the sessions.

*Powdermaker-Frank and Johnson describe many appropriate and inappropriate responses of the therapist to the schizophrenic patient, but rarely discuss them in terms of countertransference. The index to the first book contains no reference to countertransference, and that to Johnson's book of more than 400 pages lists only half a dozen brief references.

The principle of disregarding diagnostic labels and composing groups on the basis of the severity of ego pathology came to the fore during the next ten years. As stated by Johnson, "Regardless of the clinical picture put forward [by patients with overt psychotic conditions], there is severe ego psychopathology present which poses certain problems in their management in group therapy" (p. 389). On the other hand, ambulatory schizophrenics can be treated together with neurotic patients and function well with them in outpatient groups.

In composing heterogeneous groups to be treated in private practice, some therapists regard diagnosis as an inadequate source of information on how patients will function together (Spotnitz, 1971). These practitioners therefore try to ascertain the types of defenses that each candidate for a group activates in interpersonal situations. An assessment of current impulses and defenses is one aspect of achieving a balancing of personality types; this facilitates the functioning of the group as a unit.

Therapists who conduct group treatment as a primarily emotional experience seek to blend placid and volatile persons with some who tend to arouse excitement and others who check it. There are no generally accepted criteria for excluding a candidate, but reciprocal tolerance of each member for the psychopathology of his co-members is an important consideration.

SCHIZOPHRENIC PATIENT IN THE GROUP

The schizophrenic patient who undergoes treatment in a mixed group performs valuable functions for his co-members, and they for him. Even though he tries to inhibit his own tendency to engage in discharge-directed behavior, his strong impulsivity and imperious attitudes create tension in the group. Their attitudes, on the other hand, have a dampening effect on him, thus helping him develop methods of controlling and regulating the release of aggressive energy.

In a mixed group, too, the schizophrenic patient is usually the first member to express the deepest resistance of the group as a whole. Successfully dealing with his resistant attitudes often has the effect of alleviating problems of the other members.

The schizophrenic patient in a mixed group requires more attention than its other members. Because of his tendency to mobilize their aggression, the therapist may have to intervene more frequently and rapidly. Guidance of the group may be necessary to protect the schizophrenic from acting on his impulses, to help him deal with his defenses against the verbalization of his resentments, and to provide him with special psychological nourishment.

During the initial period of treatment, the therapist needs to be on the watch for a rapid exacerbation of symptoms in the schizophrenic patient—a clue to defensive regression. Does he demonstrate a need to withdraw from the group when under verbal attack? Does he need to discharge his tensions in immediate action? Does he engage in ego-damaging explosions? What is the anxiety content of his silences? Does he come in and talk "scared?" Can he be protected from attack without inhibiting the emotional interchanges of the other members? These are questions that it is desirable to investigate during the trial period. If the patient regresses rapidly and severely in situations of stress, he may not qualify at that time for treatment in an outpatient group.

GENERAL THEORY OF TREATMENT

Working Hypothesis

Schizophrenia is an organized mental situation, an intricately structured but psychologically unsuccessful defense against destructive behavior. Both aggressive and libidinal impulses figure in this organized situation; aggressive urges provide the explosive force while libidinal urges play an inhibiting role. The operation of the defense protects the object from the release of volcanic aggression but entails the disruption of the psychic apparatus. Obliteration of the object field* of the mind and fragmentation of the ego are among the secondary consequences of the defense (Spotnitz, 1969a, p. 28).

Hereditary, constitutional, and environmental factors appear to be implicated in the illness. In some cases, only one of these factors seems to produce the schizophrenic reaction; in other cases, highly specific combinations of two or all three factors appear to be involved. Regardless of etiology, the schizophrenic reaction is psychologically reversible, most readily so when the predominant factor is life experience.

Reversal of Schizophrenic Reaction

No cases have been reported in which the schizophrenic reaction has been reversed through group psychotherapy alone, but it is a valuable adjunctive procedure to long-term individual psychotherapy.

The major thrust in group treatment is the resolution of the obstacles to the appropriate release of aggressive energy through defense-freeing exercises and the development of understanding of the patterns of checking or releasing it constructively. In the course of working through these patterns, psychological growth is facilitated through verbal and emotional communications and enhancement of the capacity for emotional differentiation. The ultimate goal of treatment is personality maturation.

---

*Encompassing the earliest representations of the self as well as object representations. These overlap in the undifferentiated phase of development during which the situation appears to be organized (Spotnitz, 1969a).

Operating on the assumption that the patient enters the group in a state of psychic regression, the group therapist accepts responsibility for safeguarding him against further regression and psychotic breakdown. For the schizophrenic (and other group members with preoedipal problems) the treatment is structured as a process of self-regulated progress alternating with brief periods of retrograde movement.

From the opening session, the group members are inculcated with the idea that verbalizing feelings and thoughts is cooperative functioning and that acting on them in any way is out of order. In other words, the group is a forum for open discussion, *not* an arena for action. The distinction between communication in language and motor activity is maintained by appropriate reminders when the latter is engaged in. This approach dampens tendencies to act in, and its influence extends into the interpersonal situations of daily life.

The therapist sees to it that the treatment climate is salubrious,* and that the patient is provided with ego-syntonic communication. However, he experiences sufficient frustration to activate his psychopathological defenses against the release of aggression. These unconscious maneuvers, evoked by and studied in the transference situation, are dealt with when they interfere with progressive verbal communication and cooperative behavior in the group sessions (Spotnitz, 1969b). The patient is not exposed to pressure to give up these resistances; but, as he is made aware of them and gets to understand how they are activated in the group interchanges, he tends to give them up voluntarily.

Since explanations of the emotional logic of his behavior tend to make the schizophrenic more self-absorbed, it is desirable to withhold interpretations until he is able to freely verbalize the resentment they engender and is capable of utilizing insight in his own interest. However, resistive behavior that, if permitted to continue, would make the continuance of treatment impossible, is discussed with him as a matter of urgency. Such behavior early in treatment characteristically includes repeated absences from the sessions without advance notification to the group, chronic tardiness, and failure to adhere to the payment schedule.

The schizophrenic patient is drawn gradually into spontaneous verbalization; some degree of noninvolvement is permitted. By and large, resistances to verbal communication are sanctioned, and may even be reinforced. Such resistances are regarded as primitive modes of communication that will be outgrown as the treatment proceeds (Spotnitz, 1969b). When the group interchanges fail to resolve these resistances, the therapist may psychologically reflect (join) them—with or without feelings—, ask questions that will draw the patient's attention away from his ego preoccupations and toward

---

*A too sudden or too intense mobilization of feelings that cannot be freely and adequately released in language signifies that the schizophrenic is being exposed to an undue degree of excitation.

external objects (object-oriented questions), or intervene in other ways to minimize the counterforce to talking.

Schizophrenic symptomatology, such as delusions and hallucinations, is studied but not interpreted. Symptoms are responded to only when they interfere with meaningful communication. The patient is neither encouraged nor discouraged from revealing psychotic material in the group, but no attempt is made by the therapist in the initial phase of treatment to modify the patient's thoughts and feelings. When misperceptions and distortions of reality are accepted and objectively investigated, the patient experiences feelings of being cared for. More than that, he tends to move away from his original attitude; he may respond with feelings of appreciation for the group's help.

The schizophrenic patient mightily defends himself against experiencing and verbalizing hostility to his co-members, conveying the impression that he was inordinately sensitive in early childhood to hostile feelings—his own as well as those of his parents. He may need considerable help from others in the group to develop the ability to talk out his negative feelings. Especially difficult to verbalize are feelings of worthlessness, depression, nothingness, hopelessness, incurability.

Cathartic release is not worked for deliberately since it is of minor significance for long-term personality change. However, much of it occurs in the framework of the defense-freeing exercises that help to liberate the schizophrenic group member from the compulsive grip of his maladaptive patterns. Another important aspect of this unlearning process, mediated through identification with the other group members, is the creation of new action patterns that will facilitate the discharge of aggressive energy in personally and socially desirable ways whenever it builds up in the future.

Emotional Induction

The propulsive charge (in the form of feelings) that is needed to move a schizophrenic patient into emotional maturity may have to be provided by his co-members and the therapist—a much greater commitment than the group makes to a member who responds more therapeutically to insight into his problems. In effect, the schizophrenic is told: Feel and talk out all the bad feelings you experienced as a child with your parents and siblings. In turn, you will be helped to express these bad feelings, and we will help you deal with them. We will also help you acquire all the good feelings you needed and failed to experience in childhood.

The feelings of the schizophrenic patient arouse similar and complementary feelings in the other group members and the therapist (Spotnitz, 1969a). The induced feelings are a great aid in reconstructing the patient's primary relationships in life and in guiding him toward experiences that will help him achieve emotional maturity.

If the group commits itself to this process of emotional induction, all kinds of feelings will be experienced in relation to the patient—some disagreeable or strange, others pleasurable. The expression of these feelings immediately is not helpful. However, if they can be tolerated and sustained, the realistically induced feelings are an important source of therapeutic leverage when communicated to the patient at the proper time.

CLINICAL ILLUSTRATION

The following material, drawn from the case of an arrogant and severely troubled schizophrenic patient, illustrates the types of interventions used to reduce tendencies toward destructive action and facilitate the resolution of defenses against the verbalization of hostile feelings.

Dick was a good-looking young man, 26 years old, when he entered a group on the recommendation of several practitioners who had treated him individually over a period of eight years. The patient, a dental technician who worked in a laboratory operated by his father, was placed in an open group composed of men and women who were expected to have considerable tolerance for his psychopathology.

Within a few sessions, Dick initiated a battle for control. He tried to dominate the group's communications, making repeated efforts to limit their content and impose restrictions on the language to be used in the sessions. No member had the right to raise problems that were not, in his judgment, strictly psychological. He did not talk about other matters, and he expected the others to behave as he did.

When these attempts at group control and group censorship were hooted down by the other members, Dick threatened to leave the room or to beat up anyone who referred to him as "vicious" or called him a "lousy bastard." Winning his respect for the principle that each member had the right to speak freely without being put under the threat of physical violence required numerous explanations; these were advanced by the other patients. Dick's threats were also met with threats (joined). The therapist informed him that, if he wanted to remain in the group, he would have to accept what was said about him.

Moreover, special attention was paid to his objections. For example, he was invited to draw up a list of the epithets that provoked him. After receiving this attention, Dick changed his mind. He informed the other group members that they could express whatever they felt about him.

Dick's efforts to suppress rage led to increasing emotional tension. The suppressed rage and tension were recognized, and he was told that he had the right to express whatever he felt in language. He came to see that, although certain group members aroused intolerable feelings in him, he was able to verbalize these reactions, no matter how childish or degraded he felt when doing so. Hence, he did not have to strike anyone. When the verbal release of rage was blocked, he was told that he wouldn't be executed for having hostile thoughts or feelings or for using violent language. Dick's richest curses did not meet with damaging retaliation. In a climate of acceptance, his tolerance for his own feelings of being childish or degraded gradually increased. It was explained to him that these feelings inhibited verbal release. Eventually, he was able to verbalize comfortably his urges to strike others, and he mastered his tendencies to act on these urges.

Other destructive behavior, such as running out of the room, setting himself up as the final arbiter of group behavior, and refusing to attend sessions, slowly yielded to the same approaches. Dick was helped to perceive his own feelings. Interchanges among the other patients and the therapist bearing on the significance of their feelings about Dick served to sharpen his perceptions of his group associates. His own ego boundaries were more clearly delimited.

The technique of joining resistances figured in the process of dealing with Dick's controlling attitudes. When, for example, he announced that he wouldn't attend the next session, he was told that he wasn't required to come. On one occasion when he said that he wanted to leave the group, the therapist did not oppose the idea, and when Dick decided to return two weeks later, the therapist again joined him. At that time, Dick wrote the therapist that he would like to return but would do so only if he was invited to come back. The joining of these resistance patterns enabled Dick to talk more freely and to act more consistently in harmony with feelings that were not potentially destructive to others.

Dick's disclosure of his willingness to pay girls for dates that involved only dancing together evoked critical remarks from the men, and the women in the group speculated that his penis must be an awfully unappealing one. The group interchanges at this juncture aroused intensely hostile feelings in Dick. When he was able to describe these feelings without action, he observed—to his surprise—that the women in the group found him much more attractive. They displayed growing interest in helping him with his everyday concerns. The men expressed warm approval of his new courtship activity. The positive feelings communicated helped him acquire a sense of identification.

During the second year of group treatment, Dick's communications were marked by spontaneity. He reported that he was deriving more satisfaction in his social life, enjoying the company of attractive young women, and working more productively. He behaved appropriately in the group situation, and participated helpfully in discussions of the problems of the other members.

Emotional Change

The group experience just reviewed indicates that a domineering, hostile, and potentially psychotic individual, when placed in a suitable group, can be effectively educated to give up asocial attitudes dominated by feelings of intense hatred, infantilism, and degradation—feelings that urged him toward violent action. He responded favorably to the attention and interest of the group, to joining techniques, to the meeting of his threats with threats, to reminders of the rules he had accepted on entering the group, and to the praise and admiration that rewarded him for more mature functioning in the treatment situation and in his own social environment.

In a follow-up report several years later, Dick said that his two years of group treatment had been the most effective of all the psychiatric procedures to which he had been exposed in moving him along the road to emotional maturity.

PART THREE:

Childhood and Adolescent Schizophrenia

Chapters 14, 15, and 16 present consecutive clinical reports on a research project devoted to the treatment of severely disturbed children and adolescents. Sponsorship of this program by a private New York treatment agency permitted staff psychologists and psychiatric social workers to accept cases that were generally regarded as unsuitable for outpatient treatment in the 1940s and 1950s, and enabled me to train therapists who were personally interested in treating these young people. In some instances, parents and other family members were also provided with individual and group psychotherapy.

Reports of good results in the psychotherapy of such patients, who had long been regarded as inaccessible to such treatment, stimulated challenges to the accuracy of the diagnosis in these cases. This is reflected in Chapter 17, which shifts the focus from the therapeutic process to the differential diagnosis of adolescent schizophrenia from the "normally" psychopathological manifestations of that age group.

Chapter 18 illustrates the response of severely disturbed children and adolescents to clinical approaches designed to counteract their self-attacking tendencies. Although developed in the course of working with schizophrenic young people, these approaches have a more widespread application. The concept of constructive emotional interchange is applied specifically in this chapter to specially structured interviews with the patient in the presence of family members.

14

Initial Steps in Therapy

(A PRELIMINARY REPORT)

Coauthor: Leo Nagelberg, Ph.D.

As part of a research project, five schizophrenic children have been receiving individual analytic therapy. This has been conducted by one of us (L. N.) under the direction and according to the principles suggested by the other author (H. S.). The present report covers the content of the initial interviews and, furthermore, presents some of the considerations underlying the initial technique employed with these children.

The basic assumption of the project was that the immediate problem of the schizophrenic child is to learn how to control the discharge of a relatively powerful urge toward libidinal and destructive impulsivity. The narcissistic state serves as a defense against the asocial impulsivity. The initial interviews were to be conducted in a relatively non-stimulating and controlled setting, and were to be so handled as to make it possible for the children to understand that the therapist was aware of their fears of their own impulsivity and was attempting to assist them to a spontaneous verbal discharge of their impulses.

SELECTION OF CASES

The five cases reported on, like all others accepted for the project, were selected for treatment because both the psychiatric study of the intake material and psychological tests, including projective techniques, concurred in the diagnosis of childhood schizophrenia. Three of the cases reported on were diagnosed as schizophrenia-simple type, one with marked homicidal trends, and the other two were schizophrenia-hebephrenic type.

The therapist attempted to see each of these patients at weekly intervals. The duration of the interviews was about 45 minutes.

The technique employed was a relatively simple one. Whenever possible, it was conveyed to the patient that the interviews were not compulsory; they were being held at his discretion. If the patient desired to know their purpose, he was told that it was to help the patient in self-understanding.

The therapist attempted to behave in such a way as to demonstrate that he was content to wait for the patient to present whatever information he desired and was trying to understand what was presented. The therapist demonstrated good self-control. Questions or stimulating comments were kept at a minimum except when it was evident from the patient's behavior that these would be interpreted as a sign of mild, positive interest in understanding him.

ILLUSTRATIVE MATERIAL

The following material, summarizing case records covering many pages, was selected to illustrate symptomatology and interview material which were considered to be of value to the reader in arriving at some understanding of the impulsivity and disorganization to which the ego of the schizophrenic child is exposed.

Case 1

Samuel, referred at the age of 9, was described as withdrawn and having few friends. At school he refused to speak aloud in the classroom. He rarely left the house except when necessary. He was fussy about his food and disliked having anyone touch it. He did not allow a spoon or other utensil to touch his mouth. He took food off his plate with his teeth. He did not smile; he objected to receiving gifts. He concealed his body to an extreme degree when undressing. He said that he would like to live where there were no other people. His mother commented, "He is a glutton for punishment." He was of superior intelligence, read extensively, and kept everything about him in meticulous order.

From the age of 3½ to 9 months, he had cried almost continuously. He had many intense fears. When 3 years old, he had refused to eat or play with other children in a nursery. His mother said that he had always been different from other children. At the age of 4, he had felt that all eyes were staring at him. He had developed an impassive, immobile, expressionless appearance which indicated no emotion.

Diagnosis: Schizophrenia (simple type) with obsessional features.

Interview 1. Samuel did not sit down or touch anything in the room. Instead, he wanted to show the therapist a mathematical problem, then said that he wanted to leave. When told that it was all right for him to leave, he decided to stay and again showed the mathematical problem.

Interview 2. Samuel brought in catalogues, binoculars, puzzles, a plastic kaleidoscopic kit, and a microscope set for the therapist to look at. He did not want to talk and displayed no emotion.

After the fifth interview, he began to talk about the smell of explosives, about firecrackers, bombs, and fire-rockets. He spoke about people being burned by fire, about booby traps that kill them, and whirlwinds and tornadoes that throw them high up into the air. He set a match to some papers and, for the first time, became animated and excited as he watched the fire. He told the therapist that he cut insects apart and had burned an ant beneath a magnifying glass held in the sunlight.

His mother has reported that he has been getting better marks at school, that he has been playing with other children, and is expressing more emotion at home.

Case 2

Mary, 9 years old, was referred because of her inability to adhere to the school routine, lack of relationships with other children, and sexual preoccupations. In school, she wandered from one room to another, creating commotions. At home, she preferred to be alone, reading and playing with an imaginary club. Her I.Q., 194 two years earlier, had dropped to 124.

Her general attitude was one of slow motion and extreme suspicion. She had attacks of weeping without apparent cause and also cried when certain words were mentioned, such as "friends." In order to stop herself from crying, she would expose her underdrawers either by lifting her skirt or throwing herself back in her chair with her legs raised high. She was occasionally dazed, would sit by herself for long periods, and appeared unaware of what went on around her.

When Mary was about 2 years old, she began to have difficulty falling asleep at night. She would lie in bed for hours and sing to herself. About this time, she began to read. One of her special delights was to play in her playpen, which she fantasied was a house.

Diagnosis: Schizophrenia (simple type).

Interviews: During the first three interviews, Mary spoke about her imaginary club, giving many details about membership, attendance record, admission procedures, etc. Even though the therapist remained silent, her behavior changed. She began in the fourth interview to splash ink on paper, making many blots and designs, which she numbered and called to the therapist's attention. When he asked why she was showing him these ink dots—his first question—Mary replied that she could show them because they were not secrets. Later she began slowly to reveal things that she did not want her mother to know; she asked if the therapist had secrets too. When asked why she wanted to know this, she said she wanted to know whether he was like her. Did he have secrets, and could he keep them? Then Mary began to talk about what she did at night; for instance, she played with a blanket which represented a girl, had a teddy bear which represented a boy, and went to fairyland with them.

After five interviews it was evident that Mary had developed an interest in revealing herself and in getting to know the therapist.

Case 3

Harry, aged 13, had no friends. He avoided going out into the street or did not respond to greetings when he did. At home, he had made several attacks upon his mother; she was afraid that he might kill her. He had once put a knife to her, had jumped on her in bed, and thrown a pillow over her face while threatening to choke her. He resented any time she spent with his grandmother away from him. He accused her of not loving him, and hid her clothing to keep her at home. Once he told her that he loved her so much that he had to kill her, laughing hysterically as he said it. On other occasions, he would lie in bed for hours, pull the covers over his head, or listen to the radio. This peculiar behavior apparently began after his father died, when Harry was 5½ years old.

Diagnosis: Schizophrenia (simple type) with homicidal trends.

Interviews: When the therapist phoned him for the initial interview, Harry banged down the telephone receiver after saying that he would not come. When he arrived, he spoke in a low voice and was tense and suspicious. He forced his mother to come to the interview room with him but permitted her to remain outside. He explained to the therapist that he did not wish to come for treatment. When told that he did not have to come, he wanted to know whether he could come once or twice. When given a date, he again said that he would not come. He responded in this negativistic pattern several times to suggestions made about his coming. Finally, when convinced that he did not have to come, he said that he would come and thought it a privilege to do so. However, he could not understand why no effort was used to make him come.

Interview 2. He asked what he should do here. It was suggested that he might tell the story of his life. He asked whether the therapist was not going to help him; the therapist replied that he was here only to understand Harry. The boy then talked about himself, his interests, his reading. In the next interview, Harry stated that he could not think of anything important to tell. The therapist remained silent. Harry finally talked about his life and stated that he liked to come here, that he liked to talk, and that it was nice to have someone to listen to him.

Harry's mother phoned before the fourth interview to complain that he was "impossible," that he had threatened to kill her.

Interview 4. When Harry arrived he was told that his mother had phoned. He was silent for 25 minutes, and then wanted to know exactly what his mother had said. He was silent again for another 12 minutes and then repeated that he would like to know exactly what his mother had said. After another silence, he asked whether the therapist wasn't going to say anything. He asked why the therapist smoked and commented that if the therapist did not show self-control, how could he control other people? The therapist should know that smoking is poisonous and causes cancer of the lungs. At the end of this interview, he wanted to stay longer.

Interview 5. He was silent, and the therapist maintained silence. Finally Harry asked whether the therapist couldn't suggest a subject to discuss. Why? He thought it would be a good idea; they could exchange ideas and he could find out about the therapist. He then talked at length about war developments in Korea. He was not interrupted.

Case 4

Betty, 16 years old, was referred because of temper outbursts, dizzy spells, inability to concentrate, and truanting from school. She was extremely hostile to, and jealous of her mother. After a quarrel with her, Betty would worry a great deal about the right and wrong of her behavior. She appeared to be oversensitive and resentful of direction. She worried about her weight and diet, and was often forgetful. She would leave the house late at night and walk up and down the street. On one occasion, she became sleepy and rested on the back seat of an unlocked car.

When she was 3 years old, she had been very aggressive and cried when this was least expected. There was a marked change in her behavior between the ages of 11 and 14; she became defiant, unpredictable, overtalkative, mischievous, and would not participate in school activities. She took to slapping people on the back.

Diagnosis: Schizophrenia (hebephrenic type).

Interview 1. Betty wore slacks. She said that she was bothered but did not know about what. She never wanted to be told what to do. She had difficulty in concentrating. Her father and brother screamed and cursed; they had unruly tempers. She too had a nasty temper, which she had been trying very hard to control.

Interview 2. She asked what she was to do. She was told to tell the story of her life. She began to speak of her fears of being drowned or killed in an automobile accident. She felt that she was a scatterbrain who could not think logically; people did not understand her. She mentioned three memories. At the age of 2, she tore up another girl's rag doll and her parents punished her. Her next memory was of riding up and down in an elevator for a long time. Her third memory was of her mother's fear that Betty had poisoned herself by sucking the color off her glove.

She called attention to the fact that she could not stand regulation. She would like to do things her own way, but everybody suggested different things for her to do. She did not want her father to tell her what to do, but he did not understand. She liked to read and was interested in philosophy.

Case 5

Sheila, aged 16, was disinterested in school and truanted. She preferred to daydream and lie around the house partially dressed. On some occasions, she felt too confused to talk to anyone. She would like to be a hermit and go to deserted places. She believed she could change herself into a man or a horse. She complained of funny feelings; she felt like crying, dancing, giggling, and said she could not control these feelings. At times she had dizzy spells. Occasionally when she was excited, her speech became jumbled and disconnected, and she would stare, apparently listless and oblivious to her surroundings. She frequently resented the fact that her mother spent time with other people. Sheila's appearance was usually dishevelled.

Diagnosis: Schizophrenia (hebephrenic type).

Interview 1. She spoke in a welter of words. She complained that her grandmother did not understand her, and that she was not allowed to kiss her own mother. She felt that she herself was weak-willed, scatterbrained, talked too much, and had bad habits she couldn't control, such as smoking and lying.

Interview 2. She spoke immediately about seeing a customer go into a store, where she was kissed by the owner. Sheila said that she used to give in to all her urges. She had become convinced that she had no willpower. She did not think that her mother had any either. If she heard an argument, she felt like screaming. People told her that she had a nasty temper. Then she spoke about horses; she liked the beauty and rippling muscles of a wild horse. She did not understand herself; she did not want to help her mother and yet she had to think about her mother's wishes all the time. If she wanted something, nothing on earth could stop her. She talked about people starting rumors and then stated, "We all have a certain idea of civilization but we are savages underneath. A person who becomes crazy just becomes a savage. If we go crazy, we have a rage which turns us back centuries. But one can't do that because one would kill the other. If any person becomes a murderer, he actually goes back centuries."

Interview 3. She spoke of her willpower slipping and said that she was fascinated by death. Talking about death, she remembered that once she had thought she would kill her grandmother. "It's so terrifying if one cannot control one's feelings. I was not angry at grandmother, I just wanted to kill her because she was in my way."

Interview 4. She talked, among other things, about how she hated having people come close to her. "If people are not close, then I want to come near them. But if they come close, I have to pull away."

In subsequent sessions, she continued to talk in a confused, but sometimes more coherent fashion. She looked less dishevelled, talked more to the point. At the same time, however, she began to speak about feeling that she had two different personalities. There were two persons inside her, one just the opposite of the other. One was meek, submissive, weak; the other was cheeky and forceful and did whatever she pleased. She looked upon the therapist as an inhuman, controlled personality. She could not even imagine that he slept, shaved, or did other human, earthly things.

CONCLUDING OBSERVATIONS

Reservoir of Destructive Impulsivity

The schizophrenic reaction in these children appears to be a defense against the acting out of the oedipal triangle. On the one hand, libidinal drives seek instinctual gratification from one or both parents; on the other hand, there is a marked destructive impulsivity, which appears to be a reaction to excessive gratification or frustration of the schizophrenic child in his relations with one or both parents. The most outstanding problem of all these children seems to be that as a result of their life experience, they have been left with a huge reservoir of destructive impulsivity which they are attempting to control.

The lack of emotion, the disorganization, the withdrawal from contact with other human beings, and the attacks on their own egos appear to be aimed primarily at preventing the release into action of murderous impulses toward their parents or parent-surrogates. These children provide many examples of unbridled aggressiveness, uncontrollable rages, violent opposition, and tendencies toward direct assaultiveness, which they attempt to control by releasing their impulses—by expressing them in fantasies, imaginary games, and outbursts of profane or abusive language. If these methods of release are not sufficient, the children attempt to withdraw from emotional contact with other human beings in order not to be stimulated to injure them. The children then try to control their behavior by developing non-feeling states; they do not feel their impulses so that they do not have to act on them. They attempt to destroy feelings that might lead to dangerous action.

Ego Sacrifice

The primary motive for this defense appears to be the need to protect the lives of people who are important to them.

It is our impression that the schizophrenic child—unknown to himself—is a highly social being who is willing to sacrifice his own ego to protect his parents from destruction by himself. He attempts to destroy his own ego by making it incapable of functioning in an organized way. He seems willing to destroy his ego in order to protect parents or parent-surrogates from his uncontrolled aggressiveness. It appeared clear to us that if the child's final defense—destruction of his own ego—was not successful, he would then burst into homicidal behavior.

Role of Therapist

It was evident that the presence of a controlled and understanding therapist increased the capacity for self-control sufficiently in these children so that they began slowly to release their overwhelming destructive impulses in play material or through verbal expression. The gradual decrease in their destructiveness and their increasing capacity to control the acting out of their impulsivity appeared to make them more capable of feeling their impulses and of expressing them in language.

It is our impression that the key to the successful initial technique in dealing with the schizophrenic child is the ability of the therapist to help the child increase his control of his own impulsivity sufficiently so that he can dare to feel and express some of it, initially in fantasy material and later in words with appropriate affect.

15

The Attempt at Healthy Insulation in the Withdrawn Child

Coauthors: Leo Nagelberg, Ph.D.
Yonata Feldman, M.A.

In a preliminary report (Chapter 14) some material from a group of schizophrenic children was presented and desirable initial steps in their treatment were outlined by Nagelberg and Spotnitz. The purpose of the treatment was to cope with the excessive impulsivity which, it appeared, made necessary the development of the schizophrenic syndrome in the children described. The present report concerns one aspect of that syndrome— namely, the mechanism of emotional withdrawal, which seems necessary for some children in order to insulate themselves from the strong pressures of the environment or, specifically, from the excessive emotional impact of their parents.

THE NEED TO WITHDRAW

Freud suggested the problem when he wrote:

Protection against stimuli is an almost more important function for the living organism than *reception* of stimuli. The protective shield is supplied with its own store of energy and must above all endeavour to preserve the special modes of transformation of energy operating in it against the effects threatened by the enormous energies at work in the external world (1920, p. 27).

The child needs to be protected against any overwhelming stimulation. Insufficiency of the stimulus barrier, as mentioned by Bergman and

Escalona (1949), may lead to the formation of a premature ego organization that may dispose a child to the development of a psychosis.

The relatively healthy child has learned through parental understanding, care, and protection, to differentiate himself from his parents. The child whose parents are too stimulating or fail to shield him from overstimulation, is deprived of the protection he requires; his protective barrier is inadequate, and his health and survival are threatened. Such a child may therefore tend to withdraw emotionally in order to obtain the necessary insulation through a substitutive process.

CLINICAL ILLUSTRATIONS

The therapeutic sessions briefly described herein were conducted (by L. N.) with the possibility in mind that the children were using emotional withdrawal as a method of achieving adequate insulation. Whenever possible, therefore, the therapist kept the emotional impact of his own personality at a minimum and maintained as much emotional reserve as possible.

Material is presented from three cases treated at the Child Guidance Institute of the Jewish Board of Guardians, New York City. Our intention was not to provide complete case histories, but to demonstrate, through the statements of these children, what withdrawal meant to them and the purpose it served.

Case 1

Samuel, 10, was withdrawn. He had few friends. He refused to speak out loud in class. He would not leave the house without his mother. She described him as abnormally modest, terrified of her seeing him naked. He never smiled or laughed out loud. He mumbled when he spoke, his facial expression was extremely rigid and impassive, he often ate alone in his room, and he would not permit anyone to sing in the house. He would not accept gifts or show any enjoyment when things were offered to him. He had an IQ of 152.

Samuel was the oldest of three children. The two younger ones were girls. The parents' marriage was not a happy one; they separated several times and finally obtained a divorce when Samuel was 5½. He was not wanted by his father. His birth was a difficult one; the mother was in labor 48 hours and low forceps were used. Samuel was breast-fed only for three weeks. From the age of 3½ to 9 months, he cried constantly because of insufficient food. From the day he was born, his stool was caught in Kleenex. He was never permitted to soil. At 19 months, his tonsils were removed. At 20 months, the child had a tantrum and his father slapped his face until Samuel was exhausted. At the age of 2, he had a severe jaw tumor requiring surgical treatment; as a result, many of his teeth had decayed. At 3½ years of age, when he annoyed his mother and she pushed him, he fell on a lawn mower, sustaining an injury that permanently crippled his thumb.

Interview 1. Samuel's eyes were alert but his facial expression was rigid. He refused to sit down and *kept at a distance* from the therapist. He looked at the objects in the room but did not touch any. He asked questions about the therapist's work, and if he had read *Problems by Ripley.* These problems, he said, often may take "a million years to solve." In revealing his interest in higher mathematics, in complex problems, he seemed to be telling the therapist: My difficulties are very complicated, and it will take you a long time to help me solve them.

Interview 2. Confirming this impression, Samuel brought in a kaleidoscope and showed the therapist "complicated designs." He told how he looked into freight cars, threw stones at hogs and bulls, and frightened animals. The bull made a noise like the atomic bomb. He suggested that the therapist read the *Book of Knowledge,* which "gives you all the answers." Did he know why old people die? At the end of this interview, he told the therapist, "You don't seem to understand me. Your language is different." One wonders whether Samuel had an inkling that he spoke in the language of symbols; only someone with understanding of this language could reach him.

Interview 3. Samuel brought in binoculars. The therapist was to look into other people's windows and solve puzzles. In this interview, Samuel went one step further. He told the therapist to read a book that "will teach you to become a detective"—a hint that things that are so dangerous to look at have a criminal flavor. Samuel, furthermore, promised to bring in a book "full of interesting facts"; namely, it told how a man could remain in ice for 1,000 years and then come to life again; also the ice (apparently freezing of emotions) could be used against cancer.

Interview 4. Samuel brought in a science magazine to show the therapist an article about healing through hypnosis, and also showed him the picture of a sea mask, which allowed one to swim under water for a long time. Then he produced a book on "personal magnetism," and another one on "how to read people's minds."

In all of these interviews, Samuel suggested the insulating aspects of his withdrawal: One must protect oneself from danger, must freeze oneself, must preserve oneself in ice and not come to life prematurely, must hide under water. Convinced that the therapist remained at a distance and did nothing "to throw stones and to infuriate the hogs and bulls" (refrained from stimulating his aggression), Samuel felt sufficiently at ease to throw some light on the nature of the danger created by these "animals," from which he must insulate himself or withdraw.

Interview 6. He built a tower and made a little ball, which he rolled toward the tower; while doing this, he held his hand over his mouth. Expecting the tower to collapse, he jumped back as the ball came close to it. In this interview, Samuel for the first time moved freely around the room and explored objects.

It should be noted that around this time, the mother phoned to say that Samuel had shown improvement in behavior. He now went to the park and played with other children.

In the interviews, Samuel discovered, as if for the first time, that the therapist was a person. He bored a hole in clay, rolled another piece and tried to put it in the hole. At the same time, he talked about animal movies which, he said, people risked their lives to take.

In subsequent interviews, Samuel displayed aggression directly. He brought in guns; he demanded 100 firecrackers. He said he liked the smell and the noise. One could make a booby trap with fireworks. Perhaps, he added, this trap would be too small to kill a person. He said he had killed a caterpillar. The smell of firecrackers reminded him of the smell of camels. He set a fire in the room. His aggressive activity, gaining momentum from interview to interview, led to memories. One was of a whirlwind on his grandfather's farm. "If it hits you, it will throw you right into the air!" Throughout these aggressive reports, Samuel held his hands over his mouth, as if to prevent his real wishes and drives from escaping, suggesting the primitive belief in the magic of the word. Putting a thought of doing something into words was, for Samuel, equivalent to doing it.

The therapist, becoming somewhat impatient with Samuel's activities, asked him why he was coming and to talk about his present and past life. Samuel said he did not wish to know why he was coming; if the therapist would tell him what his problem was, he would stop coming. Under the pressure of the therapist's desire that the boy talk, his productions became confused. Samuel commented angrily that the therapist observed everything about him and that he was not able to move around. On various occasions, he hid under the clothes rack or crawled under the desk.

When the therapist stopped asking questions, Samuel resumed his aggressive activities during the interviews. The therapist joined Samuel in whatever discussion he initiated. If he talked about maps, the therapist would talk about maps. If Samuel discussed cars, inventions, wars, the therapist would start talking about these topics. As he went along with Samuel's resistiveness and, so to speak, took part in it, the boy's stiffness was replaced by behavior that was more natural for a 10-year-old. Samuel then spoke about his feelings for the therapist. Positive feelings emerged. He did not like his mother to smoke but he did not mind if the therapist smoked. He would like the therapist to visit him in his home. Though he still told of "stink bombs one might suffocate from," he also asked the therapist to get him a volunteer who would be a Big Brother to him and take him out on weekends.

At the end of the 40th interview, the boy discussed plans to go to camp or visit his father, who lived in another city. Though he still had compulsive symptoms, the immediate signs of his withdrawal had almost entirely disappeared.

The material presents evidence that Samuel was a traumatized child, and that he feared injury to his ego. When he discovered that the therapist would not overstimulate or traumatize him, the boy began to feel free to express his own aggression in impulses, feelings, and thoughts.

Case 2

Mary, aged 9½, was referred to the agency by her father because of her inability to adjust to other children. She preferred solitary activities at home. She read excessively, covering 400 pages a day. Occasionally she appeared oblivious to what was going on. Until recently Mary had clowned at school; refusing to do what other children were doing, she would walk out of the classroom. At times, she picked up her skirt in class and put it over her head. Yet she was intellectually capable of keeping up with her class. At the age of 7, she rated an IQ of 194 on the Stanford-Binet; two years later she was retested and rated only 124. Her inability to relate to children had been observed when she was only 5 years old. At that time, strong aggressive tendencies were also in evidence; she showed unusual sexual curiosity and used obscene language in a compulsive way. As time went on, her remoteness from people became more pronounced.

Mary's father was a conscientious, unemotional person. Her mother ran from school to school, and constantly interfered in the child's affairs. She did not permit Mary to cross the streets alone or to dress herself, even though she was 9 years old.

Interview 1. Mary said she had come to talk about herself. Yet she spoke at great length about an imaginary club consisting of 10 girls and 11 boys. In her fantasies, the membership steadily increased, but the proportion of males and females was kept intact. As Mary formulated her problem to the therapist, she seemed to want to belong to a normal group but could not realize this wish.

Interview 2. She enlarged upon why she had withdrawn from the group. Speaking of Jim, a member of the imaginary club, she said he had shot Rose, hit Martha with a drumstick, and crushed three animals. He was excluded from the club.

Interview 3. Mary spilled water over her dress and cried out, "My mother will think that I messed all over myself in the bathroom." For a 9½-year-old child, it was rather unusual that the act of spilling water should immediately lead back to infantile wishes and memories of strong maternal prohibitions.

From then on, interview after interview, Mary messed around with ink, spilling it and making blots. Guilt over messing expressed itself in a game of hanging. "You hang the person who is wrong," she said. Asked to talk about her troubles, she replied, "I hope you will not ask me questions about my troubles, because it almost makes me cry." As the therapist slowed his pace and shifted from ego-oriented questions to questions about objects, she told him that there was a time when she had played with real children.

Having experienced his permission to play and mess with ink, she could make the next step. She said, "I am curious about things but I am afraid to know what I am curious about." Another child might have said that she was ashamed to talk about her curiosity. Being "afraid to know" seemed to point to a much more primitive fear, and suggested that forbidden impulses were much closer to the surface, aroused greater anxiety, and also that more energy had to be invested in repressing them.

Then came the day (12th interview) when Mary wore a new dress and told the therapist that she was not going to dirty herself. This was the first development of an ability to control herself in the therapeutic setting. She made bizarre drawings and uttered meaningless sounds, which she asked the therapist to repeat after her. Mary said, "I can do it here and it is not crazy, but if I do it outside, people will call me crazy."

A growing attachment to the therapist manifested itself. She wished to stay longer with him and to hold his hand; she wanted him to accompany her downstairs. As he permitted her to say "crazy" things, she felt that he accepted her infantile wishes. They could come to light and be understood. She could invest her energies in more appropriate behavior. She could give up her "crazy" behavior.

In a subsequent interview, she produced an old memory of a couple standing beside an infant's crib. The father said, "How cheap this crib is." Mary interpreted that the father did not mean the crib was cheap; he wanted to say that the infant was ugly. It was Mary herself who was ugly and crazy and afraid of what she was curious about. Again the therapist did not push away this "crazy person"; he took her hand and led her down the stairs after the interview.

Messing with ink led to more creative work with clay, and joy at producing real objects, including a Menorah that her mother and brother could admire. She made a gift for the therapist, a paperweight—something real and useful.

She began to talk about real children in school. She was then attending a progressive school where the free expression of aggression was permitted.

Mary cried and begged to be allowed to change schools. In the meantime, she had acquired a girl friend. Mary was transferred to another school. Then her mother reported that Mary was so busy with school activities that she no longer had time to see the therapist.

The predominant theme of Mary's interviews was that she could not tolerate the sight of aggressive behavior in other children. The acceptance demonstrated by the therapist gave her the feeling that she was worthwhile, and had the right to assert herself and demand that she be placed in a school where children were less aggressive. Her ego had been threatened by exposure to an extremely aggressive environment.

Case 3

Harry, referred at the age of 13, usually talked in muffled tones in a low, monotonous voice. Invariably, he spoke haltingly and, at times, was devoid of spontaneity. Although he was a brilliant student, he was losing interest in school; often he truanted, spending the day in bed, listening at times to the radio with a sheet over his head. He preferred to be with his mother. When out in the street, he walked close to buildings. His mother complained that he had no friends, and told her that he did not want any. When his acquaintances came to the house at her invitation, he was annoyed. When they phoned, he would ask his mother to inform them that he was not at home. He would lock her out of his room. At times, he hid in closets, bundled up in a blanket. Once when she undid it, she found him rolled up like a cocoon, perspiring profusely, and quite exhausted.

Sometimes he told his mother that he loved her very much; at other times, he said he had to kill her. He spit at her, took the belt off his pants and hit her with it, and threatened to commit suicide. He would put a rope around his mother's neck, jump on her, and threaten to suffocate her with a pillow.

She said that his difficulties began after the death of her husband, when Harry was about 5. They then lived with her own mother for two years. That period with the maternal grandmother, she felt, had caused the boy's present problems.

Interview 1. Harry expressed unwillingness to come. He had nothing to say about himself. He summed up his life by stating, "I was born and am still living!" When told he didn't have to come, he decided that he would come. The therapist did not put any pressure on him and Harry asked, "Why don't you persuade me to come?" No encouragement was given, and he volunteered, "I understand it's quite a privilege to come." Had the therapist applied pressure, Harry might have withdrawn from the treatment situation; he was free to venture into it because he was not pushed to come.

The therapist continued this nonstimulating approach. Harry maintained his isolation, talking impersonally about his interest in science and planetary problems.

Interview 4. Harry said that he felt better when he talked and when there was someone to listen to him. He maintained his suspicious attitude. He asked, "Would you consider it impolite if I would say that psychiatrists are not on the level?" He indicated that nobody was on the level, and that he had to protect himself against a threatening environment.

Interview 5. He asked why the therapist smoked. Had he heard that cigarettes contain nicotine? That nicotine was poisonous, dangerous? The therapist should show self-control. Harry asked, "How can you control others when you cannot control yourself?" Nicotine might go into the lungs and thus cause cancer. Again Harry demonstrated his fear that other people would not be able to control themselves, projecting his own fear that he could not keep himself in check, as if he thought that an explosion would ensue if people did not keep at a distance. He told a story about a cripple who actually had benefited from his broken leg; people gave him money. Harry said, "It's better for people sometimes if they are sick." It was an advantage not having to participate.

Interview 6. He initiated a method that he clung to for some time. He inquired about the therapist's thoughts on political issues, explaining that this was a way of keeping the therapist at a distance. Harry needed to avoid talking about himself or drawing attention to himself. On the surface, he seemed to be showing an interest in the therapist. Actually he was not at all interested in the therapist as a person.

Interview 7. Harry said he was impelled to talk about impersonal objects, hobbies, museums, a stamp collection, in order to keep the therapist away. "However, I realize that you are not interested when I talk about impersonal things. I know, because if I don't talk about my personal opinions, I will not be helped." Harry was now more ready to discuss personal matters.

Interview 8. Harry looked much better and showed more spontaneity. He was friendly, and although he still spoke in a muffled tone, exhibited some animation. He said he himself was surprised that he now liked school. He had a friend who bred fish, and his own hobby now was to protect fish. "Female fish devour their own eggs, and when eggs are produced, one has to separate the eggs from the female fish."

Interview 9. Harry returned to the theme of big fish eating little ones if he did not separate them. Separation was necessary. A balance had to be maintained, too, to keep the tank clean. This suggested the idea that he had to continue his withdrawal, that it was necessary for him to maintain a balance. In the same interview, he went a step further and suggested the next problem, namely, that of his confusion about male and female identifications. After speaking about baseball and the World Series, he returned to the fish. Referring to a book he had bought on fish breeding, he explained how one distinguished between female and male fish. Then he said, "I hear little fish cannot be distinguished yet as to whether they are male or female, but in time I will be able to do so."

Interview 10. He discussed different types of fish and drew a picture of an angelfish. It was in danger he said, because it could not stop by itself, and might drop dead if it brushed against a rock.

Interview 14. Harry discussed his mother. They had argued because he had not gone to school that day. They had lots of arguments. He had insulted her and then thrown up his meal. He said, "If mother only would not take me so seriously, but she won't. Mother wants me to go out but I like to read, practice my clarinet. My mother interrupts me and wants me to go on errands but I don't want to."

Interview 17. He said that he had decided to talk more openly to the therapist. The week before, he had cried and thought that nobody loved him. "I often thought that I can only get satisfaction from myself; that is, I have to like myself because nobody likes me. No one really understands me; for this reason, I prefer to stay home and not go out."

Later he spoke more freely about his mother. He said, "I do homework much better when Mother leaves the house and *I work best if I'm separated.*" In one interview, after making a number of critical remarks about her, he looked at the therapist and said, "I feel you understand. You certainly know that I really love my mother even if I say that I don't love her. One part loves my mother and the other part does not."

Interview 19. Harry said that he had joined a club and would like some suggestions about how to run it. He thought the therapist could give him some good ideas because "you have the right psychology and I might use it for the club. It's important to use the right psychology. One teacher asked me to recite a poem. First I said no, but the teacher did not bother me and then I became interested and I was willing to recite the poem. If people are direct and tell me what to do, I will say no, but if they say I shouldn't do it, I'll do it." Harry again demonstrated his negative suggestibility, *his need to go contrary to all direction because he felt he must separate himself sufficiently from other people before he could participate on his own.*

Again he said that the therapist used the right psychology. "You showed discretion, didn't show any interest but I continued to come. If you had said 'Come,' I would have laughed to myself and said ha-ha, and surely I would not have come. Secondly, you showed the right psychology because you arranged it in such a way that you helped me to find a solution for myself. I think that you and I actually always have the same idea. A good psychologist is a person who makes the other person express what the psychologist thinks, and then the other person feels happy about it."

Several times he tried to extract advice from the therapist, to test out whether he would intervene. For instance, Harry wanted to know whether he should or should not fight with other boys or with his mother. But the therapist remained noncommittal. On returning to the same subjects later, Harry repeatedly said that the therapist had used the "right psychology" in not intervening.

The boy became more and more interested in finding out how the therapist operated. He said, "I know you watch me and put pieces together, but how do you do it? I think you do it because you listen to me, watch me; you watch me even if I yawn. I would like to get from you complete instructions on how to put pieces together. I think I have to learn something from you, and this is how one goes about putting people together. These are the rules; First, listen. Second, don't rush to get all problems. Third, wait until the other person has something to offer too."

His drive to become a good psychologist became stronger. He said he was interested in becoming one himself. The therapist asked him, "Suppose you become a psychologist, what would you get out of that?" He replied that he would no longer need to come. Evidently, if he should become like the therapist, then the latter would be superfluous.

The need to become like the therapist had some positive aspects, in that Harry wanted to identify himself with, or incorporate a "good father." Still, one should not fail to recognize that Harry was also demonstrating his defensive technique, that of swallowing up the dangerous object. The therapist or outside world was a menace against which he could defend himself only by becoming like the object. On the surface, this attitude suggested compliance, interest, a need to please, flattery; but these were also defensive devices to get the therapist out of the way. Harry continued to say that he wanted to read books on psychology so he would be able to handle people. He brought in a psychology book which, he said, helped explain how to handle people. "If I understand it, you will be superfluous." He became furious, complaining that the therapist was not teaching him psychology. The therapist asked, "Suppose I teach you psychology, what will there be in it for me?" The therapist would get nothing, Harry replied; he didn't want to give the therapist anything at all.

After 40 interviews, Harry was able to divulge personal material more freely. He spoke about his dreams, his sexual urges, his difficulties at school, and his arguments with his mother. He joined two clubs; he attended school regularly and enjoyed going; and he talked more about his fear of being different from other children, his nausea and vomiting, his instinctual drives, particularly his concern about masturbation and his voyeuristic impulses. At home the situation improved considerably. As Harry explained, "I used to fight mother because I had to let off steam and give expression to my energies in some way. Now I try to understand myself." He still spat at his mother occasionally, but he had given up most of his violently impulsive actions. In school, Harry was one of 10 graduates, in a class of 600, who were awarded medals.

Mother's treatment. Harry's mother,* 45 years old, was a gifted person, but with many bizarre traits. She had strongly hostile feelings toward her mother, but was afraid to disobey her and was completely under her domination. Her happiest years, she claimed, were with her husband, who loved her, understood, and protected her. When he died suddenly, she felt lost. Her father wanted her to return to the parental home, but her mother was jealous of her husband's affection for her daughter and her son, and set out to make their life a torment. She blamed her mother for Harry's problem.

Finally forced to move to a furnished room with her son, she surrounded him with constant flirtatious attention. Though they had separate beds, they slept close to each other and exchanged beds on weekends. There was a fuss made by both about dressing and undressing, and a constant pushing of each other on the bed. The mother often provoked fights. Then, as if in retaliation, she slapped her son, spat in his face, locked herself in the bathroom, and indulged in the same antics as the boy. After scenes of violence, she would write poems to Harry urging him to enter "a harmonious relationship" with her "as mother and son should have."

In her interviews, she often referred to Harry's violence toward her as "a funny way to show his love." She remarked that "he always likes to be on top of me." She was torn between "two animals, my mother and Harry." As an escape, she wrote poetry and music. She said that Harry too "can write lovely poetry and can compose music." Her bizarreness is evident in the way she explained conception and childbirth to her son: "It is like tonsils—you don't know where they come from but the doctor takes them out!"

When the mother first came to us, she too was withdrawn from the circle of her family—sisters and brother. As treatment advanced, she resumed her social contacts, showed better control of her impulses, and was firmer with Harry. She herself felt that Harry would not have developed his present problem had there been "someone to take over when my husband died."

In summary, the predominant theme of Harry's productions was that he needed insulation in order to separate himself from other people so that he would not be injured by their overstimulation.

---

*Treated by Betty Gabriel at the same agency.

VALUE OF THERAPIST'S EMOTIONAL RESERVE

The withdrawal reaction, as it appears from the material presented here, seems to be a defense against the acting out of preoedipal and oedipal strivings both in their libidinal and destructive aspects. The child has a great need to *increase his control* of his impulsivity so that he can dare to experience it, to think about it, and to express it to some extent, first in fantasies and eventually in language with appropriate affects. *Adequate insulation* or a *good protective barrier* makes this control possible. In the absence of adequate insulation, emotional withdrawal is used as a substitute.

Our study has revealed one consistent finding. An attitude of emotional reserve on the part of the therapist, which was intended to be as nonstimulating as possible, had the effect of making the children reported on here less withdrawn in their behavior, first with the therapist and later with other people. The verbal and play material presented by these children during their interviews suggested that they used withdrawal as a method of removing themselves from overwhelmingly dangerous reality situations with their parents.

In view of their inadequate protective barrier against overstimulation, they were in a twofold danger: (1) parental overstimulation with inadequate insulation created a constantly accumulating state of instinctual tension with concomitant states of pain, anxiety, and terror; and (2) the continual danger that loss of impulse control might cause them to behave destructively to people whom they loved and ultimately to themselves, or both situations occurred in varying degrees. Their ever-intensifying state of instinctual tension increased their desire to release their tension in destructive behavior. The attempt to withdraw emotionally served a dual purpose: If they did not feel the people around them, the children were more insulated against excessive stimulation, and they were also under less temptation to discharge impulses in actions that might destroy these people.

In a comparatively healthy environment with an adult who did not stimulate them excessively, one with whom their protective barrier was adequate and with whom they could verbalize and discharge their destructive feelings in a controlled and measured way, these children no longer needed to withdraw. They felt sufficiently insulated and separated from the therapist so that they could function with greater independence of thought, feeling, and action; this increased their insulation. They had been rescued from the ultimate fate of the schizophrenic who, "having abandoned object relations in order to avoid dangerous stimulation from the outside world and having taken steps to block reality excitations, is in the position of the child that falls asleep" (Glover, 1949, p. 228). *The experiencing of an insulating, protecting environment gave them a sufficient feeling of insulation to render withdrawal unnecessary as an impulsive defensive process.*

MEANING OF WITHDRAWAL

Withdrawal, then, may be viewed not only as a defense mechanism but also as a protective coating. It is designed to give the individual a period for gradually developing within his personality a mechanism whereby outside emotional stimulation will be kept at a minimum and thus will evoke only a muffled response in harmony with the total personality.

Such additional understanding of the meaning of withdrawal should add another dimension to the therapeutic approach; namely, one should guard against too early an attempt to break the closed circle of the withdrawn child. Any attempt by the therapist to further a positive relationship by showing understanding of the meaning of the child's material too early in treatment may create more confusion and disorganization, and thus delay or even prevent healing.

Social Significance

What is the social significance of an understanding of withdrawal as an attempt on the part of the child to develop a healthy insulation against an overstimulating environment? Our study suggests that it is the duty of parents, educators, therapists, and caseworkers to help provide an environment in which children, especially oversensitive children, are sufficiently protected from overstimulation so that they do not need to withdraw emotionally. The child's need for insulation and protection has to be studied and understood on an individual basis. It is important that a healthful environment be provided, one in which the child is shielded from overstimulation, so that he feels free and secure enough to express a fair measure of his own creative personality and to begin to realize his potential for functioning in a socially useful way.

16

Ego Reinforcement

Coauthors: Leo Nagelberg, Ph.D.
Yonata Feldman, M.A.

The present report, like two earlier studies on other aspects of the treatment of childhood schizophrenia, deals with techniques and findings drawn from a research project in which the authors are associated. Two of us, in outlining techniques used in beginning analytic therapy (Chapter 14), stressed the child's need for an understanding therapist, one well "insulated" and goal-directed. The significance of the therapist's insulative capacity in such situations, it may be helpful to note, is developed in our discussion of casework training (Feldman, Spotnitz, and Nagelberg, 1953) Our second study of childhood schizophrenia set forth the view that the withdrawn child, because he lacks the insulation necessary to protect himself from his own impulsivity and from unfavorable environmental pressures, makes use of emotional withdrawal—an inadequate substitute—as a defense against such pressures (Chapter 15). If the treatment process helps him develop the insulation he requires, the substitute becomes unnecessary. Another specific type of inadequate substitute for insulation to which the schizophrenic child resorts is pathological narcissism. Its treatment, employing highly specific methods of ego reinforcement, is the subject of the present study.

That the schizophrenic individual suffers from a high degree of pathological narcissism has long been known (Freud, 1914b). Primarily, this has been regarded, and correctly so, as a manifestation of excessive self-love; what has not been so well recognized is that the schizophrenic individual attempts to utilize pathological narcissism to strengthen his insulating or protective barrier.

The accumulation of excessive self-directed impulses from which the schizophrenic child suffers includes not only libidinal impulses but destructive ones as well. Moreover, he cannot cope with his excessive libidinal and destructive impulsivity toward others, which may express itself in open oedipal manifestations, disorganized and assaultive impulsivity toward a parent or parent surrogate. To prevent himself from being stimulated to injure himself or any other person concerned in that disequilibrium, the child sacrifices his ego (sacrifice of ego for object). He develops a condition of nonfeeling, withdraws, maintains his ego in a "perfect" state from which objectionable and "crazy" impulses must be shut out, and resorts to pathological narcissism in order not to feel, think, and act on his destructive impulses toward others.

The Narcissus myths, it might be observed, support the idea of the presence of excessive narcissism for the purpose of increasing inadequate insulation (Chapter 9). The fact that Narcissus gazed at his own image may be regarded as a pathological effort at ego reinforcement—an attempt to strengthen the ego by re-emphasizing and revitalizing toward the self whatever behavior patterns exist within it.

It is well known that at certain ages children tend to find in other children similar to themselves a sort of ego support. The ego of one twin is strengthened and reinforced by the presence of the other; at the age of four months, twins actually mirror each other (Burlingham, 1952). It is characteristic of adolescents to seek out other teen-agers like themselves; their participation in gangs, clubs, and the like has ego-strengthening value.

APPLICATION IN PSYCHOTHERAPY

The use of ego reinforcement in treatment requires thorough understanding of the "contact functioning" of the ego, that is, its method of disobeying the implied or stated demand of the therapist that the patient give an emotionally significant account of his life. Sooner or later, in the course of the interviews, the child refuses to do so and tries to evoke a response from the therapist. The process whereby the therapist reflects these attempts at contact—mirrors and reinforces them—is referred to as "ego reinforcement."

If the child is silent, for example, the therapist is silent. If the child questions the therapist, he in turn questions the child. If the latter remains self-absorbed and does not address the therapist directly, even though communicating indirectly, the therapist remains silent. He responds only to *direct attempts* to elicit his response, and only in kind. Thus, the timing is regulated by the child's direct attempts to elicit such response. The contact functioning of his ego is the thermostat that guides the therapist throughout this process. And any replies he gives are designed to reinforce the defensive structure of the child's ego.

Analysis, judgment, and understanding are continually required. Essential to the success of this type of treatment is the therapist's sincere desire to understand. This desire is transmitted to the unconscious ego of the schizo-phrenic child. The therapist will not prematurely accelerate the pace of the child's ego development. Nor will he break or penetrate the fragile defensive structure of the ego.

The therapist addresses himself primarily to the child's psychological needs. He respects and responds to them, as we have just indicated, in the manner outlined by the child. In this psychological twin image, the child is to feel himself recognized and understood, is to feel that he is loved. He sees that the therapist has become "like" him; and in preoedipal terms, "like" is equivalent to being loved. Instead of having only one person, isolated and self-absorbed, in his world, the child now has two.

He is thus enabled to relate, first on a narcissistic basis, to another person (the therapist) and then to investigate, in the treatment relationship, the twin image he has of the latter. When the child has learned to *judge* whether or not that twin image is *real*, he has learned to distinguish between the illu-sory aspects and the reality of the therapist (object relationship).

In brief, the child is helped to find the mirror image of his own ego in the therapist. The ego thus obtains a wholesome type of reinforcement. His understanding has enabled the therapist to reproduce, at times psycho-logically, methods of child rearing which are normally associated with pa-rental care and protection, methods which will enable a child to develop healthy object relationships, identifications, and differentiations.

CLINICAL ILLUSTRATIONS

The interview material which follows was selected from the case records of two boys who received analytic therapy at the Child Guidance Institute, Jewish Board of Guardians, New York City. Through their statements, we shall attempt to indicate what pathological narcissism meant to them and the effect of ego reinforcement upon their understanding of themselves.

Case 1

Howard was referred at the age of 11 because of his struggle with his mother when the time came for him to go to school each morning. As soon as his father had left for work, Howard would throw a temper tantrum. Jumping up and down, he would scream, "You don't love me; that's why you send me to school." As an excuse to remain home, he complained con-stantly that his stomach or head ached.

Mother was concerned about other aspects of Howard's behavior too. *He was constantly standing in front of the mirror and making funny faces and noises.* He handled all his problems on an infantile level, preferring to play with younger girls and boys. He threatened to run away if he did not get his own way. Once he went up to the roof and threatened to jump off. He had become fussy about food, picking meat apart for fat and veins. Mother didn't understand him; other children thought he was peculiar. *He would giggle and laugh for no apparent reason.* Mother believed that Howard was excessively preoccupied with sexual matters. She was afraid to leave him alone in the house because of his wrestling and possible sex play.

The parents had been married for 17 years. Father was regarded as extremely weak and inept in handling the boy, yielding to Howard's pleadings and often countermanding the mother's orders. A very tense and anxious woman, she hovered about the boy, accompanying him whenever she could, and worried about what he would do next. When he got out of control and beat up other youngsters, she would become hysterical and proclaim that he would be the death of her.

Interviews with Howard

Interview 8. Howard said he'd like to live forever, make a million dollars, have a mansion. He said nobody wanted to die. He wanted to remain young forever. He believed in reincarnation; there couldn't be a blackness at the end of life. He would like to be reincarnated as a dog. (Excessive narcissism.)

Interview 14. Howard told his mother that other boys went to bed at a later hour than she permitted him to, but she didn't believe him. Mother washed all the time. *She wanted him to be just like her, and would tell him what a good girl she had been.*

Interview 21. Howard said, "When we talked about stealing and you asked *why I don't steal more* (ego reinforcement) I stopped stealing. If you had told me not to steal, maybe I would have stolen more. It would have made the hour more exciting for *you*."

Interview 22. He was no worse than other boys, Howard said. Even when he did bad things, he could always control himself and stop doing them. *Also, he was always in the company of another person so he wouldn't take the rap by himself.* (Need for ego support.)

Interview 23. Howard was both a bad boy and a good one. He'd given up stealing, particularly because he didn't want to be the worst boy. He wanted to be just average. Though he still rang doorbells, he did not smash car windows. He had even told his parents he cursed, but not the words he used. He could repeat them to the therapist, however, because he "had something" on the therapist, *who had said that he was out to teach Howard to be bad. If Howard let other people know about the remark, something might happen to the therapist.* That was why the boy was pretty sure the therapist wouldn't tell on *him*. (Initial effects of ego reinforcement.) The therapist told Howard he didn't have a chance. People would rather believe the therapist than Howard.

Interview 28. Howard, because he did not want the hour to be too boring for the therapist, would tell him about some mischievous doings. Animatedly, he related how he had stolen bottles from a fire escape, after making sure the owner wasn't around, and had shown off the bottles. That would teach people not to leave beer bottles outside their apartments. Gleefully, he talked about how surprised they would be when they discovered that the bottles were missing. To the therapist's observation that Howard liked to have his revenge but took it in such a trifling way, the boy replied that it would be too dangerous if he weren't careful. *The therapist suggested that Howard should become invisible;* than he could do practically anything. Smiling, Howard said that the first thing he would do would be to rob the Yankee Stadium; then he would rob the bank and have lots of money.

About a year after Howard had come to the Institute, his treatment (with L.N.) came to an end because he said he did not wish to continue. About seven months earlier, however, he had persuaded his mother to come for treatment (with Y.F.). Over a period of 20 months, there were about 45 interviews.

Interviews with mother

Interview 1. Mother disclosed that she and her husband felt that Howard made a point of annoying and spiting them. He was out to torture and kill them. He was always asking for toys and gifts, and was never satisfied, never had enough. He nagged his parents, and chattered incessantly. (Aggression as basic problem.)

Interview 3. Mother commented that Howard's therapist had acted very "crazy" with Howard. *Mother thought the therapist had acted that way to show Howard that it isn't so terrible to "be crazy." At times, even grownups can act like babies. The normal way a father would play with a baby might appear "crazy" to adults.* (Ego reinforcement.)

Interview 5. Mother blamed herself for Howard's difficulties. When he was little, she had demanded too much of him. (Excessive frustration led to excessive aggression.) She couldn't stand dirt or disorder. Now she knew better, but thought it was too late. The damage had been done.

Interview 23. Mother reported that Howard was chairman of his class. He had been afraid to run at first; but she had helped with his speech, and he had been elected. His teachers were bestowing honors upon the boy, but he complained that they brought added responsibilities. If she could only force herself to leave him alone, not nag him, perhaps things would be better. *She got too anxious and couldn't control herself.*

Case 2

Interview 14. Harry remarked, "If only mother would not take me so seriously!" He complained that she wanted him to go out, but he liked to read and practice the clarinet. She would interrupt him to run errands for her, and he disliked doing them.

Interview 17. Harry had been crying recently because he felt that nobody loved him. *That was why he had to love himself and get satisfaction from himself.* He preferred staying home to going out because no one really understood him or liked him. (To get love for himself, he had to become narcissistic.)

Interview 20. Harry was interested in the therapist and wanted to know what he was like. (Clash between self-love and object love.) He wanted to know how smart the therapist was. Harry was always thinking that the therapist might put something over on him; that was why he had to be on his guard, and had to give the "right" answers. *He was always thinking of himself. It was always "me, me, me."* He felt that his mind existed apart from his body. He was always observing himself.

Interview 21. The therapist had been helpful, had given Harry a solution. The therapist *had shown discretion* in *not* seeming to care whether or not Harry continued to come for treatment. Had the therapist said "Come," Harry would have laughed to himself, and he surely wouldn't have come. Besides, the therapist had used the right psychology because *he had helped Harry find a solution for himself.* And it was the very solution that Harry had in his own mind. (Fusion and identity between subjective and objective ideas; satisfaction value of psychological mirroring.) In Harry's opinion, a good psychologist made the other person express the psychologist's idea, which makes the other person "feel happy about it."

Interview 22. The therapist encouraged Harry's suggestion that his mother take the initiative in getting treatment for herself, through regular channels. (Encouragement of Harry's ego identification with his mother.)

Interview 26. Harry felt he was smart, that he was more intelligent than the rest of his class.

Interview 27. Discussing a quarrel he had with some other boys, Harry angrily asked, "What are you waiting for? Why don't you tell me what to

*Case 3 in Chapter 15, which provides information on the presenting problems and earlier interviews. Many techniques were employed in Harry's treatment, but the material presented here was selected to illustrate only the use of ego reinforcement.

do?" After a pause, he said he realized that he had to decide for himself whether or not to fight. If he should decide not to fight, he wouldn't fight. That was at least a temporary solution.

Interview 28. Harry explained, "If you had said 'Fight' and I wouldn't have fought, then I would have been puzzled. If you had said 'Don't fight' and I didn't fight, then I would have been puzzled too, because I would have thought that I shouldn't fight if I had fought; so everything is all right."

Harry felt superior because he felt stronger. He was thinking of inventions, such as a gadget for wings—to fly, run fast, and be ahead—and a radio-television combination to be attached to the wrist.

Interview 30. He hoped that his mother, after she had seen a caseworker, would "get off" all the bad things about him. Then she could tell all the things she loved about him.

He explained that he answered his own questions when the therapist raised them again in order to prove that he could find an answer. He understood himself a lot better now. He could see how smart the therapist had been to say that Harry came so that he could understand himself better. It had occurred to him that if he understood himself too well, he would not have to come any longer. However, he wanted to continue to come for treatment.

Interview 33. If the therapist had wanted Harry to come for treatment at the beginning, he would not have come; but *if the therapist acted* as if he didn't care whether Harry came or not, then he would decide to come. (Psychological reflection of indifferent attitude of child is understood by the child to be only a "protective cover"; despite the I-don't-care attitude, the therapist has nonverbally conveyed his real interest in helping the boy.)

Interview 34. In discussing a homosexual experience of his early childhood, Harry crossed his arms and sat stiffly. Looking at the therapist, he said the thought had suddenly come to him: What does a therapist think about that makes him sit so erect? It was a kind of mental telepathy. His mother told him to sit straight, and he really felt better when he did. He was wondering whether the therapist had noticed it. (Delayed obedience made him feel better.)

Interview 35. Harry had told himself that he would be normal for a week. To be normal meant to be like everybody; it meant not to do what others don't do. This determination lasted five days. He said, "To be normal also means to say anything that comes into your mind."

Interview 36. The more his mother pressed him to have friends, the less inclined he was to have them. He had discovered a psychological technique that could be applied to his mother. He would say to her, "Keep talking to me about having friends." Then she would stop asking him. *He wished his mother would not push him so much.* The ideal person was one who did not push. The most important thing he had learned from the therapist thus far was that playing at being indifferent got results.

Interview 39. Harry realized he did not have to know about everything. He would get interested in knowing about something, but he quickly lost interest in it once he knew the answer.

Interview 42. He felt that he understood himself much better, but was not sure he understood everything about himself. Take the argument he had with his mother. When he fought with her, somehow he watched himself fighting, as though he were another person. Since he would regard the other fellow as silly, he found himself silly—so he stopped fighting. *He had the idea that he thought too much about himself, worried too much about himself, and was self-conscious. But being self-conscious meant that he looked upon himself as if he were another person; and that self-consciousness kept him from fighting.* (Statement of an attempt at ego mastery through pathological narcissism.)

Interview 66. Harry thought that the therapist understood himself and could control himself. If he knew how the therapist behaved, he could try to behave the same way. Then he too would be able to understand himself.

Interview 69. Harry had the idea that coming here would enable him to understand himself 100 per cent. He also had the idea now that he might be a "hard case," and might have to come a long time. He had the feeling that coming here would make him happier, but still he wanted to know if he was a hard case. "Is that correct?" he asked.

The therapist remarked, "Suppose I think you are a hard case, or suppose I think you are not. . . . If I say you are, you may get the idea that I consider your case hopeless. What then?" In that case, Harry replied, *he would have to go back to himself and find happiness only in himself.* (Use of pathological narcissism for consolation.) But that wasn't possible either. "Then why don't you want to hear from me that you are a hopeless case?" the therapist asked. Harry answered that there was a question in his mind whether the therapist was interested in him and really cared for him. If the therapist considered Harry hopeless, that would indicate he did not care for Harry.

Harry had a double attitude toward the therapist. On the one hand, he thought he knew the therapist very well; on the other hand, he had the idea the therapist was like any other ordinary human being. But to think about the therapist in relation to himself was something Harry did not like. He could look on while the therapist treated another boy, could imagine that the therapist might like the other boy and have some feeling; but Harry said that he did not want to think about that feeling with respect to himself. Harry often had the idea that the therapist was a logical piece of machinery and didn't show too much feeling. Harry himself did not want to show or say too much that he might be needing or liking another person. He was asked what was wrong about showing that one likes or needs another person.

"Now we're getting somewhere," Harry answered. "I have an idea that we always move very slowly. Psychiatrists move much faster by giving a word association test. I finally get the idea that you are driving at. You would not mind if I feel toward you as if you were my father."

Elaborating, Harry said that he was afraid of expressing feelings of love because they might be homosexual. He only got love from his father but even then, as a small child, he remembered hating his father for being a rival for his mother. Harry remembered that his father had given him a present, an electric train. The gift had stuck in his memory because he felt that he hadn't deserved it; he thought he had hated his father, and his father should have hated him. In a way, he was glad that his father was dead, because now he could possess his mother all by himself. After his father's death, he had come to hate all men. He didn't want his mother to remarry. He clung to the idea that men hate one another; he couldn't conceive of their loving one another, even of a father loving a son or a brother loving a brother. But now he could see that he had been wrong. It was possible for father and son to love each other without being accused of homosexuality.

Interview 105. Harry was called upon to review and explain various therapeutic measures that had been effectively applied during the course of the treatment.

When his worries about masturbation were discussed in previous interviews, the realization that the therapist not only did not want him to stop worrying but might even wish him to worry some more about the matter brought him relief. "When you come for treatment," the boy observed, "you put your worries into words and unload them on the therapist. I like other people to do the worrying for me, but then again I don't like it because you remain indebted and won't be free. I used to think you didn't want me to worry about masturbation, so a load was taken off my mind when *I thought I had the right to worry*. Then I stopped worrying." Harry added that it is not human to remain perfect, that is, in the mother's womb. Being human is "to be imperfect, to worry, to be responsible, and to be free."

Expressions of unhappiness and depression had been voiced in some interviews. Harry recalled how he had wanted to be made to feel happy immediately; therefore, the thought that the therapist might want to see him even more depressed had made him miserable. That meant he had little chance of getting attention. He had wanted the therapist to be bothered about his depression. Harry went on, *"Since I did not get a reaction out of you, I decided there was no use bothering about my depression and so I started to get to work to understand myself."* He had decided that feeling depressed wasn't such a bad thing; after crying over himself, he would feel much better. (Apparent acceptance of sadness and depression as inevitable in life, as something his ego could tolerate.)

Harry also referred to his previously expressed desire to kill himself. Self-destructive impulses rose up in him when he felt that his mother, others in his family, or the therapist did not measure up to his ideal of them. Then too, when he felt he wasn't loved, even by himself, he would question the use of living.

The therapist, had he responded to those disclosures by telling Harry not to kill himself, would have been acting, according to the boy, like a "guidance counselor with a family approach." To have been told not to kill himself would have been pleasing to Harry, but would also have been frustrating. He would then have thought to himself: Why is he so against my killing myself when I see no reason for living? Had the therapist shown sympathy, Harry said he might still have gone ahead and killed himself after something disagreeable happened later on. He continued, "When you said, 'Why don't you kill yourself?' I thought, Why don't *you* kill yourself first? And I resolved that I wouldn't kill myself."

Harry felt that *encouraging him to live would just have pushed back his desire to kill himself, whereas being asked why he did not kill himself left him free to re-examine the whole question of whether he should, or should not, kill himself.* He felt that the response given him (a response, obviously, that could be voiced only in the proper context and after the establishment of a healthful emotional relationship) *made him feel that it would be better to try to work out his own problems than to commit suicide.*

The boy expressed himself in similar fashion about their discussions of his fears of being insane, of being watched, of being a freak, a sex maniac, and a homosexual. If he had been told that all those fears were groundless, Harry said that he would have continued to feel them.

"But when I thought that you might want me to be insane or a pervert," the youngster went on, "I felt miserable at first. I thought you were crazy and should see a psychiatrist. I thought I would let other people send me to an insane asylum but I wouldn't let you do it. I also had the feeling that you wanted to make yourself disliked. I disliked you very much, though I didn't want to dislike you. I felt you were joking, and that you were purposely making yourself disliked, to help the treatment.

"I was miserable, but then things began to brighten up. *If everything is down at the bottom, everything above—even if it is bad—looks good.* At first, I felt that everything we had done had gone to pot; but looking back, I prefer your approach. When I thought you might want me to be a homosexual, my whole body got tense. Then I thought that there is no pleasure in being a homosexual. *It also became easier for me to talk about my thoughts. I learned that it is all right to talk crazily without having to act crazily. Now it seems strange that I once felt watched and talked about by people.* (Hallucinatory trend.) *If you can admit to yourself that it may be all right to have all sorts of crazy impulses, it is easier to control them and they no longer bother you."* (A basic principle for the treatment of the schizophrenic child.)

Discussing his feeling that the therapist was not perfect, Harry said, "I always want you to be smart. If I feel that you are not perfect, how can I feel good inside and want to keep coming here?" It disappointed him to think that the therapist might have problems; but it was also disappointing to think that he might be "high up and unattainable." Harry went on, "I liked to break you down to my level, although it hurt me. When you behaved as if you had problems, I thought that maybe you were self-destructive. My illusions were broken, but it also made me more alive and you became more human. You mixed me up but it is comforting to talk to you. We have a common meeting-ground, and I have a chance to be like you. If I can think that you may have faults, it is easier to talk about my own."

On his own initiative, Harry disclosed his feelings about some of the therapist's prohibitions. He had both liked and resented being told not to masturbate, not to threaten his mother, and not to peep at women undressing. He had wanted, and yet had not wanted, to be told to stop doing those things. Then he said he had realized that the therapist was telling him what to do for therapeutic reasons. He went on, "I knew that eventually I had to stop those activities, and I felt that you were trying to help me stop." (Actually, the therapist's directions had not been given to influence Harry's behavior outside the session but for their stimulating effect during the session.)

Permeating the interviews, and developing over the months with a crescendo of intensity, had been this theme: the boy's yearning to be adopted by the therapist and his wife. Harry would become depressed after it was discussed, and again refuse to go to school. Reviewing his feelings about the matter, he said, "I expected you to tell me you would never adopt me. You didn't say that, so adoption was left as a possibility. Then I thought to myself: Why doesn't he hurry up and adopt me?" He recalled his depression over not being adopted. He remembered that he had been surprised to hear the therapist ask, "Harry, why don't you adopt me?" Harry said he always tried to outwit the therapist, but never knew what he would come up with next. The boy felt that he was too weak to do anything for the therapist. "Besides," he observed, "how could I be your father? But at any rate I stopped wanting to be adopted by you. Then I realized that you wanted to indicate to me that I was being selfish, that I had not done enough for you. And I decided that the best way for me to be loved was to be working with you in our therapy." He was still mixed up, Harry remarked, but he was coming out of his muddlement. Airing problems was more important than adoption, he had decided. His thoughts were not blocked, and the road was being kept open so that he could discuss things and become a useful member of society.

Interview 134. Harry said he had recently been wondering how much longer he would have to come. Not that he would want it to be thought that he did not want to continue coming; in fact, he felt quite the reverse about it. But what was on his mind was that the purpose of therapy was to help one justify what one did and thought, and Harry now felt that he could justify his own thoughts and actions by himself. Besides, it had occurred to him that if he did not come, he would not raise problems and then those problems would not exist.

He did not want it to be thought that he did not wish to come any more, Harry repeated, but he felt that the therapist might not be satisfied with the things Harry talked about during the interviews. (In the preceding session, the therapist had pointed out that there were other areas of discussion; in earlier interviews, the boy had discussed rather vaguely, and also in an obsessive manner, the topic of self-understanding.)

If Harry wanted to discuss the subject of understanding one's self, the therapist asked him why he had to do it in such a repetitious way. The boy replied that he always hammered away at one problem at a time. He went on to say, *It's like shutting myself up in a back room and shutting out everything else. I hammer away and it is like grabbing for some security, and also justifying myself that I am right."* This is an illustration of insulation by (1) self-isolation; (2) shutting out of stimuli; (3) forceful repetition as a protective pattern; (4) clinging; and (5) self-justification.

The therapist asked why Harry could not also be insecure or wrong. Harry remarked, smiling, that he was predominantly the type of person who sought security. Becoming more animated, he went on to say, "Gee, now I'm really interested, but I'm afraid that any minute now you'll say that our time is up."

Harry could talk to the therapist 24 hours a day; if they could be together all the time, the therapist would satisfy him very much. To the therapist's rejoinder that he was not supposed to satisfy Harry, the boy replied, "You are doing a good job not to satisfy me." (Psychological mirroring, used to induce frustration and increase tolerance to frustration.)

The therapist pointed out that one has to learn to take frustration in life, and that therapy was helpful because it enabled a person to adjust himself to frustrating situations. Harry expressed awareness of the fact; he knew that it wasn't good to live in fantasy. Then he added, "But in the meantime it's me who suffers. It's horrible to think that our time will soon be up."

When he then asked how much longer he would have to come, the therapist asked Harry what he would think about having to come for the rest of his life. In that case, Harry replied, therapy would not be worth the effort was putting into it. If he had to do that, it would also prove that he wasn't a worth-while person and that the bad things he used to think about himself were true.

When Harry repeated his question and was told that he might have to come for the rest of his life, he smiled and said he didn't believe it. But he really was not interested in finding out about that. What he really wanted was the chance to discuss how he would feel if he imagined either that he would have to come for the rest of his life, or only for a limited time. To come for the rest of his life would mean that he would never be independent, would never marry. To come for a limited time would mean that he would be independent and stand on his own feet. Harry then said that the length of time and the matter of whether he would be dependent or independent didn't really concern him. The important thing was that he should get the opportunity to investigate with the therapist those problems about himself. Now that he had discussed them, he expressed surprise that the question of how long he would have to continue coming seemed so much less urgent. (Increased tolerance to impulses.)

Interview 154. Harry was becoming more confident but "in the back of his mind," he sometimes wondered how long this self-confidence would last. He used to feel tense and fearful when he had to speak up; now he speaks to people freely because he is no longer mad at them, and no longer feels that they are mad at him.

Interview 161. Harry remarked that he used to be secretive with people, and regretted that he had been brought up to be that way. Now, though, it was good to know the contrast of speaking freely. He used to hold back thoughts from the therapist while asking himself whether it would "pay off" to disclose them. Now, he was willing to put everything that went on in his mind into words, even if this did not always "pay off."

Interview 166. One's difficulties in life can be traced to the fact that one does not feel liked; this gives a person a mixed-up feeling, he observed, and makes him feel that he has no right to have bad, abnormal, or antisocial thoughts. If a person feels liked, on the other hand, he will speak up to people and talk freely about himself to a therapist.

Interview 167. He tried to think the way the therapist did, Harry said, because he felt safer when there were no differences between them. Actually, though, there were stability and instability, certainty and uncertainty, in the world, and one could accept all of them. Instead of taking over the feelings of other people, it would be better for him to follow his own. And if he felt his own feelings first, it would be easier to understand what other people were feeling.

When she first referred him for treatment, Harry's mother felt that he might have to be institutionalized. She has recently expressed satisfaction over her son's improvement. His schoolwork is excellent; he has friends; and he belongs to social clubs. Except for occasional situations when he is under stress, he no longer speaks in a low monotone. He can be direct and outspoken. His general bearing suggests increased self-confidence as well as greater interest in the world around him.

Harry is now 16. He occasionally visits girls, but feels that he ought to be more comfortable and relaxed in their presence than he is able to be at this time. He thinks that he should go on with his treatment, in order to gain further understanding of himself.

MASTERING PATHOLOGICAL NARCISSISM

The case material would seem to indicate that the narcissistic child, with the good offices of the psychotherapist, can utilize his wishes, fears, and projections as a springboard from which to plunge into further therapeutic investigations which will reinforce the narcissistic ego. After the therapist has revealed himself to the child as an individual who is both rational and irrational, perfect and imperfect, constructive as well as destructive and self-destructive, the child comes to accept the wide range of his own emotions as part and parcel of human existence.

To achieve his purpose, the therapist may find it necessary at times to make a presentation—by "acting out" or talking out, at the right moment and with proper understanding—of the repudiated, imperfect, or "crazy" ego structure of the narcissistic child. The latter, when helped to externalize the "imperfect" element of his personality, is able to reap the benefit of therapeutic investigation.

Instead of remaining helplessly locked in struggle with forces that he can neither inspect nor combat—his own impulses—the child emerges to find in the therapist a person whom he can see before him, whom he can battle with, whom he can also love. Hate and love, externalized according to a deliberate plan, may be directed toward another person in a wholesome and reciprocal fashion after it has become possible for the narcissistic child to acknowledge, as part of his ego, all of the pre-ego impulses he had formerly been shut out. These impulses can then be channelized and discharged in socially acceptable ways.

Pathological narcissism—an excessive amount of self-viewing, self-preoccupation, autistic activity, and fantasy—appears to be a defense against the acting out of preoedipal and oedipal strivings, especially in their destructive aspects. It is vital that the schizophrenic child have enough control of those destructive impulses to be able to feel, think, and express some of them, initially in fantasy material, and later verbally with appropriate affect. Such control is made possible by adequate insulation, or a good protective barrier; in its absence, an attempt is made to achieve insulation through pathological narcissism. It is found, however, that this inadequate barrier can be discarded when the child's ego is reinforced by the presence of an understanding therapist. By mirroring the child's contact functioning, the therapist enables the child to play out, to feel, and eventually to verbalize his desturctive impulses. This has the effect of increasing his tolerance to frustration.

Pathological narcissism serves to guard the schizophrenic child against undesirable stimulation from others. Because of his inadequate protective barrier, he is faced with two dangers: (1) that such improper stimulation may create a continual state of instinctual tension, with concomitant states of pain, anxiety, and terror; (2) that loss of control over his impulses will be destructive to others or to himself, or to both in varying degrees. The continually rising state of instinctual tension makes it more and more desirable that impulses be released in behavior. Narcissistic activity, a positive factor in that situation, serves to produce carefully controlled stimulation and discharge of activity, both directed toward the self. Whatever disequilibrium may be present is thus primarily the result of the child's own activity and, while endangering himself, will be a protective factor in his relations with other persons.

A therapist who responds to the child or. y in the manner indicated by the child's own contact functioning presents stimuli that are carefully controlled by the child and which, consequently, tend to reduce the amount of narcissistic activity to which he will resort (Fenichel, 1945b). The therapist provides the stimuli in the exact proportions and sequence needed to build up the child's protective barrier. As the need for pathological narcissism decreases, the ego's narcissistic energy may be used for the appropriate expression of the child's own healthy impulsive attitudes toward people. The experiencing of a relationship with a therapist who provides the narcissistic supplies required to build up the insulating barrier eliminates the necessity of utilizing pathological narcissism in a process of defense against destructive impulses. The therapist has performed the service of reinforcing the child's ego in the area where reinforcement was essential for proper contact functioning. That is, to assert himself sufficiently to obtain what he needs from others.

It should be borne in mind, of course, that careful psychological reflection of the contact functioning of the child is only one of many desirable psychological methods that may be employed in helping the pathologically narcissistic child master his unhealthy behavior patterns and develop in the direction of emotional maturity.

Precautionary Considerations

Psychological reflection needs to be used cautiously in dealing with the aggressive impulses of the pathologically narcissistic child who requires ego reinforcement. The therapist needs also to guard against providing narcissistic supplies in a manner not properly conducive to ego reinforcement (Wexler, 1953). Any apparent attempt on his part to further a treatment relationship through anger, goading, reassurance, emotional support, and like manifestations, or by disclosing understanding of the meaning of the patient's material at an inappropriate stage of treatment, may have the effect of further disrupting the insulating barrier of the extremely narcissistic child. Such disruption might lead to heightened narcissism and the further development of a psychosis. For these reasons, we do not recommend indiscriminate use of the method, despite its effectiveness when it is cautiously employed by an understanding, goal-directed therapist.

TESTING OF SOCIAL INSTITUTIONS

We have observed that a child is generally the first member of a highly narcissistic family to be referred to our agency for treatment. The show-me attitude of the parents would appear to be the following: If you can cure the child, then you may be able to help us, for we are the main problem. But we won't admit it unless you can demonstrate that the child can be cured and we can be cured.

The treatment of the child often serves, therefore, as a test of the agency's ability to handle the emotional problems of the family concerned. As soon as the central figure in the test case shows positive signs of improvement, it is a normal occurrence for other members of his family to introduce themselves and apply for emotional therapy. The mother is frequently the first to appear, but the father or any other siblings in the family group may precede or follow her.

Parents, educators, caseworkers, and therapists who deal with individuals suffering from pathological narcissism must exercise the utmost care to ensure that their methods of dealing with such individuals will not further disrupt their insulation barrier, but will serve to strengthen it. Ingenuity should be applied particularly to developing techniques for strengthening this protective barrier in narcissistic children. A child who has been assisted in establishing an adequate insulation barrier then feels free and secure enough to express his own creative personality. When he has thus acquired the potential for functioning in a socially desirable manner, he does not have to be pressed into socializing with other children, and engaging in healthful activities. The child whose protective barrier is functioning efficiently feels and acts on socially beneficial urges.

17

Problems in Differentiation

The identification of schizophrenia as a childhood illness, with dynamic manifestations, diagnostic criteria, and therapeutic indications distinguishable from those of adult schizophrenic reactions, did not actually get under way until mid-century. A few cases were reported in the literature of 1929 and 1933. Compared with 54 items concerning dementia praecox in childhood, which appeared from 1936 to 1946, the technical literature from 1946 to 1956 contained 515 items related to the broad field of childhood schizophrenia and related disorders. Only 2 of the 54 earlier reports (4 per cent) dealt with therapy, and by therapy is meant chemotherapy—the use of metrazol; there was no report at all on the use of psychotherapy. In the following decade, 190 of the total of 515 items (40 per cent) were therapeutically oriented, and 90 of these 190 items were psychotherapeutically oriented (Ekstein, Bryant, and Friedman, 1958).

Schizophrenic reactions are loosely related disorders replacing the formerly recognized disease entity of dementia praecox, and they comprise a wide range of disturbances. Among these are the simple, the hebephrenic, catatonic, paranoid, schizo-affective, acute undifferentiated, chronic undifferentiated, residual, and childhood types. All are vaguely described in the 1952 diagnostic manual of the American Psychiatric Association as "marked by a strong tendency to retreat from reality, by emotional disharmony, unpredictable disturbances in the stream of thought, by regressive behavior, and in some, by a tendency to 'deterioration' " (p. 26). These schizophrenic reactions may or may not be of a psychotic nature.

Since descriptions of the various symptom pictures in adults dominated the literature for many years, it is relatively simple for the psychiatrist to make a diagnosis of schizophrenic reactions of one type or another in the person who has achieved at least physiological maturity.

RECOGNITION OF ADULT SCHIZOPHRENIA

When the clinician perceives a strangeness about the adult facing him, he quickly begins to explore the possibility that he is observing some type of schizophrenic reaction. The patient will generally seem withdrawn and will exhibit an emotional flatness and lack of drive. His affect will also be inappropriate, his thought processes confused, and in one or more respects his behavior will seem incongruous or even bizarre. If he is suffering from simple schizophrenia, he will convey the impression of a general slowing down in his physiological functioning, sometimes to an extreme degree. If he hallucinates, one may associate this with the catatonic, hebephrenic, or paranoid form of the disease. If this is actually present, the adult will also show some marked defect of ego functioning, such as stereotyping, posturing, disorientation as to time and place, and a pathological degree of self-preoccupation matched by his reluctance to associate with other people.

In establishing a diagnosis of schizophrenia, one takes into consideration many different factors, and the more of these factors one has knowledge of, the easier it becomes to reach the clinical diagnosis. These include such functions of the patient as his general performance and behavior in his life situation, any disturbances of control, relationships to others, thinking, memory, learning, perception, reality testing, etc. It is in the early stages of the disease, when one is most likely to lack information on these aspects of functioning, that the principal mistakes in diagnosis occur. Estimates of incorrect diagnosis reportedly range from 16 to 50 per cent, and appear to indicate that women are more frequently misdiagnosed than men. The most common mistakes reported are to categorize the illness as one of anxiety reaction, hysterical and phobic reaction, a manic-depressive or depressive reaction, a neurasthenia, or a psychopathic personality (Weiner, 1958).

The study of diagnostic criteria for the establishment of schizophrenia in the patient who has not reached adulthood leads us into a much more uncharted area than when we are dealing with the disease phenomena in the older patient. Least ground has been broken in the study of schizophrenia in adolescents. Let us approach it through the territory of childhood schizophrenia.

Why should we do this? Because, in the same way as adolescence is the meeting ground of childhood and adulthood, adolescent schizophrenia is the meeting ground of childhood schizophrenia and adult schizophrenia. To recognize the picture of adolescent schizophrenia, one has to know the childhood and adult pictures of the disorder, as well as those of adolescent psychosis and adolescence itself.

CLINICAL PICTURES OF CHILDHOOD SCHIZOPHRENIA

Although a great deal of nosologic confusion still exists and a tendency to overdiagnosis is still noted, much has been done recently to facilitate the development of diagnostic criteria for the schizophrenic reactions of childhood. Most helpful in this respect have been the clinical pictures delineated by Lauretta Bender, Leo Kanner, and Margaret Mahler—that is, Kanner's concept of early infantile autism, Bender's investigations of childhood schizophrenia, and Mahler's hypothesis about symbiotic psychosis.

According to Bender, childhood schizophrenia "involves a maturational lag at the embryonic level characterized by a primitive plasticity in all areas from which subsequent behavior develops" (1956, p. 499).

Eisenberg and Kanner (1956) regard extreme self-isolation and obsessive insistence on sameness as the primary diagnostic criteria in early infantile autism. These lead to derivative characteristics such as mutism or abnormalities in language development, unusual apathy, and failure of the autistic child to respond to the approach of people, rage reactions over attempts to alter his mechanical way of living, interest in spinning objects, and tendencies to relate to things rather than to people and to part-objects rather than to whole objects.

The conjoining of innate and experiential factors produces the clinical picture of this syndrome, Kanner has concluded. Early infantile autism is basically determined, in his opinion, by the child's own psychological structure, resulting from inherent factors combined with the dynamics of child-parent relationship.

Mahler (1949) classifies symbiotic psychosis into three groups of symptoms. The primary group includes panic reactions brought on by extreme organismic distress; alternating and unpredictable outbursts of violently destructive behavior and apparently pleasurable excitement; symptoms indicative of the fusion of the self with the nonself leading to a confusion between inner and outer reality; lack of differentiation between animate and inanimate reality marked by a tendency to devitalize the animate world; attachments to adults; and conspicuous evidence of dereistic thinking and feeling, and dereistic actions. Psychotic defense mechanisms representing attempts at self-integration comprise the group of secondary symptoms, and defenses akin to neurotic mechanisms constitute the third group.

Mahler sharply differentiates this condition from autistic psychosis. She traces symbiotic psychosis back to pathological vicissitudes of the normal symbiotic period of infantile development. As a result, the brittle ego of the child broke down and fragmented in the process of leaving the mother outside the omnipotent orbit of the self (Mahler and Gosliner, 1955).

In addition to the difficulty of diagnosing childhood schizophrenia, numerous general difficulties in diagnosing psychotic illness in children have long been recognized. One is caused by the unreliability of the histories given by parents. Even the fully objective and detached observer may have trouble detecting emotional illness in a child, because of the fluidity of a symptom complex in a psyche whose capacities and tendencies have not yet completely emerged. Moreover, the severity and significance of sudden changes in disposition and behavior are difficult to diagnose in the relative absence of adequate criteria for differentiating normal from deviant aspects of maturation in this period. The early behavioristic reports of schizophrenic children tended to obscure one important differentiating factor between adult and childhood schizophrenia. This is the fact that the child's symptoms have a special meaning in relation to his developmental and maturational age level.

From a pathognomic point of view, the concept of fluctuating ego states is a major diagnostic feature in all types of childhood schizophrenia (Ekstein and Wallerstein, 1954). Marked and frequent fluctuations in the ego states of many schizophrenic children under intensive clinical observation led to Ekstein's hypothesis that there were similarly fluctuating ego states in the children in response to the stimulation and reactions emanating from their relationship with the significant mothering figure. Ego regression alternating with progression characterized the functioning of the extremely sensitive and fluid ego organization of schizophrenic children. In their regressed state, they produced markedly oral fantasies with such underlying themes as fear of separation, abandonment, or bodily disintegration and distortion of body image. Fantasies of giants devouring their victims, and primitive outbursts of rage were also characteristic. These fluctuating ego states are especially marked in adolescence.

The multiple symptoms and paradoxical picture of acceleration alternating with retardation of development have led to various other theories. Bender's concept of the plasticity underlying the schizophrenic manifestations has already been mentioned. There is Hartmann's (1953) concept of dedifferentiation—that a reversal of the normal course of ego differentiation takes place. Bergman and Escalona (1949) conceptualize a precocious ego undergoing fragmentation in the course of stressful development and experience. Erikson (1950) presents an interesting concept of interference with the psychoembryological schedule of ego functions.

DIFFERENTIAL DIAGNOSIS IN ADOLESCENCE

Concepts such as these often prove helpful to the clinician who has to make a difficult differential diagnosis in the case of a child. When he is dealing with an adolescent, however, he has few such accepted guideposts. In comparison with the now abundant literature on schizophrenia in adult life and in childhood, he does not find many directional signals to facilitate his entrance into the territory of adolescent schizophrenia. To compound his difficulties, what he would have to regard as an extreme manifestation of psychiatric disorder in the adult is apt to be no more than a normal phenomenon of development in the adolescent.

The nature of the difficulties confronting the diagnostician is suggested by the following quotation. As an exercise in differential diagnosis, the passage is cited before identifying the author or the subject discussed. Mention is made of the latter's

anxieties, the height of elation or depth of [his] despair, the quickly rising enthusiasms, the utter hopelessness, the burning—or at other times sterile—intellectual and philosophical preoccupations, the yearning for freedom, the sense of loneliness, the feeling of oppression by the parents, the impotent rages of active hates directed against the adult world, the erotic crushes—whether homosexually or heterosexually directed—the suicidal fantasies, etc.

Yes, this is adolescence as it appears to Anna Freud (1958, p. 260). She goes on to say that adolescence is

by definition an interruption of peaceful growth . . . The adolescent manifestations come close to symptom formation of the neurotic, psychotic or dissocial order and merge almost imperceptibly into borderline states, initial, frustrated or fully fledged forms of almost all the mental illnesses. . . . (p. 267) Such fluctuations between extreme opposites would be deemed highly abnormal at any other time of life. At this time they may signify no more than that an adult structure of personality takes a long time to emerge, that the ego of the individual in question does not cease to experiment and is in no hurry to close down on possibilities (pp. 275-276).

All of this adds up to the idea that an adolescent may temporarily appear like a psychotic and *not* be psychotic. On the other hand, this picture may actually reflect the beginning of a psychosis.

Memory Romances

Another concept I have found helpful in understanding adolescence was suggested to me by a passage in the paper (1906) in which Freud modifies his earlier views on the significance of adult memories of sexual seduction during childhood by parents or older children. Freud points out that recollections of this nature, which could not be corroborated, probably represented fantasies of seduction, most of them occurring during puberty. These fantasies are referred to in the definitive translation of the paper as "imaginary memories" (1906, p. 274), but in the *Collected Papers*, where I first read the paper, I encountered the more picturesque translation, "memory romances" (Vol. I, p. 277).

Memory romance is a term that beautifully characterizes the period of adolescence. I have the impression that adolescents are less dependent than either the child or the adult on external objects for emotional gratification; perhaps this is because adolescence is a pinnacle where one may enjoy striking new glimpses of the panorama of childhood and also stargaze at will into the future.

Though life has to be lived forward, it can only be understood backward. The Danish philosopher Kierkegaard made that statement a century before we entered the era of dynamic psychiatry. Some adolescents seem to be less interested in living forward than in understanding backward. As gonadal and other physiological changes of puberty (such as rapid growth, the reawakening of pregenital impulses, and stimulation toward genital dominance) begin to affect the adolescent's psyche and heighten his sexuality, he seems to derive much satisfaction from going back in memory to the family romance of the oedipal period and reliving it in a way that will restore to him some of his infantile sense of omnipotence. Elaborating on his memory traces of the family romance, he spins it out endlessly into the richly embroidered romantic fantasies of adolescence. There is a line in a play by James Barrie to the effect that God gave us our memories so that we might have roses in December, and adolescence is the December of childhood.

Emotional Hunger

Certainly, adolescence is a time of great emotional yearning. The adolescent has a great hunger for the approval of his family, the acceptance of his peers, and popularity with those of the other sex. He needs favorable recognition for his performance at home and in school, on the athletic field, and in social situations. When such emotional gratification is not forthcoming, however, the adolescent appears to have a greater facility than either the child or the adult to derive from fantasy life the satisfactions which his real life denies to him. Within reasonable limits, romancing with oneself provides some desirable relief amid the too brief satisfactions and stormy vicissitudes which the process of being socialized may bring. Loving oneself is at least the beginning of a lifelong romance, as Oscar Wilde pointed out.

An adolescent's great emotional hunger is not invariably due to an absence of gratification in his life. The hunger may reflect primarily some inability to absorb and assimilate emotional satisfactions which actually are available to him. Hypersensitivity, tendencies to overreact to certain stimuli will make it difficult for him to tolerate the company of other people, let alone to obtain the normal quota of satisfaction from associating with them. In that case an adolescent will tend to spend much time alone or with a relatively constant, nonstimulating figure—a twin image. Or he may withdraw into a life of fantasy, of memory romancing. In extreme cases he will attempt to deny the existence of the ungratifying outside world and search for nirvana in an all-inclusive psyche, an ego device which Silverberg (1947) calls the schizoid maneuver.

The fact that the adolescent is able to derive a great deal of gratification from his self-preoccupations may help to explain why schizophrenic breakdown is less likely to occur in early adolescence than in its later years, or in early adult life. Sooner or later, though, he may reach the point where his fantasies become too pallid, too worked out to give him further gratification. As he moves toward that point, more and more frustration-aggression develops, and what the adolescent does about this is a crucial factor. When the satisfaction value of the memory-romance period has been exhausted, the adolescent has two choices. The first is to establish new sources of satisfaction in external objects. That is the choice of the healthy adolescent. The other alternative is to run the risk of ego breakdown from lack of emotional satisfaction and from the psycho-toxic effects of his undischarged frustration-aggression.

Persistence of Symptom Picture

Since it is about as difficult to prove the presence of a schizophrenic reaction in an adolescent as it is easy to suspect it, how does one differentiate between typical adolescent defenses and true schizophrenic reactions? There is virtually complete agreement that the persistence of a symptom picture is one of the most reliable differentiating criteria. Periods of seclusiveness, despondency, and sexual or philosophical preoccupations do not last long or lead to a break with reality if the ego is an essentially healthy one which is undergoing one of the transient states of fragmentation normally associated with adolescence. If such behavior is prolonged, however, one must investigate the possibility of a schizophrenic reaction. Pervasiveness as well as the persistence of the symptom picture, and also its apparent inexplicability, are other diagnostic criteria mentioned by Weiner (1958). And one must also examine the history for previous disturbances of personality and relationship in the patient and his family.

Self-Attacking Tendency

How the adolescent handles his frustration-aggression seems to me to be an equally important key to the differential diagnosis. If he demonstrates a strong tendency to attack his own ego rather than his object, this is an important indicator of his vulnerability to a schizophrenic reaction.

The first male adolescent schizophrenic I treated was a youth who used to go through a bizarre routine of singing, dancing, wisecracking, and showing off whenever he was in the presence of girls. Since he did not enjoy their company, this clowning helped him to keep his distance and to get some of the admiration which he craved. He could always admire himself, at least, even if he didn't impress the girls. Needless to say, they would try to avoid a repeat performance.

Quantitative Differences

The differences between behavior such as this and behavior within the range of normality for adolescence are primarily quantitative. Adolescents traditionally go through stages when they are overstimulated by the presence of the other sex, and act accordingly. A normal youth who was treated by a girl as the patient I have just discussed was treated might make some other attempts to get her to know him better and to like him, but, after a few weeks at most, he would write her off as "lousy" and find himself another girl. Occasionally, my patient would describe a girl who shunned him as "rotten," but it was always himself whom he treated as "rotten." He consistently attributed any failure in social relationships to some defect in himself, and the defect was his own feeling. He clung to the idea that if he just made a great effort to change his feeling, the girl would eventually come to like him. In other words, he had a strong tendency to attack the feeling rather than the external object causing it. When such attitudes last for many months, or even years, they are certainly to be regarded as deviant.

The great need for admiration and attention—for emotional gratification—drives the adolescent schizophrenic to extreme lengths in his attempts to make a favorable impression on those around him. Fully anticipating rejection, he tries to forestall it with demonstrations of his right to a place in the sun. Hence, boasting and bragging, verging on outright mendacity, are prominent aspects of the schizophrenic reaction in adolescence. To one adolescent I treated, talking about the inventions he was completing seemed to be a good way to attract attention. But inventing was no more than an idea of his; if this bid for admiration failed, he would seek satisfaction in fantasy and masturbation. In his attempts to gain popularity, the adolescent schizophrenic may unwittingly disclose more than he intended.

Sometimes, he shows an eagerness to share the benefits of his own inexperience with others. For example, a schizophrenic youth in basic training boasted to his squad mates that he and his girl friend "used to take a shower together every Friday night."

"And then what did you do?" Jimmy was asked by his expectant buddies.

He could only flatly reply, "Why we dried each other" (Erikson and Marlowe, 1959, p. 108).

THRESHOLD FOR SCHIZOPHRENIC REACTION

Adolescence itself does not precipitate schizophrenic reactions. What it does, rather, is to expose young people to special pressures—social pressures and those attendant upon rapid growth and personality changes—which typically lead to fleeting states of ego fragmentation. These accumulating states of episodic ego fragmentation may serve as the straw that breaks the camel's back; that is, they may suffice, in certain situations, to push a fragile and defectively functioning ego over the threshold into the schizophrenic reaction.

How hard or how easy it is for this to happen depends on how high or low the threshold is. I have the impression that each person has a highly specific threshold for the development of a schizophrenic reaction. This is determined by three interacting factors—heredity, constitution, and life experience. A person's upbringing, and especially what he learned to do in his childhood with his frustration-aggression, is a crucial aspect of the life experience. If, in the absence of adequate emotional nourishment, he discharges his frustration-aggression into his body, for example, he will develop some psychosomatic complaint. If he discharges frustration-aggression into his superego, this will produce depression. It is when he does not discharge the frustration-aggression, but tends to mobilize it and let it accumulate in an emotionally impoverished ego, that the optimal condition exists for the development of a schizophrenic reaction. It is primarily the corrosive effects of frustration-aggression mobilized in the stunted ego, rather than the lack of emotional gratification, which breaks down the ego—interrupts or reverses the growth process—and, if severe enough, produces the schizophrenic reaction.

Securing the release of frustration-aggression is, therefore, the crucial element in the treatment of the schizophrenic patient. This requires a favorable environment, and, of course, a certain degree of emotional nourishment, but I have found that the emotional gratification itself is a secondary factor in the treatment process.

The following case is presented in considerable detail to elucidate the various diagnostic possibilities it presents.

Case Report*

A 13-year-old white Jewish girl had four admissions to Kings County Hospital Psychiatric Service. The first, at 6½ years of age, was occasioned by the implication of the father by the mother in the sexual seduction of the child. She was diagnosed as a child with "multiple symptoms consistent with the diagnosis of conduct disturbance with neurotic traits." Stealing, temper tantrums, and exhibitionism were manifest, as well as phobias, nightmares, and somatic complaints. The child's illness was considered to be reactive to the mother. Although therapy for the mother and child was recommended, there was little likelihood that the mother would change.

The second admission was at the age of 8 years. The mother alleged two sexual episodes: "The man next door took out his penis and took out dirty pictures." She also said that the child was molested at school. The child also was said to have put iodine in her urine, telling her mother it was bloody. The mother brought the child to the hospital "to get her away from sex." She remained for three weeks.

In the report on her mental-status examination, it is stated: "On coming to the interview, she stood back and appeared to be reticent before any rapport could be obtained. A period of time had to go by in which she played with a mechanical toy and was flattered for her proficiency. Her speech was clear and to the point, and her emotional responses were appropriate. Some depression appears to be present. Innate intelligence is at least average, and the child can read and do arithmetic. Later on in the interview, she told me she did not like me, and said that I reminded her of someone else, but she refused to elaborate. She guessed that I knew about the incident of an elderly neighbor exposing himself, and she feels that this is the reason why she is now in the hospital. She stated that this was a horrible experience and that she has had no interest in such things. She stated that her mother had told her that the devil comes into men at night and they do terrible things; that men are made to do bad things. She stated that if she went out into an alley a man would be likely to put something around her neck and strangle her. No thinking disturbance is

*Prepared for presentation by Dr. Lewis Ward, under the supervision of Dr. Henry I. Schneer.

elicited. The hallucinatorylike phenomena that were present 1½ years ago, she now feels, were her own imagination and occurred mostly at night. With help, she recalled these phenomena in which some woman-like creature supposedly was telling her that her mother was to leave her, and after she would hit at it, 'things would come out.' "

On the ward she was initially depressed, refused to eat for several days, and created conflict between her mother and the hospital with tales of un-just treatment. She engaged in provocative sexual play which she tried to deny and for which she tried to place responsibility on others. An attempt to suggest placement was refused by the parents who, though loathsome to each other, agreed to remain together and took the child out against advice. At that time it was felt that her diagnosis included adjustment re-action of childhood, conduct disturbance, sexual behavior, neurotic traits, and anxiety reaction.

The third admission occurred at age 13 when a finding of neglect was made and the patient was remanded to the hospital. In the years since the last hospitalization, the patient was achieving at school, but the home situation steadily deteriorated. The mother was in group therapy at Kings County Hospital for 1½ years, and the patient was seen in group also for about two years. During this period the therapist felt that the patient was in need of residential treatment, and she began to press for it. Receiving no cooperation from the parents, she eventually instituted neglect pro-ceedings against the parents in November, 1958.

The mother related incidents preceding this event that illustrate the friction between mother and daughter. The mother said that she would tear up the patient's books if she was up late. The patient began to use vulgar language to the mother and father, who, the mother stated, was still attempting to sexualize his relationship with the patient. The patient inquired of her mother about her sex life. She refused to let her clothes touch her mother's in the closet. She "got too clean," and the mother "couldn't take it." At the same time the father was coming in at midnight, waking up the patient, and offering her pizza and ice cream. In October, 1958, during an argument, the patient was burned on the left arm by an iron which, the mother states, she was handing over while saying, "If you want it, here it is."

A note on the patient's mental status follows: She related very poorly, alternately laughed and cried, and productions in general were coherent but irrelevant, rambling, and marked by loosened association. No halluc-inatory experiences were elicited. Content was concerned with her feeling that she has first to experience suffering before she can experience plea-sure. She became frightened that she would be examined by a man, be-cause this would make her ashamed. She talked of her parents as being unfit, later changing this. She asked that I not interview her now becuase later she might be sorry for what she said today. She plans not to eat, and only to take medication by force so as to punish herself. When asked why, she responds that she has pride and that it was humiliating to be dragged in by ambulance. She pleads not to be sent to a ward with girls her own age but at first cannot tell me why, then says that she really feels much superior to those other tramps and bums. She plans to be a psychiatrist because she has such great sympathy and understanding for other patients. Mood was apprehensive, tearful, and depressed as well as agitated. Affect was labile and not appropriate to expressed ideation.

Psychological tests supported a diagnosis of schizophrenia, and the patient was placed in the custody of her aunt to await placement. She was taken to her mother's house, against the express order of the court, for two weeks before going to the treatment center where the hunger strike and this history started.

Her fourth and present admission to Kings County Hospital was occasioned by a hunger strike which started immediately after she arrived at a residential treatment center to which she had been sent by the Children's court. She was making an apparently good adjustment except for the refusal to eat. This was not complete, however, since she occasionally took liquids and sweets. She lost 8 pounds in seven days, and early signs of dehydration were noted during physical examination. She refused to be examined by a female physician, and refused to submit a urine specimen. Concomitantly, according to the center's psychiatric report, she developed "marked introspection and seemingly compulsive thinking with regard to her spirit." She constantly referred to the various transformations which the spirit goes through in leaving the body. She visualized various positions over one's body best suited for the spirit both entering and leaving the body. There was more than veiled intimation of the relatedness of suicide to the spirit leaving the body.

Some similar distortion of thought processes was also seen during the psychiatric interview when, knowing that if she did not eat and went to Kings County Hospital she would be forcibly fed, she said, "It is terrible to think that they will forcibly save my physical body but will leave my spirit die." For some minutes after making this statement, although she knew that she would have a psychiatrist seeing her at the hospital, she seemed markedly agitated and depressed. She also showed marked preoccupation with illness and with what cancer does in terms of the nature of the disease and the nature of the crippling symptoms.

Of her hunger strike at the treatment center, she said that she had taken this action in order "to get even with the court" because the court couldn't make her do what she didn't want to do. But then she ambiguously added, "I didn't begin to eat at the center because I had another reason for going on a hunger strike but I forgot that reason. I don't think I'll ever remember the reason and so I won't ever be able to stop being on a hunger strike." At another time, she said that she wanted to be on the adult ward at Kings County Hospital because "you meet so many interesting and intelligent people."

On the hospital ward, her predominant mood was an anxious depression. She spoke in superlatives of her stay at the treatment center and how she loved her social worker. She said that her urgency to be on the adult ward was to avoid being seen by a girl whom she knew at school. She denied hallucinations, and no delusional system was elicited. She made a vigorous denial that her starvation was suicidal.

The patient's family constellation consisted of her two parents and a half-brother from her mother's previous marriage. The mother, 46 years old, has been recognized by several observers to be "aggressive, demanding, impulsive, provocative, functioning on a borderline level." The father, 61, appeared passive, withdrawn, and given to periodic outbursts of anger. The mother came from Russia at the age of 6. She failed several times in grade school. She said she was "cross-eyed and didn't have glasses." She blamed her mother for poverty, deceit, and promiscuity. Her older brother had a "nervous breakdown" at 57 and was given electric shock treatment. She had three marriages previous to her present one. She has accused her present husband of molesting her son as well as her daughter.

The mother supplied few facts relative to the patient's early life. She felt that the child was born out of sin because she did not marry the father until the child was 6 years old. Difficulty with feeding or toilet training was not recalled. The half brother, who was 14 years older, diapered the patient and even "baby sat" on his honeymoon.

DISCUSSION

Diagnostic Possibilities

In making the differential diagnosis of the 13-year-old subject of our case report, I considered it necessary to investigate five diagnostic possibilities before reaching a decision. The four disorders which were suggested more or less strongly by various symptom pictures, but which were successively ruled out, were anorexia nervosa, reactive depression, reactive psychosis, and affective depression.

Anorexia nervosa. The hunger strike this girl started after the court ordered her placement in Pleasantville obviously suggested the presence of anorexia nervosa, a condition found almost exclusively in adolescent girls and young women. This condition begins most typically as an attempt to lose weight through dieting, and will have been preceded by demonstrations of hysterical tendencies and, perhaps, minor obsessional traits. A family history of mental illness or psychopathy is also associated with the condition, and its course will be marked by amenorrhea or other menstrual disturbance, which in some cases predate the most obvious signs of lack of appetite. Peculiar reactions to food and disturbances in bowel functioning are other signs mentioned by Sandor Lorand (1946). In a case of anorexia nervosa, reported by Lorand, the patient lost her appetite and taste for food—indeed, had a definite disgust for it. Other symptoms were dryness of the mouth, gagging at the sight of food, and periodic vomiting, all of which were aggravated if she forced herself to eat. Depression was also present.

Some of the information in our own case report would sustain a diagnosis of anorexia nervosa. Besides the refusal to eat, I am alluding to the family history of mental illness and such constitutional factors as the earlier demonstration of hysterical tendencies and minor obsessional traits. The girl may also have suffered from amenorrhea, though no mention of menstrual disturbance is made in the case report itself. What seemed to me to differentiate this case most strongly from anorexia nervosa, however, were the indications that the girl's refusal to eat was motivated by her consciously revengeful and self-punishing attitude rather than by any peculiar reactions to food or loss of appetite. Unconscious fantasies of self-punishment and revenge are not necessarily inconsistent with a diagnosis of anorexia nervosa, but these would not be so open and pervasive—not the important elements they are in this case. This seemed to me to be the most important differentiation.

There was, moreover, no conclusive evidence about an actual loss of appetite in connection with the hunger strike. The case report notes that the girl occasionally took liquids and sweets at the residential treatment center; her awareness that she would be forcibly fed on her return to the hospital if she went on with the hunger strike is also noted. Be that as it may, anorexia nervosa would not have accounted for the evidence of deep-seated personality disturbance, the thought disorder, and the pervasive nature of the oral regression, and it was quickly dismissed from the list of diagnostic possibilities.

Reactive depression. There was also some superficial evidence that would permit one to entertain a diagnosis of reactive depression—that is, a neurotic reaction precipitated by the immediate trauma of separation from parents and home when this girl was sent to the residential center. Against such a finding, however, it was necessary to weigh the long history of disturbance before the court ordered her transfer to Pleasantville. In view of the longitudinal nature of the girl's disturbance, the environmental and family background, and the diagnostic picture at the time of her three preceding admissions to the hospital, depression over the situational change could hardly be regarded as the major factor of the illness. Somewhat more diffuse depressive episodes had been reported in the earlier history of the illness.

Rather than stressing a fixed depressive reaction to the separation from home and parents, the case material suggests somewhat ambivalent reactions to the stay at the center and at the hospital. At the center, the girl insisted that she wanted to go back to the hospital; back at the hospital, she is reported to have spoken "in superlatives about her recent stay at Pleasantville." From this point of view, in addition to the fact that a reactive depression would not have accounted for the intensity of the thought disorder, her condition was differentiated from reactive depression.

Reactive psychosis. Another possibility to be considered was that this girl was suffering from a reactive psychosis of adolescence. Warren and Cameron (1950) reported six such cases, involving youngsters from the ages of 11 to 16; they had transient episodes of psychosis which proved very difficult to diagnose. All were model children who yearned for parental approval and were fearful of criticism. In each case the psychotic episodes had an acute onset and were followed by much anxiety, insomnia, and pervasive night fears or concern about the parents' welfare. In this condition, from which the patients just referred to eventually recovered, the early history of development and maturation as well as the adjustment to the home were favorable, and the thought disorder was relatively insignificant. Reactive psychosis would not begin to explain the multiple and sustained symptoms in this case, let alone the developmental history, the progressive nature of this girl's disorder, and the disturbances in her thinking and affect, so that it was not seriously entertained as a diagnostic possibility.

Affective psychosis. Affective psychosis is a label which is sometimes attached to patients whose refusal of food cannot be fully accounted for by inertia of their digestive and metabolic systems and seems, rather, to be just one aspect of a more generalized depression. Patients suffering from a depression of this nature may give evidence of strong convictions about their own unworthiness and may express suicidal wishes. In a case of affective psychosis, however, one does not see obvious reactions to what is going on around the patient, as were observed in this girl; her overreactiveness to the environment and extremely labile affect would argue against a finding of affective psychosis. For this and other reasons, her disturbance has to be differentiated from affective psychosis.

Schizophrenic reaction. There were present, on the other hand, many factors which would justify a diagnosis of schizophrenia and certainly no presenting symptoms that would preclude such a label. Let us consider, for example, the most obvious presenting symptom—the hunger strike. Early in the century, Bleuler pointed out that "in no other mental disease does complete refusal of food occur so frequently and so persistently as in schizophrenia" (1911, p. 162). Anyone who has observed schizophrenics in the hospital wards knows how difficult it is to get some of them to eat. The necessity of tube feeding some of these patients, especially if they are in a catatonic condition, is recognized.

I have already called attention to an equally persuasive sign—the tendency of the emotionally malnourished ego, overwhelmed by the weight of undischarged frustration aggression, to punish itself instead of the object. This kind of self-punishing attitude, the essence of the schizophrenic reaction, is strongly manifested by our patient. The statement that she couldn't remember why she went on the hunger strike, so she has to stay on it, is typical schizophrenic thinking.

Her family history, her own developmental history, and the many traumatic events in her life which are detailed in the case report are familiar precipitants of such an illness. We find prominently represented the three elements which Weiner (1958) found to be precipitating factors in many cases of schizophrenia: domestic discord, the frustration or deprivation of emotional needs, and emotional alienation or separation from others.

Is this case of schizophrenic reaction new in onset, or has it existed since childhood? This question, because of its significance for the prognosis and the form of treatment required, ought always to be answered when one diagnoses schizophrenia in an adolescent or preadolescent. The longer the history of this condition, the longer the treatment required.

In my opinion, this girl's schizophrenic tendency has been developing since childhood and was accentuated by normal pubertal changes and the traumatic environmental factors reported in the case. The three which seem most significant to me are the apparent sexual seduction by the father, the quarrels with her mother, and the group therapist's intervention which the girl probably experienced as an act of rejection, since it led to her forcibly removal from her home and her therapy group. I want to make it clear that this assessment of the therapist's move is based entirely on the case report, and might not be borne out by direct and more detailed information. Hence, it is mentioned tentatively, in the absence of more complete, and possibly contradictory, information. In any event, there were the two other precipitating circumstances involving the parents. The seductive behavior of the father and the quarrels with the mother were also experienced by the patient in her childhood; but the cumulative effect of these relationships and the girl's greater vulnerability in the period of pubertal change could explain the frank outbreak of the disease at this time.

The case report strongly suggests that this girl's parents are both potentially schizophrenic individuals, and reference is made to the mental breakdown of an uncle at the age of 57. But, whether or not there is any hereditary disposition for the disease in the family, the patient's developmental history supports the hypothesis that there was an experiential transmission of the disease. One is tempted to speculate whether she was already a schizophrenic at the ages of 6½ and 8, on her first two admissions to the hospital.

In that connection, it will be noted that she was then diagnosed as having a conduct disturbance with neurotic traits. Various forms of overt aggressive behavior, which probably protected her against a schizophrenic reaction, are mentioned in the first diagnostic report. The diagnosis made on her second admission refers to "anxiety reaction," to reticent behavior, evidence of depression, and to the difficulty of establishing rapport with the child. When she was 8, she spoke about devils taking possession of men's bodies at night and making them do terrible things, an idea of splitting implanted by her mother. There is no information about how the girl was handling her frustration-aggression during this period, but, from the first two diagnostic reports, her condition certainly appeared to be one of neurosis.

On the third admission, however, a tendency to bottle up her frustration-aggression was evident. Now, on the fourth admission, following her return from Pleasantville, she is well bottled up, and the growth process appears to have been interrupted by the undischarged aggression. Now she gives evidence of oral regression and of typical schizophrenic thinking and attitudes.

Prognosis. One sign that this girl may not be irreversibly ill is that she does well at school. Given the kind of treatment that is needed to get her growth process under way again, the prognosis would, in my opinion, be favorable. The vital factors in her treatment would be small doses of emotional nourishment and the development of outlets for the release of frustration-aggression. What made her schizophrenic was not emotional hunger but the psychological consequences of that hunger, which allowed the frustration-aggression to be mobilized and, thus, to damage the ego.

The presence of such aggression, and in some cases an unconscious fear of it, gives some therapists the feeling that they cannot get into contact with a schizophrenic patient. In my experience, however, the patterning of adequate outlets for the release of aggression in feelings and language, combined with an ego-strengthening process of emotional nourishment, will generally lead to the resolution of the schizophrenic reaction (Chapter 16). Then the sole vestige of the illness is the scarring caused by the healing of the defective ego.

The prognosis in a case does have some significance for diagnosis. The fact that the diagnostician has sound reason to anticipate that a patient will deteriorate without therapeutic intervention does tend to confirm a diagnosis of schizophrenia. I would vigorously challenge the notion, however, that such a diagnosis is disproved if the patient responds favorably to treatment, or that it is confirmed if he fails to respond. Failure to respond merely indicates either that the therapy itself was inadequate or that the environmental situation was so unfavorable that it prevented or seriously interfered with therapeutic progress. My impression is that the schizophrenic reaction can be resolved if the patient secures the kind of object he needs, a setting conducive to emotional reactiveness, and the right kind of retraining and life experiences.

18

Object-Oriented Approaches

APPLICATION IN ADOLESCENT CASES

Contradictory opinions on the response of adolescents to analytic psychotherapy, and even doubts about their "true analyzability," are reported. The literature also stresses the paradoxical nature of the differential diagnosis of psychopathology and the transitory emotional upheavals experienced on the developmental level between puberty and adulthood. The rite of passage from late childhood to early maturity is characteristically associated with the use of defenses that are often difficult to differentiate from florid symptoms.

The inherently problematic nature of the transition is suggested in formulations that link symptomatology with normality—for example, Anthony's reference to the "normal depression of adolescence" (1970) or Sugar's theory of "normal adolescent mourning" (1968)—and by Anna Freud's identification of the absence of turmoil at this stage of life as an indication for treatment (1958).

Undoubtedly, psychic reactions to the attainment of physical genitality and the reproductive capacity, coupled with the reawakening of pregenital impulses, confront the practitioner with problems he does not have to contend with in the treatment of children or adults. The process of detachment from parents and experimental approaches to new love objects are reflected in rapid fluctuations in the transference relationship. The adolescent's wish to be helped is typically stronger than that of the child. So too is the mental

*Based on a paper presented at the Conference on the Adolescent in Family and Group Psychotherapy, American Society for Adolescent Psychiatry, New Orleans, January 1971. For an earlier version of that paper, see Spotnitz, 1972.

suffering of the adolescent, and in many cases he mobilizes powerful and subtle defenses against experiencing it.

CAUSES OF FAILURE

Another reason why psychotherapy in this critical phase is complex is that the patient is part child, part adult. To treat him as a child is to insult the adult components of his personality; to treat him as an adult entails some degree of failure in meeting the maturational needs of the child. Even though the general principles of psychotherapy with adults are applicable, each adolescent presents a special problem and has to be understood as an individual.

The large number of failures reported in the treatment of adolescents has built up the impression that they are unsuitable candidates for analytic therapy. The major reason for these failures, however, appears to be the tendency to expose these patients to undue pressure for progress. Usually they respond favorably when their vulnerability to the development of high states of tension is borne in mind and they are permitted to proceed at their own pace.

In supervisory work I find that therapists who report difficulties in working with adolescents have usually been trying to get them to *do something*. Typically, the psychotherapist beginning to work with this age group demonstrates, in one way or another, great interest in helping the patient improve his immediate functioning. That attitude often leads to disappointment because, as the adolescent begins to "unwind," his behavior tends to worsen.

When, on the other hand, he gets the message that the therapist is more interested in dealing with the obstacles to cooperative communication that the patient encounters in the relationship than in helping him change his behavior, the case proceeds more smoothly. Given permission to be himself, the adolescent eventually becomes interested in understanding what is going on in the relationship; at that point, he begins to make noticeable improvement.

By and large, the approaches that are most effective with teen-agers are less stimulating than those employed with children. The therapist needs to maintain an exploratory attitude and use interpretation sparingly. He intervenes only when the patient asks for information or when a communication is clearly required to preserve the relationship.

AGE-SPECIFIC RESISTANCES

In operational terms, the main problem in treatment of the adolescent is the failure of the customary interpretive procedures to resolve his resistances to communicating freely. He presents special patterns of resistance that do not respond directly to understanding and insight because they are upheld by powerful maturational needs. At a time when the ego is in a state of rapid flux, explanations of immature functioning are traumatizing and at times have a paralyzing effect. Interpretations mobilize a great deal of aggression, thus stimulating aggressive acting out.

Responsiveness to Indirect Approach

But when these age-specific resistances are dealt with *indirectly*—that is, by facilitating the resolution of the maturational needs that maintain the patterns and by helping the patient verbalize his aggressive impulses— movement in the direction of personality maturation gets under way. The indirect approach may resolve the resistance only temporarily, but it reduces his need to resist. In short, interventions are based on recognition of the patient's resistances and defenses as attempts to control aggression or as the product of maturational needs (Spotnitz, 1969a).

That recognition dictates a more time-consuming approach to resistance than exerting analytic pressure on the patient to overcome it; however, the more regressed the patient, the greater his need for the indirect approach when he enters treatment. Eventually he is able to profit from insight and asks for it; interpretations of his defective functioning are then helpful rather than ego-damaging.

NEED FOR SPECIFICITY

Adolescents with mild oedipal-type disturbances are responsive to individual, group, or family treatment. Those with severe psychoneuroses, behavior disorders, character disturbances, schizophrenia, and other preoedipal conditions are not equally responsive to these modes of treatment. Combined treatment is indicated in some of these cases. In order to achieve the degree of specificity required to resolve these problems, careful evaluation of each patient is essential. The therapeutic approaches discussed in this chapter are generally applicable to adolescents with deteriorating conditions.

Choice of Treatment Setting

Individual psychotherapy is indicated for the emotionally overcharged adolescent, who requires little stimulation from the environment. The therapist facilitates the maintenance of a calm treatment climate by timing and formulating his communications to reflect the patient's "contact functioning"—that is, his conscious and unconscious attempts to elicit a response—and by intervening primarily to deal with questions posed by the patient. When contact functioning is employed as a guide to interventions, the patient is, in a sense, provided with emotional feeding on a self-demand schedule. For example, a highly excitable teen-ager for whom this approach has been very reassuring is an obese youth who developed a pattern of overeating to relieve his anxieties. Assisted to talk without interruption in a kindly but cool climate, he becomes less anxious and is able to moderate his food intake.

Obviously it is easier to provide communication on a self-demand basis in the one-to-one relationship than in a group. Some adolescents, however, cannot tolerate a situation in which there is little communication from the therapist. This problem may arise in the individual psychotherapy of an emotionally hungry, narcissistic adolescent with strongly regressive tendencies. Although he may later require individual treatment to deal with his more intimate problems, he is usually more immediately responsive to a group therapeutic experience.

Unlike the schizophrenic adult, who tolerates long periods of silence and minimal communication from the therapist, the schizophrenic adolescent tends to either regress or become explosive in a non-stimulating treatment climate. In the absence of immediate emotional communication, he may activate primitive defenses or his condition may become static. It is easier to provide him with the additional emotional stimulation he needs in the group setting, where other patients confront him with different reactions simultaneously. He can be placed in an adult group but one composed exclusively of adolescents is preferable when the need for friends—peer reinforcement—is primary.*

Group treatment is also indicated for the drug-prone teen-ager. Such drugs as marihuana and the amphetamines appear to neutralize the influence of the therapist as transference object. In relatively benign cases, the patient may give up the drug after a series of individual sessions, but serious addictions are more responsive to a group experience with peers who do not take drugs.

In either treatment setting, the severely disturbed adolescent often activates patterns of resistance that are intractible to the customary therapeutic procedures. The pathologically narcissistic patient becomes preoccupied with his defective ego functioning and tends to control his aggressivity by withdrawing psychologically from the treatment situation (Spotnitz, 1969a). A special approach to this resistance is often required to counter his introspective tendencies.

---

*Therapeutic management in adolescent group therapy is the subject of an excellent report by Leslie Rosenthal (1971).

OBJECT-ORIENTED QUESTIONING

Retrospectively I recognize that the orientation discussed here was suggested by my early experience with patients beginning treatment in a psychotic state. They were usually incapable of talking, let alone talking about themselves in an emotionally meaningful way. Given some assistance, however, they were able to talk about inconsequential subjects, and this proved to be a relatively efficient way of establishing contact with them. They were therefore asked many questions about numerous aspects of their daily routine—for example, what they had eaten for breakfast, how they had slept, whether hospital attendants or family members were giving them proper care, and the like. As long as the labile phase lasted, they were asked only about aspects of their current activities that would have been perceived by an ever-present and observant companion. Such questioning helped to bring them out of psychosis relatively quickly, and also proved effective in the early stage of treatment when they tended to relapse.

In working with patients in post-psychotic conditions, it is sometimes necessary to help them talk first about external events and other impersonal matters. For example, a man who had expressed eagerness to address himself to his emotional problems during the initial interview, and was otherwise able to comply with the requirements for office treatment, was unable to express himself coherently during his first year of psychotherapy. Although the last of several courses of electroshock therapy he had undergone had been completed some years earlier, he still betrayed their mentally disorganizing effects. When he was too troubled or confused by his jumbled ideas to answer questions, I talked to him about external realities such as current events, books, and the theater. After the psychic obstacles to the formation of a cooperative treatment relationship were thus gradually resolved, he was able to apply himself effectively to his emotional problems.

Special Values

Object-oriented investigations have special values for the severely disturbed adolescent, particularly one in late adolescence. He is hypersensitive to direct probing into his problems. If one tries to induce him to talk about them, he often feels that he is being put "on the spot." He then becomes more anxious and feels more resentful about whatever is bothering him at the moment. On the other hand, interventions that do not focus on his deficiencies and difficulties are very reassuring to him. Moreover, when his attention is repeatedly directed to other persons or emotionally insignificant aspects of his daily experience, he becomes curious about why his problems are not being investigated. One adolescent said, "I don't see how it's going to help me to talk about football and the war in Vietnam." Another patient became annoyed after being questioned at length about a schoolmate he had met at the movies that week. He asked, "Why should I waste time telling you his name and what he looks like? Why don't we talk about the things that are troubling *me*?" That was the first time resentful feelings were verbalized by these patients, and the first time they demonstrated the ability to communicate freely.

Group treatment is by its very nature an object-oriented experience. Each participant has just a fraction of the time to talk about himself and drifts naturally in the direction of involvement with his co-patients. Since group processes militate against prolonged self-preoccupation, the group therapist is not called on to do much talking to check it. In those relatively rare situations when an intervention is indicated for that purpose, however, there are various ways he may intervene to draw the patient's attention to his present objects. The therapist may, for example, ask someone else a question or "go around" the group inviting each of its members to verbalize his impressions of another person's functioning or problems. Consequently, it is more difficult for a patient to remain self-absorbed and uncommunicative in the group.

The deteriorating patient. From time to time, one encounters an adolescent who is totally unresponsive to treatment. Neither individual nor group therapy checks his deterioration, and he continues to indulge in behavior that is dangerous to himself or others. In such a case, it may be necessary to investigate the responsiveness of that patient to an experimental procedure.

CONSTRUCTIVE EMOTIONAL INTERCHANGE

One such procedure, evolving from the object-oriented approach, is conceptualized as constructive emotional interchange. Although its application is not limited to adolescents, their age-specific vulnerability to self-disclosure and defensively hostile attitudes to adults make them ideal candidates for the procedure. It has been effectively employed with several adolescents, and its application is discussed here in the context of that age group.

Use of Family Setting

Constructive emotional interchange emancipates the adolescent from the role of patient. The implementation of this operational principle is highly specific, depending on the adolescent's underlying problem, current reality situation, and reactions to the other participants in the interchanges—usually both parents and, when appropriate, his siblings. But regardless of the overt content of these verbal exchanges, the adolescent is *not* asked to talk about himself and attention is directed away from his intrapsychic problems. He is helped, instead, to deal with the problems he creates for the family. The therapist structures the sessions to bring into strong focus the reactions of the participating family members to the adolescent's behavior and to help him deal with these reactions.

Despite the participation of family members in constructive emotional interchange, I do not regard it as a variant of family therapy. "In its strictest sense," Ackerman stated, "the term family therapy refers to a systematic method of psychotherapeutic intervention, designed to alleviate the multiple, interlocking emotional disorders of a family group" (1972, p. 440). Constructive emotional interchange is based on a principle that can be broadly applied in both family and group psychotherapy, but the specific application discussed here is not family therapy in the sense of the strict definition just mentioned. The family members who participate are not diagnosed; their problems are not investigated or discussed, except tangentially and in terms of their effect on the adolescent. The presence of family members is essentially a therapeutic tool for treating the adolescent indirectly, that is, in terms of their current reactions to his behavior. Constructive emotional interchange is therefore viewed as treatment of the young patient in the family setting.

Even if one equates the use of the family setting with family therapy,* it is questionable strategy to refer to the procedure discussed here as such when one tries to secure the participation of the adolescent's family in constructive emotional interchange. In some instances, the parents cooperate only because they think their presence will eventually be helpful to the patient; they are motivated solely by their anxieties about his condition, anxieties that effectively mask whatever problems they may have. They do not regard themselves as candidates for psychotherapy and they do not want it; the notion that the family is to be dealt with as a treatment unit would give rise to insurmountable resistances in these parents. On the other hand, the formulation that constructive emotional interchange would help another member of the family evokes a favorable response in the parent, as in the adolescent.

Procedural Factors

---

*Where family therapy begins and where it ends has yet to be determined. It is still, in Ackerman's words, an "extremely fuzzy" field. In one of his later communications on the subject (1972), which includes the strict definition of family therapy quoted above, he more loosely identifies as family therapy ten diverse psychotherapeutic procedures that entail the participation of the family. Constructive emotional interchange could be covered under a few of these broader definitions.

PROCEDURAL FACTORS

Constructive emotional interchange with the adolescent is predicated on two observations:

1. Whereas the dominant problem of the adult patient relates in some way to his adjustment to society, that of the adolescent is contending with his inner urges. At this stage of life, the magnification of feelings, especially those that he does not want to experience, may cause excruciating suffering. The task of dealing with his endogenous impulses is compounded when he is bombarded with feelings of people around him that he cannot assimilate healthfully. A refusal to experience these feelings may drive him into deviant forms of behavior. And the tendency of the adolescent to act on feelings is exacerbated by the new dangers that beset mankind today—the technological threats to human survival as well as the new sexual freedom, the overstimulating effects of information on violent acts, and the greater availability of drugs, knives, and guns.

2. Parents are highly significant objects to the adolescent. For many years I have been impressed with the need demonstrated by young people recovering from severe emotional disturbance to influence their parents, help them release feelings, and to change them. After verbalizing such wishes, they often add, "If only I knew how!" The need to reach out and help a parent is strong in the adolescent who was exposed to a great deal of positive feeling but so inconsistently or inappropriately communicated that the desire to reciprocate it was stifled.

Patient as Helper

In constructive emotional interchange, the customary policy of enlisting the cooperation of parents on behalf of the patient is reversed. The young patient is cast in the role of helper. The therapist so manages the interviews that the adolescent takes the initiative in helping his parents deal with their feelings. He assists them in verbalizing their feelings for him with awareness and regard for his reactions to their communications.

This procedure is tailored to provide the emotional ingredients needed by the emotional hungry adolescent with narcissistic problems. The greater his desire to help his parents—whether or not he is conscious of this desire—the more responsive he is to the procedure.

Participation of Family Members

Parents who qualify for constructive emotional interchange are those who have appropriate feelings for the patient and can be educated to control their expression. Usually they have exposed him to feelings at the wrong time or in the wrong dosage, or they may have lacked the verbal facility to communicate these feelings effectively. The participants may also include siblings of the patient, provided that they too demonstrate strong interest in committing themselves to mutually helpful communication.

The Agreement

The parents must eventually agree not to be verbally assaultive or to humiliate the patient in the sessions. Untimely or overly strong expressions of feelings may overwhelm the adolescent and may stimulate suicidal impulses in him, as well as rebelliousness, accidents, and behavior destructive to others.

The treatment is structured to provide a non-damaging and mutually beneficial experience. The value for the parents is that, in the process of being trained to provide the kind of psychological food the patient needs at the tempo he can digest it, they secure his help in controlling their communications. The patient benefits in four ways: (1) functioning in the role of helper boosts his ego; (2) the feelings he helps his parents verbalize appropriately serve to meet his maturational needs; (3) in working on their problems, he discovers problems of his own that he would not otherwise be willing to recognize as such, and is thus able to accept help for himself; and (4) the feelings of love that are communicated to him by the parents serve to greatly increase his self-esteem.

The clinical material that follows illustrates the use of this object-oriented, investigative procedure in the treatment of an adolescent who had not benefited from individual psychotherapy or hospitalization.

Clinical Illustration

A bright, somewhat moody boy, Paul had been a model student and seemed to be developing favorably until the age of 12. The emergence of his emotional problems coincided with the departure of his older sister from home. He then became the focus of his parents' attention, at times receiving more of it than he wanted and at other times being neglected because of their active social life. Both individually and as a team, they handled him inconsistently.

His mother, an attractive and energetic woman, was inclined to act on impulse. When her impetuous behavior got her into difficulties, she would become frightened and try to reverse herself. Paul reacted to her occasional attempts to discipline him by locking himself in his room or storming out of the house. The father, a successful manufacturer, was given to fits of anger.

He oscillated between entrusting Paul's mother with full responsibility for his upbringing and suddenly stripping her of that responsibility when Paul defied her. Though the parents were happy together in many respects, their son's behavior had become a source of much friction between them.

Paul began individual psychotherapy at the age of 12, when his emotional problems became apparent, but he continued to deteriorate. Although he expressed willingness to cooperate at the start, he soon manifested strong resistances to communicating, withholding important information from the psychiatrist. The individual treatment was terminated when the patient attempted suicide—a panic reaction to threats from boys with whom he was taking drugs. He was 14 years old at that time.

Paul was hospitalized after the suicide attempt, which culminated a series of failures at school and growing strife at home. He had been truanting from school to go on drug trips with cronies whom his parents regarded as undesirable companions, and was taking money from his father's wallet to pay for pep pills and pot. When reprimanded for his failing grades, Paul threatened to drop out of school. Although he was a talented violinist, he had already dropped his music studies. But hospitalization also failed to check his deterioration. Within a year he was transferred from one hospital to another and discharged from the second, after several months, as an incurable schizophrenic.

At this juncture, his parents, greatly alarmed, again consulted the psychiatrist. A series of family interviews was proposed, with the idea that the son would take a leading role in investigating and helping his parents deal with their anxieties about him. Confronted with the alternative of a third hospitalization—this time in a state mental institution—Paul expressed willingness to cooperate to that extent, though he had no confidence that the interviews would be of any help to him.

During these sessions, conducted weekly, rules of conduct that were calculated to allay parental alarm were enunciated as needed. Each deviation from the rules was studied and, when the reason for it was understood, attempts were made to correct it. For example, the parents agreed to restrain their expressions of anger since these tended to heighten the general state of alarm. When the father exploded in rage, Paul told him to "cool it" and explored with him the reason for the outburst. Over a period of months, it was discovered that the father's explosive anger was connected with fears provoked by Paul's frequent misunderstanding of his directions, and by the mother's evident anxieties. Another rule, occasionally implemented to help her control her impulsivity, was that she was not to talk until Paul gave her permission to do so. His feeling of being stifled by her gradually diminished, and he developed a sense of power and control in their relations.

One of the major sources of disturbance in the family was each member's misperception of the feelings of the others. Paul, for instance, interpreted his mother's nagging at him to stop smoking pot as an attempt on her part to impose her will and deprive him of freedom of action; he did not recognize that she was reacting to intense fears that he was damaging himself. Similarly, his father's anxieties and explosions of anger induced feelings in Paul that his father was trying to humiliate him, and he characteristically reacted to these feelings by avoiding contact with his father. Initially the youth insisted that, if his parents had the right to drink Scotch, he was entitled to take drugs. The parents viewed this attitude as a deliberate defiance of their wishes, whereas the son saw himself as being merely self-assertive. Their strong pressure for compliance, he said, obliged him to make an effort to assert himself. Furthermore, he contended that he had a right to do anything that would make life more tolerable for him. In view of his manifest difficulties, their highly emotional reactions irritated him and he considered them to be inappropriate.

In the sessions, Paul demonstrated growing interest in helping his mother resolve her tendency to behave impulsively when frightened. He became more and more aware of the connection between his own behavior and her acute anxiety; eventually, he realized that she nagged him because she was anxious. He verbalized feelings of sympathy for her plight and then, after the interviews had been conducted for several months, moved forward from sympathy to action. He announced that he would give up drugs in order to relieve her. He said he did not really need drugs.

This dramatic change of attitude greatly reassured his mother and transformed the emotional climate of the home. Equally notable were the steady improvement in Paul's performance at school and his more discriminating choice of companions. He formed new friendships with boys his parents approved of. Before the end of the first year of interviews, he had resumed his music lessons and was contemplating a career as a violinist under the aegis of an outstanding teacher.

DISCUSSION

Paul's Impressions

When Paul agreed to help his parents deal with their feelings, he did not believe the psychiatrist's statement that helping them in this way might help him too. Nothing else had worked for him, so the "crazy" psychiatrist had dreamed up that scheme. But Paul agreed to participate to avoid being rehospitalized.

When the interchanges with his parents heated up, he began to study the effects of their feelings on him and his feelings on them. It slowly became clear to him that what he had personally experienced as verbal attacks were, from their point of view, the involuntary responses of concerned parents who really loved him and had trouble dealing with the fears he stirred up in them by getting himself into precarious situations. Increasing recognition of their affection and concern stimulated strong desires in Paul to allay their anxieties.

Later he came to recognize that these anxieties were also affecting his parents' behavior toward him outside the interviews and accounted for many of the restraints they imposed on him. It dawned on Paul that his difficulties in getting along with them waxed and waned somewhat with their emotional states. He experienced them as reasonable, even benevolent, when they were relatively free from anxiety, whereas he felt that he was being crushed by iron hands when they were wrought up about his behavior, as they frequently were.

Paul also discovered that their anxieties about him were adversely affecting their own relationship. They spoke despairingly at times of having failed with him. Occasionally one parent blamed the other for Paul's problems. His mother verbalized feelings of worthlessness that induced intense rage in his father. In the course of investigating the emotional influence that each parent was exerting on the other and on himself, Paul experienced wishes to relieve their suffering and to disengage himself from patterns of behavior that were triggering conflict between them. These wishes grew stronger as the interviews continued.

After he understood the marital stress in which he was a factor and became aware of his power to alleviate it, Paul wanted to help his parents deal with emotional difficulties in which he was not directly implicated. He became interested in knowing them as people—not just as parents. He questioned his father about business matters, his mother about community causes to which she devoted much time. Their openness to his opinions and suggestions regarding their pursuits, especially their responsiveness in terms of behavior, made it seem more natural to him that they should guide him in managing his own life.

Mutual Improvements

As Paul began to feel more at ease about venturing into areas of his parents' lives beyond the home with suggestions for changes, his rebellious defiance gave way to cooperative self-assertiveness. His ability to help his parents master the expression of their feelings and to allay their anxieties gave him some confidence that he could play a favorable role in their lives. The parents, by meeting Paul's maturational need for expressions of warm positive feelings—love, admiration, and respect—made it easier for him to improve his behavior.

Reorganization of Memories

Any new experience has the potential for reorganizing existing memories. New and ego-syntonic emotional interchanges with parents during the labile period of adolescence may thus reduce the tension connected with the developmental task of separation-individuation. Sugar, focusing on one aspect of that task, has theorized that depressive moods and various other affective manifestations reflect those processes by which the adolescent mourns for "the parents from whom he is separating—the lost infantile objects" (1968, p. 268). Adaptation to that loss appears to be facilitated for the adolescent who, in the process of giving up his infantile objects, gains objects that are both similar and dissimilar—like the lost objects in that they are his real parents, and different in that they now function to meet his present maturational needs.

Mourning reactions did not figure prominently in the case of Paul; they were overshadowed by his strivings to rid himself of the influence of the old objects. But he was glad to accept his parents' influence as new and different objects. Given the opportunity to explore their current reactions to him, the youth acquired impressions that were more favorable than his past impressions of them. The new impressions were a powerful therapeutic force.

The remarkable improvement observed in Paul's functioning at the end of the first year of constructive emotional interchange greatly surprised him. He did not concede that this could have resulted from the change in his parents' behavior. After two years of constructive emotional interchange, it was easier for him to recognize that mutual helpfulness and understanding can produce significant alterations in all of the participants. During the third year, a subject that had frequently come up for discussion was the mother's inability to lose weight, as recommended by her physician. After she had volunteered information about her lack of progress, Paul helped her select a diet that she would be most likely to adhere to and then helped her to do so. In a situation when she was reporting progress, he interrupted her to direct attention to a problem he was becoming aware of in his social life. He reported various difficulties in forming good relationships with girls, and added, "Do you know, I really think now that I need some treatment myself."

But this statement reflected an attempt to escape from the family situation rather than a strong desire to accelerate his improvement. It is possible that Paul, now nearing his twenties, will develop a firm resolve to work on his fundamental problem in individual analytic psychotherapy. At the present time, however, he continues to meet with his parents.

Emotional Ingredients for Security

Constructive emotional interchange emerges as a by-product of controlling communication in the interviews in terms of its effects on the patient. Interventions are made primarily to influence the timing and dosage of expressions of feelings by members of the adolescent's family, so that the emotional ingredients that he wants and needs are verbalized in ways that make him feel more secure.

The therapist operates on the assumption that the adolescent who experiences certain types of communications from his parents as agreeable and other types as disagreeable will strive to alter the conditions that lead to the disagreeable emotional reactions. He does not see his own behavior as a problem; what he does recognize as the problem is his parents' behavior. He would like them to experience feelings that would enable them to relate to him in a consistently agreeable manner. In the sessions he becomes aware of their positive feelings for him and his own positive feelings for them. These feelings stimulate him to change his behavior.

Exchanges of positive feelings, combined with assistance in verbalizing them, help the adolescent deal with his conflicts in ways that make inner change possible. The process of learning to communicate with his parents in mutually agreeable ways becomes so rewarding, personally and socially, that he develops strong desires to preserve these gains. When constructive emotional interchange with highly significant objects becomes ego-syntonic, the patient really wants to work to resolve his own emotional problems.

The adolescent's willingness to help his parents deal with their feelings, and their reciprocal needs to help him and cooperate with him in his efforts to help them, are the fundamental prerequisites for this approach. The existence of these attitudes opens up the possibility of resolving one of the major obstacles to harmonious family relations—that is, the inability of its members to influence each other's feelings agreeably. Addressing itself consistently to this problem, constructive emotional interchange equips the therapist with a powerful instrument for improving the adolescent's functioning in the family milieu and also in his social relationships.

PART FOUR:

Group Psychotherapy

Seven chapters are devoted to scientific observations, clinical experience, specific issues, and appraisals of progress in the therapeutic use of the group setting.

Chapter 19 reports an early study of the phenomenology of the setting. After perceiving certain connections between the emotional currents that operated and the communications of the subjects of the investigation, it seemed important to determine the influence of these forces in arousing and resolving resistance to the therapeutic process. Findings that emerged from this related study are reported in Chapter 20.

Having gained the impression that certain types of resistance are more easily resolved in the shared treatment experience than in the individual relationship, I placed a borderline schizophrenic patient in the first group I treated. The results are discussed and illustrated in Chapter 21.

As it became clear that more could be accomplished through this modality than the alleviation of symptoms, it seemed important to clarify more significant goals to which the group therapeutic process might be oriented. A report on that subject is presented in Chapter 22. One finding discussed is the tendency of members of an effectively conducted group to strive for more ambitious goals as the treatment proceeds.

Chapters 23 and 24 discuss specific problems encountered in analytic group therapy. The concept of touch countertransference reflects the proliferation of innovative methods that began in the late 1960s.

The concluding chapter in this section presents a brief evaluation of the field from the vantage point of the 1970s.

19

Phenomenology of the Setting

A STUDY OF ADOLESCENT GIRLS

In the course of regular psychiatric consultations on the treatment of a group of adolescent girls, it became clear to me that certain emotional forces were influencing the group proceedings. The purpose of the present report is to indicate the nature of some of these forces and to show how they manifested themselves during the group sessions. The report considers the group as a unit,* and illustrates the emotional currents and countercurrents that operated as the therapy progressed.

THE GROUP

Presenting Complaints of Members

The group originally consisted of six girls, selected on the basis of mutual compatibility; that is, several outgoing and active young women were accepted for treatment with others who tended to behave appropriately but

*The results obtained by the individual members are not discussed here. The improvements achieved by one member of the group are the subject of a previous report by Betty Gabriel **et al.** (1947). Mrs. Gabriel, who conducted the group, recorded the material presented by the girls, as well as her own observations, which she made available to me. Her record of one of the therapeutic interviews is incorporated in the present report. Fruitful discussions with her assisted considerably in its preparation.

It is my pleasure too to acknowledge my indebtedness to Samuel R. Slavson, whose recognition of the need for a report of this nature stimulated me to write it.

were less active. Only two of the original six were still in the group at the end of about two years of therapy (95 sessions). In all, ten girls were treated during that period, generally not more than six at one time. The group met about once a week, with time out for summer vacations and holidays.

To facilitate understanding of the material, the complaints about the ten girls when they were referred to the treatment agency are specified, and they are identified by names that indicate when they were placed in the group and how long they remained.*

Ann was 15 years of age when she began group therapy. Referred by her mother because of feelings of inferiority and self-criticism, she appeared generally to be repressed. She was unable to make friends.

Belle, 15, had been referred by her mother at the age of 13½ years because of her inability to make friends, her tendency to hang around the house, be moody, mistrustful, cautious, and depressed.

Celia was referred by her father because she had been apprehended by the police for a runaway experience. She had been disobedient at home and difficult at school. She was 15 years old when she began group therapy.

Della was the only member of the group who did not receive individual therapy from Mrs. Betty Gabriel, who conducted the group. She had been referred to the Jewish Board of Guardians at the age of 12½ years, and began group therapy at the age of 17. The original complaints about her, by the visiting teacher who referred her, were that she laughed hysterically in the classroom; at home she had been irritable, antagonistic to her mother, and had used obscene language.

Ethel, 16 years of age when she began group therapy, was referred by her brother's psychiatric social worker. She complained of having difficulty in making friends and in sleeping at night.

Fay, 15 years old, was referred by her guidance teacher because she had been truanting from school and stayed out late at night.

Gertrude, 15 years of age, was referred by her school because of truancy. At home she had been disobedient, sloppy in her personal habits and had shown her mother a "big mouth." She had fears that God would punish her for her attitude toward her mother.

Hilda, aged 15 years, was referred by her mother because she had been abusive toward her family. Her mother complained that Hilda went around the house with a superior air and called her parents stupid and ignorant.

Ida, 16 years old, was referred by her mother because she felt herself to be

---

*This information is suggested by the first letter of the given name of each girl. Ann, Belle, Celia, Della, Ethel, and Fay were the original members of the group, and were treated as a unit for a period of one year (39 sessions). Ann and Belle remained throughout the two-year period; the other original members are listed in the order in which they dropped out of the group. The names of the other four girls are similarly coded to indicate the order in which they joined the group.

inferior. She did not go out much, was somewhat apathetic and was not making full use of her capacity. Clothes appeared to be her only interest.

Jill, aged 17 years, was referred by the visiting teacher because she was performing below her potential in school and had been unhappy at home.

Special Features

These girls constituted a highly specialized group in the sense that all but one of them were receiving individual and group therapy from the same therapist. Della was in individual psychotherapy with another psychiatric social worker.

The contacts of the girls with one another were not strictly limited to the group situation. They met on the outside, and also had social activities in the group. They ate together before the group meeting and, under exceptional circumstances, went to the theater together, and invited boy friends to a group party.

The girls selected what they wished to talk about. They were encouraged to engage in spontaneous exchanges of their life stories, ideas, and feelings. Meeting around a conference table, they spoke as they pleased to the whole group, usually one girl at a time. They had pencil and paper beside them and doddled if they wished to do so.

The therapist limited her verbal participation as much as possible.

PATTERNS OF EMOTIONAL EXPRESSION

In general, the material presented during the group interviews followed a certain consistent pattern throughout the therapy; that is, certain driving forces appeared to determine the course of the interviews and the type of material discussed. Initially, these forces seemed to be essentially of two types: forces that tended to bring the group together, and forces that tended to disrupt it or threatened to dissolve it. Later, it was recognized that the binding forces and the disruptive forces were the same—the basic needs of the girls. Essentially, these forces were emotional drives tending to provide each girl with the satisfactions of which she had been deprived by her life circumstances. The same forces could be both binding and disruptive to the group! What determined their binding or disruptive character was the relative stability of the group situation.

The function of the group was essentially to provide an arena for emotional expression and emotional understanding. As long as the developing emotional expressions and increasing understanding led in the direction of removing the obstacles to emotional gratification, the needs of the girls served to bind them to the group. But when the group became a growing source of frustration and failed to increase their ability to obtain emotional satisfaction, the same forces became disruptive and tended to break up the group.

Among the various emotional forces that operated during the course of the therapy, two constellations are focused on here. Their changing function as binding and disruptive forces, as the therapy progressed, was studied.

Let us first consider the constellation of forces represented in the desire to have sexual congress, become pregnant, give birth to a healthy, normal child, and bring up that child to become a healthy, normal adult. This constellation operated in the first interview and was more or less in evidence, in one form or other, throughout the therapy, giving expression to what all in the group agreed was a desirable goal.

What blocked them from the realization of that goal? And what blocked the gratification of impulses leading in that direction? The realization of these drives required a degree of physical and emotional maturity which the girls had not as yet attained. They were blocked then by another constellation of forces. They knew that, in order to have sexual congress in our society, to bear and raise a child in a satisfactory manner, certain physical and emotional requirements had to be met. They were unable to meet these requirements because of certain limitations: They were not old enough; they were not sufficiently aware of the dangers involved in solving these problems; and they were not sufficiently integrated to advance in the direction they wished to go. In short, their physical, emotional, and integrational inadequacies deterred them from the realization of their ultimate goal. As a result, they experienced varying degrees of tension, were subject to painful and anxious states, or developed symptoms of neurotic or behavior disorders.

How did the group therapeutic process mediate between the emotional drives of the girls and their individual inadequacies? In this critical situation, group therapeutic process intervened to help the girls become physically, emotionally, and integrationally adequate to operate in terms of their reproductive drives.

ILLUSTRATIVE MATERIAL

In presenting the material that follows, I propose to
(1) illustrate how the drives to have sexual pleasure, to marry, to conceive, and to raise children properly manifested themselves in the course of the group discussions. This emotional current is referred to as the *reproduction constellation;*
(2) provide evidence given by the girls of their physical, emotional, and

integrational inadequacies. These factors are referred to as the *inadequacy constellation*; and

(3) indicate how the girls assisted one another to overcome these inadequacies, how the reproduction constellation conflicted with the inadequacy constellation, how the group functioning served to resolve the inadequacy constellation, and how its resolution promoted individual integration.

Reproduction Constellation

From the beginning of the therapy with these adolescent girls, it could readily be seen that they were working in the direction of attaining the gratification associated with being good wives and good mothers to children who would develop in a healthy and socially useful way. The forces that were driving in this direction assumed various forms.

In the first interview, when the girls were just getting acquainted, they found subjects of mutual interest, namely, their attitudes toward dolls and dollhouses. They talked later about what was inside a doll. One of them had found it was just sawdust; she had been curious about what went on inside a baby, the makings of a real baby, and felt that having only a sawdust doll was a frustration not worthy of further interest. The question of proper care of children also came up, and each girl attempted to indicate what her personal problems were in taking care of herself. After taking a small step in the direction of self-care, the girls became interested in discussing legitimate and illegitimate ways of getting a man. The illegitimate course led to all sorts of dangers, which they pointed out to one another: the possibility of contracting venereal disease, social disapproval, conflicts with the law, and so forth.

In the process of getting a man, they were worried about how far to go at their present ages. Should they let themselves be petted by a man? Should they go out on double dates? Was there greater security in double dates than in one-couple dates? How would their parents feel if they associated with men? Could marriage be successful without love? Eventually, they speculated on whether a marriage entered into just for sexual gratification could lead to real love, which would make the marriage worthwhile.

Later, they delved into more intimate subjects: They spoke of the difference between male and female sexual organs, at first daring only to hint at it in a symbolical way. The girls felt that they should sublimate the drive toward a fusion of the genital organs—sexual intercourse.

Then they began to discuss their own genital experiences. Had there been sexual contacts with persons of the opposite sex, and what were the consequences? What should they do when in the company of a man, and when they felt sexually stimulated? They were worried about pregnancy. Illegitimate children frightened them; legitimate children were also frightening, because of the pains and dangers of childbirth and the new responsibilities it brought. Some felt that it might be better to avoid these dangers and limit themselves to gratification by masturbation. But masturbation had its hazards too; the hymen might be ruptured, and they might bleed. They recalled their initial menstrual periods and their fright and concern at that time. To have full self-respect, they must have intercourse with a man to whom they were married. And some were concerned about how a girl behaves with her first love.

If they were afraid of Jewish men, who often reminded them too much of their fathers, what were the problems connected with religious intermarriage? Was that a safer course to pursue? Would that not turn the home into a madhouse? Some felt that "the whole problem was one to despair the human soul." One girl said, "What is the use of it all? You are born, you grow up, you marry, you have a child, you die." Since death is inevitable, is any action necessary? Wouldn't it be nicer to retire into some state of sleep and return a hundred years from now and see where the whole thing was going? Sex could lead into grave dangers; there was the problem of rape, which all of them feared. There were the dangers of intercourse with father; insanity could be a consequence. On the other hand, life without sexual gratification was not worthwhile. However, men were such dangerous creatures; they might attack you and kill you. Women were also dangerous, they might kill you if you attempted to take their men away; even a mother might destroy her own daughter if she felt that threat.

As these subjects were explored, the girls gathered more courage from both theoretical discussions and discussions of the sex life of othe people. They became increasingly free in talking about their sexual fantasies and dreams. Gradually, with hesitant steps forward and backward, they also got around to describing their petting with men and their movement in the direction of sexual intercourse. They began to feel that they made a worthwhile appearance and might, in a legitimate way, meet men who actually found them attractive, but they still demonstrated tendencies to act quickly and enjoy sex illegitimately. If they did have children legitimately, what problems would they have with their children, what caused these problems, and how could they be corrected? There were discussions of parental attitudes toward children and the girls talked incessantly about doing a better job in bringing up their own children than their parents had done with them. They displayed growing interest in developing their own latent talents and furthering their own education, so that they could get better husbands and fathers for their children and become better wives and mothers.

After about two years of therapy, in the main, there had been definite movement from curiosity about children and how they are conceived to greater interest in producing and taking proper care of children.

Inadequacy Constellation

Some of the material presented above inevitably reflects the operation of the inadequacy constellation, as it inhibited the reproductive forces and led the girls into detours rather than toward the goal of the reproduction constellation.

In the early interviews, although the girls were interested in having children, they felt themselves to be inadequate to cope with these emotional drives. They had not been taking care of themselves properly; they had developed behavior-disorder symptoms and symptoms of neurosis. Since they were emotionally immature and needed to be taken care of themselves, they were in no position to take care of children of their own. Being afraid of where their own drives might lead them, they found it reassuring that their group associates had similar problems. They called attention to their own neglect, by themselves and by their families. They were afraid, too, of their own hostile feelings for one another, and for their parents; each girl was also afraid of her hostile feelings for herself.

Because their parents had been unsatisfactory, the girls did not want to settle into the life patterns of their parents. Should they act illegitimately? They were afraid of the social consequences and greater dangers that might ensue from illegitimate behavior. Their present lives were difficult enough; they found that they were inadequate to the demands of school and work; they tired easily. The girls denied the reality of many of their own desires since their fulfillment was felt to be impossible. They concealed their own defects from one another because they wanted to be liked and felt that nothing could be done to correct these defects.

They made dates with any man who came along, because they needed to feel wanted. They considered prostitution and having illegitimate children because it seemed unlikely that they would ever have legitimate sex relations and legitimate children. They tried to conceal their thoughts and feelings about sex and menstruation, which indicated to them that they were inadequate and defective human beings whom no one could love. They had to hide their deficiencies at school because they blamed only themselves for not being more successful.

They did not see the connection between emotional disorders and pathological functioning. The hatred they felt for one another and their jealousies proved to them that they were defective rather than being basically healthy human beings who were exposed to undue emotional deprivation in childhood. If they could not tolerate frustration in the group, they felt that this was a weakness to conceal, not one to be discussed, understood, and mastered.

They viewed life as too difficult for them, and insanity and death as escapes from dangers lurking around them. They felt unequal to defending themselves from attack or to repelling attempts at seduction that men might expose them to.

At first the girls felt that they, and they alone, were responsible for their personal inadequacies. Later they found similar inadequacies in the other girls and began to recognize that these had something to do with the type of background in which they had developed. They then became interested in revealing their inadequacies and finding out how to correct them. The girls became more and more aware that their relationships with their parents had contributed to their deficiencies, and that these were natural in view of their ages and difficulties in finding the sort of companions they wished and the male affection they craved.

It became increasingly clear to them how defective their parents really were. The girls recognized the areas in which their parents were most inadequate, and also their good qualities. After pointing to parental shortcomings that helped to account for their own, the girls became interested in correcting inadequacies in themselves. In the process of connecting some of their emotional difficulties with lack of parental affection, the girls became aware of their own affection for one another. They began to accept the inevitability of sibling rivalries, that it was natural for siblings to hate each other, and that it was not monstrous to have desires to kill them or destroy parents.

The girls gradually discovered that many of the inadequacies they dwelt on were not actual but were fancied, primarily on the basis of social disapproval. As they learned to tolerate the group disapproval, many inadequacies turned out to be assets; others tended to disappear as the girls were able to express their feelings more freely and developed more liking and understanding of one another.

They learned of the problems that parents have with each other and with their children. They came to understand that some parents preferred boys and others, girls; that some preferred infants to older children; and that there were times when parents did not want to have children. They recognized that the economic, social, and emotional inadequacies of parents have an important effect on their children. The significance of parents' feelings in terms of the present inadequacies of the members of the group was discerned.

The girls spoke with increasing freedom of tendencies toward incest in their own families, and came to understand the influence such problems had played in the development of their own anxieties about sex. They learned that the ages at which parents married was important for the child, that religious intermarriage might raise new problems, that parents could act like infants. The girls became aware that their own defenses served to protect them from emotional attack by other girls.

Other learning went on in the group sessions as they discussed the causes of suicidal impulses, French kissing, flight into homosexuality because of fear of heterosexuality, symptoms and anxiety caused by the repression of painful memories, theories of infantile sexuality, killing leading to pregnancy, what lack of respect for another person's privacy may do, and the need to fight for privacy.* The girls learned that they must lead their own lives and exert themselves to get what they desired out of life.

They mastered these principles on the basis of personal life experience and that of the other girls in the group. As they interpreted the meaning of these experiences to one another, they became impressed with their reality.

ANALYSIS OF ILLUSTRATIVE MATERIAL

The behavior of the girls in the group indicated that they were aware of the essential purpose of their being together, that by expressing their ideas and feelings they were to work in the direction of solving their own problems and mastering their individual inadequacies. This was made easier by their presence in a group. The fact that they were about the same age and had similar experiences seemed to give them a feeling of union and greater strength than they would ordinarily have had. Furthermore, they found that it was safe to talk about what they really felt in the group, and that they could expect more assistance than sabotage from one another.

After one girl spoke of her individual problems, the others brought up their own similar problems. Some had greater insight than others. Frequently the ventilation of problems also clarified them.

Throughout the therapy, each girl manifested a basic desire to be the center of attention and get group approval. To accomplish this, she found that she would have to share the group's attention and also take a certain amount of disapproval.

The reproduction constellation was introduced repeatedly in some form or other by different girls. It became clear to them that they had similar desires, that they were not isolated individuals battling a hostile world but a community with similar aspirations transcending their own desires, and that the gratification of their own desires was important not only to them as in-

*The topics are listed in the order in which they were brought up.

dividuals, but also to the others. The success of one made it more likely that the others would succeed.

It did not take them long to get some inkling of the fact that their individual defects were part of a basic problem characteristic of all mankind. As individuals, they had many inadequacies and had attempted at times to solve their conflicts in disadvantageous ways. The inadequacies of family life, and the problems of parents and siblings had influenced them and were reflected in them, but they could do something to resolve these problems by increased emotional understanding and emotional expression.

Some of the methods employed by the girls to assist one another during the development of therapeutic group process are delineated below.

The girls were ready to praise one another for whatever individual talents they possessed and sought to encourage the development of these talents. They exchanged ideas on how best to deal with troublesome situations that confronted them at that time or might develop in the future. They criticized extreme forms of behavior employed or discussed during the group sessions, thus fostering the development of more mature patterns. They encouraged exchanges of ideas and manifested desires to understand why they differed in modes of behavior, abilities, and tastes. Each girl was encouraged to verbalize her dissatisfactions in a cooperative spirit. They battled verbally in the sessions, rejecting unjustified criticism and ventilating hostile feelings. The recounting of dreams and fantasies was encouraged; and they attempted to interpret them and uncover the meaning of their fantasies. Whatever improvements occurred in the course of therapy were accepted as natural, and they stimulated one another to account for these changes. They gave thought to their own problems and analyzed themselves.

Illustrative session. As demonstrated by the record presented below, the girls were aware of their own inadequacies and were willing to admit and discuss them. The session began with such a discussion: They described their respective difficulties in getting the food they needed before the session. They were willing to cooperate to solve the problem. They went on to discuss their lack of boyfriends and how they attempted to get them, expressing approval or disapproval of some methods mentioned. Then they showed through their fantasies that they desired to go in the direction of the reproduction constellation of emotions. However, they were held in check by fears about the dangers to which they might be exposed. Men such as Nazis hated and might injure them.

They had unresolved oedipal problems and problems of sibling rivalry which they had been afraid to express openly and come to understand. Throughout the session, however, one could observe the basic trend of this whole series of therapeutic interviews, extending over a two-year period. In effect, the girls were saying, over and over again: I need care. Help me to take care of myself and to get what I want, a child. I want to help that child grow up and become a better person than myself, and to have more advantages.

RECORD OF GROUP SESSION*

This meeting took place on a beautiful springlike day, although it was rather cold.

In the order of their appearance, Della, Ann, Belle, Hilda, Fay, and Ethel were present.

When Ann came in, she apologized for her absence last week, stating that she had feared she would take cold and therefore stayed away. She was given some recognition for having been more regular in the past. As we sat around eating cheese and jelly sandwiches and having coffee, Ann told us about a recent adventure.

The girls expressed themselves as feeling that too much time was wasted in preparing the food.

I spoke of the difficulties of serving here and wondered whether some other arrangement could be devised.

Fay said that if she were to stop and eat before coming here, it would be too late and she doesn't have enough money to eat out. Ethel works in a factory, where she polishes diamonds. She carries her lunch, and feels it would be too difficult to carry food for both meals. Belle, too, would find it difficult because she rushes to her job as soon as she leaves school, and she does not know how she could manage. And so it went down the line.

The girls recognized the expense. When I said that our budget was running rather low, almost in unison they said they would be willing to get along on as little as possible. But they felt that they must have something as they get too hungry.

Della said that she always comes early and would be willing to set the table in addition to bringing whatever food we have. She would also put the coffee on. With everything ready when the girls get here, the food could be dispatched quickly and the meeting could continue without interruption.

Ann then told of her adventure. She was going to work on the subway, when she met two boys. She did not talk to them, but they looked at her and seemed ready to pick up a conversation. She did not give them an-

---

*The 46th session, held in March, 1945. Notes supplied by Mrs. Gabriel constitute the record of the session. For information on the participants, see pp. 240-241.

other thought, but on the way home, "by coincidence," she met them again and when she stepped off the train, they followed her and talked with her. One of the boys was an Italian and the other one's name was Tony. They walked home with her and made a date with her for the following day. She introduced the boys to her parents, and her mother liked Tony. The father did not care for either boy, but the mother encouraged her to keep the appointment. It seems that Tony invited her to his home and she found four boys there. They behaved like gentlemen. Later, a girl friend of one of the boys came along, and they went car-riding. Again the boys behaved like gentlemen, but she did say that she thought the girl had had too much liquor.

Almost before she finished, the girls pounced, as it were, on Ann.

Della told Ann that she had no right to engage in conversation with boys in the hallway, that such behavior always gives rise to gossip among the neighbors.

Ethel said she could understand why Ann did not take the boys into the house because Ann fears her father. Ann does not quite agree that she fears her father, but she said that her father quarreled with her mother and called her stupid for having encouraged Ann to keep the appointment.

Ethel, speaking in motherly fashion, told Ann that she was too nice a girl to get herself involved with pick-up acquaintances. "I don't want to sound like a grandmother, Ann," and Ethel went on and on, lecturing Ann.

Fay commented sarcastically about Ann being so shy.

Belle said Fay was right. In a previous meeting, Ann had commented that she had hesitated to ask a clerk to see a pair of panties "and yet she goes in for pick-ups."

Della believes that Ann should have been afraid of strangers. Della always whistles loudly whenever she enters her hallway because she never knows who's on the stairs. Her mother always recognizes her whistle and would come to her assistance in a moment.

Ann seemed to sit very securely in her chair, not at all abashed. She said with a good deal of firmness, "I feel I can take care of myself."

Fay asked, "Are you sure?"

Ann questioned the girls. They all know her pretty well by now. Do they think she is cheap?

With great emphasis, all said "No!"

Ethel said to Ann, "That is why we are all so upset, because we know you are so innocent and you could be misled." Ann must never forget that when she is out with a pick-up acquaintance, she can expect that it will be "a fellow's strength against a girl's."

Ann remarked that she had faith and a strong feeling that nothing could happen to her.

Ethel suspected that she knows what is wrong with Ann. Ann feared that she would be an old maid. "It's mutual, Ann, but don't forget that pick-ups are not up your alley."

Ann questioned: What if she should happen to pick up the right one?

Della was sure that Jack would never pick up; in fact, they had often discussed it, and he was very much against it. Della then remarked that the name Tony did not sound Jewish, and she didn't know that it was.

The girls pounced on Della. Why should she be upset because Ann was out with an Italian. Doesn't Della have Italian friends? At first Della vehemently denied it, then reminded herself that Joe was Italian. Moreover, laughingly, she said he was a pick-up acquaintance. She then told in detail how she met him in the library. He threw a penknife in order to get her attention, but she paid no attention to him because they had not been properly introduced. In the end, she gave in and they became good friends.

Ethel commented that she has been having some very bad dreams. It has got so that she dreads going to sleep because sleep surely means that she will have some horrible dreams. She dreamed of having a fight with a horse in front of her aunt's house. Her cousin, Jack, was angry and was screaming. Ann interrupted to ask Ethel if her cousin Jack was the horse.

Ethel paid no attention to Ann and continued. In her dream she yelled and screamed for help. Her aunt passed right by her without offering any sympathy or interest in her predicament. The horse, which by now she described as a child's toy horse with a disfigured nose, began jumping all around her. Ethel feared that she would be struck. As the horse raised its hoof, she grasped it in her hand. The horse tried to bite off her hand while she tried to push the hoof away from her.

Ann said that Jack must have been very angry at Ethel. Ann was quite sure that he was the horse. She asked her whether Jack had been angry at her lately. Ethel gave me a meaningful look.

Again Ethel said she dreaded going to sleep.

Della told her to think beautiful thoughts before she falls asleep.

Ethel said that she had another terrible dream. Encouraged by the girls to tell it, she said: "I dreamed I was in school in a large room. There was a table full of cake there and next door my girl friend had a birthday party. All her presents were laid out on a table. There was a beautiful compact and a gorgeous pin in the form of a bouquet of flowers. The Germans had come to America. Fearing what they would do, I quickly suggested hiding the cake for food will be needed. Alas, I was too late; the Germans had already reached the room.

"I remember there was one tall, ugly-looking Nazi, who came over to me and sat down beside me. I tried to be friendly to him, though underneath I was scared to death, for he was trying to be nice to me, not recognizing that I was Jewish. I asked him how they would come, that is, the rest of the Nazis. He answered, 'We will come down the Concourse with music; America is ours now and we will stay here.' My girl friend, who sat beside me, laughed and said, 'The aristocrats will come, not you.' I kept on pinching my friend to be quiet. I was wearing a black dress with a big bow, the biggest bow I ever saw on a dress, and a necklace with a Jewish star was hidden by this bow; but my friend took out the Jewish star, so it was exposed. I begged her to leave me alone, otherwise I would be killed.

"Suddenly the lights were turned off, and the Germans were making speeches while I felt that ugly Nazi pulling my chair toward him constantly. I begged my girl friend, 'Julie, please don't leave me, stay with me.' Then the dream changed. I dreamed that I had a baby, and the father of my baby was an old man with a white beard. I came to tell my mother, who then traveled with me to Brooklyn to see my baby. But there was so much confusion, as there were so many trains to take, and every time I changed, I had to pay a nickel. Then I woke up."

Belle and Fay both thought that Ethel was very anxious over the war situation.

Hilda wondered why she never dreamed, or if she did, why she never remembered a dream.

Fay did not dream. In fact, none of the other girls, with the exception of Ethel, have such dreams or dream at all.

Ann thought that she had improved in so many ways. She felt she was growing up sort of inside herself and, since she was growing up, she did things so much better than formerly. She was more aware of keeping appointments, she groomed herself much better, and she went to school regularly.

Ethel still hankered for a college education, and was very indifferent to her job. She would like to study psychology; she daydreamed about being a doctor.

Belle daydreamed about wanting to be a nurse. She would like to work in a hospital.

I asked whether that was to show up the doctors and nurses who have attended her.

Belle laughed and admitted that she did not always get the treatment she liked.

Della was doubling up at school. She was carrying many subjects now in order to get out next January, so that she could go to work and help the family.

Hilda could not think of what she would be "because nothing nice ever happens to me."

Ethel could identify with Hilda because her plans were really not plans, but daydreams. In reality, she could not expect very much, because she has never had anything pleasant come to her.

Belle was absent the last time because she had to go to the doctor for another examination. Her accident case was coming up in court.

Hilda asked Belle whether it was worth suing. Belle said, "No." There was some discussion about this. All the girls felt that, unless Belle had actually been seriously injured, there was no point in going through all this fuss. Moreover, Belle was very worried because she had been instructed by her lawyer to tell a certain story. Much of it was true but, when cross-examined, she feared she might not be able to stick to the story completely, although actually the accident was not her fault.

Ethel felt a little like Belle. She had to be awfully sure of things. In fact, she always was that way from the time she was a little girl.

I asked whether she would like to tell about this.

Ethel said that when she was a little girl, her father used to buy many fine dolls for her. She didn't get satisfaction from just playing with the dolls and accepting them as they were. She had to know what was inside them.

I asked what happened then.

As soon as she saw that there was just sawdust inside, she lost interest.

Ann said that she had had dolls, but always broke them.

Hilda expressed surprise as she heard these girls talking, because it seemed to her that they all liked to indulge in impersonal things. They seemed to have imagination; they daydreamed. She and her sister, particularly her sister, never had any imagination. Her sister was just "a regular down-to-earth person." As for Hilda herself, she never played with dolls; what she wanted was a real baby. Actually she began early to take care of babies.

Della said that when she was little, they were rich and she had enormous dolls. She may have thought of them as being real. She knew that she always slept with them.

Ethel believed that the real reason why she gave up dolls was that she too used to sleep with her dolls and perhaps had a lot of fantasy about them. But one night her father took her doll away from her. When she awoke in the morning, she still recalled, though she was a little girl then, that she felt guilty; she had a kind of shamed feeling because she actually had liked that doll. But all her love for it left her, and the next day when she found the doll, she threw it into the garbage can.

I wondered whether she felt guilty.

"Because I pretended I was the mother." Ethel then asked if that was why she hated all games, was afraid to pretend, and now felt at least twenty years older than her actual age.

Hilda wondered whether Ethel felt ashamed because she was too old for dolls. I questioned whether she felt ashamed because of a possible tie-up to the father.

Della spoke of her sisters.

Everybody was surprised, as it was the first time she had ever spoken of them. When this was brought to her attention, she flushed and said that they were all right. She liked them; they were not in her way.

The meeting ended on that note.

MANIFESTATIONS OF EMOTIONAL FORCES

The material presented by a group of adolescent girls in group therapy over a period of about two years (85 sessions) indicates that the basic driving force that held the girls together and interested them repeatedly was their common desire expressed in the reproduction constellation of emotions.

Intensification in Group Setting

While one would expect adolescent girls to be interested in sexuality, the significant feature of the present study is that their union in a therapeutic group served to intensify the force of these emotions, to bring them more readily to discussion, to make them more acceptable for conscious fantasy, and to make it easier for the girls to act in harmony with these emotions.

In conflict with the reproduction constellation, there could readily be discerned what has been labeled as the inadequacy constellation. These were feelings of inadequacy, tendencies toward misbehavior that interfered with the development and operation of the reproduction constellation. It was apparent that these emotions were brought into play as a result of the economic, familial, and social deprivations to whcih the girls had been exposed. As they developed an emotional understanding of the origins and operation of this inadequacy constellation, its force tended to diminish, and the individuals progressed in the direction of increased maturity.

The resolution of the inadequacy constellation of forces and the strengthening of the reproduction constellation enhanced the feeling that they would be able to produce children who would be better equipped to deal with the problems of life than they themselves were. They hoped that their children would have more ability to love, to express all kinds of desires, and to act in harmony with socially useful purposes.

The group was held together by these two constellations of forces and tended to be broken up when this feeling was not experienced. The group situation had to be so flexible that the girls felt that it was increasing their capacity to operate in harmony with their basic drives; otherwise, they would not attend the group sessions, would not participate in its activities, or would sabotage them.

Transference and Countertransference

There is no doubt that the therapeutic group process fostered the development of a transference neurosis. The material demonstrated that the neurotic conflicts and behavior-disorder symptoms of the individual members of the group operated in relation to the group situation, and that the group as a whole resisted individual attempts to monopolize attention and induce group passivity.

The character of the transference, both positive and negative, was difficult to follow. One complication was that the transference was of at least two types: one to the group leader, and the other to members of the group as a group, and, possibly, also as individuals. It would be desirable to investigate further the type of transference neurosis, the forms of the resistance, and the positive and negative transferences that develop in the course of group therapy. The present group was a special one in that the same social worker conducted the individual therapy and group therapy of the girls; consequently, the situation was further complicated. Although she did not in the early stage of the therapy make a conscious effort to recognize and deal with resistances and transference material, it was clear that at times the therapist and the group were regarded as a mother by the individual girls; sometimes, too, they developed a countertransference and tended to act like fathers or mothers to one another.

POSTSCRIPT

Subsequent to the publication of the above report on the operation of the reproduction and inadequacy constellations, evidence for another grouping of forces was noted (Spotnitz, 1952).

Negative Reproduction Constellation

These forces—termed the "negative reproduction constellation"—make themselves felt in the desire to prevent sexual congress, to prevent conception, to produce defective and unhealthy children, and to deter the healthful development of children so that they will die at any early age or fail to surpass their parents in any respect. Depending upon the state of organization of the individual's ego, he is more or less aware of these forces in the form of thoughts, feelings, and behavioral tendencies.

The members of a group do not appear to shift directly from the reproduction constellation to the negative reproduction constellation. The inadequacy constellation tends to operate as a transitional state. In other words, at times when they complain of their inability to engage in creative accomplishment, for example, to have and bring up healthy children, they may eventually be dominated by urges to be utterly destructive, to block themselves from achieving what they most desire in life.

The disruptive forces of the negative reproduction constellation, it was noted, operated in a non-therapeutic way unless they were discharged in language with feeling (anger, resentment, etc.) in the group setting.

When the instinctual energy supplying the various constellations of forces is blocked from discharge into consciousness, ordinarily it makes its appearance through symptoms of neurosis, or psychosomatic or psychotic states. The group setting tends to facilitate the discharge of impulses into consciousness in the form of feelings. Thus, it is easier to recognize the presence of emotional currents in the group setting than in the bipersonal setting, and also to determine which constellation of emotions, singly or in combination, are operative at the moment.

20

Resistance Phenomena

A STUDY OF CHILDREN AND MOTHERS

Coauthor: Betty Gabriel

In a report on a group of adolescent girls, it was indicated that some of the emotional forces that operated during the course of the therapy formed two constellations: a reproduction constellation of forces, and an inadequacy constellation of forces (Chapter 19). The present report deals with our study, under the same direction, of four additional groups,* two of mothers, one of adolescent girls, and one of preadolescent girls and boys. In each of these groups, as in the first one studied, it was found that, if the instinctual aims of the members were frustrated, destructive forces appeared. These forces, which disrupted the group's operation and sabotaged its therapeutic aim, supplied energy for various forms of resistance to the spontaneous emotional expression, in words, of the feelings, thoughts, and memories of the individual members of the group.

The purpose of the present report is to indicate how the forces of the inadequacy constellation and the reproduction constellation operated as resistances to the therapeutic process. These took three forms: (1) resistances of the individual members of the group to presenting a spontaneous, emotionally significant accounts of their life stories; (2) resistances of the group as a whole; and (3) resistances induced in the therapist by the group. A general discussion of how they operated will, we hope, clarify the usefulness and meaning of resistances during analytic group therapy.

---

*These groups were conducted by the coauthor, who contributed the clinical material on which the present study is based. Notes taken by Mrs. Gabriel during two group sessions are incorporated in the text.

THE FOUR GROUPS

Group A consisted of six mothers who were treated in the group for about one year (36 sessions). The diagnosis of four of the members was anxiety hysteria. One had a mixed psychoneurosis with depression and psychosomatic symptoms; another appeared to have an impulse disorder. Their ages ranged from 34 to 47 years.

Group B, consisting of four mothers within the same age range, had been in existence for three months, having had nine sessions at the time this report was prepared. Three of the mothers had been diagnosed as anxiety hysteria; the fourth was considered to have a mixed psychoneurosis with preoedipal conversion symptoms.

Group C consisted of four adolescent girls who were treated over a period of one year (34 sessions). Their primary diagnoses were anxiety hysteria and mixed psychoneurosis; schizoid trends were present in one individual, compulsive trends in a second, and preoedipal conversion symptoms were present in a third. They were all 16 years of age.

Group D consisted of two boys and two girls, who were either 11 or 12 years old when the treatment began. Two were diagnosed as primary behavior disorder. The third member had a preoedipal behavior disorder, and the fourth was diagnosed as a psychoneurosis with compulsive trends. This group was treated over a period of two years (about 75 sessions).

Most of the individuals in these four groups were at the same time receiving individual psychotherapy from one of us (BG). A few were receiving such treatment from other psychiatric social workers. In the sense that the members were undergoing group and individual psychotherapy at the same time, these were highly specialized groups.

Contacts among the members of each group outside the group situation were discouraged. The role of the therapist was generally limited, when feasible, to studying the defenses of the individual members of the group and to questioning that would make them aware of the presence and meaning of their resistances.

CONCEPT OF RESISTANCE

While the members of the groups reported on here were under treatment for therapeutic purposes, our primary intention was to treat them in the group situation along lines analogous to a certain extent to individual analytic therapy. Each member was to say whatever occurred to him in the group setting and, in addition, help the other members of the group do the same. They understood that they were to relate their life histories, feelings, and thoughts in a spontaneous, emotionally significant way. Naturally it was anticipated that they would find it difficult to do so, and the voluntary and involuntary methods they used to avoid presenting the desired material were considered to be the resistances.

The group therapist was directed by the psychiatrist to be primarily concerned with the forms of these resistances and, when feasible, to call attention to the form a resistance was taking by asking a question about it. The therapist attempted to enlist the assistance of the group members in understanding the meaning and origin of these resistances. The extent to which these resistances were made voluntary was considered to be of significance for the group therapeutic process.

ORIGINS

Inadequacy Constellation

A summary of the inadequacy and the reproduction constellations of forces has been formulated in the brief statement, "I need care. Help me to take care of myself and to get what I want, a child. I want to help that child to grow up and become a better person than myself, and to have more advantages" (Chapter 19). The inadequacy constellation encompasses the forces that the members of a group become aware of when they feel themselves inadequate to produce better children.

Group A: The mothers began their verbalizations with statements to the effect that they were inadequate wives because of their children; the mothers wanted to help support the family but could not leave their children. The fact that their husbands were inadequate to providing proper economic and emotional support disturbed the members of the group. Furthermore, in this situation they found themselves inadequate; they also lacked the proper emotional attitude towards their children. Discussion of their own inadequacies led to the recognition that these were connected in some way with having had inadequate parents, and the group members then became interested in the parental deficiencies that had resulted in their own.

This emotional trend gradually led them to react to the fact that the therapist was doing little, actively, to make up for the deficiencies they had suffered at the hands of their parents. These reactions took various forms: failure to attend group sessions, coming late, ignoring the therapist, not answering her questions, resenting her lack of active help, defending her from the attacks of others in the group, and attempting to be independent and to do without the therapist's assistance.

Group B: These mothers, beginning treatment in the same way, called attention to their inadequacy in handling their problems with their children. It was emphasized that taking care of their children was a duty they must perform, but they did not know how to do so. The members hoped that they would be repaid by having their children take care of them in their old age; they also felt, however, that parents, when no longer useful to their children, should die off. They related to one another according to the principles of identification and reaction-formation, pointing out similarities or differences in their backgrounds. The fact that they had similar inadequacies served to strengthen them individually and stimulated them to give more information about themselves. Reacting to the comparative silence of the therapist, they recognized that she had good self-control, and then tended to identify with her in this way (identification as defense).

Group C: The inadequacy constellation manifested itself in this group of adolescent girls in statements to the effect that their parents were inadequate —individuals with problems. The girls then saw that the transmission of these problems caused them to be inadequate individuals. They were afraid of dealing with people. They could not understand their mothers and battled with them. They strove to assist one another in these conflicts with their mothers.

The girls also found themselves inadequate to the demands of the group situation. They would rather play than talk; they arrived late, or were absent from sessions because of illness. Each of them felt inadequate to cope with her own problems, but these seemed less important than their common problems as individuals of the same age. The situation with the therapist reminded them of their past fears of their parents; but instead of revealing these fears, they voiced present fears of rape, burglars, of the dark, and they described fearful fantasies. They spoke of their various physical defects (cysts, nose defects, and so forth), their own present illnesses, or those of relatives. They discussed their theories of love, their fear of injections. They attempted to conceal defects by flippant remarks. They spoke of their failures in school examinations. The more alike they felt themselves to be, in terms of their common defectiveness, the more strength they seemed to muster to cope with their common problems with the group therapist.

Group D: The youngest of the four groups, treated over the longest period of time, was also unique among them in pairing two individuals of the same sex with two others of the opposite sex. The bisexual character of the group of preadolescents served to intensify and to magnify their desires and tendencies to engage in motor activity in the sessions. Their inadequacy was immediately manifested through their apparent lack of motor control. They spoke less than the members of the other groups, and acted more in the treatment situation. These inadequacies—less ability to inhibit their impulses to act and to play, or to transform action impulses into talking patterns—resulted in more instinctual gratification, which then became a powerful resistance. Inadequate to control their impulses, these individuals acted for immediate pleasure. As one of them said, "I just can't stop myself when I see something that I want."

The general picture, then, was one of action rather than talking; nevertheless, the same type of material was presented: problems with their parents that the children felt inadequate to cope with. The members of the group were compelled by their parents to do things they did not wish to do. Gradually they began to talk about hating their parents. The fact that they acted out repeatedly in the presence of the self-controlled therapist and, when restrained, recalled similar situations in which they had engaged in motor activity, resulted in their becoming more self-controlled. In order to deal with the group therapist, they began to help one another master some of their inadequacies. They got along well together and, after accepting a "must" from the therapist, began expressing hostility to her because her inquiring attitude made her appear uninterested in helping them.

The individual resistances used by the members of each group in relating to one another were similar to the patterns they manifested later in their dealings with the therapist. They vied for favor, attacked when frustrated, ignored one another, and each member tried to set herself up as a model for the others. It was only as they came to recognize that they would have to unite to deal with the group therapist that they made some effort to understand the significance, history, and origin of their individual patterns of resistance.

As gathered from the study of the four groups, the basic trend of the resistances derived from the inadequacy constellation of forces was as follows: Confronted with a request from the therapist to tell their life stories, the group members reacted with inadequacy when they received little or no help or approval from the therapist. They operated to resolve one another's individual inadequacies so that they could eventually unite in dealing with the therapist who was not granting their wishes for personal gratification —who appeared to be only a little less inadequate in relating to them than their parents had been.

Reproduction Constellation

The inadequacy constellation of forces verges on the reproduction constellation. As individuals become less inadequate emotionally to deal with their immediate life problems, they also tend to cope more adequately with problems associated with the reproduction constellation.

Group A: The latter constellation operated as resistance when the mothers devoted their energies to learning how to get greater genital pleasure with their husbands. Problems of contraception were discussed. At times when they felt that the welfare of their children was more important than their own, the mothers became more interested in utilizing the group situation to benefit their children than in telling their own life stories. For example, the mothers were concerned with thoughts of future child-bearing because their children desired more siblings.

Group B: Additional resistances were brought out in the second group of mothers. They concealed information about themselves and talked at times for enjoyment. For example, they derived pleasure from dwelling on the idea that one should hide the fact that one masturbated and enjoyed it.

Group C: Considerable time was devoted to attempts to attain emotional gratification by talking about their actual sexual experiences. The girls spoke of their desires for sexual pleasure and of hating their parents for preventing them from having it. Objecting to marriage as legalized sexual activity, the girls thought it would be desirable to "play the field"—diffuse impulsive behavior aimed at immediate pleasure without regard for the consequences.

Group D: The preadolescents were strongly influenced by impulses originating in the reproduction constellation. They played games about furnishing a house for a doll. They attacked one another verbally and attempted to do so physically. They eventually spoke of bashing their heads in (as a symbol of sexual intercourse). The spoke of how they would like to see one another undressed. They compared their various possessions. At times they reversed identifications, the girls addressing the boys as mommy and the boys addressing the girls as daddy.

Thus the reproduction constellation (frustrated in the group setting) served as a resistance in all four groups. It tended to sway the individual members in the direction of getting immediate gratification for genital and related pleasures rather than stimulating them to understand themselves and one another. When faced with the non-participation and latent disapproval of the therapist, they attempted to assist one another to redirect their impulsive activity into language, to understand their need for immediate action. This led to controlled behavior.

Induced Resistances

Inevitably the attempts of the therapist to guide the group in the direction of emotional remembering and articulation of their memories served to induce in her impulses responsive to the needs of the group members that would have interfered with the therapeutic functioning of the group.

Some of the induced resistances based on the inadequacy constellation of emotions were as follows: The therapist became aware of a strong desire to help the patients with their individual problems, to correct their personal deficiencies, and to prevent or control any misbehavior in the sessions. She became aware of a tendency on her part to break up the group when they behaved in an uncontrollable way. She also tended to avoid subject-matter that might expose her to expressions of hostility from the whole group. Because of the pressure of the latent feelings of hostility in the group as a unit, she tended to behave so as to prevent such feelings from developing; if they did develop, she tried to ward off their expression in hostile tones and language.

The presence of the inadequacy constellation in the group thus influenced the therapist in two ways. It stimulated desires in her to (1) correct the inadequacies of the group members because of her positive feelings for them; and (2) forestall the expression of hostile emotions provoked by their frustrations.

The reproduction constellation of the group induced tendencies in the therapist to operate in harmony with this emotional current. For example, she was able to lead the group of adolescent girls into appropriate discussions of sexual matters and socializing with boys, and also to help them report and dwell on their sexual experiences and thoughts about having children.

As the group therapeutic process advanced, one could discern from the study a definite trend in the groups, because of the initial inadequacies of the members, to identify with the therapist's controlled and understanding attitude. It was clear that they developed an interest in helping one another and in doing away with their hostility and rivalry, apparently because they wanted to become more alike—more understanding and more controlled. Would they then be able to deal more effectively with the therapist's opposition to their attempts to secure the immediate gratification of their impulses?

As yet we have not studied a group over a sufficiently long period of time to determine whether the impulses aroused in its members might eventually be so organized that they would deal constructively with such opposition instead of by either ignoring it or insisting on compliance with their demands regardless of the therapist's wishes and intentions.*

Regular conferences with the psychiatrist were of considerable assistance to the therapist in dealing with the intense emotional pressures to which she was subjected in conducting the four groups discussed here.

---

*Subsequent studies (unpublished) indicate that patients in an advanced stage of group therapy often recognize and allude spontaneously to the emotional stresses entailed in treating them. By calling attention to the difficulties they provoke, they help the therapist deal with countertransference resistance.

ILLUSTRATIVE GROUP SESSIONS

Group C, 26th Session

One session of the group of adolescent girls was selected to illustrate the tendency to attack the therapist in an increasingly hostile way. The material also hints at their recognition that a process of emotional evolution was under way in the group setting.

Bertha had been studying very hard. Her English teacher made her chairman today and she really worked well. Everyone thought her marks were very good. Her father suggested that "at this age" she should concentrate more on school; she could wait until she was 17 or 18 to go out with boys.

At this point I commented on Adele's late arrival. Was there any reason why she felt like insulting me? She said that her tardiness was certainly not intended as an insult; it was due rather to a lack of responsibility "or possibly callousness."

Edith could not be so ill-mannered as to come late without a very good excuse. She could not even break into an interesting conversation; that would be poor manners.

Dora had a definite reason for coming a little late today. They had just gotten a phone and the whole family was involved with it. She couldn't tear herself away.

Edith said directly that she considered me to be a bad leader because I was not helping them. I sat by and let them struggle along; I did nothing. If they could help themselves, they really wouldn't need a leader.

Dora told Edith, with some feeling, that she had not been in the group long enough to really appreciate it, and practically asked what gave her the privilege of accusing me so directly. Both Adele and Dora spontaneously said that "personally" they had been helped. Edith persisted, however, and in a way tried to show me how to conduct the group. I should introduce a topic or, if one of the girls did and the others broke in when anyone started to talk, I ought to control the discussion and see that they followed through to the end.

Dora told Edith that they were distinct individuals in the group; each had a definite problem. In a way, this was a kind of, let's say, individualized group treatment.

According to Adele, Dora had tried to say that "we have to have a stream-of-consciousness technique because we are in the group." Edith remarked that we only skimmed the surface. She objected to the lack of depth in what was going on. Adele said that what Edith lost track of was that this was a demonstration of "evolution rather than revolution . . .

and, Edith, if you follow, you will find that you slowly become conscious of it."

Bertha also criticized me, in a way. She thought we should concentrate on one person at a time.

Edith then criticized me for not asking questions.

Dora commented that at school, in the laboratory, when all was quiet and she was wishing that something would explode, she spontaneously expelled flatus. Adele said that somehow this pointed to all of them having many blocks here. It was hard for her to say what she wanted to because she did not have enough ego to defend herself. Dora could not be uninhibited; even with her best friend "it just doesn't come out." She feared to express herself. That was one of the reasons for her being in the group. She couldn't even admit to herself certain things about herself. She pushed these things far back. Bertha too was afraid to find out about herself.

Adele said she had wasted all of last summer and realized it. She had picked up young boys and really got no pleasure from doing it. Suddenly she had a revelation; she realized that she made bids for attention. Maybe that was what she was so preoccupied with last summer when she went through the park picking up strangers; "maybe I want my father." It was like a game of chess, Adele continued. Actually, even at school she found herself going after all of her male teachers.

Reminded of her previous treatment here and of the Big Sister who had been assigned to her, Adele said she had always felt she had to please the Big Sister, as though she were with a stranger. She wondered about the name "Big Sister" for a woman who was actually a stranger; maybe she should have been called something else. Adele then got to thinking about why this stranger had taken her places and done things for her. At that period she had read the novel *Nana*. It had harmed her. She thought that she wasn't ready to read all about sex at that time. At that point she turned to Dora, remarking that she hadn't said anything. Dora said, "Boo."

Adele went to a dance on Wednesday evening and thought she had a victory. She knew that she looked very nice, even pretty, in fact, that evening. Joe was there and noticed her. She described what she had worn. She had discovered that "you can be near a person and yet appear as though you don't know that they are living." Adele now recognized that she really liked her mother, who had seen to it that she had a pretty dress to wear and that everything was ready for her.

At that point, the girls noticed that Edith was perhaps a little impatient and told her that she was nervous. No, she was not nervous, Edith said, just impatient. Bertha observed that Edith jumped to conclusions fast. That was what Adele liked about Edith; she was quick and alert.

Edith said that life was too fast for her. Actually she wanted to jump ahead so that, in the end, she could take it easy.

That ended the meeting.

Group D, 51st Session

The operation of the reproduction and inadequacy constellations is illustrated in the material presented from the group of preadolescent boys and girls. The session also indicates that these children recognized, to some extent, how they had developed in the group, and how they continued to resist the therapeutic process by aiming at immediate gratification. They secured it through motor action and play, but their use of language to express feeling had been gradually increasing.

Bob was absent and the others asked about him when they arrived. When I told them that he was ill, they immediately busied themselves making get-well cards for him. Ordinarily, this is not done after a one-time absence, but I had remarked that Bob's mother had phoned to say that he was very ill.

Al seems to have improved enormously in his drawing. He now attempted composition. Beth too demonstrated some ability. Ann did not seem to have any creative ideas; her card was the simplest of the three that were made.

Al then began to build with the blocks while Ann modeled with clay and Beth just chatted. She talked about her ambition to be a nurse. As a hobby, she would like to write plays—"for pleasure," she added.

Ann will sing when she grows up, but her father said that she only screeches. I wondered whether that made her angry. She smiled and said she would sing anyway. But her ambition is to marry a millionaire "but not for money." Her real ambition, she said with considerable frankness, is to marry, and to have a home and children.

Al played very aggressively, flinging the blocks around, building and destroying, building and destroying. He built as high a tower as he could with the blocks, and then watched it totter and fall. I observed that he seemed to get a feeling of pleasure as the blocks fell. He then remarked that he was so happy that he hadn't gone to Hebrew School that day. There was some kind of celebration there, but he preferred being here.

Again, I asked what the group was doing for them. Al thought that it was good for "destructive kids." Asked what he meant, he said, "Well, here we destroy. Sometimes we destroy what others build, but in the beginning we used to destroy a lot of things, but now it is only fun." I asked, "You mean you don't feel like really destroying things anymore?" No, he doesn't.

Ann said that she had learned in the group how to get along with other children. Now she has many friends; formerly she did not have so many. She had also learned to play nicely with her friends.

Beth thought she could say the same. Once she had problems in school and on the outside. Now she has only friends, her teachers like her, and she doesn't have any more trouble at school.

Everything would be much better for Al if he just didn't have to go to Hebrew School, but coming to the group had taught him to accept even this. "I learned to accept a 'must'." His mother forced him to go. In the beginning, he had fought it all the time, but he doesn't anymore, even though he wasn't happy about going.

Ann went out to get some water. Then she got very busy emptying the dollhouse. After she began to clean it, Beth moved over to help her. There were rather noisy children in our hall. Ann said quite loudly that they were so noisy that it was impossible for her to work, and then the noise stopped. Ann made a remark about it. While working she complained that time went so fast here. She recalled a time when it went more slowly. They seemed to have just arrived, and soon they would have to go home.

Somehow the children settled down to work. Al drew while Ann and Beth gave the dollhouse a thorough cleaning. Then they put back all of the furniture, giving the dollhouse a very livable and clean appearance.

Energy Sources and Management

As illustrated above, the verbal productions of two groups of mothers and two of children, treated over periods ranging from three months to two years, indicated that both the inadequacy constellation and the reproduction constellation provided material that served as resistance to the spontaneous reporting of the life histories of the members of the four groups. It was evident that the resistances contributed by the inadequacy forces were based on the infantile needs of individual members that their parents had not responded to sufficiently, and that those of the reproduction constellation originated in instinctual urges toward genital gratification. Both types of resistance apparently obtained their energies from drives that operated in the child-parent relationship.

In an apparently lawful way, the reactivation of a problem in that relationship initiated resistance in all of these groups. The mothers, who at first emphasized that their children created the problem, later recognized that they also contributed to it. Initially the children blamed their parents but eventually perceived that they shared responsibility for the problem.

What function was served by the maintenance of resistances? It helped the members of the group and the therapist adjust to the immediate stresses of the treatment situation. The fact that this mobilized either binding or destructive forces made it necessary for them to contain these energies. The utilization of resistances served to preserve the status quo and to maintain the existing relationships. The resistances could be given up in a voluntary and satisfactory way only when the mobilized energy did not threaten the therapeutic situation and relationships. Too much pressure for resolution of the superficial resistances might have led to the utilization of deeper resistances, the operation of which might have endangered the equilibrium of the individual personalities.

Of considerable significance appeared to be the observation that the initial therapeutic endeavors of the group members were directed to understanding what made them different, uncooperative individuals. Apparently the ultimate aim of this understanding was not actually to help one another but to transform themselves into a unified, cooperatively functioning group capable of either forcing the therapist to heed their need for gratification or of neutralizing her influence.

The initial effort of the group to push aside individual problems that might impede concerted action by the members in their struggle with the therapist may have accounted, to some extent, for most of the therapeutic results achieved at an early stage. An important factor was the intuitive understanding that persons with similar problems offer one another. Competition for individual favor and feelings of sibling rivalry were sacrificed as they united to deal more effectively with the frustrating therapist.

An extremely difficult problem confronted the group therapist. She was exposed to emotions that were multiplied and intensified by the number of individuals in the group. As they strived, on the basis of their own understanding, to bend her to their will or ignored her, it required great sensitivity and skill to sense their latent emotions and to mold them into a cooperative team capable of furthering the development of the group members and the therapist.

It was evident that such cooperative functioning served to facilitate the gradual emotional evolution of all the participants. The group treatment provided new experiences, and new thoughts and feelings that enhanced their power, flexibility, and adaptability.

21

The Borderline Schizophrenic

A number of factors have led to the increasing acceptance of group psychotherapy for the borderline schizophrenic. First of all, as we have come to know more about the apparently reversible forces surrounding his illness, and have been able to demonstrate the effectiveness of psychological methods of treatment, there has been a growing confidence in *all* psychotherapy, whether administered individually or to a group.

The community as a whole is becoming aware that it reaps social and financial dividends every time a patient is enabled to remain with his family and keep up his productive role in life while he is learning how to resolve his difficulties through psychological methods of treatment. And the dividends which accrue to society from keeping one patient out of a mental hospital are multiplied every time a therapist is able to create an emotional climate in which a whole group of patients undergo simultaneously a process of arrest, repair, and emotional release that enables them to resolve their problems, improve their functioning, and avoid psychosis.

Aside from its own intrinsic values as an instrument of treatment, group psychotherapy obviously has important social implications, not only those flowing from the greater availability of treatment for the vast number in need of it, but also the broader implications of providing a more constructive means of tackling the grave problem of schizophrenia and greatly minimizing the potential for it.

These observations and impressions of the borderline schizophrenic in the course of group psychotherapy, though based primarily on my own experience in treating or supervising the treatment of this type of patient for the past ten years, also reflect the experience of many other therapists, some of whom have been carrying on group treatment for borderline schizophrenic patients, among others, for a much longer period.*

APPROACH TO RESISTANCE

Freud's frequently recalled conclusion that the narcissistic neuroses (psychoses) do not respond to psychoanalysis serves as a constant reminder of the difficulties encountered in treating schizophrenic or near-schizophrenic patients. My own experience with such patients has confirmed Freud's conclusion that their resistances do not yield to analysis. Since these cannot be overcome as resistances are overcome in the so-called transference neuroses, a totally different approach is required.

The recent development of such an approach to severe mental illness allows us to look forward to the day when the great majority of these patients will be restored to health in the community setting and when confining them to institutions to protect society and themselves will be an exceptional practice. The approach referred to is analytic psychotherapy, which is employed not to overcome resistances, as in psychoanalysis, but to master them in a different way: by reinforcing them until they have become so firmly secured that the patient no longer finds their use essential and can subsequently outgrow them. In brief, the resistances are not overcome but *outgrown*.

To clarify this important distinction, let us assume that one of these patients comes very late to a group session. He looks very withdrawn and has a guilty expression on his face as he apologetically attributes his tardiness to some circumstance beyond his control, such as a traffic tie-up. The therapist seemingly accepts the explanation and answers in such words as these, "That's all right. You have a right to be late." If this response satisfies the latecomer, that ends the matter for the time being. If, however, he continues to dwell on the unintentional nature of his lateness and expresses a desire to be punctual thereafter, the therapist points out how the patient may avoid getting into the same situation in the future—by making an earlier start, say, or by taking a different route or means of transportation.

Thus, instead of focusing analytically on the tardiness, instead of making a frontal attack upon it as a pattern of resistance to treatment, the resistance is first supported and reinforced. Finally, but not until the patient himself expresses genuine interest in such an investigation, the unconscious basis for the tardiness is investigated. This is done both to help him understand the

*I am glad to acknowledge, in particular, the cooperation of Betty Gabriel, who contributed some of the illustrative material incorporated in the present report.

psychological need that has forced this resistance to treatment, and to help him express the need in some other way.

Through such a procedure, the patient is prevented from utilizing the investigation of the resistance as a weapon for self-attack, as an excuse for self-examination, or as a justification for self-punishment, to which he is especially vulnerable in view of his tendency to be pathologically self-dissecting.

Analytic group psychotherapy is conducted to provide a truly therapeutic experience, as well as to give each member of the group a good understanding of his own problems. The optimum objective is to arrest the illness, repair its ravages, and help the patient to develop a mature personality capable of adjusting to our present democratic society.

DIAGNOSTIC CONSIDERATIONS

Borderline schizophrenia appears to have many possible determinants— hereditary, congenital, and experiential. Any one or more of these determinants may operate in a particular case. Prominent among the possible experiential factors are unfavorable familial attitudes or experiences of the first two years of life, which are so crucial for the maturation of personality. The schizophrenic or near-schizophrenic individual appears to exhibit one very specific type of failure in the process of maturation.

Influencing Factors

Whatever factor or factors may have contributed to the disruption or interruption of his psychological development, the result is that his mental apparatus is exposed to excessive accumulations of latent destructive energy, which facilitate regression and may even drive him into psychosis. The ego's survival is threatened by these vast amounts of latent destructive energy as long as there is danger that the energy will be mobilized by some external factor; thus, the longer the energy fails to find proper release, the more inadequate the ego becomes to deal with it and the greater the likelihood that the ego will fall apart. To prevent this, the individual tries to avoid all situations that might lead to the mobilization of destructive energy and thus accelerate the process of ego disintegration. However, if he is ever forced to make a choice between fragmenting his own ego or damaging an emotionally significant external object, his involuntary choice will be the former. He is willing to sacrifice his own ego, to destroy his precious self, to prevent himself from harming such an object. *

---

*This conception of the nuclear problem in schizophrenic illness was first presented in 1952, in a report on childhood schizophrenia (Chapter 14). Giving eloquent expression to the same idea, Lewis B. Hill stated that

But *how* does he attempt to protect this external object? My impression is that the illness itself constitutes the attempt. Gradually, the individual eliminates his feeling for an object, and then he goes on to eliminate his awareness of it. His attitude to his therapist might be expressed in these words: "I have destroyed my feeling for you, and I am not aware that you are here in the room with me." Thus, he unconsciously prevents himself from hating, and hence destroying his therapist. In this way, the individual delays a motor act against an object as long as he possibly can. If, however, his latent destructive energy ever does explode into action, it may be the type of action that would make his commitment to an institution inevitable.

The regressive tendencies are not as crystallized in the borderline schizophrenic as in the schizophrenic individual, and the former has a quantitatively greater attachment to reality, which makes it easier for him to maintain himself, financially and socially, in the community. Under normally tolerable conditions, he can support himself—sometimes others as well—and his behavior is not apt to endanger any of his associates physically, or otherwise bring him to the notice of the constituted authorities.

Nevertheless, his severe ego defects are easy to observe. Autistic patterns dominate his behavior, and he has a strong tendency to isolate himself socially and to be emotionally oblivious to his environment. His identifications are extremely defective; his regressive tendencies become obvious from time to time; and his reactions reveal marked anxiety. He is troubled by aggressive fantasies of a destructive nature, which reflect his inability to release energy appropriately. His tendency to react very destructively from time to time during prolonged periods of discomfort suggest that he is being subjected to intolerable pressure from the mobilization of too much destructive energy in his mental appartus.

In essence, consequently, his behavior will often be strongly reminiscent of that of the infant shortly after birth, when responses are directed toward discharging impulses rather than to any outward goal. The borderline schizophrenic's disagreeableness under stress is like the infant's loud wails; it testifies to some intolerable discomfort but does not indicate exactly what is causing the discomfort.

Effect on Diagnostician

Contact with a patient of this type may leave a diagnostician with a feeling of emotional uncertainty. Is this neurosis or psychosis? he may ask him-

---

the schizophrenic individual "does not have any belief in the possibility of self-realization, except in terms of sacrifice to preserve the mother" (Hill, 1955, p. 150).

self as some reaction strongly suggestive of psychosis pierces the patient's strong neurotic facade. From one examination to another, there may be a change in the diagnosis. Indeed, the personality changes may occur so often and so rapidly that the diagnostician will find himself shifting from one to the other within a matter of hours, or even minutes, as the patient traces and then retraces his steps along the road to psychosis. The diagnostician will finally decide that the patient is suffering from borderline schizophrenia; or he may prefer one of the other labels which are sometimes used to describe more specifically the borderline condition, such as pseudo-neurotic schizophrenia, latent schizophrenia, prepsychotic states, or postpsychotic states. Any of these labels signify a more readily reversible illness than schizophrenia, because the attachment to reality is stronger and the regressive trends more transient. Unless the borderline schizophrenic's basic difficulties are resolved, however, there is a distinct possibility that they will lead him into a fullblown psychosis.

COMPOSITION OF THE GROUP

Let us assume that we decide to make group psychotherapy available to a borderline schizophrenic patient. What kind of group shall we put him in? And once he has become a member of the group, how do we help him overcome his problems?

The type of group which I have found to be most therapeutic for this patient is one composed of individuals with more or less similar economic, social, and educational backgrounds; common life experiences, occupational activities, and interests facilitate identifications. A group may number from five to ten individuals; eight has been the average number in my groups. Some of them have been mixed, while others have been composed exclusively of men or of women.

Divergence in personality structures is as vital for good functioning as similarity in life status. Interaction with other types of personalities, such as hysterical, obsessional and depressive individuals, usually benefits the borderline schizophrenic patient. When several different types of psychological make-up are personified in a group, the diversity necessary for good ego integration is generally assured. Needless to say, sufficient flexibility for psychological change is an important prerequisite for group membership.

The ability of the members of any group to work together therapeutically cannot be determined purely on the basis of personality types, however. This depends primarily upon the emotional intensity with which they can respond to one another. If members of a group can transfer strong feelings of love or hate and learn to prevent these feelings from seriously interfering with their functioning in the group setting, their association can be a very therapeutic one. Feelings of love and of being loved by others in the group have great significance for the borderline schizophrenic, who wants and needs to feel that he is important to others.

Psychodynamic Factors

Along with instigators of emotional intensity (Slavson, 1943), a group needs members who can qualify as good regulators of emotional release. Their presence will serve to influence the amount of energy mobilized, and enable it to be released gradually and rhythmically, with whatever amount of dampening the immediate situation may require. The need for instigators of feeling and regulators of emotional release is dictated by the very nature of the group process, the psychodynamics of group activity. A group will behave as though it is dominated by two powerful drives. The first drive is to come together, both physically and psychologically, and is reflected in the tendency of members of a group to agree on everything. The other drive —diametrically opposite—is to move as far away from one another as possible, again both physically and psychologically. It is reflected in tendencies to disagree, to create as much difference of opinion as possible, to explode emotionally, to offend and disrupt the group, and to refuse to take part in its activities. A strong desire to eliminate one member of the group, or to shorten or cancel a session are other reflections of the drive to move apart.

Since members of a group put up various kinds of resistances to feeling, thinking, or expressing the group drives in language or behavior, these drives are rarely manifested openly. But the resistances are not always good regulators of energy; they may allow too little, too much, or the wrong kind of energy to be released for the particular occasion. The type of emotion that the group process should create will make it possible for members to communicate significant details of their life, and to do so spontaneously.

If the group process is truly therapeutic for the members of a group, these patients will gradually become able to maintain the proper psychological distance from one another, as the two basic drives tend to balance each other. If they dominate and recede alternately and rhythmically in the course of group activity, the members will be able to develop healthy patterns of adaptation. These patterns will then be used to maintain the proper position of each member of the group and enable him to release his surplus energy—both libidinal and destructive—in the form of verbal communication. The key to the successful evolution of a group is the creation in each of its members of adequate regulators of energy and adequate channels for its release.

Trial period. Six weeks are usually sufficient to test out the capacity of those assembled to work together therapeutically. In a group that can provide a borderline schizophrenic patient with truly beneficial experience and associations, his functioning will not have become more seriously disturbed at the end of that trial period, although he may have become aware of more disturbing feelings. He may even have begun to make progress, gradual and continuing improvement that will satisfy both the therapist and the patient himself.

FUNCTIONING OF THE GROUP

The general plan of treatment is as follows: Talking is the chief activity. No other kind of motor activity is required. And any activity that might contribute to the development of extreme states of excitement is to be avoided. The members of the group are eventually told that each of them is expected to tell the story of his life. In addition to significant details about both the remote and recent past, they are encouraged to talk spontaneously about their thoughts, feelings, dreams and fantasies. Comment on events of immediate and general interest is also in order. The members are slowly educated to a process of communication which approaches free association.

Certain patterns of conduct are sanctioned. Members are expected to keep silent and pay attention while someone else is talking. From time to time, they may be asked to repeat the actual words he used, or to demonstrate their grasp of what was said, or the feelings behind it, by restating the gist of his remarks. They are expected to talk on their own initiative, but with due respect for the rights of other members to a fair share of the treatment time. Constructive evaluations and responses from one member of the group to another are encouraged. Approval is given to reactions which provide reassurance, as well as to responses which stimulate the verbal discharge of feelings or counteract any tendencies to suppress feelings.

As the group carries on, the various resistances which its members display to communicating their life story are studied by the group therapist, who tries to help resolve them. They are eventually interpreted and explained to the group if their significance has not already been made clear by group members.

Therapeutic Factors

The primary emphasis is placed on meeting two basic needs: (1) the need for adequate psychological nourishment in the form of emotional communication or attitude; (2) adequate psychological release for the high accumulations of destructive or libidinal energy in the mental apparatus of the borderline schizophrenic. *Adequate* nourishment and *adequate* release are specified because too much or too little of either one is not therapeutic for this type of patient.

With these needs provided for, the members of the group can concentrate on the repair of their own energy systems. When put in good condition, these systems facilitate the simultaneous accumulation and release of moderate amounts of energy.

Interpretation is not particularly therapeutic for the borderline schizophrenic. A therapist who focuses upon explaining to such a patient how his ego is disintegrating is either wasting his time or not using it to good advantage. In the course of such interpretation, the therapist may himself be contributing to the disintegration process. I do not mean to imply that the use of interpretation is never indicated; it is, in fact, if the patient desires it to help him improve his immediate functioning. For this purpose only, however, are knowledge and understanding of value to him during psychotherapy. If, on the other hand, the patient does not request interpretation, or if it appears likely that he will use it simply to help him become more absorbed in himself, interpretation is contraindicated. To help the borderline schizophrenic become completely absorbed in himself is destructive rather than therapeutic. When told that his problems are such-and-such, he thinks that he is being told that he is no good. That is one way to make him more schizophrenic.

IMPRESSIONS OF OTHER PATIENTS

How does the borderline schizophrenic patient respond to the group setting, and what resistances does he exhibit? While the neurotic may be wondering if the group is good enough for him, the borderline schizophrenic is probably deciding that he is not good enough for the group. His apparent astonishment over the willingness of the other members to accept him may be cloaked in an attitude of superiority and condescension. Even so, I have the impression that he feels that his associates in the group have overestimated him and will be driving him from their midst the moment they discover how worthless he really is.

As a patient of this type begins treatment, his withdrawal tendencies are very marked. He seems to have no feeling, and no regard for the other members of the group. He seems disinterested in what is going on, and tends to behave egocentrically. He has great difficulty in releasing his feelings into language. He generally warms up to treatment much more slowly than a neurotic patient, who often talks just because he wants to be cooperative. Later on, the borderline schizophrenic may blossom into a would-be prima donna; but if he talks during the initial stage of the group's operation, he usually does so simply because he wants to be defiant or provocative.

The first impression he makes upon the other members of his group can be very surprising to his therapist. Once, in introducing a borderline schizophrenic, I warned the other members of his group that they would soon find out how mean he could be. During the first few sessions, however, he turned out to be so quiet and well-mannered that they were soon trying to convince me that my description did not fit the man at all. One of them told me, "The trouble with you is that you just don't understand Tom." After a few more sessions, though, Tom gave them a rude awakening. He became very offensive, insulting one or two of their number repeatedly and mouthing obscenities which shocked them all. His hunger for attention seemed insatiable; he wanted the group's undivided attention. Did Tom's rough conduct lead to his expulsion from the group? Not at all. The neurotic patients were soon working on him, and trying to make him more cooperative and interested in the group's functioning.

Tom's behavior in the group setting was characteristic. The experience of sharing the therapist's time and attention with several other patients is first-rate training for the borderline schizophrenic. It strikes at his most vulnerable area—his tendency to suppress rage over certain types of frustration. The potential for frustration is much greater in the group setting than in individual treatment, since the overweening desires of any member of a group for full and immediate gratification are bound to meet with severe rejection.

The borderline schizophrenic is apt to feel completely rejected because the therapist and the other members of the group do not like or respect him at the moment, just as he once felt that incestuous activity was forbidden to him because his parents hated him and held him in low esteem. It seems impossible for him to believe that frustration can be dictated by love. He may have this attitude because he actually did receive very little love from his parents. It may also be due to the fact that, after so much rage has accumulated in his mental apparatus, the frustration of another impulse is like the last straw.

CHARACTERISTIC RESISTANCES

The various behavior patterns of the borderline schizophrenic in the group setting represent three basic types of resistance.

1. He resists spontaneous verbal communication. He is often unwilling to talk, or his remarks are inappropriate when he does.

2. A disinclination to function democratically, with proper respect for the rights and sensibilities of the other group members, is also characteristic. The borderline schizophrenic patient may show marked rivalry or tend to be jealous of other members of the group. He is also apt to be ill-mannered. Since his behavior, as I have already suggested, may be directed to discharge rather than to any independent goal, if he feels like belching or spit-

ting or laughing inappropriately, the presence of others does not deter him from doing so.

3. He exhibits strong resistance to releasing his hostile or libidinal feelings in language. At times, he may seem devoid of emotion; at other times, he may suddenly and involuntarily explode with feeling. He may occasionally go into a state of intense anxiety, or even panic. This type of resistance must be outgrown if the borderline schizophrenic's treatment is to be effective. The destructive and libidinal tensions that have accumulated in his mental apparatus may have already led to the fragmentation of his ego. The discharge of these feelings in language is the crucial factor to which his treatment is directed.

PROBLEMS IN MANAGEMENT

The group therapist dealing with borderline schizophrenic patients has the same kind of problems as the mother of quintuplets. In a sense, though, the therapist's may be the more difficult task. Like each of the quintuplets, each patient resents the presence of the other members of the group. In addition, the borderline schizophrenic patient resents any slights and deprivations to which he may be subjected because of his childishness. He wants to receive the full attention and regard accorded the infant who has just arrived in this world, plus all of the rights and privileges enjoyed by the mature adult of his own age.

perience a beneficial one unless his patients, like the quintuplets being raised under one roof, tolerate and help one another to the best of their abilities. The *involuntary* aid they give one another—the valuable reassurance, protection, social training provided by the emotional impact of their personalities—is of the utmost importance; but at this point, I am especially mindful of the *voluntary* and *deliberate* help usually given the therapist, notably in terms of the patience and forbearance which the less seriously disturbed individuals in a group tend to display for their sicker associates. Such cooperation facilitates the digestion of the psychological nourishment which they are absorbing for emotional growth and regrowth.

The ever-watchful host who has invited the group to partake of this nourishment is thus helped to limit his own verbal communications and other interventions to the minimum required for therapeutic progress. In the role of an emotionally participating observer and helper, the therapist's major responsibilities are to recognize and help to resolve the various individual resistances to communication, and to prevent the accumulation in his patients of large amounts of mobilized destructive energy by facilitating its safe and efficient release. And the therapist must be a supplier as well as a regulator of power, since he provides the psychological energy that sparks the group's emotional evolution. Whenever the group process is in danger of grinding to a halt, he needs to catalyze it with his comments. Interesting or enlightening observations are then in order, but the fewer the words the better.

Whether investigating, studying, analyzing, explaining, or interpreting, the therapist needs to be therapeutically oriented at all times. This may be difficult. Although he invests his energy and all his other professional and personal assets in providing patients with the group experience because he is primarily interested in improving their emotional health, he may be research-oriented as well. He may from time to time be strongly tempted to modify his usual procedures in order to study various aspects of group interaction, to investigate, experiment, or test out certain hypotheses, so that any significant findings may eventually be made available to other investigators. But unless the study contemplated would be of specific value to the subjects themselves, such an orientation is inadvisable when one is treating borderline schizophrenics and it can traumatize them. Indeed, the more seriously disturbed his patients are, the less research-oriented the therapist can afford to be.

The borderline schizophrenic patient regards the group experience as one that was organized primarily for his own personal benefit. But "benefit" may not convey his attitude correctly, for he seems less concerned with the end results of treatment than with securing direct and immediate satisfaction. One patient told me, "You don't care how I feel. To you, the important thing is the final result. Well, that's important to me too, but I can't wait that long to feel good. I want to feel good now, while you are treating me, today." So great is the immediate pressure in such a patient for comfort that dangerous forces may be mobilized if it is not forthcoming. To prevent this from happening, the therapist must look to the borderline schizophrenic's immediate psychological comfort in the group, even if this means slower going in collecting information. On the other hand, the therapist must take care not to overindulge this patient with comfort. *Mild* comfort is desirable —just enough to prompt him to struggle for more.

Checking Regressive Tendencies

It is also important that the members of the group concentrate their attention upon the realities of the moment. They should clearly understand that the therapist's interest in understanding details of their past is primarily motivated by his desire to help them improve their functioning that very day, hour, and moment. The therapist's dual emphasis on comfort and on the here-and-now serves a common purpose: to prevent too strongly regressive forces from developing in the group setting.

For the same reason, the therapist recognizes the immediate needs of the individuals gathered around him, and assists them in communicating these needs to one another. They are encouraged to release the impulses of the moment, and also the counterimpulses. For example, a member's impulse not to talk may be investigated by the group and, in the process, it may be canceled out by a growing impulse to talk as he observes the group's eagerness to have him do so. After they have become aware of their own needs and discussed them in the group setting, the therapist helps them to determine how these needs are being frustrated, so that their mobilized aggression may be utilized to promote their mental health.

Ever on the alert to prevent destructive energy from overloading the mental apparatus of the borderline schizophrenic, the therapist should try to forestall the development of situations during which such hostile impulses are most likely to accumulate in the group setting. I have observed that the more significant a group experience is in terms of the patient's past life, and the more unwilling he is to become aware of the feelings it arouses, the more destructive energy he will tend to accumulate and the greater the pressure of this latent energy. Its mobilization is also very harmful to the ego, so that the patient's need to release destructive energy in language is particularly urgent on such occasions. In this connection, it may be helpful to keep this fact in mind: When the patient is receiving praise and reassurance from his group, or when its general attitude to him is favorable, his accumulated destructive energy is less dangerous for his ego than it is apt to be when the group's attitude to him is negative.

Facilitating Verbalization

What can be done to facilitate the verbalization of hostile impulses which are causing too much pressure on the ego of a borderline schizophrenic in group treatment?

The patient is more willing to discharge his destructive energy verbally, I have observed, when he recognizes that this will not be damaging to any significant object present, and when he feels that such verbal release will meet with the approval of the group, including the therapist. The more desirable an object the group becomes to him, on the other hand, the more he tends to inhibit the discharge and, hence, the sicker he will become. That is why special structuring may be necessary during some group situations in order to facilitate the patient's verbal release of high accumulations of destructive energy. Their voluntary and regular release is the key to the cure of the schizophrenic reaction.

PREFERRED SETTING

The time is long past when borderline schizophrenics (or, for that matter, any other patients who have been difficult to handle or unresponsive to individual treatment) are placed in a group because the therapist hopes that they will cure themselves or one another. The unique and particular values of group psychotherapy are now too well recognized for it to be regarded as a catchall for frustrated therapists. We must have some basis for determining when to use the group setting, when to use the bipersonal setting, and when combined treatment is required. What, then, are the comparative implications of the two settings for the borderline schizophrenic?

My own impression is that neither setting is better, equally good, or less desirable than the other. They are *essentially different* experiences, each of which has its own values and limitations. These ought to be carefully explored in relation to a patient's specific problems before a decision is made for or against either one (assuming, of course, that either is available) or for both types of psychotherapy. It seems to me, on the whole, that for the majority of borderline schizophrenic patients, the group setting should be made available in combination with individual treatment rather than as an isolated experience. The decision for one or for both, the element of timing, and similar factors require fresh consideration in each case, however, so that this matter cannot be dealt with dogmatically. My general approach to such a decision may therefore be helpful.

The group setting represents a valuable instrument for the treatment of the borderline schizophrenic, whether used in combination with individual treatment or as the only instrument. Group interaction will generally help him to improve his immediate functioning, although not necessarily his immediate feeling of well-being.

In the more formal bipersonal setting, the patient's reactions are limited to the two individuals he can actually perceive—his own self and the therapist. Moreover, the therapist's behavior is circumscribed by the professional relationship he must maintain with the patient. In contrast, the group setting offers a wealth of opportunity for reacting to several different types of personalities at the same time, and for experiencing different feelings for each of them. It can be especially useful in countering the tendency of the schizophrenic or near-schizophrenic individual to respond to each person he encounters with either an overwhelmingly positive or an overwhelmingly negative reaction. The opportunities which group treatment may provide to experience different sets of reactions to other individuals may enable the patient to learn how to temper this all-or-nothing tendency with the discrimination and balancing reaction of which the more mature personality is capable.

For patients who have few social contacts, the group setting represents an ideal opportunity to interact for a couple of hours a week with various persons and to learn how to respond spontaneously to many different situations. A rich social environment in itself, the group setting opens up broad new perspectives. For the patient who has no friends or only the wrong kind, it serves as an antidote to loneliness. For the patient who has never gotten a real argument out of life, it provides a forensic training ground where he can develop skill in channelizing destructive energy into verbal sidewipes, thrusts, and parries at those around him. The give-and-take of words in the well-functioning group generates first-rate exercise in "blowing off steam."

Clinical Illustration

The presence of other patients may make an even more direct contribution to the effectiveness of the group psychotherapeutic process. Some of them may become therapeutically valuable objects for a borderline schizophrenic patient. This is illustrated by material drawn from the treatment of a group of six professional women, all of them mothers. The condition of four had been diagnosed as psychoneurotic depression, and that of the two women figuring in this incident—Rose and Edith—as borderline schizophrenia. Both women had marked withdrawal tendencies.

During the 11th group session, Rose, who was in her middle forties, began talking about her first girl friend, through whom Rose had met her husband. They had rarely seen each other since they and their husbands had vacationed in the same resort several summers before Rose started treatment. Her old friend wanted to renew their friendship, Rose remarked with little affect; she went on to say that she did not know what to do about it.

A most unexpected reaction to this statement came from the other withdrawn woman in the group. Edith, who was in her early thirties, snapped back instantly. In a voice that shook with anger. Edith accused Rose of treating her old friend shabbily because she had no further use for her. Then Edith went on to say that Rose reminded her of the ruthless housekeeper in the novel *Rebecca*.

The therapist asked why Edith was so upset about Rose's reference to her old friend. "Because she reminds me of my own brother," Edith replied. In answer to a question from one of the other members of the group, Edith made it clear that she regarded her brother as a mean and miserable human being.

But that did not end the incident. After listening to this scathing criticism of her treatment of an old friend, Rose hit back at Edith with these words: "You're just as cruel to me as my father used to be."

After that, the two women found it easy to hate each other. They also began to feel more at home in the group. And, before treatment ended, they had also experienced feelings of love for each other. Each was able to help the other to express herself, because Edith had found a "sounding board" in Rose, and Rose had found a "sounding board" in Edith.

SPECIAL VALUE OF GROUP SETTING

A traumatic experience or intimate relationship described by one group member often has an explosive effect on another member, who will immediately begin reliving a similar experience or relationship. Such opportunities to speed the verbalization of significant aspects of one's past can mean a great deal to a borderline schizophrenic.

In investigating the relative advantages of the two treatment settings, the therapist has another factor to consider: the different types and degrees of emotional intensity they provide. A problem involving a patient's relations with several individuals, such as the various members of his family, may be relived with a maximum intensity of emotion in the group setting. On the other hand, it tends to inhibit the communication of unipersonal problems, and the borderline schizophrenic's problems usually center around his most intimate relations with the person who was closest to him in the first years of life—his mother. Such problems are reactivated with maximum intensity in individual treatment.

But if a patient becomes overexcited when he refeels crucial experiences or traumatic relationships for the first time in treatment, it may be more therapeutic for him to reactivate his problems with less intensity in the group setting. This is especially indicated for a borderline schizophrenic patient, whose ego is in danger of being overwhelmed by too much feeling when he reactivates a unipersonal problem with greater intensity in individual treatment.

The group setting may serve, too, as a protection against the development of too powerful a negative reaction to treatment itself, or it may prevent too powerful a negative transference when either is likely to be created by the closer and more direct contact which obtains in individual treatment. For a person who cannot face a therapist alone without undue anxiety, the group setting dilutes the threat of the therapist's presence, thus making possible the development of a milder transference. For such patients, the group setting may recommend itself as a preliminary to individual analytic psychotherapy.

The borderline schizophrenic patient derives certain types of reassurance from the group setting. Other members of his group often help him muster up the effort necessary to resolve his difficulties. The opportunity to engage in emotional interchange with patients whose troubles are much like his own may inspire an extraordinary amount of confidence in his own ability to improve. Contact with patients whose condition is less serious can be even more reassuring, because of their tendency to underestimate the severity of his illness. I have observed this time and time again, especially when patients first come together in a group. During their first contacts with a borderline schizophrenic like Tom, referred to earlier, neurotic patients tend to comment favorably on his behavior. In doing so, they manage to make him feel that they do not consider him to be as ill as he feels, or as the therapist recognizes him to be. This can be very reassuring indeed.

The group experience, consequently, is likely to have an immediate and spontaneous appeal for our patient. The setting itself, with its many potentialities for an individual who needs to improve his functioning, serves as a sort of laboratory for testing out responses to various types of interpersonal situations. The reactions of other subjects assist our patient in determining which of his responses are appropriate and which will have to be improved when he has to cope with relatively similar situations amid the stresses and strains of the outside world. This training should help him build up a more integrated personality, capable of improved functioning in his home, at work, and as a member of his community. In that respect, group psychotherapy represents a direct attack upon the schizophrenic process.

Clinical Illustration

To illustrate this value of the group setting, I want to tell you about a borderline schizophrenic patient who went on into group treatment after receiving individual analytic psychotherapy from the same therapist intermittently over a period of ten years.

Early in life, Ronald had been exposed to many biological and psychological traumatizations. The possibility of hospitalizing him had been considered on several occasions because of his acute anxiety states, obsessional ideas, intolerable absorption in himself, and because of his hostile attitude toward all of those with whom he was closely associated.

But Ronald never did enter a mental institution and, in the course of treatment, he learned to accept his wife and the child who was born to them. After working for someone else, he and an associate became partners in a sales organization. All in all, during that decade, he managed to become a fairly respectable member of his community.

Nevertheless, Ronald still felt insecure; and his strong tendency to withdraw and become self-absorbed was not resolved. He had not completely overcome his anxiety either, although he knew how unnecessary it was. He still disclosed a need to be defiantly selfish, and to have his own way about everything, irrespective of the effect this might have on others. He also wanted to obtain approval for feeling and acting the way he did.

Ronald was admitted to a group formed about four years ago. Among the other members were a borderline schizophrenic patient, an epileptic patient, one suffering from anxiety hysteria, and another with a severe psychoneurotic depression. A male homosexual joined the group later.

The group situation turned out to be highly beneficial to Ronald. If I had to explain in a few words why this proved to be the case, I would say that it was largely due to the acceptance and love he received from the other patients, and their influence on him.

He discovered, for example, that the others could tolerate him when he verbalized some primitive attitudes or expressed strong feelings of love or hatred for them. Even his disclosure, in obscene language, of a perverse extramarital relationship which he was then carrying on did not lead to rejection. Instead, the other group members expressed warm interest in his family and business activities. They also exerted pressure upon Ronald to develop a mutually cooperative relationship with his wife, which he eventually succeeded in doing. Ronald was astonished that the women in the group found him sexually attractive. Two of them indeed would have been very willing to have intimate relations with him. It was not too hard for them to resist the temptation, however, because they were principally concerned with their own improvement in the group situation. Nevertheless, the fact that these women were genuinely attracted to him was very reassuring to Ronald.

He talked spontaneously, and often with much feeling and appreciation, of his own difficulties. Among the statements he made to the group were several references to his own anxiety.

The first time Ronald brought it up, he remarked, "I have a lot of anxiety; that's my main problem. I'm fearful all of the time." Another time he expressed himself in this way: "In any present situation, something from the past will always come up to worry me. It surprises me that you people have the same trouble."

"Some goods I ordered a long time ago haven't arrived, and I'm worried about them," Ronald told the group on one occasion. "Where can they be? . . . I have a compulsion to solve the problem." Later he said, "Tell me, how do I break the worry habit?"

During one session, he harshly criticized a woman in the group who had been weeping. "That's my opinion of you," he went on. "You judge everyone else critically but you are really crying for yourself. You think people are too selfish, but the trouble is you can't accept people having low-level needs."

Ronald reported some dreams to the group. Here is one as he told it: "I had an interesting dream that I was walking down the street with my mother and father. In the dream I was about the age I am now. Mother was telling father that he had never done anything for her. I defended my father; I said that he had done the best he could. I felt very sad; I could feel myself weeping because they were divorced. I awoke with a groan. My wife has often told me the same thing that my mother told my father in that dream."

He expressed awareness later that he resented the fact that his parents were divorced. How could he displace that awareness and come to feel more secure? "New feelings should displace old feelings. So it should be unimportant that I once felt destitute without my mother. Now I am independent."

He often expressed his feelings about the other members of the group. Once he said that he couldn't "respect the feelings of the evasive people in this group." A few sessions later he blurted out in great fury: "None of you people talk properly here. You don't understand me and you don't express your real feelings." On another occasion, he said that he hated all of them, and that they were all "sex organs" (using obscene words at this point). As early as the seventh session, he remarked that he hated all the "old women" in the group. "I like Elaine though," Ronald continued, "I could have an affair with her."

At another time, he insisted that he ought to be able to "neck with anybody I want anywhere" without anxiety. He remarked, "All women are sexually exciting to me, even my daughter." In describing a dream, he said, "I dreamt that a man was grabbing and pulling at my penis. Then my wife was putting her mouth to it. She used to hold it a lot for me before we were married. But now she won't do it."

About the time that Ronald's third year of group treatment began, his wife started her second pregnancy. She gave birth to twin girls prematurely, and one of them died. Ronald was able to express mixed feelings about the infant's death, as well as about the twin who survived. First, he greatly resented having to support her; then Ronald expressed deep feeling for the child and his intention of being a good father. He was able to understand both his feelings of loss over the other infant's death and his relief at having one less mouth to feed.

As soon as Ronald found out that he could accept these mixed feelings, he decided to "graduate" from his group. The residue of anxiety after ten years of intermittent individual treatment was completely dispelled during the three years of group therapy that followed. During that period, he also learned how to control his tendency to act impulsively. He discovered that he could feel love and be loved, feel hate and be hated, and that he could express such emotions in the presence of others without impairing his own functioning. Confident that he could carry on appropriately in his own life setting, Ronald left the group, at his own suggestion and with the consent of the other members. His painful uneasiness and hostility toward himself and society had vanished. For the first time in thirteen years of treatment, Ronald really "felt cured," and he said so!

Use of the Setting

Analytic group psychotherapy provides an excellent instrument for the treatment of borderline schizophrenia. Whether its use will actually be beneficial in a given case, however, depends upon the skill with which the instrument is wielded. Will the therapist be able to structure sessions and situations so that the patient obtains the exact amount of psychological nourishment he needs, at the moment that he needs it? Will the therapist also succeed in creating a climate conducive to appropriate release, and an atmosphere in which a fragmented ego can heal and synthesize itself? The group therapist who can provide such benefits will be able to assure his patient of immediate comfort and to lead him on toward eventual cure.

22

The Concept of Goals

The therapeutic value of the group setting has been known since the pioneers in the field began to report their results. Their findings on the phenomenology of group process have been substantially amplified by recent investigators in the field of group research. Wedded to knowledge of this sort in determining our functioning is another kind of knowledge—the scientific understanding which psychoanalysis has brought us about human behavior and, especially, about the significance of its unconscious aspects.

We have learned from psychoanalysis how to explain and how to predict behavior. We have also learned what is the constructive way to influence and to modify it. Psychoanalysis has taught us not only how to recognize and to understand the obstacles which prevent an individual from functioning in a desirable way and how these obstacles specifically affect his functioning; it also taught us how to remove the obstacles. To effect cures by helping to resolve the emotional difficulties which prevent healthful functioning is therefore our primary concern in administering analytic group therapy. It has the same ultimate goal as individual analytic psychotherapy —the creation of mature and well-adjusted human beings.

The obstacles dealt with in psychoanalytic treatment are what we call the resistances. We tell group members to talk about themselves in an emotionally significant way in order to recognize and understand, and help them understand, and resolve their resistances. We do not try to help them realize their potentialities by support or suggestion, by direction, persuasion, or exhortation, but basically by trying to remove the obstacles which seem to be preventing them from realizing their potentialities. We carry on a process of emotional reeducation to enable them to outgrow their need for emotional education and be capable of imparting it to others.

GOALS OF PATIENTS

Does this coincide with the goals of the group members themselves? I shall present some clinical material to indicate their typical motives at various stages of the treatment process. I shall then go on to examine the implications of the process as it finds its reflection in the goals of the group therapist himself.

Clinical Illustration

A meeting of a therapy group can encourage unusual kinds of analytic activity. In one session of a group of eight adults, Madge, a trim and attractive woman in her late twenties, suddenly plunged into an analysis of the manners and posture of one of her co-members, Herman, a 34-year-old-sanitation engineer. Madge's verbal scrutiny of his general gaucheness testified to her efficiency as the personnel executive of a sales corporation. She called his attention to his often disrespectful attitude to the group leader and rudeness to his co-patients, his stony silence when rebuked for interrupting one of them, his poor diction, and the way he slouched in his chair.

At first the "victim" vigorously defended himself. No one had ever called him ill-mannered before this and he always tried to be considerate of others. He was not aware that there was anything amiss in his deportment. He knew all the rules of polite society and could conduct himself impeccably at the most elaborate dinner party.

"I'm not talking about using the right fork," Madge said, "But how about treating us with a little common courtesy in these sessions? If you're not aware of how improperly you're behaving, it's about time you should be."

This statement opened up a frank discussion of Herman's conduct in the group. He stopped being defensive and listened intently to her observations, some of which surprised him; he also asked her opinion on aspects of his conduct which she had not mentioned. Then he thanked her with a great deal of enthusiasm and added, not wholly in jest, that he would seek some further advice from her before meeting people on whom he wanted to make a good impression.

The other six members of the group registered no objection to this use of ten or fifteen minutes of their session time. They quietly approved of the woman's earnest efforts to be helpful and of the man's constructive acceptance of her suggestions. What most impressed me about this episode was the striking change in attitudes which it demonstrated after little more than a year of group functioning.

When these men and women embarked on this group experience, they understood that it would have one general goal—cure. They had previously been in individual psychotherapy with other therapists or with me; two of them had also undergone some group treatment. In joint agreement with me, each of them had decided to try to resolve some residual emotional insecurity or social handicap in the group setting. All of them gave lip service to the same general goal of cure; but each tended to interpret this goal narrowly, in terms of his immediate and pressing needs.

For example, our expert on the social amenities entered the group because of interpersonal difficulties. Madge had married a man who pleased her mother. She divorced him a few years later, apparently because she thought that this would please her first analyst. In individual treatment with me, she had repeatedly complained that it was as hard for her to find the right kind of associates as to leave the wrong kind.

She introduced herself to her group mates as a "well analyzed" person who had no need for the services of amateurs. In other words, her contract was only with the group leader. She was in the group for only one reason: to learn how to relate better to people in close contact. She hoped to accomplish this, she explained, by acting out in the group "what I feel toward my mother and father, my oedipal conflict, and my life and death drives."

Madge was the storm center of many early sessions. Her lengthy pronouncements were always about herself and were always directed to the group therapist. She rarely commented on the problems disclosed by other patients, and their comments on her own easily infuriated her.

As her constructive criticism of Herman's conduct demonstrates, a rather amazing change took place in Madge's own behavior. It was a change brought about gradually, and almost in spite of herself, by the phenomenology of the treatment process. Madge ceased to be a monopolist. She developed a sincere interest in her co-patients. She acknowledged that they had helped her to understand herself better and had helped her in other ways too. She was grateful to them for talking her out of an unnecessary operation. She developed a real need to express her thoughts and feelings about their problems, and volunteered many helpful suggestions.

Herman's response to Madge's criticism represented a substantial departure from his initial attitude. The bachelor engineer had entered the group complaining about the emptiness of his life and career difficulties. He did not recognize the offensiveness of his behavior and described himself as being "overcontrolled." The angry feelings he characteristically poured back on himself practically immobilized him at times. He tended to underparticipate as much as Madge overparticipated. He rarely commented on the communications of the other patients and seemed to feel that there was nothing they might say that would mitigate his own basic feeling of worthlessness.

But Herman too was drawn into the group interchanges. His ability to stand up to Madge's criticism and then to make the most of it reflected his growing awareness that he had some real stake in what was going on in the group.

Fred entered the group with the intention of participating only on an intellectual level. He was almost apologetic about being there. He was an insurance broker in his early forties, married, and the father of three children. He maintained that he was not really uncomfortable, just slowing down in his work. Aside from some rather sarcastic comments on the emotional problems revealed by more cooperative patients, he adhered to an attitude of watchful waiting for about four months. Then he became more seriously involved in treatment. He told the group that he had come to recognize that keeping up with his sales record was not the only thing that bothered him. He also had a serious family problem to resolve.

Grace tended to use the group sessions simply as an antidote for loneliness. She was an unmarried newspaper woman, 41 years old, who spent her spare time writing fiction for a women's magazine. Her interpretation of the group contract was one that enabled her to sit quietly most of the time and listen to the other patients. From time to time she would chatter at length about some current dispute with her managing editor and about her own distaste for the life of a reporter. Then, with the air of one who had discharged her bounden duty, Grace would retire to her listener's post again. It took a long time for her to respond verbally to the disclosures of her co-patients or to talk with sincerity about her own emotional problems.

By contrast, Alfreda was positively loquacious. The mother of a teenage girl and a businesswoman who outclassed her husband as a family provider, she seemed at first to be carrying the world on her shoulders. She tried to use the group initially just as a setting where she could carry on in tête-à-tête with the group therapist. She was openly indifferent to the others present until she began to experience some benefits from their comments on her problems.

When she entered the group, Alfreda suffered from a hearing impairment in her left ear, and this cleared up rather quickly after she became genuinely involved in the group experience. Gradually her reliance on her sound right ear lessened until the time came when she announced, with an air of excitement, that she could hear equally well with the other ear. After further movement in her case, she connected her previous hearing impairment with a morbid fearfulness about listening to group members whose comments had hurt or offended her. She recognized later that she had reactivated in the ·early stage of treatment an unconscious defense against painful communications, a defense which relaxed as she resolved her specific oversensitivity to the opinions of other patients. The auditory deprivation which she had involuntarily imposed on herself ended when she ceased to experience listening as fraught with hazard.

The improvement in Alfreda's hearing was an unexpected dividend rather than a goal of treatment. After it occurred, however, she became interested in understanding the origin and development of her hearing difficulty. From then on, self-knowledge was the significant goal in her group treatment.

Jim, 39 years old, was a businessman who had trouble getting along with women. In their company he either became withdrawn or extremely aggressive; he was ostracized by the wives of his business associates because of his primitive attitudes and vulgar expressions. To his surprise, the women in the group turned out to be more tolerant. They criticized him in a good-humored way and made an effort to understand his point of view. He in turn became increasingly interested in theirs. After using and abusing their presence in order to learn how to relate better to women generally, he developed a strong desire to help the female members of the group resolve their difficulties with men. Helping people, he learned, gave him a great deal of satisfaction.

Phyllis, a spinster in her late thirties, resented Jim's obscenities at first. "There are men in my office who use the same dirty words," she said, "and every time I hear them I want to curl up and die." To her surprise, the other women were not so touchy; she heard them mouthing similar expressions on occasion. Her hypersensitivity to Jim's primitive language was explored in the sessions, and Phyllis came to recognize that she regarded the use of swear words in her presence as insulting to her personally because they made her feel that she was not a worthwhile person. After a while she was able to accept the idea that such expletives are a form of visceral language that has its time and place in the lives of most people. After having learned to tolerate this language, Phyllis became interested in investigating the feelings of inferiority which it aroused in her.

The initial attitude of the eighth member of the group was exceptional. Ernest, a commercial artist, had worried for years about his inability to settle down and raise a family. His own home life as a child had been miserable. He transferred to the group because individual treatment had not given him the feeling of being a patient. He hoped to acquire this by identifying with other patients. He was the only one in his group who sought or anticipated getting some help from his co-patients. Paradoxically, Ernest complained after some months that he had not received any, whereas all of his group mates were indebted to him for some fresh insight into their own problems. He had not regarded being helpful to others as one of the ingredients of his group treatment.

Initial Attitudes

The attitudes just discussed are typical. The members of a group usually start out with goals that are different, and so limited that they can best be referred to as *part-goals*. Each member tends to concentrate on the specific symptoms or inadequacies of which he is most aware or finds most troublesome. Instead of approaching the group experience as a general process of reeducation or retraining for life, he may commit himself to it rather naively, as if he were taking a short cut to whatever his individual goal happens to be—the eradication of a symptom, a good marriage, the promotion of a career, more authority in facing authority figures, or greater ease in social situations. "Full steam ahead" without sidestops or detours is what he hopes for.

These initial goals of group members have two common elements. The first and most obvious is that they express a need and a determination to *change the status quo*. The greater their current distress, the more importance they give to their presenting symptoms and the more urgency they feel about resolving them. A second prominent element in the initial design of patients for a group experience is that they look to the *therapist to do the whole job*. They do not deliberately accept the responsibility of participating in the therapy and have little confidence in one another as therapeutic agents. The superficial and fundamentally egocentric goals of the patient beginning group therapy are only natural, and most experienced group therapists take them for granted.

Patient as therapist. The basic concept of patients being able to treat other patients is still so strange in our culture that it can produce unusual fantasies in the mind of a patient. One woman who was becoming oriented in a therapy group related a daydream in which she found herself in the waiting room of her family physician. Other patients had preceded her, and as she seated herself, she wondered how long it would be before her own turn came to enter the examining room. "You can't imagine how many hours of my life I'd already spent in that waiting room," she went on, "and how many ideas I'd thought up to get my doctor to operate more efficiently."

In her fantasied visit, though, the woman had little time for meditation. She looked up from her magazine to find the physician standing at the door to his consulting room and cheerfully inviting all of those awaiting his attention to follow him in at once. "I've decided to see you all at once today," he told them. "You can help me attend to all of your complaints together, and it will be a good experience for all of you."

The woman reported that her immediate reaction to this invitation was one of intense annoyance. "I had come in to talk over a serious medical problem," she said, "and I had no intention of bringing it up before a bunch of strangers. Besides, the whole idea seemed absurd. How could I help a doctor treat his other patients? Then I became excited at the thought of paying out good money for such shenanigans. I didn't calm down until it dawned on me that the situation was all a trick of my imagination."

Later on, the woman thought some more about her fantasy, and she finally decided that it wasn't as crazy as it had first seemed to her. The only thing that was odd about it, she has concluded, is that it happened in the office of her family physician. "What I was really dreaming about," she announced, "was you and this group. You really do treat us all together here and we help you do it. And I suppose that soon I won't be thinking twice about giving away my most intimate secrets here. Where else could such a thing happen?"

Expansion of Goals

To what should one attribute the relatively rapid expansion of goals that characteristically occurs among patients during the early stage of analytic group process? This undoubtedly takes place because the presenting symptoms tend to be alleviated rather quickly in a favorable developing group experience. Later on, when the individual resistances have been pretty well dealt with, often by the patients themselves, they tend to develop common resistances. Resolving these is the essence of analytic group psychotherapy. As these patterns are being dealt with, the group members frequently feel as if they have reached a standstill; but that is another story. Long before the stage has been reached, the presenting problems command less and less attention. They drop out of the communications of some patients altogether.

The desired change in the status quo actually gets under way when they begin to experience their presenting problems as less painful or urgent. Almost inevitably, patients then begin to move closer to their nuclear conflicts. A writer whom I treated some years ago may have put his finger on the unconscious dynamics of the goal-changing process when he talked in his group about his own development. He recalled that he had felt driven until his first book was published. Then the feeling of being driven left him. He explained this in a way which seems to me to express what happens to group members as the pressure of their obvious symptoms begins to relax. "What I once saw as the prize of success no longer seemed like very much," he said. "Then I had to find some more important goals."

As the members of a group become more and more concerned with the deeper aspects of their functioning, their own goals for their treatment tend to converge with those of the group therapist. The more therapeutic the experience, the greater the degree of harmony one may expect to emerge between the two sets of goals.

GOALS OF THE THERAPIST

Are the goals of the group psychotherapist subject to similar modification? Can he too begin with limited or indefinite goals and permit himself to be moved along on the shifting group tides?

If he functioned in such a way, it seems to me that he would neither be measuring up to his professional responsibilities as an instrument of scientific treatment nor responding adequately to the needs of his patients. It should be clear that, before he assumes the functions of analytic group therapist, he ought to be fully qualified to meet the requirements of this complex and exacting role. It requires a mature therapist, one who is and acts consistently as a well-analyzed person, and who does not project his own values and prejudices onto his group. Of course, since none of us is completely mature and free of conflict in social situations, let us recognize that we may, in the course of treating a group, acquire some special personal goals. Notably, we may strive to make a group experience therapeutic and educational for ourselves as well as for those we are treating. Goals of this nature, which are separate considerations, may well be subject to change. But hypothetically, at least, the analytic therapist's overall goal for his group must, in my opinion, be fixed and inviolate from the start.

That goal, of course, is to achieve cure. The question may arise: Whose cure? The group's cure? Not at all. The group is just a laboratory where originally traumatic emotional situations can be re-created and re-experienced, so that their harmful effects may be mastered and outgrown. Since emotional release and the activation of earlier patterns of functioning tend to be stimulated by this family-type setting, it is a uniquely valuable laboratory for establishing that identity of perception between new and old situations for which the mind strives (Freud, 1900). But however highly we value the laboratory, the plain fact is that, when a treatment experience is over, all that remains of the group itself are fading memories in the minds of those who composed it.

Some group psychotherapists do postulate that they treat the group, but no one disputes the fact that the goal of treatment is to cure each of its members.

Slavson, the father of psychoanalytic group therapy as it is commonly practiced in this country today, regards it as a process taking place within the individual through the instrumentality of the group (Slavson, 1954). Our primary interest is not in the group as a composite; all our efforts are directed toward turning each member into an emotionally mature individual. If and when we succeed in doing this, of course, we have a group of mature individuals. However, it is not the group good but the good of each person in it for which we work.

Work Entailed

But must we really *work*, and if so what kind of work must we do? A casual observer watching an analytic group in session may get the impression that things just happen. However, things are not always as they appear to be. Our goal may not be ostensible, but it must structure and dominate the entire treatment process. That is, the individual contributions to the group interchanges—the communication of feelings and thoughts and the functioning of the members in harmony with these expressions—are all food for analysis, the raw material needed for analysis of the resistance patterns. These may also have to be dealt with to some extent through reenforcement, reassurance, suggestion, and other methods congenial to the personality of the group therapist and responding to the immediate needs of his patients; but in analytic group therapy, the principal way of handling the resistance patterns is through their analysis.

Hence, an important treatment objective is that of structuring the group as a setting where work can go on. This does not mean that the group leader works while the group members play, or that they work while he watches. Analytic therapy is no sinecure for anyone concerned. The energy and force which are collectively expended by everyone in the group to overcome the impediments to the maturation of each personality are the measure of the combined resistances to therapeutic change.

The Meaning of Recovery

What is to be regarded as therapeutic change, and how does it lead to cure? Analytic group therapists spell out these immediate and ultimate goals in different ways. I conceive my general objective as one of transforming the patient into an emotionally mature and emotionally versatile personality, that is, a person who is able to feel and express appropriately, in words and behavior, love and hate. He is also able to accept both appropriately. The give-and-take is important. He is capable, too, of assuming the various productive roles which life assigns to healthy members of our society—to work, to raise a family, and to contribute in accordance with his potentialities to social progress.

The truly therapeutic group experience enables the patient to function eventually in certain specific ways: (1) He behaves as if he understands that all group members have the right to talk and to listen. His democratic sharing of time and attention reflects this awareness. (2) He demonstrates through his behavior that the group members' exchange of communications about their problems have a positive value for him. (3) The group experience enables him to function as if he recognizes the value of *belonging* to a group. (4) His conduct reflects his acceptance of the fact that emotional problems are universal. (5) He demonstrates through his behavior that he appreciates the differences in the perspectives and attitudes of the people around him. When he is able to understand and respect these differences, he has made an important move toward the acceptance of reality.

Emotional maturity and emotional versatility express themselves in many different ways inside and outside the group. Here are some kinds of evidence on which a group may base a verdict on emotional maturity. What is looked for, first of all, is a harmonious wholeness in the patient's behavior patterns, the movements of his body, his words and his affectivity. Another consideration is his ability to communicate his emotions spontaneously and clearly. Does he appear to be thoroughly at ease with himself and in adapting himself to the various kinds of situations arising in the group sessions? Egocentricity has to give way to sociocentricity; that is, along with greater respect for his own dignity and integrity, and a sense of equality, does he demonstrate a balancing capacity to appreciate the worth of the others present and to understand their respective points of view, even when he realistically maintains his own? Does he see himself as others see him, and can he communicate this?

Does he function as if he were prepared to live forever but might die today? The patient who conducts himself in that manner is a likely candidate for "graduation" from the group!

Performance in life is, of course, the ultimate test.

A RESEARCH GOAL

To work consistently so as to facilitate the development of mature and emotionally versatile personalities and then to dissolve the group itself with a sense of fulfillment are of course what we all strive for as a group psychotherapists. Beyond these goals, however, it seems to me that group psychotherapy offers us an opportunity to make an important contribution to the development of a new science, the science of toxipsychology. This would be concerned with the toxic effects of specific interpersonal maneuvers or methods of functioning.

The group situation is ideal for such study, since the behavior of one group member frequently has a psychotoxic effect on the other members. A study of such reactions would shed new light on the kind of toxic agents that lead to emotional illness, and on how these actually operate to stimulate particular forms of illness. It is easier for the psychotherapist to observe and report on such maneuvers when others engage in them than when they result from his own responses in the one-to-one relationship.

We now know a great deal more about psychotherapeutics—about how to cure our patients and about the precise kinds of interventions which are therapeutic for them—than we know about what may be harmful in our communications and attitudes. Yet, there is an equally great need for more understanding of the types of errors that are made and are contraindicated in psychotherapy.

Our general knowledge of what is entailed in emotional reeducation, and the specific knowledge we acquire in the course of resolving various forms of resistance to the maturation of personality could serve as the foundation for another science, a predictive science that would elucidate the relation between social settings and personality change. Psychotherapeutics and psychotoxicology, in combination, would constitute such a science.

Utilized as a framework for research, analytic group process would foster the emergence of a dynamic group psychology. This would deepen our understanding of the factors that are instrumental in emotional maturation, and would also be of great significance for the prevention of mental illness.

Along with our patients and ourselves, the future has an important stake in our group experience.

23

Touch Countertransference

Much is going on in the field of group psychotherapy which invites fresh scrutiny of two contrary streams of thought that might be labeled the "touching taboo" and the "healing touch." Advocates of the former allude disparagingly to the laying on of hands, the king's touch, and other rituals of prescientific healing that were discarded several generations ago, whereas some current champions of the touch that heals prescribe it as a generally applicable technique or a valuable means of communication. But arbitrarily to connect touching with either taboo or healing is to obscure the fact that it has both pitfalls and values. These elude us when we attempt to view in wholly objective terms a practice that has only subjective validity.

THE SUBJECTIVE FACTOR

I do not advocate or oppose the practice per se. The use of touch in psychotherapy depends on whether it will contribute an essential *maturational* ingredient to the treatment relationship. This it does for some patients; sooner or later in the course of psychotherapy, they have to be touched. But I would like to call attention to certain vicissitudes and problems connected with touching and to discuss its indications and contraindications.

Perceptions

Some who espouse the use of touch refer to it as controlled skin contact and characterize such contact as a reliable mode of communication with patients. Little is gained by arguing for or against touching in that narrow sense. Touching has broad ramifications, and to employ it without knowledge of them is to venture into a nonspecific and potentially damaging technique. Touching stimulates not only the skin but all aspects of the personality, and it does so in circuitous ways. To use it constructively, one needs to understand the known principles according to which the sense of touch operates.

Reactions

Modern neurophysiology supports three observations of psychologists about touching: (1) the same touch can have divergent meanings for different recipients; (2) the message one is attempting to convey through touch can be modified by the attitude of the recipient; and (3) repetition alters the meaning of a touch. These observations suggest that direct touching of the skin of another person is at best an uncertain conduit for conveying emotions. The message communicated will not be routinely correlated with the *conscious intent* of the stimulator.

For example, in touching a patient in a mildly positive way to convey reassurance, one may also arouse strong cravings for sexual intimacies. The unfulfilled "promise" may provoke anger, outbursts of rage, or depression.

Touching is of relatively little significance to the person who is able to control his impulses; but it may stimulate the anxieties of the neurotic patient, and he may subsequently become more anxious. It is possible that he will eventually drop out of treatment, fearing that loss of control will lead to sexual misbehavior.

The more difficult it is for a person to control himself, the more likely he is to respond to the therapist's touch as a releaser for action. Even a gentle tap on the arm may incite violent action; such behavior has occurred in therapy groups. It is uncertain at times whether a schizophrenic or borderline patient will be able to talk out his impulses or whether he will vent them destructively. Because the dominant impulses of these patients are aggressive, therapists who utilize physical contact and who work with very disturbed patients in mental hospitals rely on assistants or other hospital personnel to protect themselves against assaultive behavior. Such precautions are not only in the interests of the therapist's own physical safety; they are also an elementary safeguard for the patients against the damaging results of psychotic reactions.

In ambulatory practice, the regression of patients during therapy sessions needs to be sufficiently controlled so that they will be able to pursue their daily activities. Touch, with its capacity to arouse the deepest infantile cravings, has the power to precipitate severe regression. There have been reports of patients who were unable to leave the therapist's office because of an emotional state brought on by touching; eventually they had to drop out of treatment. Touch needs to be used judiciously to avoid uncontrollable disturbances in functioning.

Potential Values

If touching can have deleterious consequences, why employ it at all in psychotherapy? There are various answers to that question. One is that it is essential for human beings to have some natural physical contact with one another. Another reason is that touch has considerable reassurance value. It has the effect of strengthening one's sense of reality. Touch may make one more aware of feelings for others. When employed for its personality-growth potential rather than for its pleasure value, it can have a strong maturational effect.

FEELING STATES

Feelings influence us to touch and also influence how we touch. It is important to understand the relation between touching and the emotional climate of the group when it occurs.

Emotional climate refers to the total constellation of feeling states of the patient-members of the group and the therapist. As one studies this dynamic configuration, it becomes clear that two types of feelings primarily account for the need to touch and be touched in the sessions. The first type is referred to as *touch transference* and the second type—the reciprocal (induced) feelings—as *touch countertransference*.

The latter phenomenon is identified solely with the therapist in the schema of individual analytic treatment. In the group setting, patients also relate, however peripherally, to one another; each comes under the sway of the transference emotions of the other members. In other words, they experience countertransference as well as transference feelings for one another. Moreover, in the more lifelike setting of the group, all of the participants are under a greater temptation to act in both types of feelings. Hence, touching stimulated by induced feelings is more difficult to understand and control in group psychotherapy than in the dyadic treatment situation.

In the early stage of group treatment, patients rarely experience a need to touch one another. But as they go on talking together, transference develops. Verbal interchanges focused on the inner realities of their lives gradually arouse in each member feelings similar to those experienced for emotionally significant persons in his childhood. As he relates to a co-member or the therapist in terms of those feelings, he becomes aware of a growing desire to touch that person or engage him in some other form of direct physical contact.

Touch transference evokes touch countertransference; these feeling-responses are either subjective or objective, and each type may be positive or negative. The reaction is subjective when the respondent, for one or another reason connected with his own patterns of adjustment, reacts atypically to another person's transference emotions; it is objective when the member is reacting purely in terms of the feelings induced by the other person. For example, a group member may experience a maturational need to be caressed by another member. If the latter experiences an urge to respond with a sharp blow, the reaction is subjective and negative. If, on the other hand, the respondent really feels like meeting the need for affectionate contact, the touch countertransference is objective and positive.

Neither type of reaction is objectionable *qua* feeling. However, whereas the objective response is usually predictable and appropriate in the situation, subjective touch countertransference is not predictable and it may provoke destructive behavior, irresponsible and unplanned actions that may be deleterious to other members of the group.

Under the influence of feelings aroused (induced) by the transference emotions of someone else in the group, a member may engage in libidinal behavior, aggressive behavior, or both. Erotic feelings, for example, easily incite seductive behavior more appropriate in courtship and in love-making than in sessions of group therapy. Such behavior is particularly tempting because of its gratification value. Therapy that affords a high degree of gratification has an immediate appeal for the patient but later leaves him depressed, guilty, or no better than he was before.

As Freud pointed out when he identified the touching taboo as the central mechanism in obsessional neurosis, "a thing that is forbidden with the greatest emphasis must be a thing that is desired" (1913, p. 69). In the present context, study of the touch countertransference is suggested because it helps to enlighten the group therapist on whether he wants to touch a patient because it is the best way of dealing with the problem the patient presents or whether he wants to do it to gratify his own need to touch. A taboo against touching for the therapist's gratification, the patient's gratification, or for their mutual gratification is wholly justified. A group experience that is primarily gratifying smothers the incentive for change and fixates the patient at his current level of development.

Significance of Touching

Spontaneous and unplanned physical contact between the therapist and a group member, or between two or more group members, may be mutually gratifying but it is not therapeutic activity. Touching is of little or no maturational value unless the intervention is predicated on an understanding of the transference needs and the countertransference needs and occurs spontaneously in terms of the realistically induced feelings, that is, the objective touch countertransference.

The feelings induced in the therapist and other group members by a patient's behavior contain clues to the precise meaning that the patient would attach to being touched in his immediate transference state. In states of positive transference, patients usually interpret a gentle touch as an expression of acceptance, reassurance, or support. The touch may mitigate feelings of alienation. Patients may recognize one another as sources of gratification. They may want to move their chairs closer together, hold hands, nudge or lean against one another, and talk of sexual intimacies. But being touched carries far different meanings to patients in negative transference states. The mildest physical gesture may be interpreted as a sign of disrespect or condescension. The gesture may implant the notion that the other group members or the therapist are unaware, corruptible, seductive, untrustworthy, that they cannot control themselves, and that they are physical threats. Paranoid ideas may appear; the touch may mean, for example, that other group members have designs on the patient. States of anxiety and rage may develop, so that the patient declares that he cannot remain in a group where he is physically molested. Threats of violent response to being touched may be articulated.

INDICATIONS FOR TOUCHING

On the basis of such clues, emerging from recognition of the objective touch countertransference, the therapist and the other group members need to determine whether touching in the presence of such feelings is indicated. If, for instance, positive touch countertransference leads one to make some gesture of affectionate intimacy toward a schizophrenic patient who is defending himself against the release of hostility, that gesture will have an antitherapeutic effect; that is, it will help him maintain his infantile pattern of bottling up his aggressive impulses instead of verbalizing them. In short, to feel like touching a patient is not sufficient reason for proceeding to do so.

To avoid deleterious conduct, it is advisable not to touch when the countertransference is dominated by strong affectionate sentiments or feelings of violence and the patients and therapist are not certain of their ability to control their behavior. It is also good policy not to touch a patient at times when there is some likelihood that he will respond assaultively.

Patients in states of intense emotion may attempt to trap other group members and the therapist into physical contact. One member may, for example, act as if to strike another in pursuit of a strategy to force his co-members or the therapist to intervene physically. The preferable policy is to try to prevent such action by verbal direction; physical restraint serves to encourage a repetition of the maneuver.

The therapist's touch frequently conveys permission to engage in infantile behavior. The group members may thus be encouraged to act on sexual and hostile impulses instead of verbalizing them.

One needs to bear in mind, too, that a touch may communicate the invitation to touch back. A young woman lightly patted the arm of the man seated beside her in a group session as a calming gesture; he responded just as spontaneously with a stinging blow to her face. Her touch had unleashed a desire to destroy her. For many of the severely disturbed, touching means violent touching—destroying the object.

BASIC PRINCIPLES INVOLVED

In principle, touching, like other patterns of behavior in a group assembled to work for personality maturation, is governed by the therapeutic contract. The importance of verbalizing one's genuine feelings is emphasized because such communications greatly increase the therapeutic leverage of the group. Rules are promulgated, explicitly or implicitly, about other forms of behavior to help the participants operate in mutually beneficial ways—in other words, to engage in constructive emotional interchange. Since touching may be destructive in some group situations, the members are educated to the idea that they are not to engage in it. When touching occurs, it is investigated, like other patterns of uncooperative behavior, to determine whether it has a constructive or destructive effect in the immediate group situation. In the first instance, the behavior may be tolerated (resistance joining); in the second instance, the therapist works to eliminate it (resistance resolution). Touching that is consistently destructive to the physical or mental well-being of individual members of the group may eventually necessitate its dissolution.

Facilitating Transference

The two main justifications for employing physical touching as a therapeutic agent are, in technical terms, to facilitate transference and to resolve resistance. Verbal interventions are usually preferable. In theory, direct contact should be regarded as an ancillary technique to be employed when indirect contact cannot produce the effect sought.

A person whose earliest interpersonal relations were characterized by a great deal of physical intimacy may experience strong feelings of unreality that militate against the development of a viable transference relationship. The use of touch may be indicated when one is working on the problem of strengthening his feelings of reality. This procedure should not be used indiscriminately, however, because repeated touching can arouse realistic expectations to the point of dissolving transference.

Resolving Resistance

As one works to facilitate constructive emotional interchange, touching is often found to be an effective resistance solvent. I refer to touching in a cooperative spirit; that is, the type of physical contact that is naturally engaged in in everyday human relations, such as shaking hands on appropriate occasions, helping someone on with his coat, giving a comforting embrace to a person who is suffering. Destructive touching—for example, punching, kicking, biting, and other assaultive actions that may be physically harmful to another member—is not a permissible form of behavior.

Touching may figure in the long-range plan for resolving a pattern of resistance that is being maintained by a preoedipal personality need. A need to be touched, for example, may be met to help the patient outgrow the need. This is an aspect of the strategy of physically reflecting or joining resistance patterns that do not yield to interpretations or other verbal interventions. The therapeutic task is one of helping the patient recognize his need to be touched, to understand its origin and current intensity, and to verbalize this understanding. After he has achieved the freedom to be touched or not to be touched—whichever is appropriate in a situation—the resistance needs to be permanently resolved. This requires verbal communication.

As an early step in resolving obstacles to cooperative functioning in the group, the use of touch figures chiefly in the treatment of an individual whose progress entails regression to the polymorphous-perverse stage of development. The patient has a right to be touched or to touch if acting on his infantile needs in the treatment sessions will have an essentially maturational effect. Not to touch a patient when therapeutic progress dictates such an intervention is as objectionable as touching him when this might foreclose therapeutic progress.

Precautionary Consideration

One needs to guard against the overuse of physical touching in analytic group psychotherapy. When patients enter a group they are implicitly asked to give up direct physical gratification for indirect verbal sublimation. The principle is established that they do nothing but talk together, and progress hinges on their giving expression to all of their wishes in language and securing understanding responses in language. Verbally communicated understanding that meets their maturational needs helps them to achieve constructive change and move into emotional maturity. When understanding communication does not fully meet these needs, patients may have to seek some gratification outside the treatment setting. If, on the other hand, they have to engage in physical contact with the group therapist, and with one another, for purposes of gratification, their capacity to achieve personality maturation through that group experience is curtailed. After they have managed to obtain a substantial amount of gratification, they will no longer be able to tolerate the sublimated relationship.

24

Acting Out

As a technical term, "acting out" has survived about two-thirds of a century, but it has not passed the test of time with flying colors. In addition to confusions about terminology, there is discontent with the proliferating nature of the concept. Amid rumblings that the conceptual breaking-point has been reached, one hears predictions that the term itself is on the way out. But this may be wishful thinking; it does not appear likely that we will dispense with either the term or the concept. I shall therefore address myself to some of the confusions and try to extract what all of us want and need— theories of acting out that, when applied to our patients, will help to liberate them from tendencies to function in personally and socially damaging ways.

To dispose first of a point on which there is no disagreement: Acting out is not the exclusive prerogative of likely candidates for psychotherapy or those undergoing it. Acting out is a normal phenomenon; all of us are actors-out on occasion. But our special concern with this human phenomenon is justified because we utilize instrumentalities that activate it, for better or worse. The individual analytic situation is a natural breeder of acting-out forces, and the group setting is an even more efficient incubator.

GENERAL USAGE OF THE TERM

Originally the term was applied to behavior during (as well as between) treatment sessions, and it is still used in that sense; but acting out in the treatment situation is more specifically referred to now as "acting in." The latter term, however, has acquired other connotations. One author employs it, for example, to designate psychotic acting out as distinguished from neurotic acting out. Perhaps we shall be introducing other prepositions in the future. Menninger suggests that the social misbehavior of the patient in the course of treatment might be appropriately referred to as "acting up" or just "acting" (1958, p. 108).

Definitions and Distinctions

But it is easier to tidy up the term than its meaning. Acting out (neurotic) has been defined as "acting which unconsciously relieves inner tension and brings a partial discharge to warded-off impulses (no matter whether these impulses express directly instinctual demands, or are reactions to original instinctual demands, e.g. guilt feelings); the present situation, somehow associatively connected with the repressed content, is used as an occasion for the discharge of repressed energies; the cathexis is displaced from the repressed memories to the present 'derivative,' and this displacement makes the discharge possible." (Fenichel, 1954a, p. 197).

There is scarcely any type of unconsciously determined action to which that definition does not apply. On the other hand, in the more than three pages devoted to other actions in Hinsie and Campbell's *Psychiatric Dictionary*, one finds definitions that also apply to acting out. The definitions of compulsion and repetition-compulsion would seem to apply too; the former is defined as "action due to irresistible impulse" and the latter as a "blind impulse to repeat earlier experiences and situations quite irrespective of any advantage that doing so might bring from a pleasure-pain point of view."

The establishment of clear distinctions between acting out and other behavior awaits the formulation of a comprehensive and generally acceptable theory of the different types of actions that human beings engage in. A developmental theory explaining how action evolves in the life of the individual, from the reflex action of the infant to the integrated action of the mature organism, is greatly needed. It is generally accepted that acting out is not reflex action; nor is it integrated action, well thought out, purposeful, and expressive of the total personality. On a continuum of human action, acting out would have to be placed somewhere between these two extremes, along with many other types of action that have been identified—for example, impulsive action, compulsive action, symptomatic acts, mob action, raptus action, trial action, and random action. Acting out occurs in an area of immature functioning between reflex action and integrated action.

Some of this functioning is action prompted by feeling. Everyone seems to agree that feelings carried over from an earlier situation are implicated in acting out. But some contributors to the literature also apply the term to impulsive and compulsive acts. Impulsive behavior circumvents feelings and affects; the impulse is released directly in motility. Compulsive behavior is characterized by rigidity and the absence of pleasure and it is not necessarily related to a previous situation. These are among the objections that have been raised to stretching the concept of acting out to include behavior that is not ego-syntonic, not related to past situation, and that does not implicate emotions. All three elements figure in definitions of acting out that have won general acceptance.

REVIEW OF THE LITERATURE

Introduction of the Concept (Freud)

The first reference to acting out in treatment appears in Freud's well-known report on the case of Dora (1905). In the original version of the report, one finds the German word *agierte*. Translated literally in the context in which it is used, the word means "putting emotions into action" or "emotional action."

Dora's unexpected breaking off of her analysis was characterized as an "unmistakable act of vengeance" (p. 109) in a state of negative transference. She "acted out an essential part of her recollections and phantasies instead of reproducing it in the treatment" (p. 119). Freud's speculations on how he might have prevented Dora's precipitous departure are highly instructive, and I shall discuss them later. The postscript to the report suggests that he was primarily interested at the time, not in acting out per se, but in how patients can be prevented from abandoning treatment prematurely.

Whereas Dora explicitly informed Freud at the beginning of her last session that she had decided to withdraw, the elderly woman referred to in "Remembering, Repeating and Working Through" dropped out after one week in a state of intensely positive transference and apparently without any awareness of her motive. Such behavior accords with his reformulation of the concept of acting out in that essay: ". . . we may say that the patient does not *remember* anything of what he has forgotten and repressed, but *acts* it out. He reproduces it not as a memory but as an action; he *repeats* it, without, of course, knowing that he is repeating it. . . . As long as the patient is in the treatment he cannot escape from this compulsion to repeat; and in the end we understand that this is his way of remembering. . . . The greater the resistance, the more extensively will acting out (repetition) replace remembering" (Freud, 1914c, pp. 150-151).

Later Psychoanalytic Formulations

Many ideas on acting out that have wide currency today were systematically explored by Fenichel and Greenacre some decades ago. Fenichel (1945b) connected such behavior with unconscious attempts to secure the "belated gratification of repressed impulses . . . or at least to find relief from some inner tension" (p. 506). He called attention to the ego-syntonic character of the act, and linked it with insufficient differentiation between past and present, and also with an unwillingness to learn. The relative unimportance of the partner, as a person, in the action engaged in impressed Fenichel.

He also observed that persons with oral fixations frequently react with violence to frustration, but tend to repress all aggressiveness "out of fear of loss of love . . . of getting still less in the future" (1945a, p. 200). Spontaneous acting out may facilitate the mastery of experiences that aroused too much excitement to be controlled in the normal way, but these attempts to rid oneself of traumatic impressions may be pervaded by fear because of the painful character of the repetitions. The psychoanalytic mobilization of unconscious impulses often induces acting out in oral personalities, even among those who have not acted out previously, but persons with other psychic structures may also act out during treatment as a form of transference. The action itself frequently affords valuable insight to the analyst and denotes progress when first observed in an introverted, rigid patient. Nevertheless, since confrontation of the ego with unconscious material is impeded by acting out, Fenichel suggested that it be invariably regarded as resistance.

Greenacre (1950) stressed three additional genetic factors: a distortion in the developmental relation between speech and action resulting in a disproportionately greater tendency toward motor activity than verbal expression; visual sensitization that produces a bent for dramatization; and possibly a more or less unconscious belief in the magic of action. She questioned whether preverbal experiences giving rise to acting out could be recalled and communicated verbally. Subsequently Greenacre referred to acting out as "memory expressed in active behavior without the usual sort of recall in verbal or visual imagery" (1966, p. 145).

In other recent contributions to the literature, acting out has been linked with hyperactivity of a constitutional nature, faulty and insecure identifications, developmental defects in ego differentiation, the failure of secondary processes to win ascendancy over primary processes, over-reversibility of the delay mechanisms between impulse and discharge, a specific bypassing of the ego, and hypersensitivity to the id impulses of other persons. Acting out has been viewed as a form of experimental recollection as well as a form of experimental action, as a detour on the road to memory, and as a phase-

specific and adaptive mechanism in adolescence. Psychosomatic disturbances have been regarded as acting-out equivalents.

Reports on Group Psychotherapy

The fostering influence of the treatment setting has been a major theme of
group therapists focusing on the destructive aspects of acting out. A significant difference between acting out in individual treatment and in the shared
experience—that is, the greater pressure and the greater opportunity to act
out in the group, because of the presence of more transference objects—has
been repeatedly mentioned. Nathan Ackerman (1949) pointed out that in
the group setting "the urge to express conflict through 'acting out' is, to
some degree, natural. Group psychotherapy is intrinsically an 'acting out,'
rather than a 'thinking out,' type of experience."

The tendency of group members to continue interacting outside the treatment situation was attributed by Jerome Frank (1957) to the displacement of
hostility from group to environment. The members of a therapy group
characteristically form relationships that readily lend themselves to the
dramatization of conflicts, according to Foulkes and Anthony (1957). In another reference to the phenomenology of acting out in group treatment,
Helen Durkin called attention to its "high voltage character" (1955, p. 650).

Thea Bry (1953) suggested that even though acting out represents resistance, it has therapeutic and diagnostic functions in analytic group treatment, serving as the basis of working through, permitting attempts at
reality testing, facilitating socialization, and often contributing to the con-
solidation of therapeutic progress. Among authors who have stressed the
negative connotations of acting out, Henrietta Glatzer (1958) recommended
interpreting such behavior as soon as it is detected and stimulating understanding of its motivation and inappropriateness until it becomes ego-alien.

Slavson (1964), viewing acting out as an invariable sign of a relatively
weak ego and regression, frequently induced in the therapeutic group setting, comprehensively classified its determinants and functions. In another
classification, by Lawrence Abt (1965), typical patterns of acting out are
discussed in terms of interpersonal operations and assembled under three
headings: (i) aggressive-destructive; (ii) aggressive-controlling; (iii) pas-
sive-resistive and assertive-dependent.

A challenge to the traditional dichotomy between motor discharge as resistance and verbal discharge as cooperative functioning is implicit in the
notion of *verbal* acting out or talking *out*. Thomas Hora views verbalization as a form of acting out when the patient, using language for the purpose of reducing tension, "communicates little" and "clarifies nothing"
(1968, p. 135). Obviously, more discrimination is entailed in the identification of such resistance.

FUNCTIONS OF ACTING OUT

It is well known that patients often engage in emotional action to avoid experiencing other feelings. A pattern of gorging oneself with food, for instance, may originate in a desire to ward off rage of anxiety or psychic pain (protective or defensive action). Sexual acting out may serve to foreclose feelings of emptiness and of being unloved. Patients with whom I have investigated such problems have eventually recognized that they often acted to avoid, mask, or change certain impulses or feelings that they could not tolerate. (Repression of these unbearable impulses and feelings may precipitate psychosomatic disease, for example, hypertension, gastric ulcers, and gall bladder malfunctioning.) The specific action, though not particularly pleasurable in itself, was somewhat gratifying and tension-allaying when it warded off the unbearable feelings. The discovery that it would serve that purpose appears to be connected with experiences of blotting out the unwanted impulses and feelings through that action.

My observations support the idea that emotional action may also be linked with urges to convey dramatically information that a patient is incapable of communicating verbally or through his dreams. A significant factor in habitual acting out may be the need to re-feel traumatic events with action in order to master them. Such emotional actions may thus facilitate the long-range goal of personality maturation. I have found too that emotional actions are of great value in reconstruction, particularly so in developing constructs of the preverbal period.

For some patients, acting out serves the function of preventing psychosis. It protects them from being overwhelmed by tensions and feelings that they cannot tolerate.

A fascinating case in which emotional action had to occur for the mastery of problems was that of a woman with a severe oral condition. If she was inhibited from engaging in one pattern, she would activate another that was more destructive. When sexual acting out with a co-member of her group was discouraged, she engaged in it with several men outside the group. Indulgence in this promiscuous behavior became such an urgent need for her that, when she was put under pressure to desist, she experienced strong urges to turn to prostitution. Hence, the focus in the case shifted from discouraging acting out to helping her confine it to patterns and situations that were least likely to lead her into serious personal and social difficulties.

Unquestionably, there is no dearth of explanations of the tendencies of patients to act out, whether habitually or sporadically. One or another of the theories just mentioned may seem plausible and clinically useful. However, one is justified in questioning its validity for a particular patient unless its application helps him master a tendency toward resistive emotional action. General explanations are not a satisfactory substitute for persistent analytic study of the behavior until one succeeds in helping the patient improve his functioning in the immediate situation.

Crucial Factors

It is my impression that the therapeutic significance of acting out has not been sufficiently studied as a total problem. To do so would entail thorough scrutiny of three basic factors. First of all, what are the forces in the patient that account for this emotional action? Secondly, how does the therapist contribute to it through errors of omission or commission in conducting the treatment? And thirdly, what is the influence of the external environment?

Attention has been directed primarily to the first factor; the literature on the intrapsychic forces is now voluminous. But there has been little systematic investigation of the facilitating influence of the therapist and the therapeutic situation (although general warnings against countertransference resistance and passing references to unconscious encouragement or complicity in acting out are the first step in that direction) and the environmental factor. In short, there is a widespread tendency to maximize the patient's contribution, to minimize that of the therapist and the group, and to overlook the external factor—the patient's current realities and interpersonal relationships. With the advent of family interviewing and family therapy, important new avenues of investigation have opened up; studies of individual patients in their social environment offer opportunities to enrich our knowledge of the significance of the external contribution to acting out.

EMOTIONAL ACTION

In conducting treatment in either setting, it is important to recognize that the therapeutic process inevitably entails action. Talking is a form of action. It also serves the purpose of therapy to classify the patterns now so vaguely identified as acting out as various types of emotional action that need to be evaluated and dealt with in terms of their potential contribution to, or interference with, desirable behavioral change and personality maturation.

In individual treatment, the patient is expected to communicate his life story verbally and, in the process, to acquire understanding of himself and, eventually, of the analyst. In the group, the patient is asked to engage in the special action of talking in the presence of other patients as well; he is also called on to help them talk, and to get them to help him understand what he is saying. Eventually, too, he is expected to understand what they are saying.

In the group setting, he encounters the same type of obstacles that are experienced in the individual relationship. The patient may not be able to remember; he may experience intolerable affects; he may have other desires that interfere with cooperative functioning. In addition, the shared experience exposes him to a more highly charged stimulus situation. This is usually attributed to the presence of additional transference objects—target multiplicity—but the necessity of dealing with the increased feedback and making an effort to be empathic with several individuals simultaneously also makes for more tension. When the patient's inabilities and conflicting feelings and wishes interfere with meaningful communication, they are recognized as resistance.

Emotional behavior that interferes with talking for communication and understanding constitutes a particular form of resistance—resistance through emotional action, or resistive action. The emphasis commonly placed on differentiating acting out from other types of action serves little therapeutic purpose; the first question to investigate is whether the patient is engaged in *resistive* action. If so, the general theory of dealing with resistance is applicable. The therapist's task is to determine why the patient activates that pattern of resistive action and to help him direct the energy being consumed by it into the special action of talking consistently in the interests of personality change (Spotnitz, 1969b).

Some of the emotional actions engaged in, even though they interfere at that time with verbal communication in the group sessions, turn out in the long run to further the purposes of therapy. An emotional action may prevent psychosomatic illness or irreversible organic disease; it may spur learning; or it may meet a maturational need. The mastery of preverbal problems often entails the symbolic reliving of early experiences. A patient who achieves discharge and mastery of an impulse by acting it out has engaged in *constructive* emotional action. If such action, besides facilitating the mastering of that impulse, leads to behavior on a more mature level, it might be qualified as a *maturational* emotional action.

The therapeutic implications of some of the emotional actions that patients engage in are difficult to determine; these actions may or may not further the long-range goals of treatment. The emotional actions that fall into this gray area have to be regarded as *indeterminate*.

But as the group members continue to react to the intensity of the emotional climate generated by the therapeutic group setting, the therapist may observe patterns of emotional action that are definitely *destructive* to the group as a whole or to one or more of its members. These patterns, especially acting out or acting in whose persistence would threaten the continuance of the group as a unit or might be physically or socially damaging to any of its members, need to be dealt with much more urgently than other types of resistance. It is the therapist's task to try to head off destructive actions triggered by the treatment process and to concentrate on dealing with them when they occur in the therapeutic group setting or when their occurrence in other situations comes to his attention.

Destructive Emotional Action

The first patient reported in the literature to have engaged in emotionally destructive action was Dora; I referred earlier to Freud's report on the case (1905). Dora was apparently the first person to drop out of analysis. Inasmuch as the "dropout resistance" is a pattern of destructive emotional action that is frequently encountered in group treatment today, Freud's conjectures on how he might have prevented her premature departure are pertinent in this context.

He did not say, "I made a mistake when I accepted her for treatment." Nor did he write her off as an ungrateful wretch on whom he had wasted precious time and thought. Freud took it for granted that something he had or had not done led to the failure of the case. Operating on that assumption, he reviewed the evolution of the relationship and pondered on how he might have averted its untimely termination.

One of his conclusions was that he had made a technical error in not making Dora aware of the transference nature of the act. Although her first dream had given warning of her desire to abandon treatment, he had not listened to the message, nor communicated it to Dora and investigated with her her motives for leaving. In addition to the inadequate communication of understanding, Freud attributed her premature departure to the fact that he was unable to experience and communicate to Dora the feelings that she wanted him to have. Such an admission, which takes great courage, reflects Freud's deep interest, at the turn of the century, in enhancing the power of therapeutic interchange.

Implicit in his discussion of his inability to meet Dora's emotional needs in the relationship is the idea that certain feelings for the patient must be present in the therapist even though the actualization of these feelings is, as a rule, contraindicated. His behavior ought to be such as to convince the patient that the therapist would not under any circumstances depart from his professional role. Freud thus called attention, though unintentionally and obliquely, to the therapeutic potential of countertransference feelings.

When the feelings a patient needs to experience are unavailable to the therapist in the one-to-one relationship, stalemate may occur. In group treatment, on the other hand, when the therapist cannot meet a patient's immediate maturational need for specific feelings, there is usually at least one member who can do so.

Inadequate communication of understanding and failure to meet the patient's emotional needs—the two factors mentioned by Freud—figure in some of the destructive emotional actions that occur in the course of group treatment. Such actions can often be averted when they are dealt with as group resistance. Ormont (1968) has elucidated the rationale of dealing with a threatened dropout as a group resistance.

A factor that Freud did not mention in his report on Dora, that of an unfavorable external environment, may also be implicated in destructive action. If the therapist is unable to help the patient master a currently acute reality problem, he may drop out of the group. If such a problem, when it is discussed in the group sessions, is focused on as an external resistance, it may be possible to avert the dropout. It is my policy to try to help patients remain in treatment for two years. During that period, they are helped to deal with external as well as internal factors that may lead to destructive action.

Clinical Illustration

In a case reported elsewhere (Chapter 13), both factors were implicated in the aggressive acting out of a young schizophrenic man who completed two years of group treatment. Dick's case also provided a wealth of illustrations of constructive and maturational acting out and acting in. His destructive acting out appeared to be connected with the feelings he associated with bowel control. The support of an authoritarian male and an accepting, approving female group member enabled him to tolerate the pain he experienced with the verbal release of hostility.

In the course of his first few months in the group, Dick repeatedly threatened to drop out and, on one occasion when his attempts to control the group's communications failed, he absented himself from two sessions. The condition he stipulated for his return, an invitation from the therapist to do so, was accepted (resistance joining).

Dick derived several benefits from his continued participation. His group training led to his firm commitment to freedom of speech, first for the other group members and eventually for himself. The group interchanges became more and more pleasurable for him. The understanding, approval, and support he experienced from female co-members put him on the road to sexually satisfying experiences.

The destructive action that abruptly terminated his treatment during the third year occurred during a period when he had to cope with overwhelming environmental pressures, including the sudden and severe illness of his father. The loss of masculine support and the inadequacy of the group therapist and members of the group to mitigate these pressures, along with the group's excessive demands that he continue to maintain the mature level of functioning that he had achieved, became too painful for Dick. Reactivating his early pattern of adjusting to painful situations by retreating from them, he withdrew from the group. No attempt was made to bring him back.

Follow-up a few years later indicated that he was maintaining himself on the plateau he had reached through the group experience.

FACILITATING CONSTRUCTIVE ACTION

In general, I operate on the assumption that the group situation, by creating an intense emotional climate, will arouse preverbal impulses that patients will be under pressure to actualize in damaging ways. Experience in treating severely disturbed individuals has taught me that the occurrence of destructive action in the group setting can be minimized by adherence to five general principles.

1. Careful control of the degree of excitation to which patients are exposed in the group sessions in order to prevent a too sudden or intense mobilization of feelings that cannot be freely and adequately released in language.

2. Conditioning of the group members, from the opening session, to articulate and describe their emotions. They are educated to the idea that verbalizing their feelings, thoughts, and memories is cooperative functioning and that acting on them in any way without prior discussion is uncooperative behavior.* The distinction between verbal communication and motor action is maintained by appropriate reminders when the latter occurs. This conditioning dampens tendencies to act destructively without thought in all life situations.

Patients are given the freedom to do whatever they want between treatment sessions provided that it does not interfere with cooperative functioning in the sessions. Over and above the fact that the policy of issuing prohibitions is often ineffectual, another objection to it is that it offers a tempting premium—the special pleasure of engaging in a forbidden activity. Even more objectionable, it is an infantilizing approach, which does not help patients develop a sense of responsibility for their own actions. It is preferable to train them to exercise their own judgment, which puts them under pressure to evaluate critically their behavior in different contexts and decide for themselves whether they are facilitating or interfering with therapeutic pro-

---

*If action on emotions or preverbal impulses can be inhibited long enough to permit adequate group discussion, an impending destructive action can be turned into a constructive action. If the gratification associated with destructive action can be decreased, and the pleasure associated with its elimination increased, destructive actions tend to diminish. On the other hand, if the gratification associated with constructive action can be intensified by significant personal, social, and group approval, the group therapeutic situation may be instrumental in moving the patient along the road to personality maturation.

gress. In short, the operational principle of permitting the group members to participate in decisions on what is resistance and what is cooperative behavior applies to their conduct outside the group as well as in the sessions.

When, for example, a group member reports extra-session contact with a co-member, they are not told that this is not allowed; they are told that such behavior is against the rules, and discussion of its pros and cons is encouraged. Whether one or another form of destructive action reported by the patient himself or by someone else will be tolerated is, however, a decision that the group itself must make.

3. The principle of focusing early in treatment on resistance to the verbalization of aggressive impulses reduces the possibility that the group members will act destructively in terms of these impulses in the group sessions or in daily life. In a climate of negative transference, which develops when the therapist remains relatively inactive, he works first to resolve the obstacles to the discharge of frustration-aggression in language. It is recognized that, if the positive transference is permitted to become too strong, the group members will tend to bottle up their negative feelings to the point where these may erupt in destructive action. The policy of calling attention to such tendencies and helping the group members secure adequate verbal release for their pent-up emotions lessens the danger of their leaving the sessions in a state of high tension.

4. It is borne in mind that patients with inadequate opportunities for self-expression in daily living are likely to resist the therapeutic process through emotional action. Accepting responsibility for maintaining the integrity of the group and helping its members complete the treatment, the therapist deals with patterns of emotional action that are destructive to the group as a unit or to individual members more urgently than resistive actions that only interfere with communication. Whereas the latter may be tolerated, encouraged, or reinforced as appropriate until they yield to the usual interpretive procedures, destructive actions call for immediate and firm management.

5. The group therapist studies all of the factors that mobilize internal and external resistances. If necessary, he enlists the cooperation of the group members in dealing with those factors that might provoke destructive action.

Clinical Illustration

Roger, a man in his early thirties, was an English teacher whose primary presenting problem at the time he entered individual psychotherapy was his inadequacy in dealing with his wife and four young children. His tendency toward sexual acting out in work situations, which he became aware of later, following his promotion to chairman of his department in a large high school, accounted for his placement in group treatment.

Roger was an only child of the union between his parents. His father had deserted his mother when Roger was a baby. A sexually promiscuous woman who later had children with other men, she had turned over Roger, then 10 years old, to a social agency when she found his upbringing too onerous, and he had been shuttled from family to family. His schooling, however, had been uninterrupted. A diligent student and a good athlete, he had worked his way through college. After graduating with high honors, he enlisted with the Peace Corps. Shortly after his return from overseas, he married a college classmate, a somewhat overbearing and controlling girl who was determined to have him for her husband. They had two boys, aged 6 and 4, and twin girls who were 2 years old at the time Roger entered the group. At that time, he was exceedingly disturbed by his improper behavior with the attractive young women who came to his office for assignment as substitute teachers. He felt degraded by his seductive conduct with them, helpless to control himself, and fearful of the consequences—in the grip of an overpowering need to destroy his career. Two of the substitutes had expressed reluctance to accept further assignments from him, and the husband of a third had threatened to lodge a protest with the school principal. Roger told the group that he could not understand why he was tremendously attracted to these young women; otherwise, he had no difficulty being faithful to his wife.

In the group, he was immediately attracted to a thin blonde who reminded him of his domineering wife. On being introduced to her in his first group session, he gazed at her intently and said, "I would like to get together with you this evening." Other members informed him that they were just supposed to talk together in the group sessions and that contact outside the treatment situation would violate the rules of the group. Nevertheless, Roger persisted for several weeks in his attempts to form a sexual relationship with the young woman. He invited other female members of the group to have coffee with him after the sessions or tried to arrange other dates with them. He was frequently reminded that this was improper behavior.

A few months later, during a period of sexual estrangement from his wife, Roger became enamored of a pretty young woman, a substitute teacher whom he assigned to do some administrative work in his office. The principal, referring to some rumors floating around the school that Roger had been instrumental in the refusal of other substitute teachers to accept assignments in the school, warned him against behaving improperly with his new department assistant. Despite the threat to his career, Roger found himself under great temptation to kiss and hug her when they were alone in the office and seduce her into an affair. At a time when he was greatly worried about the situation, he brought it up in the group and asked them for help.

Discussion and analysis revealed that the danger of making passes at his assistant was greatest during periods when he was very resentful of his wife. It also became clear that the female members of the group were most appealing to Roger at times when his wife was particularly domineering and when they became sexually unattractive to each other.

A detailed investigation of the various ways his wife aroused his hostility was conducted by the group. These discussions clarified the nature of his problems with her and a gradual improvement in their relationship followed. Roger also recalled many incidents during his childhood when he was sexually stimulated by his mother, and he talked with great bitterness of his continual torment over her unreasonable demands and repeated rejections. Memories of his strong desire to see his father cropped up, and he spoke resentfully of his mother's refusal to tell Roger where the father was or permit him to visit them.

After he learned to get along harmoniously with his wife and cooperate with her in bringing up their children, the group encouraged him to attempt a reconciliation with his mother, whom he had not visited for several years. The reunion was mutually gratifying and his mother subsequently helped Roger establish contact with his father.

As Roger developed a sense of security, he reported that he had little need to engage in destructive behavior. On the contrary, he experienced strong urges to be a good husband and father, and to advance his teaching career. In the group situation, he demonstrated eagerness to understand his co-members and help them develop the kind of feelings that facilitate mature, constructive behavior.

The constructive emotional interchange that occurred in the group tended to discourage Roger's destructive behavior and to enhance his constructive behavior.

We appear to be on the road to developing a science of constructive emotional interchange leading to constructive action.

25

The Therapist's Emotions

EDITORIAL

Scientific psychotherapy, which originated in Josef Breuer's treatment of Anna O. (Breuer and Freud, 1893-1895), appears to be completing a highly instructive cycle in its development as the centenary of that case (1880-1882) approaches.

In formalizing a method based on Breuer's findings—that talking can be therapeutic, that the verbal expression of feelings has a profoundly beneficial effect, and that the communication of thoughts, feelings, and memories can lead to personality change—Freud was influenced by Breuer's disclosure that he had broken off the case in a state of panic on recognizing the strong reaction the patient was provoking in him.

Eliminating Emotions

Theoretically, Freud solved the problem of safeguarding practitioners of psychoanalysis from disorganizing embroilments with patients by eliminating the analyst's emotions as a factor in treatment. Rigid adherence to the notion of countertransference as an invariable source of resistance, however, retarded the development of an effective psychotherapy.

Sanctioning Emotions

Breaching the self-defensive rigidity of the classical method in the quest for better results, many psychotherapists have found that feelings for the patient, rather than interfering with treatment, actually facilitate it, provided that the practitioner's behavior is consistently oriented to resolving the obstacles to emotional maturity that emerge in each case. This lesson, evolving from Breuer's theraputically rewarding albeit traumatic experience, is restoring emotional communication to the armamentarium of psychotherapy.

Accepting Emotions

One modality that has escaped this hobbling is group psychotherapy. It has always drawn on the feelings that group members, serving in effect as cotherapists, develop for one another as an instrument of treatment. But the group therapeutic setting is an exceptionally powerful vehicle for arousing emotions, and how to exploit this force without exposing patients to damaging action is still an unsolved problem. The communication of feelings in language is constructive; venting them in action is destructive. (Spotnitz, 1961). Mastery of that distinction is, I believe, one of the crucial tasks confronting the field, for unless emotional action is inhibited, emotional communication fails to achieve its purpose.

Contemporary Problems

Contemporary group therapy demonstrates various symptoms of primitivism. For example, the values, limitations, and goals of each new method reported are rarely delineated; all too often its exponents imply that it is generally applicable. Failure to give due consideration to the specific therapeutic needs of the patient persists, despite some movement toward specificity (Spotnitz, 1971).

Specificity. The introduction of new techniques and new factors to be controlled may presage a system of group psychotherapy that is firmly grounded in accurate diagnosis and that encompasses specific interventions to resolve the psychotherapeutic problem at hand. Malfunctioning of the human mind cannot be corrected unless one ascertains the developmental level at which it has occurred.

Most claims of good results achieved through group treatment pertain to malfunctioning at the oedipal level, which can be corrected with relative ease by many different approaches. But the correction of disturbed functioning at the preoedipal level, which is implicated in the severe psychiatric disorders, usually entails highly specific procedures in each case.

Experimentation. Therapeutic experimentation in the areas of schizophrenia, psychotic depression, and severe psychosomatic disorders is a pressing need today. Acquisition of the understanding and skills necessary to resolve these conditions consistently and expeditiously would greatly enhance the role of the group psychotherapist in the resolution of the whole range of psychologically reversible disorders that beset mankind.

PART FIVE:

Clinical Research

Recognition of the responsiveness of schizophrenic patients to psychological therapy has stimulated the expansion of the field of psychotherapy to encompass the treatment of the other preoedipal conditions. This expansion has been accompanied by a sharp upsurge in experimentation.

Inasmuch as the modern psychoanalytic approach requires special training and modifications in the personality of the therapist, some research-oriented practitioners are endeavoring to develop less personally demanding systems of treatment. Others engaging in experimental activity are motivated primarily by the obvious need to increase the frequency with which the long-range goals of the treatment are realized. Although the effectiveness of psychotherapy in the preoedipal conditions has been repeatedly demonstrated, the task of making it more *consistently* effective looms ahead.

Chapter 26 suggests some general principles for conducting experimental work in psychotherapy.

Chapter 27 comments on a method of multiple therapy, in which a group of therapists concerted their efforts to resolve an acute psychotic outburst in one schizophrenic patient.

Chapter 28 points out the danger of exposing patients to a non-specific method—for example, marathon therapy—without establishing proper safeguards.

26

Experimentation in Psychotherapy

Research in the practice of healing human beings has always been a highly sensitive undertaking. The practitioner is confronted with complex responsibilities and ethical issues that do not challenge the advancement of knowledge in other fields. A famous scientist whose experiments involved fossils and plants said, "I love fools' experiments; I am always making them." That remark was made by Charles Darwin. He could afford to be lighthearted, because his research efforts did not expose him to the risk of being held liable for negligence. How different would have been the fate of Edward Jenner had his first innoculation been damaging to the 8-year-old boy he vaccinated with smallpox virus obtained from a diseased cow!

ETHICAL CONSIDERATIONS

Some of the special issues involved in medical research are highlighted in a popular novel of the 1920s—Sinclair Lewis's *Arrowsmith*. The novel focuses on the ethical conflict surrounding the withholding of cure from some of the afflicted while attempting to establish the value of a new medicine. If you are familiar with the novel, you will recall that Arrowsmith did not continue to contemplate the fate of his controls with scientific detachment after his wife died of the same disease. Thereupon, the controlled experiment ended; everyone got the vaccine.

EXPERIMENTING WITH THE PATIENT

In recent years, there has been much concentrations on the opposite concern—that is, the degree of protection and knowledge afforded those individuals on whom new treatment methods and unknown drugs are tested. A code reflecting this concern was adopted by the World Medical Association at a meeting in Finland in 1964, and approved two years later by the American Medical Association.

The Therapeutic Factor

The great significance of this so-called Helsinki Declaration is that it introduces a fundamental and clear distinction between "clinical research in which the aim is essentially therapeutic for a patient, and clinical research, the essential object of which is purely scientific and without therapeutic value to the person subjected to the research"—in other words, without immediate value. Where research is combined with professional care, the Declaration asserts that "if at all possible, consistent with patient psychology, the doctor should obtain the patient's freely-given consent after the patient has been given a full explanation." The emphasis on freely-given consent and explanation of the research goes beyond the criterion of family or self-volunteering referred to in the Nuremberg Code.

Also relevant to this discussion is the revision of the so-called consent clause of the Food and Drug Law in 1967 to emphasize the factor of patient knowledge—informed consent to serving as test subject or controls in the administration of any drugs that are being used for investigational purposes. These broader developments serve to illuminate the search for guides to professional responsibility in psychotherapy.

Destructive Effects

Experimentation that leads to destructive effects is by no means limited to social work or medicine. In a sense, life itself is the outcome of an experiment in nature. Predictably, the merger of an egg and sperm cell will, over a period of nine months, produce a child. The mother-child relationship, similarly, is an experiment in biological and psychological growth. We know many types of ingredients are necessary in a relationship to make this a constructive experiment, one that will facilitate the maturation of the child. We also know many factors that will influence the experiment of individual development in the direction of personal destructiveness or impede the growing individual from realizing his potentiality in life. It is when the favorable continuity of the relationship is threatened or has been blocked that the psychotherapist is called upon to intervene.

In working to defeat the forces that threaten a person's physical or psychological survival, we apply two basic rules: (1) do not harm the patient; and (2) help the patient—alleviate his suffering, help him to become healthy, to enjoy life, to be more productive. Both rules are, in a sense, the controls we apply in participating in the broader life experiment of each individual we are concerned with in our professional capacities. Obviously, then, destructive experimentation violates the fundamental rules of the healing professions.

Variables

What factors may be varied in our experimentation? In analytic psychotherapy, our intangible assistance is limited to what can be provided through verbal communication. Such assistance can be conveyed with or without emotional language. Diagnostic considerations, factors of timing, family relationships, environmental crises, and many other concerns dictate the necessity to function empirically even when we are exclusively concerned with psychotherapy. It is therefore difficult indeed to draw a clear line between therapy and experiment.

Trial contact. Even the initial decision to form a therapeutic relationship is made on an experimental basis. All that is agreed to is a reasonable period of trial contact. At the end of this period, the patient enjoys the same right as the therapist to terminate the relationship. Moreover, the process of changing oneself involves the capacity and the willingness to explore and test out new modes of relatedness. The unlearning of undesirable patterns requires much effort, and a high degree of psychic discomfort or pain often accompanies the acceptance of new and better ways of coping with problems. We cannot help a person change if he insists on remaining rigid. His consent to engage in the experimental process is as implicit in therapy as in research.

I started to work recently with a young man who utilized the period of trial contact to investigate the extent to which I would permit him to control me. He was interested in finding out how I would react to his expression of intense feelings of rage at his father, who had exacted strict subservience to his every demand on the patient.

Through his testing-out maneuvers, the young man discovered that I was willing to let him control me—that is, control on the verbal level. His initial therapeutic need was for an atmosphere that would enable him to experience and communicate the rage his father did not permit him to express.

Sharing information. In considering the advisability of sharing information with the patient, one needs to bear in mind that the effects of doing so are often unpredictable, and can be damaging. You may have heard about the man who, after being informed of his therapist's impression that he (the patient) was homosexual, committed suicide. On the other hand, sharing information can be very beneficial. This is illustrated by the story (whose source I don't recall) about the man who told his psychiatrist that evil people pursued him wherever he went, and was terrified that they might catch up with him. The psychiatrist regarded this as a delusion until the day he happened to observe from his office window a man seating himself at a bench across the street as the patient entered the office and departing as he left it. At the next session, the psychiatrist told the patient, "It is my impression that you are being followed." "Who is following me?" the patient asked in a state of alarm. When told about the man on the bench, however, he heaved a sign of relief and said, "Oh, that's just the man I hired to protect me from the others." Besides allaying his anxiety, the information initiated a productive examination of his unrealistic fears.

But one needs to foresee how a patient would react to information before volunteering it. Is he capable of using the information in his own interests? Adult patients at times need the same kind of protection that a young child requires from information that would be too wounding or which they are unable to cope with in stressful circumstances.

Consent. Clearly, what we are allowed to do with our patients is to engage in verbal communication. This is the essence of clinical research in psychotherapy, and requires no special authorization. But any other mode of intervention ought to be regarded as a form of experimentation that requires the sanction of the patient, his family, and the community.

In medicine, experimentation denotes the application of a new method for the sole aim of curing an otherwise incurable condition; if the method turns out to be a life-saving procedure for the first individuals exposed to it, it eventually becomes the subject of medical research. But as long as its outcome is uncertain and its hazards undetermined, it is classified as experimentation. Before experimenting, the physician has the duty of obtaining the consent of the patient or, if he can not be told about it, the consent of some responsible member of his family.

One would assume that the consent would be gladly given unless the risk factor appeared too great to the persons concerned. However, as I discovered early in my practice, consent may be withheld for other reasons.

Many years ago, I was engaged in the treatment of senile psychotic patients in a public mental institution. They did not respond to the accepted modes of treatment, and the prognosis was that they would spend the rest of their lives in the hospital. Insulin subcoma for ambulatory patients had been introduced and was proving effective in the treatment of other conditions; but its potentialities in the treatment of senile psychoses and the risks entailed were unknown at that time.

A colleague and I were very much interested in investigating the effects of insulin subcoma for this group of patients. We explained to the responsible members of their families the risks involved and also the possibility that the patients could return home if the experiment proved successful. The families were unwilling to cooperate but not—to our great surprise—because they feared the patients might not survive the experiment; the families did not relish the prospect that their aged relatives might recover sufficiently to leave the hospital. There was no room for them at home, family members explained; besides, their care would be burdensome. Consequently, the experiment was stymied not because it was hazardous but because it might succeed.

Being wanted. One gets to recognize that therapeutic research is retarded by many other factors besides the unwillingness of the subject to engage in it. The hazard involved may actually be a relatively minor consideration. Perhaps the most powerful incentive to therapeutic research would be the establishment of a social setting in which those who participate in mutually beneficial research projects are wanted people whose future well-being is of great value to themselves, to their families and to the community at large.

Conflicts of Interest

Conflicts may arise between protection of the privacy of clients being treated in a social agency and the safeguarding of a research design. Some medical scientists incline to the view that such patients should be charged with responsibility for cooperating in the research programs of the agency providing their treatment. In the opinion of one well-known research psychiatrist, all those who benefit from the use of facilities and services that operate with community support have a "moral obligation" to take part in research projects oriented to the improvement of diagnostic and treatment procedures. Social agencies exist primarily to serve their clients, and respect for the welfare of these individuals should be the paramount consideration. Rather than representing participation as a moral obligation, I would support the idea that agencies should try to help their clients to cooperate in these projects. But if the personal problems of one or another individual interfere with his participation, in my view it is inadvisable to subject him to pressure to participate.

EXPERIMENTING WITH THE THERAPIST

Should we allow our patients to experiment with us? Instead of answering that question directly, I want to recall the fruits of one experiment by a patient.

She was an attractive and highly accomplished young woman who entered treatment in Vienna some ninety years ago for a severe emotional illness. Her physician diagnosed it as a "psychosis of a peculiar kind"; hysterical mechanisms were accompanied by alternating stages of consciousness. The patient talked, and the more she talked, the more she improved, so she called the treatment her "talking cure."

The name of her physician was Josef Breuer. He reported that the young woman's improvement through talking took him "completely by surprise, and not until symptoms had been got rid of in this way in a whole series of instances did I develop a therapeutic technique out of it" (1893-1895, p. 46). Breuer was so impressed with the effects of talking that he discussed the case with a junior colleague and friend, Sigmund Freud. Freud persuaded Breuer to report it, and it appears in their joint work, *Studies on Hysteria*, as the Case of Anna O.

The identity of this patient-experimenter is now known because Ernest Jones believed that she deserved credit as the discoverer of the cathartic method. Seventeen years after her death, in his biography of Freud, Jones (1953) identified her as Bertha Pappenheim. He also revealed that, after recovering from her illness, she became the first social worker in Germany and, indeed, one of the first in the world. This famous case is excellent precedent for permitting experiments by patients in the course of psychotherapy—that is, experiments in the framework of verbal communication.

MAKING EXCEPTIONS

In conclusion, therapeutic experimentation is as desirable in psychotherapy as in clinical medicine. It is preferable that such experimentation be carried on with the full knowledge and consent of the individual concerned, and it is important to have his full cooperation. It goes without saying that his integrity and personality need to be respected.

In the field of research, however, these principles cannot be applied as hard and fast rules. Exceptional situations arise where a partial violation of the principles may be necessary for the benefit of the client and the community. But whenever an exception is in order, it should be made with the consent of the pertinent authorities and with adequate protection for the interests of all persons involved in the experiment.

27

Multiple Therapy in Acute Psychosis

Dr. Albert Scheflen watched Dr. John Rosen, several times a week for two years, demonstrate his system of psychotherapy with schizophrenics. He also held regular discussions with Rosen, studied his patients and their families, repeatedly audited tape recordings, and analyzed films of the treatment sessions. A product of this carefully documented study of the practice and theories of direct analysis is a dispassionate and enlightening book (Scheflen, 1961).

AN INVESTIGATION OF PSYCHOTHERAPY

Appropriately, Dr. Lawrence Kubie in the preface commends Rosen for submitting his operations with patients to the "microscopic scrutiny" of a multidisciplinary team of experts, and Scheflen for the "sympathetic empathy and objective critique" that pervade his study (p. x.). Beyond its value as a scientific appraisal of one widely discussed system whose precise nature and effectiveness have been obscured by both the extravagant claims and the heated counterclaims it has evoked, the book has a broader significance. It constitutes a model for psychotherapeutic investigations by a third party. Its ultimate contribution, as its author suggests, may be to "methods of observing and describing the process of psychotherapy" (p. 9). These should facilitate comparative evaluations of treatment methods and clarify their common aspects and significant variables. Investigations of the psychotoxic forces that operate in human relationships could be conducted in the same way.

THE METHOD

Use of Assistants

Rosen treats one person at a time and his assistants have generally been regarded as strong-armed attendants required to assure his personal safety. But Scheflen makes it clear that Rosen's assistants reinforce him psychologically as well as physically. "It soon became apparent," Scheflen writes, "that the interaction with a group of assistants was basic in direct analysis" (p. 10).

He provides considerable data on this interaction, which occurs in the daily treatment sessions lasting from a few minutes to six hours as well as around the clock in the small residential center of the Institute for Direct Analysis. The custodial care, supervision, and companionship provided the patient by the assistants mirrors and reinforces the immediate clinical situation. They develop emotional ties with him and serve as models for identification. Functioning as sibling or parental figures, they maintain the same attitude as Rosen, strengthening his ties with the patient and helping him in other ways to accomplish his objectives.

Presence of Observers

In addition to the few assistants who invariably participate, observers attend the sessions. The presence of the latter is also exploited as pressure on the patient; at times he interacts directly with an observer. Fellows in training as associate therapists, along with members of the research team, swelled to from ten to fifteen the number of persons assembled in the home-like living room. There they sat "as a family would" (p. 18), according to Scheflen. Rosen often turned from the patient to speak to them like a "father speaking to guests about his child" (p. 15) or addressed observers and patient simultaneously. He did not continue his intimate conversations very long and "seemed to frequently signal that this was a group relationship, not simply one to one" (p. 192).

Use of Psychological Force

The descriptions of how patients are handled in direct analysis are excellent. On the basis of the clinical material selected from the unedited tapes of the sessions, some misunderstanding of Rosen's interventions is evident; but, by and large, the author's analysis is sound.

Disputing Rosen's assumption that he gives insight to his patients, Scheflen points out that the treatment is designed to force them to give up their psychotic attitudes. He presents ideas which promote understanding of psychotics. Especially instructive are the author's observations on the approaches and feelings involved in establishing a relationship with an acutely psychotic patient and on the psychiatric formulations and emotional language to which the latter will respond.

Authoritarian Attitude

The techniques described in the book are skillfully employed, with much switching of levels of communication and tactics. Though Rosen presents whatever kind of image he believes will bring the patient out of psychosis, the therapist's dominant attitude is overtly authoritarian and fosters over-dependency. With individual and group techniques, he does an emergency job to establish speedy contact, eradicate "craziness," and return the patient to the community as soon as possible.

Focus on misbehavior. These goals are short-sighted, in view of the psychological scarring which results from the forcible suppression of an acute psychosis. Scheflen also recognizes Rosen's lack of regard for the anal period of development. Rosen appears to be oblivious to the ego's role both in releasing aggression and in defending itself against the release of aggression. He considers misbehavior to be the main problem, caused by the mother's lack of love for the patient, and does not investigate the possibility that the misbehavior may be just a symptom and that aggression may be the nuclear problem.

Rosen is able to tolerate whatever hostility the patient manifests, which may help to explain why he focuses on the misbehavior instead. As Kubie points out: "The therapist's aggression may block and overwhelm the patient's aggression prematurely, thus forcing a patient to simulate adult restraints" (p. x.).

RESULTS OBSERVED

Rapid Improvement

Evident symptomatic improvement was observed within a few days or weeks in the eight cases whose clinical course was studied by Scheflen. Four of the patients made a community adjustment; two did briefly, and two others not at all. "With a symptom-reduction standard," he writes, "at least three-quarters of the eight are in the direction of success, with an adjustment standard half of them are in the direction of success and with a maturational frame of reference at best a quarter are in that direction" (p. 233).

Direct analysis appears to be an approach that relieves psychosis quickly and brings some schizophrenics out of acute psychotic states. But a system which is consistently effective with these patients and, when necessary, meets their maturational needs as well, still awaits development.

Simultaneous Interactions

Despite his errors and the shortcomings of his method, Rosen is revealed to be a gifted and dedicated therapist with the natural forte and drive to relieve acutely psychotic patients, however he has to go about it. Though not the first to do this through psychotherapeutic intervention, he has undoubtedly done more than anyone else to alert us to the possibility of handling these cases through psychological methods.

Has he also alerted us, however inadvertently, to an area of investigation that may hold great promise? His results suggest that the group therapeutic situation of several therapists in simultaneous interaction with one patient could be forged into a powerful instrument for the relief of acute psychosis. Certainly, the potential value of the group setting for that purpose merits serious study.

28

Dangers

Some interesting scientific ideas are presented in Dr. Frederick Stoller's report (1968) on an intensive (weekend) experience for individuals whose purpose and motives in committing themselves to it are said to resemble those of patients undergoing treatment on an ambulatory basis. In this so-called accelerated interaction, the group leader sets the tone for "honest, direct, and open communication" (p. 222) by engaging in it himself. Pressure is exerted to produce behavioral breakthroughs; it is hoped that "important and enduring changes" (p. 220) will occur; and the "here and now" experience so well described is one of mounting emotional involvement apparently culminating in a sort of manic excitement. Good results, as well as definitely undesirable ones, are reported.

EVALUATION AND DIAGNOSIS

A new treatment instrument cannot be evaluated purely on the basis of its rationale; theory occasionally lags behind practice. An inadequate hypothesis that yields good results is better than an adequate one that does not. Nevertheless, it is pertinent to scrutinize the assumptions underlying accelerated interaction and the special values attributed to it.

It is true, as Dr. Stoller points out, that "effective change is not necessarily a function of long-term contact" (p. 222) but it is not necessarily a function of short-term contact either. The method he recommends is founded on an assumption that has yet to be tested. Until it is ultimately proved or disproved on the basis of adequate evidence, accelerated interaction should be clearly identified as an experiment in group process. Its acceptance as a therapeutic instrument must rest on experiential data contradicting the well-established principles of diagnosing a condition before prescribing a treatment for it and then helping the patient to master the specific psychological constellation in which his difficulties are rooted.

CLINICAL CAUTION

When people are "given the expectation that they will be able to take care of themselves," Dr. Stoller believes that they "do a remarkable job of doing just that" (p. 222). In my experience, this is not necessarily true. To feel exhilarated and renewed is not invariably therapeutic. The dropping of masks and "learning that the masks are not so necessary" (p. 225) disregard the fact that some masks are vitally needed ego defenses. Some patients are unable to build bridges until they have outgrown their need for barriers.

In short, the primary shortcoming of this paper is that it argues for the exposure of patients to an experience that may be desirable for some and undesirable for others without establishing any objective criteria for participation. A selection of candidates for accelerated interaction based primarily on "the feelings of the group leader" (p. 233) seems to me to be a rather hit-or-miss policy.

Even the so-called sensitivity training groups sponsored by various business and professional organizations for their personnel, screening procedures are "sorely needed" (Garwood, 1967). In a recent account of the use of intensive process groups as a training procedure for mental health workers, Dr. Milton Berger (1967) mentioned instances in which emergency psychotherapeutic assistance had to be administered to participants. Elementary clinical caution would seem to dictate the exclusion of persons with serious emotional disturbances from groups of this nature.

Consensus. In discussing the leader's participation, Dr. Stoller states that if the group does not echo the leader's response, he should regard it as a "special distortion of his own" (p. 226). I would challenge the view that consensus is decisive. The leader (or, for that matter, any member of the group) can be right and the others can be wrong. Repeated discussions of the point at issue are in order. They will either lead to common agreement in conformity with objective data or, equally important, establish the right to disagree.

POTENTIAL VALUE

To return to the major question raised by this report: Can an emotional experience such as Dr. Stoller describes, highly concentrated in time and created in a situation with a built-in sense of urgency, produce significant personality change? The simple truth is that we do not know the answer. If periods of excitement in a new situation can free an individual from the effects of past traumatic events, such an approach may have therapeutic potential. It might, for example, help to mitigate or nullify the effects of another type of deeply emotional experience, such as a paralyzing reaction to the death of a loved one. This possibility might bear investigation. But, in my opinion, there is little likelihood that the method described will be recognized as a form of psychotherapy.

It has been discovered and repeatedly demonstrated that people suffering from psychoneuroses and other psychologically reversible illnesses have been forced into personally and socially undesirable patterns of adjustment from which they have to free themselves before they can develop patterns more appropriate to their life situation. The process of liberating them from the old patterns entails reawakening the patterns with their original impulse intensity; any new form of treatment, to have long-range effectiveness, must address itself to reviving the old traumatic constellation. There is no evidence that the task can be accomplished simply through exposure to new experience, however profound such exposure is in its emotional impact.

GRATIFICATION VERSUS MATURATION

A group experience such as Dr. Stoller describes is very exciting for some patients. They discover that the give-and-take in situations of intense feeling can be highly enjoyable. It also encourages impulsive behavior, which may have immediately thrilling—and not so thrilling—consequences. It is my impression that these experiences are gratifying rather than therapeutic and that they increase the resistance to working to develop the ability to resolve one's own problems.

Dr. Stoller's observations on the responses of patients to those with whom they share a treatment experience conducted by the regular method are at variance with my own. Analytic group psychotherapy is a powerful instrument for desirable change. The disadvantages or limitations he ascribes to it are, in my experience, the result of errors in technique. When the group members are studied and understood, and when this understanding is effectively communicated to them, they become mature and considerate individuals.

The standard procedures for analytic psychotherapy in both individual and group treatment settings have been painstakingly worked out over many years, and their effects have been carefully studied. There is room for further improvement in both modalities, and they may not be the best techniques for dealing with every emotional problem. But other procedures cannot lay claim to therapeutic effectiveness just because they are new and different.

PROFESSIONAL RESPONSIBILITY

Current interest in the so-called marathon groups suggests that we are now encountering in the field of psychological medicine a phenomenon paralleling the search, in biological medicine, for one panacea for all known disease processes. That search has been abandoned; it demonstrated the necessity of devising and refining specific procedures for the treatment of different conditions. The armamentarium is now enormous, ranging from minor forms of physical therapy to radical surgery, and in some cases if offers treatment options for one disease. The quest for the wonder drug has been given up; the pharmacopoeia lists thousands of drugs, all of which were carefully assayed during a period of experimentation.

New and better ways of counteracting toxic patterns of human relatedness than through long-term treatment methods may be discovered. The advent of procedures that would obviate the painful and time-consuming task of working through unresolved emotional conflicts would certainly be welcome. But indications, dosages, points of application, and positive and negative values should be established before a new approach is presented as a method of treatment.

In other words, theories are fine, and their possible applications merit thorough investigation with the aid of good research designs. In the course of collecting the essential data, if the procedure in question is presented to the patients who participate and the profession at large as an experimental method, a disservice to the field of psychotherapy would be avoided.

PART SIX:

Training

The individual and group treatment approaches discussed in this book make stringent professional and personal demands on the psychotherapist. Some problems encountered in administering psychotherapy to severely disturbed patients have already been pointed out. New dimensions in training are viewed and illustrated in the next three chapters.

Chapters 29 and 30 relate specifically to the training of analytic group therapists. In the first, I report on my own use of the group setting for the affect training of group therapists working with problem patients. Chapter 30 discusses the lively account of supervisory sessions in which a young psychiatrist focused on his initial difficulties in treating a group of "captive" patients (offenders).

Recognizing one's own feelings and using them effectively with patients to repair severe personality damage entails change in the therapist. Chapter 31 indicates how such change is fostered in the training of the modern psychoanalyst.

29

Affect Training of
Analytic Group Therapists

This is a report on the ongoing training, for a period of two years, of experienced therapists in a group structured in accordance with the principles of analytic group process and resistance reinforcement. The group's activity is designed to assist its members in dealing with severely disturbed patients, either in group or individual treatment.

The group functions as a voluntary training instrument since all of its members, seven women and three men, are psychiatric social workers or psychologists who have undergone personal psychoanalysis and have had many years' experience in analytic psychotherapy with children and adults, both individually and in groups. The author is the leader of the group, which meets for a two-hour session in his office every other week. This report was prepared after 32 sessions.

INITIAL ARRANGEMENTS

The group was formed on the initiative of one of its members. After consulting with the author, she had invited 13 therapists to a preliminary meeting at her home. All of them had received some individual supervisory training from the author, either in his private practice or as consultant at a social service agency. The eight persons who attended that meeting, and three other interested therapists known to all of them, composed the group when it started to function one month later. Except for the loss of one member, who dropped out for family reasons after a few months, the group has remained as originally constituted. A silent observer at each session is the recorder, from whose notes a report of the proceedings is prepared.

The preliminary meeting called by the group's founder drew up what the author had suggested: an agreement regarding the purpose, plan, and method of functioning of the proposed group. That meeting also made it evident that they wished their training to be oriented to the treatment needs of individual patients, especially those with severe initial resistances and/or poor prognoses. Practical arrangements were made at the same time for the payment of the leader's fee and, with more difficulty, for a meeting time acceptable to all concerned.

One suggestion made was that case presentations and case discussions should be employed as part of the group training process. Their individual development through this process, the members-to-be felt, would help them become better therapists. The understanding, the discharge, and the ultimate resolution of their disguised hostility and competitiveness would, in their opinion, lead to warm feelings. The eight therapists participating in that discussion also expressed interest in studying the literature and engaging in research on psychoanalytic psychotherapy, as well as in writing papers on various aspects of their group training experience.

The group's activity, as they formulated it at that time, would have these three major goals: first of all, to study the impact of the group experience on themselves—that is, its impact on "both the subject and object of training," as one of them later explained; secondly, to study the group's impact, through themselves, on their patients; and finally, to study the value of the group as a teaching tool. The therapists anticipated that their functioning in the group would help them to "spell out precisely what they were doing intuitively or awarely" and to determine "why a particular approach fails or succeeds." They hoped thereby to clarify their knowledge and consolidate their treatment methods.

Obviously, they proposed to utilize the process of communication in the group setting to augment their own understanding, knowledge, and emotional maturity in order to acquire greater facility in treating seriously disturbed patients. And they had implicit understanding that any of their impulses, feelings, thoughts, and actions which impeded the attainment of their common goals would constitute their own resistance patterns.

THE LEADER'S PLAN

Resistance patterns have been given top priority in the group leader's own plan for helping the members achieve their goals. Although he has never communicated his plan to the group directly, he has implied it through his behavior, his questions, the expression of his feelings, and other statements during the sessions. Specifically, the leader's plan is to utilize the group process to stimulate and facilitate the emergence and discharge of the individual and the group resistances, to analyze these resistances and, by reinforcing them and assisting in the verbalization or interpretation of their patterns, to help the group master them.

In this process the leader's responses, which range from mild disapproval or displeasure to approval, admiration, and the occasional highlighting of the resistance patterns, are all designed to *preserve* these patterns until they have been fully resolved. In situation after situation, he uses his personality to secure the recognition and maintenance of the resistance patterns until they have been verbalized and mastered. In essence, therefore, his plan is one of interacting with his trainees exactly as he recommends that they interact with any of their own patients manifesting the same resistance patterns.

This type of leadership is designed to produce the kind of group climate in which members will feel free to diverge in language from what, whether correctly or falsely, they consider at a given moment to be their proper goal. In other words, the leader is helping the group resist—engage in so-called resistance—so that the amount of suppressed aggression the members will have for one another at any one time, because of group pressure, will be kept at a minimum. Hence, volitional stress for the attainment of the group's goal—that is, the amount of stress to which the members will voluntarily submit—is very limited. Instead, a spontaneous drift toward group evolution is facilitated through the joining of the group resistances.

COMMON RESISTANCES

In principle, all of the members accept this approach; they share the notion that resistances ought to be joined, analyzed, understood and mastered rather than forcibly overcome or overpowered. Nevertheless, it has been interesting to observe that they have given scant attention to their leader's application of this principle during the group sessions, primarily because they have as a unit paid little attention to the common resistances which he has been trying to help them resolve. Although, by and large, the members are alert to their individual resistances—their own, those of co-members, and the counterresistances of the group leader—they do not spontaneously look for resistances in their common behavior. Hence, a pattern of behavior appears to be regarded as goal-directed when all or most of them engage in it together. Common participation usually breeds common consent, and when they all consent to behaving in the same way, this is generally assumed to be appropriate behavior.

If their collective psychological functioning appears too manifestly inappropriate to ignore, the members tend to regard it as something completely extraneous, as dissociated from their common goal-directed behavior. Failing to accept such functioning as group resistances that ought to be studied and resolved rather than exposed to attack, they have complained instead that they were individually experiencing flight reactions, feelings of chaos, boredom, helplessness, disgust, or resentment. From time to time, they exclaim that they are "floating around" or are "piddling away" their time.

Indecision about how they should function, and a tendency to form subgroups are among their common resistances. There has been a marked inability to make unanimous decisions in the group setting, despite the preliminary agreement of eight of the present ten members regarding their purpose, plan, and method. To illustrate: Although no one course of action has ever been agreed to, a majority of the members seem to have acquired the idea that the training process is under way only when cases are being presented or discussed, and that time spent in other forms of activity is being frittered away. This resistance has gradually weakened as discussions of theoretical problems or techniques and the reading of papers have proved to be worth while.

Nevertheless, the aggression mobilized by the lack of interest in the common resistances to the training process still leads to occasional attacks upon the member whose case is being reported and reviewed, to requests that he be eliminated from the role of presenter, and even to the threatened breakup of the group itself. Each attempt to hammer disagreement into agreement, instead of dealing constructively with the common group resistances, has produced only brief periods of gratification. Eventually, the unresolved resistances emerge again in some other form.

Should one be surprised that experienced therapists could function together for 64 hours without devoting serious attention to their common resistances to analytic group process? We do not regard this as extraordinary, in view of their personal motives and expectations in forming their group. Each became a part of it primarily to obtain an immediate and individual benefit—that is, to acquire greater facility in understanding and interacting therapeutically with especially difficult patients. The members were not oriented to the idea that, over and above what they could extract separately and directly from their sessions, learning to function well together would itself be an important aspect of training through analytic group process. They did not appear to realize that the better the group performance per se, the more valuable this experiential form of joint training would be for each of tem. Failure to realize that group process cannot be short-circuited caused one member to complain that the group never took the "shortest distance between two points."

EVOLVING PROCESSES

During an evaluation of their progress after the first year's activity, one group member observed: "This is a very interesting experience. Many of us feel uncomfortable because it is so different from a seminar . . . We feel guilty and upset that it takes so long, and then we regress into play. Our leader has been testing us, but we didn't have to regress. I am fascinated by the way the creative process develops and then is stymied. When the resistance was broken through in one session, we had a really fascinating evening." Parenthetically, this serves to illustrate how shifting by common consent from one resistance pattern to another at that point tended to be regarded as fascinating. Having "fascinating evenings" was not one of the group's goals.

In analytic group process, for whatever purpose it is employed, a group is constantly evolving into something more than the sum of its original parts. The group is a living, dynamic organism. When it is brought into being, its various organs are lacking in synthesis. Like those of the human infant, they are in different stages of development and have to undergo a gradual process of growth and integration before the total organism can function maturely. A group of experienced psychotherapists enjoys no greater immunity to the complex phenomenology of this process than a group of patients undergoing therapy.

Their instinctive awareness of this fact has been reflected in the trainees' expressions of distaste and impatience with their early functioning together. Few if any of them had given any thought to how much time and actual experience in interacting together would be required to form a well-integrated group, or to the desirability of becoming such a group. Their experience demonstrates that therapists electing to be trained together through analytic process may anticipate undergoing much the same basic practice in functioning together as first-rate musicians forming a new orchestra or top athletes recruited for a team. Like a good symphonic performance and good teamwork, good group work follows the process of achieving group coordination, group identity, and group spirit. And this is a relatively slow process, especially when resistance reinforcement is being carried on. The structure of this group's functioning was designed to delay the development of group coordination and identity, and to study the factors militating against their development.

This evolutionary process is continuing. The group's primary interest is still one of functioning in a pleasant, goal-bound atmosphere. The tendency to rule out any activity that does not appear to be directly and immediately related to the stated goals also persists. Although inattentive, thus far, to its common resistances—or possibly, because of this inattentiveness—the group has already made substantial progress.

PARALLELISMS

A comprehensive study of the record of its activity indicates that this training group, which is being dealt with in accordance with the principles recommended for the severely disturbed patients its members are being trained to treat, is itself tending to evolve through the same stages as one of these difficult cases when the patient's own resistance patterns are similarly dealt with. Whether coincidentally or significantly, a striking parallel has emerged between the group's unfolding resistances and those of the particular patient whose case was receiving detailed study.

To clarify this point, it should be explained that each of three case presentations has held the group's attention for a period of several months. While each presenter volunteered to report on a case he or she had personally chosen, the survival of that case for as many as eight or ten meetings may be attributed to the process of natural selection. This assumption seems warranted since the group has shown little inclination thus far to concern itself with the purely individual problems of the therapist-presenters, and has not hesitated to "kill off" each case as soon as it failed to satisfy their own psychological needs as a training group.

In the first several months of operation, dissension and divergence of views within the group forced the leader into a more or less authoritarian role. To keep the youthful organism in operation, he had to provide food for thought—digestible ideas about therapeutic concepts and techniques. In other words, he functioned a spsychological parent to sibling rivals who were vying for care and attention without any heed for the efficient functioning of the group. While all ears were being attuned to the leader's voice, the case under review was that of a passive and compliant boy who was concealing his aggression for fear of losing his father's protection.

The group then moved into an intensive study of a case in which family problems figured prominently. During that period, the group began to become aware that, instead of being haphazardly assembled for training by the same leader, they were coalescing into interdependent members of a group which, like a family, had a common purpose.

The shift in attitude became more pronounced during the extended study of the third case, that of an orally fixated patient whose dependency cravings had yet to be resolved despite repeated analysis. In meeting after meeting, the therapist-presenter was reporting the patient's incessant demands for gratification and his equally incessant complaints that he was failing to receive it. At that time, the members of the group were still remarking about its inadequate functioning, but they were learning enough to take the initiative in keeping it in operation. The difficulty of understanding and evolving toward truly cooperative functioning was stimulating them to make greater efforts to understand and meet their common needs. More and more interest was shown in helping the presenter deal with his problems in the case as well as in the analysis of the patient, his family relationships, and his broader social responsibilities.

EFFECTS OF TRAINING

Throughout this process of slow and rather painful nurturing, the group has been developing emotional tolerance to latent and mobilized frustration-aggression. This is one of the basic needs of the analytic psychotherapist who would deal with seriously disturbed patients, since the therapist functions with difficulty in such a case unless he can help the patient to accept, recognize, understand, and master his stubborn defenses against the libidinal or aggressive drives which threaten to overwhelm him. Our experience indicates that the therapeutic resolution of such patterns can be facilitated through analytic group training. It helps to insulate therapists against the intense emotional impact of the severely disturbed patient and gives them the freedom to respond to him with spontaneity and individuality.

Members of the group have reported that the training experience has had a significant effect upon them, and in certain instances upon their patients too. The emotional impact of the group situation has been especially great for the three therapists who have presented cases, although the response of each of them to the group's recommendations and the subsequent movement in the cases reported have been different in each instance. One presenter firmly rejected the group's recommendations but said he welcomed them because they had stimulated him to do his own thinking. Some therapists report that they are more susceptible to group training than to individual training; others state the reverse. The therapist-presenters experienced feelings of separation and alienation from the group. Each of them has reported that his later therapy sessions with the patient under consideration tended to focus on those aspects of the patient's material which had been scrutinized in the group setting. Significant changes in the type of material communicated by the patient were also noted subsequently.

The methods of group training described seemed to favor the development of group identity and group feeling, spontaneity, and individuality. These in turn apparently facilitated the mobilization of the therapist's insulative capacity to respond to the intense emotional impact of severely disturbed patients.

30

Supervision of the Group Psychotherapist

The development of a group therapist in supervision, a subject rarely treated systematically in the professional literature, is well delineated in Dr. Lawrence Brody's unusual report (1966). By couching it in the form of a dialogue, he conveys admirably the flavor of the preceptorial training experience, giving the reader a sense of "listening in" on the two sessions presented. In the context of the treatment goals formulated for the group under discussion, the roles of supervisor, therapist, and the group itself are portrayed in balanced perspective. Lucidly illustrated are the treatment philosophy and attitudes which motivate the practice of what might be termed emotional-catharsis therapy.

Both parties appear to be highly impressed with its therapeutic value, and their dialogue builds up the idea that group therapy is a procedure designed almost exclusively to produce "spontaneous, genuine interaction" (p. 464). But saying what one feels is not invariably therapeutic. It does not further the aims of treatment when indulged in for personal gratification rather than to appease a maturational need of the personality. Moreover, the ventilation of feelings in some situations can be damaging to other members of the group.

USE OF PARADIGMATIC STRATEGY

However, in the context of what the senior clinician was attempting to accomplish in the two sessions covered, he emerges from the report as an able teacher. Since he demonstrates through his own friendly, humorous, and nondogmatic manner the modes of communication which he recommends that his junior colleague employ in treatment, the dialogue provides a striking example of the effective use of paradigmatic strategy in supervision. Desirable clinical attitudes are voiced by the supervisor, who notably advocates, for example, that group therapy be conducted on the basis of operational principles rather than a narrow set of rules.

By engaging in emotionally spontaneous interchanges, group members provide one another with opportunities to experience emotional catharsis. The therapist is taught by example and suggestion to lead them into such interchanges by communicating genuinely himself. The implication of the supervisor's statement, "If you're being genuine, then you're doing group therapy" (p. 472) is clear: What more can one ask? Consideration of other important ingredients of psychotherapy is neatly foreclosed by that notion, but it surmounted what he regarded as the first hurdle in getting the group under way. After the therapist has become more comfortable and relaxed with the group and has thus influenced its members to verbalize their own feelings more comfortably, the idea of "being genuine" might well be supplemented by other theoretical guides (Slavson, 1966). However, when the fruits of the training experience are summarized at the end of the report, the therapeutic process is conceptualized simply as "being with someone, reaching in a natural, healthy way." The supervisor adds, "Sooner or later this rubs off on them, especially if youhelp them to see the 'neurosis' in their behavior" (p. 483).

If whatever prevents the members of a group from verbalizing their feelings spontaneously does boil down to "neurosis," it is logical to focus on helping them by suggestion and example to communicate their feelings. But many people who learn to "communicate genuinely" (p. 483) in psychotherapy are still unable to behave properly in life. More than temporary—so-called transference—improvement entails the understanding and mastery of the *obstacles* to emotionally spontaneous functioning, such as the conflicting latent feelings and inhibiting thoughts and memories. These, too, must be verbalized and resolved.

INFLUENCE OF THE INDUCED FEELINGS

The therapist might have been educated to the need for working on the obstacles to intrapsychic change in his group members had his own difficulties in relating to them effectively really been investigated and mastered with the help of the supervisor. The weakness in the report resides in its failure to delineate these difficulties, to account for their presence, and to respond to them constructively.

Individuals who have committed antisocial acts and who assemble for treatment together on a "captive" basis characteristically generate a great deal more resentment and anger in their therapist than those who undergo group therapy voluntarily. In this instance, the therapist did not know how to deal with the feelings induced in him by the offenders; he activated defenses against the induced feelings which put him "on the spot" (p. 464). The dialogue gives no evidence that his needs to be sadistic or controlling, to deny, manage, and manipulate were accepted as material for analysis. The needs per se were ignored; he was just instructed to relax and talk spontaneously.

Directions, cajolery, and other psychological pressures effectively influenced him to suppress his defensive attitudes and operate on the principle of accepting his feelings and verbalizing them when appropriate. But his personality difficulties were not resolved through this supervisory approach; they were by-passed for the time being. It is predictable that he will tend to slip back into his inappropriate attitudes with the same group or other groups until he is helped to understand and master the interfering tendencies which are hinted at in the report.

SUPERVISORY PROCESSES

The main reason for seeking help in dealing with the clinical problems that confront the psychotherapist entering practice is to avoid the costly years of trial and error which are likely to ensue if he tries to deal with these problems himself as they arise. The kind of training which he needs encompasses two separate processes. The first is teaching him directly how to deal with his patients as therapeutically as possible—the information-inculcating and technique-oriented aspect of training. Once he fully comprehends the general principles and procedures of treatment and how to apply them in a manner consonant with his own personality, an emotionally mature therapist should have smooth sailing in his practice. However, the emotionally mature or perfectly analyzed practitioner is a mythical personage (Glover, 1955). All of us develop countertransference reactions to every patient or group of patients we treat. Dealing with these phenomena constructively ourselves requires much experience and repeated self-examination. Helping the neophte to recognize and respond to them so that they will not prevent him from carrying out his clearly understood directions—in other words, operate as counterresistance—is the second process.

The trainee may need help in resolving one or another tendency to react to patients in a uniquely personal way. Winnicott (1949) implicitly classifies such reactions as subjective countertransference. Its counterresistance force is removed by successful analysis: recognition of the origin and history of the tendency in the therapist's own life experience, combined with an understanding of its current meaning.

Various kinds of troublesome feelings may be induced in the psychotherapist by the pathological patterns and communications of patients he treats. These realistically induced feelings are now coming to be accepted as countertransference reactions; Winnicott's concept of objective countertransference (1949) may be appropriately applied to such phenomena. While their counterresistance potential is an ever-present threat, they help to provide the emotional charge that facilitates the successful treatment of many seriously disturbed patients. The induced feelings may operate as counterresistance if the therapist remains unaware of their source. When he recognizes their origin and nature, they give him much information about the developmental history of the patient; the induced feelings can also be sustained and used to provide a patient with the therapeutic experience he needs (Spotnitz, 1963).

DEALING WITH COUNTERTRANSFERENCE RESISTANCE

There are differences of opinion on the extent to which countertransference phenomena should be dealt with in supervision. When the chronic failure of a supervisee to respond to preceptorial help is attributable to countertransference problems, whether subjective or objective in nature, some supervisors recommend that he resume personal analysis to deal with these problems. Other supervisors disclaim responsibility for helping a trainee resolve subjective countertransference resistance but address themselves to the objective phenomena.

My attitude is that dealing with both types of countertransference resistance comes within the purview of the supervisory situation. The policy of foreclosing or limiting the supervisor's task to the first training process is unrealistic because, in my experience, every trainee has to be educated to deal with countertransference phenomena himself. Undeniably, some forms of resistance in the therapist are so serious and deeply rooted that a return to didactic analysis is indicated; however, this course may be recommended, or the supervisor may try to overcome such resistance forcibly because he is unwilling or unable to deal with it. But whether the task is assigned to supervision or personal analysis, countertransference resistance must be resolved if the therapist is to achieve professional maturity.

31

Training in the Use of Feelings

You may have read an article in *The New York Times Magazine* about a mythical psychoanalyst whose total preparation for practice consisted in undergoing three years of personal analysis. In this way, according to the article, he "became familiar with the techniques of therapy."

Would that the acquisition of therapeutic knowledge and technical skills were as simple as that! But the process of purifying the instrument of treatment, freeing it of its blind spots, and making it emotionally mature does not teach us the best way to use it. Freud suspected that psychoanalysis, like the raising of children and the governing of nations, was an "impossible" profession (1937, p. 248), beyond human capabilities and certain to lead to unsatisfactory results. Those of us who are brash enough to commit ourselves to it eventually discover—and the sooner the better—that their training analysis, however successful, is only one of many items of professional equipment they need.

BASIC REQUIREMENTS

Psychological Talent

The most valuable item is one that can be nurtured and brought to fruition, but not acquired or compensated for through any type of training or any amount of experience in the profession. I refer, of course, to innate psy-

This paper was presented at a meeting of the Council of Psychoanalytic Psychotherapists, New York City, in 1962.

chological talent. With this native endowment, the disciplining of one's intellect and powers of observation is fostered by a good general education. Freud suggested a curriculum that included "elements from the mental sciences, from psychology, the history of civilization and sociology, as well as from anatomy, biology and the study of evolution" (1927, p. 252). All of these subjects, in his opinion, had a *direct* bearing on the practice of psychoanalysis. Were he alive today, he would probably add to this suggested program of studies.

Knowledge of the Literature

Another valuable item of equipment is a knowledge of the professional literature, past and present. In our field, there is much to learn, and much stimulus value in the findings and experiences of colleagues, however similar or dissimilar their theories and observations are to our own. But perhaps this recommendation should be ignored if you feel dismayed rather than reinforced to find at least the germ of your pet ideas in reports that others have published. I have come to the conclusion that there are few entirely "original" ideas in this field, however spontaneously they appear to grow out of our own mental activity and personal experience.

For example, I am reminded of a letter from D. W. Winnicott commenting on the publication of "The Attempt of Healthy Insulation in the Withdrawn Child" by Leo Nagelberg, Yonata Feldman, and myself (Chapter 15). Writing from London in 1953, Winnicott stated, "My attention has been drawn to your very interesting article. . . How difficult it is for us to keep in touch with the literature; the consequence being that we find ourselves doing similar work from independent sources. I enclose a reprint giving an indication of some of my own work, and I think you will see that if I had known of your article earlier, I would have quoted from it."

The Traditional Training

Now we come to what has figured in the systematic training of candidates in the psychoanalytic institutes for many years: the trinity of training or didactic analysis, the study and discussion of theory in lectures, seminars, and the like, and the treatment of a few cases under supervision.

In some circles theoretical learning and supervision in clinical work are regarded as little more than window-dressing. There is, to be sure, the alterna-approach of discovering the answers to clinical problems though one's own experience; but this usually entails the risky process of trial-and-error learning. It is more efficient to start practice with preceptorial aid, preferably with that of several senior colleagues, to avoid being unduly influenced by any one supervisor.

These, in brief, are the various qualifications or components of training that equip one for the practice of psychoanalysis, whether classical or modern. For either form, the refinement of the personal instrument and the mastery of the art of interpretation are prerequisites.

NEW ELEMENTS

In addition, the philosophy of treatment and the findings of modern psychoanalysis require the introduction of *new* elements in the training process.

The modern psychoanalyst works with the conceptual tools of resistance and transference. He employs interpretation to the extent to which it will be effective in dealing with the resistances of the individual patient. However, patients whose resistances do not yield to interpretation and working through are not regarded by the modern analyst, as they are by some classical analysts, as unsuitable analysands. Instead he regards the technique as unsuitable, and flexibly employs other procedures to meet the needs of the case. His activity is primarily analytic but his hallmark is the commitment of emotional power as well as intellectual power to the case. The general outlook of the modern analyst is eclectic, and his approach to each patient is pragmatic.

Emotional Power

Countertransference has been a basically negative preoccupation in analytic work. The neophyte in modern psychoanalysis needs to develop the ability to detect and eliminate its pitfalls; but in order to deal effectively with the most serious of the psychologically reversible conditions, he also has to apply the principle of extracting therapeutic leverage from countertransference phenomena. Their discriminative use in emotional communications to the patient is an important aspect of training in modern psychoanalysis.

Therapeutic leverage resides specifically in the feelings that the patient induces in the therapist—the normal response of the objective observer to the feelings and attitudes directed to the therapist as the transference object. Sorted out from any tendencies to react to the patient in a uniquely personal way, subjective reactions which the student may need help in recognizing and understanding, the realistically induced feelings comprise the side of the countertransference coin that has a therapeutic value.

Use of Objective Countertransference

Experience since Freud's time has taught us that many of the resistances he regarded as impenetrable are apparently upheld by the maturational needs lurking behind them. When the patient is helped to master the forces that have militated against the appeasement of these psychological growth needs, he is liberated from the compulsory and involuntary use of such resistances. This process is facilitated by certain types of interventions charged with the realistically induced feelings. In short, they serve as the key to the transformation of apparently intractable resistances into resolvable patterns, that is, resistances that will eventually yield to the standard method of interpretation and working through. Consequently, the use of the induced feelings, which Winnicott (1949) has referred to as the objective countertransference, may be a crucial factor in providing a patient with the emotional experiences he requires to become a mature personality.

PROBLEMS ENCOUNTERED IN SUPERVISION

Fear of Feelings

One of the most difficult problems in training, in my experience, is that many students are afraid to have feelings for a patient. They are averse to having them and using them. In their attempts to get rid of the feelings, they tend to operate in such a way as to get rid of the patient. They have to be helped to recognize that the issue is not one of having or not having feelings for the patient but of using their feelings to help him improve.

Anxious Aggression

Now and then the supervisor encounters an insufficiently analyzed trainee or one whose personality is not therapeutic for a particular patient. The trainee, in discussing the case, advances various problems as justification for dropping the case. For example, the patient needs a younger or older analyst or one of the opposite sex; or his treatment at this time or under his unfavorable life circumstances forecloses a successful outcome; or the patient is untreatable or belongs in a mental institution. Some such rationalization for dropping the case may disguise the fact that the trainee is experiencing a great deal of anxious aggression in handling it.

There is no objection to a trainee dropping a case; indeed, this may be preferable to continuing it if he experiences more discomfort than he can tolerate in working with the patient. But a rationalization of this nature beclouds the realities of the situation. The trainee has to be educated to recognize them and deal with them squarely. A person who is unable to evaluate himself objectively is not primed for analytic work. An important aspect of the training process is learning to communicate honestly limitations in one's understanding or skills and honestly evaluating any difficulties that one is experiencing with a patient.

Assimilating Information

It is also important to inculcate the idea that successful conduct of a case is contingent on the ability of the trainee to figure out what the patient is telling him—in other words, to assimilate properly the information provided by the patient. With a pretty well analyzed student, I focus from the beginning of the supervisory relationship on training him to recognize the main themes of the analytic session, to conceptualize them as topics, and to indicate the transition from one topic to the next, that is, the unconscious connections between them. From two to six months are usually required for such training.

When the student's resistance to concentrating on the patient's communications rather than his own is resolved, he is able to present about five sessions of a case in each supervisory session. The final ten minutes or so are devoted to a general discussion of the case.*

Focus on Patient's Communications

When given a condensed, sequential report of the patient's communications, I can usually surmise what the student analyst has told him and whether there are problems in their relationship. But the main reason for focusing on the patient's material is that, if the trainee is permitted to get into the trap of devoting the supervisory session to what he has said, this won't help him deal with the material. The patient's response to an intervention, not the intervention itself, is the paramount consideration.

Of course, this supervisory approach may deal a severe narcissistic blow to a student who is eager to report what he told the patient and to confirm the appropriateness, even brilliance of one or another interpretation. However, the interpretation that may be desirable in one case or stage of treatment may be ineffectual in another; the patient's response in the immediate situation is the decisive factor. Moreover, this approach educates the

---

*Some students prefer to present one session of four or five cases and then devote a few minutes to discussing each of them. This seems to be a more anxiety-allaying procedure for a supervisee who wants immediate assistance in dealing with different types of problems.

trainee to the idea that the less significance he attaches to what he says to the patient, the better. He is thus prepared to analyze consistently while keeping his interventions at a minimum.

Detecting Countertransference

The student has to recognize that he will develop countertransference reactions to every patient he works with, and that these have to be detected and understood, preferably by himself but if necessary with the help of his personal or supervisory analyst. In part through his identification with the latter and in part through his practical experience, the student develops the ability to deal appropriately with these reactions.

In this connection, it has to be emphasized that the principle of employing the realistically induced feelings (objective countertransference) does not imply license to be one's own emotional self with the patient. Far from it. A goodly number of practitioners have reported instances in which they intuitively responded to a patient in an emotional manner and found this to be therapeutic; but it may be harmful. Adverse consequences have also been reported.

Sanction for Spontaneity

The student is trained to operate consistently in terms of his long-range goals, and to communicate the emotional charge of the countertransference only after the groundwork has been prepared for such an intervention. He therefore needs to develop the capacity to sustain and store up the induced feelings so that they may be used, when appropriate, in a genuine but consciously controlled manner. In the sense that the modern analyst's functioning is dominated by the principle of transforming stony resistances into resolvable resistances, even his spontaneity is planned.

SPIRIT OF MODERN PSYCHOANALYSIS

The future practitioner is thus trained to engage himself, both intellectually and emotionally, in a system of psychotherapy that adheres to the Freudian framework but is oriented to the treatment of all forms of psychologically reversible illness, including psychosomatic conditions. Some classically trained analysts who deviate from the basic model in training patients with severe disorders refer to this system as "modified psychoanalysis"; however, the term "modern psychoanalysis" is preferable, for various reasons. For example, practitioners who have associated themselves with modified psychoanalysis do not invariably address themselves to the systematic analysis of resistance.

Another reason for referring to the treatment discussed here as modern psychoanalysis is that it is conducted in the spirit of modern medicine. Drugs are not administered to a person with a ruptured appendix because the physician he happens to consult is not qualified to perform surgery, nor does an endocrinologist prescribe hormones when a patient's condition dictates another remedy. Approaching the patient who consults him in the same spirit, the modern psychoanalyst informs him, in effect: I will analyze you and find out what types of interventions are needed to resolve your problem, and then assist you in obtaining them.

References

Abt, L. E. (1965). Acting out in group psychotherapy: A transactional approach. in Abt, L. E. and S. L. Weissman (Eds.). *Acting Out*. New York: Grune & Stratton.

Ackerman, N. W. (1949). Psychoanalysis and group psychotherapy. *Group Psychotherapy*, 3:204-215. (Also in Rosenbaum, M. and M. Berger (Eds.). *Group Psychotherapy and Group Function*. New York: Basic Books, 1963.)

_____(1959). Transference and countertransference. *Psychoanalysis and the Psychoanalytic Review* 46(3):17-28.

_____(1972). The growing edge of family therapy. In Sager, C. J. and H. S. Kaplan (Eds.). *Progress in Group and Family Therapy*. New York: Brunner/Mazel.

Alexander, F. (1956). *Psychoanalysis and Psychotherapy*. New York: Norton.

Anthony, E. J. (1970). Two contrasting types of adolescent depressions and their treatment. *Journal of the American Psychoanalytic Association* 18:841-859.

Aronson, M. L. (1967). Resistance in individual and group psychotherapy. *American Journal of Psychotherapy* 21:86-94.

Bender, L. (1956). Schizophrenia in childhood; its recognition, description and treatment. *American Journal of Orthopsychiatry* 26:499-506.

Berger, M. (1967). Frontiers of Clinical Psychiatry. *Roche Report*, October 15.

Bergman, P. and S. Escalona (1949). Unusual sensitivities in very young children. *The Psychoanalytic Study of the Child* 3/4:333-352.

Berne, E. (1966). *Principles of Group Treatment*. New York: Oxford University Press.

Binswanger, L. (1957). *Sigmund Freud: Reminiscences of a Friendship*. New York: Grune & Stratton.

Bion, W. R. (1961). *Experiences in Groups*. New York: Basic Books.

Bleuler, E. (1911). *Dementia Praecox and the Group of Schizophrenias*. New York: International Universities Press, 1950.

Bloch, D. (1965). Feelings that kill; the effect of the wish for infanticide in neurotic depression. *Psychoanalytic Review* 52:51-66.

Bowles, E. A. (1934). *The Narcissus*. London: Hopkinson.

Breuer, J. and S. Freud (1893-1895). Studies on hysteria. *Standard Edition of the Complete Psychological Works of Sigmund Freud* 2:3-305. London: Hogarth Press.

Brill, A. A. (1949). *Basic Principles of Psychoanalysis*. Garden City, N. Y.: Doubleday.

Brody, L. S. (1966). Harassed! A dialogue. *International Journal of Group Psychotherapy* 16:463-483.

Brody, S. (1964). Syndrome of the treatment-rejecting patient. *Psychoanalytic Review* 51:243-252.

Bry, T. (1953). Acting out in group psychotherapy. *International Journal of Group Psychotherapy* 3:42-48.

Burbridge, F. W. and J. G. Baker (1875). *The Narcissus: Its History and Culture*. Kent: Ashford.

Burlingham, D. (1952). *Twins*. New York: International Universities Press.

Burrow, T. (1927). The group method of analysis. *Psychoanalytic Review* 14:268-280.

Clevans, E. (1957). The fear of a schizophrenic man. *Psychoanalysis* 5(4): 58-67.

Coleman, M. C. and B. Nelson (1957). Paradigmatic psychotherapy in borderline treatment. *Psychoanalysis*, 5(3):28-44. (Also, retitled: Paradigmatic encounters in life and treatment, in Nelson, M. C. [1962b]).

Cook, J. W. and J. D. Loudon (1952). Alkaloids of the amaryllidaceae. In Manske, R. H. F. and H. L. Holmes (Eds.). *The Alkaloids: Chemistry and Physiology*, vol. 2. New York: Academic Press.

Davis, H. L. (1965-1966). Short-term psychoanalytic therapy with hospitalized schizophrenics. *Psychoanalytic Review* 52:421-448.

Durkin, H. E. (1955). Acting out in group psychotherapy. *American Journal of Orthopsychiatry* 25:644-652.

_____(1964). *The Group in Depth*. New York: International Universities Press.

Eisenberg, L. and L. Kanner (1956). Early infantile autism, 1943-1955. *American Journal of Orthopsychiatry* 26:556-566.

Ekstein, R. and J. Wallerstein (1954). Observations on the psychology of borderline and psychotic children. *The Psychoanalytic Study of the Child* 9:344-369.

_____, K. Bryant and S. W. Friedman (1958). Childhood schizophrenia and allied conditions. In Bellak, L. (Ed.). *Schizophrenia; A Review of the Syndrome*. New York: Logos Press, pp. 555-693.

Ellis, H. (1955). *Psychology of Sex*. New York: New American Library, Menton Book.

Erikson, E. H. (1950). *Childhood and Society*. New York: Norton.

Erikson, K. T. and D. H. Marlowe (1959). The schizophrenic in basic training. In Artiss, K. L. (Ed.). *The Symptom as Communication in Schizophrenia*. New York: Grune & Stratton.

Feldman, Y., H. Spotnitz and L. Nagelberg (1953). One aspect of casework training through supervision. *Social Casework* 34:150-155.

Fenichel, O. (1945a). Neurotic acting out. *Psychoanalytic Review* 32:197-206.

_____(1945b). *The Psychoanalytic Theory of Neurosis*. New York: Norton.

Foulkes, S. H. and E. J. Anthony (1957). *Group Psychotherapy: The Psycho-Analytic Approach*. London: Penguin.

Frank, J. (1957). Some determinants, manifestations, and effects of cohesiveness in therapy groups. *International Journal of Group Psychotherapy* 7:53-63.

Freud, A. (1958). Adolescence. *The Psychoanalytic Study of the Child* 13:225-278.

Freud, S. (1894). The neuro-psychoses of defence. *Standard Edition. . . ,* 3:45-61.

_____(1896). Further remarks on the neuro-psychoses of defence. *Standard Edition,* 3:162-185.

_____(1900). The interpretation of dreams. *Standard Edition* 4, 5.

_____(1905). Fragment of an analysis of a case of hysteria. *Standard Edition* 7:7-122.

_____(1906). My views on the part played by sexuality in the aetiology of the neuroses. *Standard Edition* 7:271-279.

_____(1910). The future prospects of psychoanalytic therapy. *Standard Edition* 11:141-151.

_____(1913). Totem and taboo. *Standard Edition* 13:1-161.

_____(1914a). On the history of the psychoanalytic movement. *Standard Edition* 14:7-66.

_____(1914b). On narcissism: An introduction. *Standard Edition* 14:73-102.

_____(1914c). Remembering, repeating, and working through. *Standard Edition* 12:147-156.

_____(1917). Introductory lectures on psychoanalysis (part 3). *Standard Edition* 16:243-463.

_____(1920). Beyond the pleasure principle. *Standard Edition* 18:7-66.

_____(1921). Group psychology and the analysis of the ego. *Standard Edition* 18:69-143.

_____(1925). Some additional notes on dream interpretation as a whole (A). *Standard Edition* 19:127-130.

_____(1926). Inhibitions, symptoms, and anxiety. *Standard Edition* 20:77-175.

_____(1927). Postscript; the question of lay analysis. *Standard Edition* 20:251-258.

_____(1937). Analysis terminable and interminable. *Standard Edition* 23:216-253.

_____(1950b). Project for a scientific psychology. *Standard Edition* 1:295-397.

_____and J. Breuer (1893-1895). Studies on hysteria. See Breuer and Freud.

Gabriel, B., H. Spotnitz, M. G. Siegel, and S. R. Slavson (1947). Interview group therapy with a neurotic adolescent girl suffering from chorea. In Slavson, S. R. (Ed.). *The Practice of Group Therapy.* New York: International Universities Press, pp. 191-218.

Garwood, D. S. (1967). The significance and dynamics of sensitivity training programs. *International Journal of Group Psychotherapy* 17:457-472.

Gero, G. (1952). The concept of defense. In Lorand, S. (Ed.). *Yearbook of Psychoanalysis* 8:128-138. New York: International Universities Press.

Glatzer, H. T. (1953). Handling transference resistance in group therapy. *Psychoanalytic Review* 40:36-43.

_____(1958). Acting out in group psychotherapy (panel). *American Journal of Psychotherapy* 12:87-105.

Glover, E. (1927, 1928). Lectures on technique in psychoanalysis. *International Journal of Psycho-Analysis* 8:311-338, 486-520; 9:7-46, 181-218.

_____(1949). *Psycho-Analysis,* 2nd ed. New York: Staples Press.

_____(1955). *The Technique of Psychoanalysis.* New York: International Universities Press.

Greenacre, P. (1950). General problems of acting out. *Psychoanalytic Quarterly* 19:455-467.

_____(1966). Problems of acting out in the transference relationship. In Rexford, E. N. (Ed.). *A Developmental Approach to Problems of Acting Out* (Symposium). New York: International Universities Press.

Hartmann, H. (1953). Contribution to the metapsychology of schizophrenia. *The Psychoanalytic Study of the Child* 8:177-198.

Hill, L. B. (1955). *Psychotherapeutic Intervention in Schizophrenia.* Chicago: University of Chicago Press.

Hora, T. (1968). Existential psychiatry and group psychotherapy. In Gazda, G. M. (Ed.). *Basic Approaches to Group Psychotherapy and Group Counseling.* Springfield: Charles C Thomas, pp. 109-148.

Johnson, J. A. (1963). *Group Therapy: A Practical Approach.* New York: McGraw-Hill.

Jones, E. (1953). *The Life and Work of Sigmund Freud,* vol. 1. New York: Basic Books.

Karpe, E. (1961). The rescue complex in Anna O's identity. *Psychoanalytic Quarterly* 30:1-27.

Kobert, R. (1906). *Lehrbuch der Intoxicationen,* vol. 2. Stuttgart: Ferdinand Enke.

Kotkov, B. (1957). Common forms of resistance in group psychotherapy. *Psychoanalytic Review* 44:88-96.

Lorand, S. (1946). *Technique of Psychoanalytic Therapy.* New York: International Universities Press.

McDougall, W. (1920). *The Group Mind.* Cambridge: Cambridge University Press.

Macht, D. I. (1933). *Narzissensweibeln-Vergiftungen durch Verwechlsung.* Salmlung von Vergiftungsfallen, Leipzig, 4:103-104.

Mahler, M. S., J. R. Ross, Jr. and Z. DeFries (1949). Clinical studies in benign and malignant cases of childhood psychosis (schizophreniclike). *American Journal of Orthopsychiatry* 19:295-305.

Mahler, M. S. and B. J. Gosliner (1955). On symbiotic child psychosis: Genetic, dynamic and restitutive aspects. *The Psychoanalytic Study of the Child*, 10:195-212.

Mann, J. (1955). Some theoretic concepts of the group process. *International Journal of Group Psychotherapy* 5:235-241.

Menninger, K. (1958). *Theory of Psychoanalytic Technique*. New York: Basic Books.

Nelson, M. C. (1962a). The effect of paradigmatic techniques on the psychic economy of borderline patients. *Psychiatry* 25:119-134. (Also in 1962b, pp. 25-50.)

_____(1962b). *Paradigmatic Approaches to Psychoanalysis: Four Papers.* New York: Psychology Department, Stuyvesant Polyclinic.

_____and B. Nelson (1962). Paradigmatic encounters in life and treatment. (See Coleman and Nelson, 1957.)

_____, M. H. Sherman and H. S. Strean (1968). *Roles and Paradigms in Psychotherapy*. New York: Grune & Stratton.

Ormont, L. R. (1964). The resolution of resistances by conjoint psychoanalysis. *Psychoanalytic Review* 51:425-437.

_____(1968). Group resistance and the therapeutic contract. *International Journal of Group Psychotherapy* 18:147-154.

Ovid (1951). *Metamorphoses*. Loeb Classical Library, 2nd ed. Cambridge: Harvard University Press, vol. 1, book 3, pp. 149-161.

Pausanias (1935). *Description of Greece*. Loeb Classical Library. Cambridge: Harvard University Press, vol. 4, book 9, p. 31.

Penfield, W. and L. Roberts (1959). *Speech and Brain Mechanisms*. Princeton: Princeton University Press, pp. 1-55.

Powdermaker, F. B. and J. D. Frank (1953). *Group Psychotherapy; Studies in Methodology of Research and Therapy*. Cambridge: Harvard University Press.

Rado, S. (1951). Psychodynamics of depression from the etiological point of view. In *Psychoanalysis of Behavior*. New York: Grune & Stratton, 1957, pp. 235-242.

_____(1953). Recent advances in psychoanalytic therapy. *Ibid.*, pp. 251-267.

Redl, F. (1948). Resistance in therapy groups. *Human Relations* 1:307-313.

Rosenthal, L. (1963). A study of resistances in a member of a therapy group. *International Journal of Group Psychotherapy* 13:315-327.

_____(1971). Some dynamics of resistance and therapeutic management in adolescent group therapy. *Psychoanalytic Review* 58:353-366.

Saul, L. J. (1958). *Technic and Practice of Psychoanalysis*. Philadelphia: Lippincott.

Scheflen, A. E. (1961). *A Psychotherapy of Schizophrenia: Direct Analysis*. Springfield: Charles C Thomas.

Schilder, P. (1936). The analysis of ideologies as a psychotherapeutic method, especially in group therapy. *American Journal of Psychiatry* 93:601-617.

Schneiwind, H. E. Jr., M. Day and E. V. Semrad (1969). Group psychotherapy of schizophrenics. In Bellak, L. and L. Loeb (Eds.). *The Schizophrenic Syndrome*. New York: Grune & Stratton.

Schwartz, E. K. and A. Wolf (1958). Irrational trends in contemporary psychotherapy: Cultural correlates. *Psychoanalysis and the Psychoanalytic Review* 45(1-2):65-74.

_____(1960). Psychoanalysis in groups: The mystique of group dynamics. *Topical Problems in Psychotherapy* 2:119-154. Basel: S. Karger.

Scott, J. L. (1898). *Bulfinch's Age of Fable or Beauties of Mythology* (Rev. Ed.). Philadelphia: David McKay.

Shea, J. E. (1954). Differentials in resistance reactions in individual and group psychotherapy. *International Journal of Group Psychotherapy* 4: 153-161.

Silverberg, W. V. (1947). The schizoid maneuver. *Psychiatry* 10:383-393.

Slavson, S. R. (1943). *An Introduction to Group Therapy*. New York: International Universities Press, 1969, 1970.

_____(1954). A contribution to a systematic theory of group psychotherapy. *International Journal of Group Psychotherapy* 4:3-29.

_____(1964). *A Textbook in Analytic Group Psychotherapy*. New York: International Universities Press.

_____(1966). Interaction and reconstruction in group psychotherapy. *International Journal of Group Psychotherapy* 16:3-12.

Smith, W. (Ed., 1904). *A Classical Dictionary of Greek and Roman Biography, Mythology, and Geography* (revised by G. E. Marindin). London: Murray.

Spotnitz, H. (1952). Group psychotherapy as a specialized psychotherapeutic technique. In Bychowski, G. and J. L. Despert (Eds.). *Specialized Techniques in Psychotherapy*. New York: Basic Books.

_____(1961). *The couch and the Circle: A Story of Group Psychotherapy*. New York: Alfred Knopf; Lancer Books, 1972.

_____(1969a). *Modern Psychoanalysis of the Schizophrenic Patient; Theory of the Technique*. New York: Grune & Stratton.

_____(1969b). Resistance phenomena in group psychotherapy (overview). In Ruitenbeck, H. M. (Ed.). *Group Therapy Today*. New York: Atherton Press.

_____(1971). Comparison of different types of group psychotherapy. In Kaplan, H. I. and B. Sadock (Eds.). *Comprehensive Group Psychotherapy*. Baltimore: Williams & Wilkins.

_____(1972). Constructive emotional interchange in adolescence. In Sager, C. J. and H. S. Kaplan (Eds.). *Progress in Group and Family Therapy*. New York: Brunner/Mazel, pp. 737-746.

_____and L. Nagelberg (1960). A pre-analytic technique for resolving the narcissistic defense. *Psychiatry* 23:193-197.

Stekel, W. (1950). *Technique of Analytical Psychotherapy*. New York: Liveright.

Stoller, F. H. (1968). Accelerated interaction: A time-limited approach based on the brief, intensive group. *International Journal of Group Psychotherapy* 18:220-235.

Stotsky, B. and E. F. Zolik (1965). Group psychotherapy with psychotics: A review—1921-1963. *International Journal of Group Psychotherapy* 15: 321-344.

Stuart, G. (1955). *Narcissus: A Psychological Study of Self-Love*. New York: Macmillan.

Sugar, M. (1968). Normal adolescent mourning. *American Journal of Psychotherapy* 22:258-269.

Tower, L. E. (1956). Countertransference. *Journal of the American Psychoanalytical Association* 4:224-255.

Warren, W. and K. Cameron (1950). Reactive psychosis in adolescence. *Journal of Mental Science* 96:447.

Weiner, H. (1958). Diagnosis and symptomatology. In Bellak, L. (Ed.). *Schizophrenia: A Review of the Syndrome*. New York: Logos Press, pp. 107-173.

Wender, L. (1936). The dynamics of group psychotherapy and its application. *Journal of Nervous and Mental Disorders* 84:54-60.

Wexler, M. (1953). The structural problem in schizophrenia. In Mowrer, O. H. (Ed.). *Psychotherapy; Theory and Research*. New York: Ronald Press.

Wieseler, F. von (1856). *Narkissos*. Gottingen: Dietrich.

Winnicott, D. W. (1949). Hate in the countertransference. *International Journal of Psycho-Analysis* 30:69-74. (Also in *Collected Papers*. New York: Basic Books, 1958).

Wolf, A. (1949-1950). The psychoanalysis of groups. *American Journal of Psychotherapy* 3:16-50; 4:515-558. (Also in Rosenbau, M. and M. Berger (Eds.). *Group Psychotherapy and Group Function*. New York: Basic Books, 1963.)

World-Wide Abstracts of General Medicine (1961):4(4):25.

Bibliography of Hyman Spotnitz

Books

The Couch and the Circle: A Story of Group Psychotherapy. New York: Alfred A. Knopf, 1961; Lancer Books, 1972.

(with Lucy Freeman): *The Wandering Husband: Love, Sex and the Married Man.* Englewood Cliffs, N.J.: Prentice-Hall, 1964. New York: Tower, 1964. Dutch edition, 1967.

Modern Psychoanalysis of the Schizophrenic Patient: Theory of the Technique. New York: Grune & Stratton, 1969. Japanese edition, 1974.

(with Lucy Freeman): *How to be Happy Though Pregnant: A Guide to Understanding and Solving the Normal Emotional Problems and Postpartum Blues of Pregnancy.* New York: Coward-McCann, 1969; Berkley, 1974.

OTHER PUBLICATIONS

Physiology (Normal and Pathological)

Messende Untersuchunger uber Sehferne [Quantitative measurement of visual distance]. Inaugural Dissertation, Friedrich Wilhelms University, Berlin, 1934.

(with C. A. Elsberg): Some neural components of the visual response. *American Journal of Physiology* 118:792-797, 1937.

(with C. A. Elsberg): The sense of vision: I. A method for the study of acuity of vision and of relative visual fatigue. *Bulletin of the Neurological Institute of New York* 6:233-242, 1937.

(with C. A. Elsberg): The sense of vision: II. The reciprocal relation of area and light intensity and its significance for the localization of tumors of the brain by functional visual tests. *Bulletin of the Neurological Institute of New York* 6:243-252, 1937.

(with C. A. Elsberg): The sense of vision: III. A theory of the functions of the retina. *Bulletin of the Neurological Institute of New York* 6:253-267, 1937.

(with C. A. Elsberg): Factors which influence dark adaptation. *American Journal of Physiology* 120:689-695, 1937.

(with C. A. Elsberg): The value of quantitative visual tests for the localization of supratentorial tumors of the brain. *Bulletin of the Neurological Institute of New York* 6:411-420, 1937.

(with C. A. Elsberg): Are vision and the olfactory sense governed by the same laws? A comparison of the results of quantitative functional tests of vision and of the sense of smell and its significance. *Bulletin of the Neurological Institute of New York* 6:421-429, 1937.

(with C. A. Elsberg): A theory of retino-cerebral function with formulas for threshold vision and light and dark adaptation at the fovea. *American Journal of Physiology* 121:454-464, 1938.

(with C. A. Elsberg): Neural correlations of vision and their significance for localization of tumors of the brain; A preliminary report. *Archives of Neurology & Psychiatry* 39:315-326, 1938.

(with C. A. Elsberg): The relative refractory period of olfaction and of vision. *Bulletin of the Neurological Institute of New York* 7:78-94, 1938.

(with C. A. Elsberg): Is cerebral activity a physicochemical process?: Studies based on the physicochemical equivalents of a formula for dark adaptation. *Journal of General Psychology* 19:263-276, 1938.

(with C. A. Elsberg): The neural components of light and dark adaptation and their significance for the duration of the foveal dark adaptation process. *Bulletin of the Neurological Institute of New York* 7:148-159, 1938.

(with C. A. Elsberg): The relation between area and intensity of light and the size of the pupil, with formulas for pupillary reactions. *Bulletin of the Neurological Institute of New York* 7:160-164, 1938.

Subjective foveal hemianopsia during dark adaptation in patients with tumors of a temporal lobe. *Bulletin of the Neurological Institute of New York* 7:170-173, 1938.

(with C. A. Elsberg): A comparison of a series of olfactory and visual tests for the localization of tumors of the brain. *Bulletin of the Neurological Institute of New York* 7:164-169, 1938.

(with C. A. Elsberg): The sense of taste. Formulas by which the relations between stimulus and reaction time can be foretold. *Bulletin of the Neurological Institute of New York* 7:174-177, 1938.

Formulas for visual distance and size: their relationship to the Nernst-Hill theory of nervous excitation. *Journal of Experimental Psychology* 23:394-402, 1938.

(with C. A. Elsberg): Relation of stimulation time of receptors to recovery time in the nervous system: visual, olfactory and auditory senses. *Journal of Neurophysiology* 2:227-233, 1939.

(with C. A. Elsberg): The growth formula of Bertalanffy and its similarity to equations for excitation and recovery in the central nervous system. *Human Biology* 11:402-407, 1939.

(with W. O. Klingman and R. W. Laidlaw): The value of blood sedimentation rate in intracranial tumors. *New York State Journal of Medicine* 40:117-121, 1940.

(with C. A. Elsberg and E. I. Strongin): The effect of stimulation by odorous substances upon the amount of secretion of the parotid glands. *Journal of Experimental Psychology* 27:58-65, 1940.

(with C. A. Elsberg): A theory of the activity of the human nervous system in response to stimulation. *Journal of General Psychology* 26:95-127, 1942.

(with C. A. Elsberg and E. I. Strongin): The olfactory-parotid reflex. Study of one hundred and fifty patients with disorders of the central nervous system; a preliminary report. *Archives of Neurology and Psychiatry* 47: 707-717, 1942.

(with C. A. Elsberg): Value of quantitative olfactory tests for localization of supratentorial disease. Analysis of one thousand cases. *Archives of Neurology & Psychiatry* 48:1-12, 1942.

Physioloigcal Psychology

(with P. Polatin and B. Wiesel): Effects of intravenous injection of insulin in treatment of mental disease: preliminary report of clinical observations. *Archives of Neurology & Psychiatry* 43:925-931, 1940.

(with P. Polatin and B. Wiesel): Ambulatory insulin treatment of mental disorders. *New York State Journal of Medicine* 40:843-848, 1940.

(with P. Polatin and A. J. Raffaele): Intravenous injection of solution of zinc-insulin crystals: its effect in treatment of mental diseases. *Journal of Nervous & Mental Disease* 95:40-45, 1942.

(with P. Polatin): Continuous ambulatory insulin shock technique in treatment of schizophrenia; Report of two cases. *Archives of Neurology & Psychiatry* 47:53-56, 1942.

(with P. Polatin): Evaluation of the effects of intravenous insulin technique in the treatment of mental diseases. A follow-up study of a group of patients treated with intravenous injection of unmodified insulin and zinc-insulin crystals. *American Journal of Psychiatry* 99:394-397, 1942.

(with P. Polatin): Ambulatory insulin shock technique in the treatment of schizophrenia: An evaluation of therapeutic effects. *Journal of Nervous & Mental Disease* 97:567-575, 1943.

(with P. Polatin): Effects of combined ambulatory insulin and electroshock therapy in the treatment of schizophrenia; a preliminary report. *New York State Journal of Medicine* 46:2648-2650, 1946.

Psychoanalytic Psychology

(with B. Gabriel, M. G. Siegel, and S. R. Slavson): Interview group therapy with a neurotic adolescent girl suffering from chorea. In *The Practice of Group Therapy*, S. R. Slavson, editor. New York: International Universities Press, 1947, 1974.

Observations on emotional currents in interview group therapy with adolescent girls. *Journal of Nervous & Mental Disease* 106:565-582, 1947.

(with B. Gabriel): Resistance in analytic group therapy; A study of the group therapeutic process in children and mothers. *Quarterly Journal of Child Behavior* 2:71-85, 1950.

A psychoanalytic view of resistance in groups. *International Journal of Group Psychotherapy* 2:3-9, 1952.

(with L. Nagelberg): Initial steps in the analytic therapy of schizophrenia in children. *Quarterly Journal of Child Behavior* 4:57-65, 1952.

Group therapy as a specialized psychotherapeutic technique. In *Specialized Techniques in Psychotherapy*, G. Bychowski and L. Despert, editors. New York: Basic Books, 1952.

(with L. Nagelberg and Y. Feldman): The attempt at healthy insulation in the withdrawn child. *American Journal of Orthopsychiatry* 23:238-251, 1953.

(with Y. Feldman and L. Nagelberg): One aspect of casework training through supervision. *Social Casework* 34:150-155, 1953.

(with P. Resnikoff): The myths of Narcissus. *Psychoanalytic Review* 41: 173-181, 1954.

The prophecies of Tiresias. *Psychoanalysis* 4:37-43, 1955.

(with L. Nagelberg and Y. Feldman): Ego reinforcement in the schizophrenic child. *American Journal of Orthopsychiatry* 26:146-162, 1956.

The borderline schizophrenic in group psychotherapy. *International Journal of Group Psychotherapy* 7:155-174, 1957.

Resistance reinforcement in affect training of analytic group psychotherapists. *International Journal of Group Psychotherapy* 8:395-402, 1958.

(with L. Nagelberg): Strengthening the ego through the release of frustration-aggression. *American Journal of Orthopsychiatry* 28:794-801, 1958.

(with L. Nagelberg): A preanalytic technique for resolving the narcissistic defense. *Psychiatry* 23:193-197, 1960.

The neurotic child. In *Professional School Psychology*, M. B. and G. B. Gottsegen, editors. New York: Grune & Stratton, 1960.

The concept of goals in group psychotherapy. *International Journal of Group Psychotherapy* 10:383-393, 1960.

Adolescence and schizophrenia; Problems in differentiation. In *Adolescents; Psychoanalytic Approach to Problems and Therapy*, S. Lorand and H. I. Schneer, editors. New York: Paul B. Hoeber, 1961; Delta Books, 1965.

The narcissistic defense in schizophrenia. *Psychoanalysis and the Psychoanalytic Review* 48(No.4):24-42, 1961. (Also in *Reports in Medical and Clinical Psychology*, No. 1. New York: Stuyvesant Polyclinic, 1961.)

The need for insulation in the schizophrenic personality. *Psychoanalysis and the Psychoanalytic Review* 49 (No.3):3-15, 1962. (Also in *Reports in Medical and Clinical Psychology*, No. 3, Insulation and Immunization in Schizophrenia. New York: Stuyvesant Polyclinic, 1963.)

Le divan analytique and le cercle. *Medecine et Hygiene*. Geneva, December 12, 1962.

The toxoid response. *Psychoanalytic Review* 50:611-624, Winter 1963-1964. (Also in *Reports in Medical and Clinical Psychology*, No. 3, Insulation and Immunization in Schizophrenia. New York: Stuyvesant Polyclinic, 1963; and in *The Active Psychotherapies*, Harold Greenwald, editor. New York: Atherton Press, 1967.)

Group counseling methods. In *Handbook of Counseling Techniques*, E. Harms, editor. Oxford/New York: Pergamon Press, 1964.

Talent in the playwright. *Annals of Psychotherapy* 5:18-22, 1964 (Monograph No. 8, The Creative Use of the Unconscious).

Hate. In *The Why Report*, Lucy Freeman and M. Theodores, editors. Purchase, New York: Arthur Bernhard, 1964.

Accidents to children. In *The Why Report*, Lucy Freeman and M. Theodores, editors. Purchase, New York: Arthur Bernhard, 1964.

Failures in group psychotherapy. In *Topical Problems of Psychotherapy*, Vol. 5. Basel/New York: S. Karger, 1965. (Also in *Group Therapy Today: Styles, Methods, and Techniques*, H. Ruitenbeek, editor. New York: Atherton Press, 1969.)

The maturational interpretation. *Psychoanalytic Review* 53:490-495, 1966. (Also in *Use of Interpretation in Treatment: Technique and Art*, E. F. Hammer, editor. New York: Grune & Stratton, 1968; and in *Journal of the Long Island Consultation Center* 4:3-6, 1966.

Techniques for the resolution of the narcissistic defense. In *Psychoanalytic Techniques: A Handbook for the Practicing Psychoanalyst*, B. B. Wolman, editor. New York: Basic Books, 1967.

Psychoanalytic therapy of aggression in groups. In *Current Psychiatric Therapies*, J. Masserman, editor, Vol. 8. New York: Grune & Stratton, 1968.

Traitement psychoanalytique de le schizophrenie. *Medicine et Hygiene*, Geneva, July 30, 1968.

The management and mastery of resistance in group psychotherapy. *Journal of Group Psychoanalysis and Process* 1:5-22, 1968.

Resistance phenomena in group psychotherapy (Overview).
In *Group Therapy Today: Styles, Methods and Techniques*, H. Ruitenbeek, editor. New York: Atherton Press, 1969.

Comparison of different types of group psychotherapy. In *Comprehensive Group Psychotherapy*, H. I. Kaplan and B. J. Sadock, editors. Baltimore: Williams & Wilkins, 1971. (Also in *Modern Group Book*, II, IV and V, H. I. Kaplan and B. J. Sadock, editors. New York: E. P. Dutton & Co., 1972).

In tribute to S. R. Slavson. *International Journal of Group Psychotherapy* 21:402-405, 1971.

Group psychotherapy in perspective (editorial). *American Journal of Psychiatry* 129:606-607, 1972.

Constructive emotional interchange in adolescence. In *Progress in Group and Family Therapy*, C. J. Sager and H. S. Kaplan, editors. New York: Brunner/Mazel, 1972.

Touch countertransference in group psychotherapy. *International Journal of Group Psychotherapy* 22:455-463, 1972.

Acting out in group psychotherapy. In *Group Therapy 1973: An Overview*, L. R. Wolberg and E. K. Schwartz, editors. New York: Intercontinental Medical Book Corp., 1973.

My philosophy of psychotherapy. *Journal of Contemporary Psychotherapy* 6:43-48, 1973.

Group psychotherapy with schizophrenics. In *Group Process Today: Evaluation and Perspective*, D. S. Milman and G. D. Goldman, editors. Springfield: Charles C Thomas, 1974.

Object-oriented approaches to severely disturbed adolescents. In *The Adolescent in Group and Family Therapy*, M. Sugar, editor. New York: Brunner/Mazel, 1975.

Supervising the psychotherapy of the schiqophrenic patient. Behavioral Sciences Tape Library, I. K. Goldberg, editor. Leonia, N. J.: Sigma Information, 1974. No. 30367.

Experiences in conducting demonstration groups. In *Group Therapy 1975— An Overview*, L. R. Wolberg and M. L. Aronson, editors. New York: Stratton Intercontinental Medical Book Corp., 1975.

Observations on child analysis. *Modern Psychoanalysis* 1:33-41, 1976.

The death of the father: its emotional impact on a group. In *Group Therapy 1976—An Overview*, L. R. Wolberg and M. L. Aronson, editors. New York: Stratton Intercontinental Medical Book Corp. In Press.

Child-Analysis. In *Understanding Disturbed Children*, R. L. Jenkins and E. Harms, editors. Seattle: Special Child Publications. In press.

Narcissus as myth, Narcissus as patient. In *Narcissism in our Lives and Times*, M. C. Nelson, editor. New York: Behavioral Publications. In press.

Aggression and schizophrenia. In *Psychoanalytic Perspectives on Aggression*. D. S. Milman and G. D. Goldman, editors.

Discussions

Political creed and character (R. M. Lindner). *Psychoanalysis* 2 (No. 2):33-36, 1953.

Benefits of combined therapy for the hostile withdrawn and dependent personality (E. Fried). *American Journal of Orthopsychiatry* 24:535-537, 1954.

Irrational trends in contemporary psychotherapy (E. K. Schwartz and A. Wolf). *Psychoanalysis and the Psychoanalytic Review* 45:74-78, 1958.

The application of group concepts to the treatment of the individual in the group (S. H. Foulkes). In *Topical Problems of Psychotherapy*, Vol. 2. Basel/New York: S. Karger, 1960.

Childhood schizophrenia and mental retardation; differential diagnosis before and after one year of psychotherapy (F. F. Schacter, L. R. Mayer, and E. A. Loomis, Jr.). *American Journal of Orthopsychiatry* 32:594-595, 1962.

A case arrested by psychoanalysis and analytic group psychotherapy (F. W. Graham). *International Journal of Group Psychotherapy* 14:282-286, 1964.

Harassed! A dialogue (L. S. Brody). *International Journal of Group Psychotherapy* 16:491-494, 1966.

Accelerated interaction; A time-limited approach (F. H. Stoller). *International Journal of Group Psychotherapy* 18:236-239, 1968.

Experimentation within the psychoanalytic session (H. Ezriel). *Contemporary Psychoanalysis* 8:253-259, 1972.

Book Reviews

Ego Psychology and the Psychoses (Paul Federn). *Psychoanalysis* 1(No.2): 73-75, 1953.

New Dimensions of Deep Analysis: A Study of Telepathy in Interpersonal Relationships (Jan Ehrenwald). *Guide to Psychiatric and Psychological Literature*, February, 1956.

The Ego in Love and Sexuality (Edrita Fried). *International Journal of Group Psychotherapy* 11:473-475, 1961.

A Psychotherapy of Schizophrenia: Direct Analysis (Albert E. Scheflen). *International Journal of Group Psychotherapy* 12:267-269, 1962.

Four Books on Dreams — *The Science of Dreams* (Edwin Diamond); *Ego Synthesis in Dreams* (Richard M. Jones): *The Clinical Use of Dreams* (Walter Bonime); *New Approaches to Dream Interpretation* (Nandor Fodor). *Psychoanalytic Review* 50:152-155, 1963.

Neurosis in the Family and Patterns of Psychosocial Defense (Jan Ehrenwald). *Psychoanalytic Review* 51:676-677, Winter 1964-1965.

Infantile Autism: The Syndrome and its Implications (Bernard Rimland). *Psychoanalytic Review* 52:137-138, 1965.

Behavioral Individuality in Early Childhood (Alexander Thomas, Herbert G. Birch, and Stella Chess). *Psychoanalytic Review* 53:144-145, 1966.

Problems of Sleep and Dreams in Children (Ernest Harms, editor). *Psychoanalytic Review* 53:148-149, 1966.

Basic Approaches to Group Psychotherapy and Group Counseling (George Gazda). *Psychiatry and Social Science Review* 3(No. 8):9-11, 1969.

Clinical Supervision of the Psychiatric Resident (Daniel B. Schuster, John J. Sandt, and Otto F. Thaler). Psychoanalytic Review 61:637-638, 1974-1975.

Interpretation of Schizophrenia, 2nd edition (Silvano Arieti). *Psychoanalytic Review* 62:351-352, 1975.

Ego Psychology: Theory and Practice (Gertrude and Rubin Blanck). *Modern Psychoanalysis* 1:107-109, 1976.

Obituary

In Memoriam: George Lawton, Ph.D. *Psychoanalysis* 5(No. 4):73-74, 1957.

Workshop Report

Fostering Group Interaction. *Newsletter*, Eastern Group Psychotherapy Society, May 1970.

Name Index

Subject Index

conditions, 20, 28, 101, 137, 213, 256, 313, 314, 316, 324, 364
Psychosomatic reactions, induced in therapist, 20, 58, 75
Psychosis, psychotic states, 49, 106 117, 119, 127, 207-208, 273, 333
—treatment of, 108, 113-114, 147-148, 154, 156, 159, 160, 227, 302, 339, 340
Psychotherapy, profession of, 18-20, 330, 359; ethical issues in, 31, 329, 330, 344; values in, 32-33

Question(ing), 85, 86, 140-141, 147, 160, 178, 227; ego-oriented, 227, 280; object-oriented, 72, 87, 114, 134, 159-160, 180, 227

Rage, 41, 49, 52, 55, 104, 123, 172
—defenses against, 155, 161-162, 277
—experiencing of, 71, 107, 151, 332
—reactions in psychosis, 106, 112-115, 131, 134
Reactive depression, 218-219
Reaction-formation, 67, 75, 260
Reactive depression, 218-219
Reconstruction, 143, 160, 314
Recovery, 297-298. See also Cure
Regression, 101, 221, 226, 272-273; clues to, 157-158; dealing with as resistance, 140; safeguards against, 140, 159, 279-280, 302
"Remembering, Repeating and Working Through," 311
Research, clinical, 279, 289, 298-299, 329, 330
Resistance, 15, 24, 43, 53, 61-62, 77-79, 83, 90, 130, 131, 139, 145, 160. See also Resistance, dealing with
—definitions of, 62, 70, 77-78; of group (common) resistance, 62, 80
—early patterns of, 142
—functions of: communication, 43, 53-54, 78-79, 145, 159; defense, 65, 78; survival, 70, 78-79, 145
—in groups, 59, 61, 62, 66, 69-70,

83, 257-261
—sources of, 78, 267-268 (see also Constellations)
—in therapist (see also Countertransference)
—types of, 62, 139 (see also External resistance; Group resistance; Status quo resistance; Transference resistance; Treatment-destructive resistance)
—value of, 63, 79 364
Resistance, dealing with, 54, 63-66, 82-84. See also Interventions
—on all levels, 79, 149
—early in treatment, 53-54
—focus on: group (common) patterns, 82, 85-90; transference resistance, 82, 84
—management (control of intensity), 86-88, 139, 146-147, 149
—nullifying destructive potential of, 70, 82 (see also Treatment-destructive resistance)
—priority system in, 86-88, 139, 146-147, 149
—reinforcement, 53, 54, 160
—resolution, 75, 85-86, 98-90, 102, 306-307
—steps in mastering, 63-66, 83-86
—working through, 85-86, 148-149 (see also Working through)

Sadistic gratification, 70, 144
Scarring of ego, 135, 221
Schizoid maneuver, 211
Schizophrenia (schizophrenic reaction). See also Adolescent schizophrenia; Borderline schizophrenia; Childhood schizophrenia; Insulation; Narcissistic defense; Withdrawal
—depressive component in, 114-115
—diagnosis of, 205-206, 209, 219-220
—ego involvement in, 121
—etiology of, 101, 104-105, 122-125, 138, 158, 213, 220, 271